Computers at Work

WILEY SERIES IN PSYCHOLOGY AND PRODUCTIVITY AT WORK

Series Editors
D. J. Oborne and M. M. Gruneberg

The Physical Environment at Work
Edited by D. J. Oborne and M. M. Gruneberg

Hours of Work—Temporal factors in work scheduling
Edited by Simon Folkard and Timothy H. Monk

Computers at Work—A behavioural approach
D. J. Oborne

Further titles in preparation

Computers at Work

A behavioural approach

David J. Oborne

Department of Psychology,
University College of Swansea

JOHN WILEY & SONS

Chichester · New York · Brisbane · Toronto · Singapore

Library of Congress Cataloging in Publication Data:

Oborne, David J.
  Computers at work.

  (Wiley series in psychology and productivity at work)
  Includes index.

  1. Computers—Psychological aspects. I. Title.
II. Series.
QA76.9.P75026 1985   001.64'01'9   84-17335
ISBN 0 471 90410 4

British Library Cataloguing in Publication Data:

Oborne, David J.
  Computers at work.—(Wiley series in psychology and productivity at work)

  1. Computers   2. Work
  I. Title
  306'.36   HD6331
  ISBN 0 471 90410 4

Typeset in England by The Whitefriars Press Ltd., Chichester and Tonbridge
Printed by St. Edmundsbury Press, Bury St. Edmunds

To Susan,

my wife and very best friend whose encouragement and support greatly eased the task of writing this book.

Contents

Acknowledgement

I should like to acknowledge the help given to me by Mr Paul Wood, of the Swansea Psychology Department, in the preparation of the figures for this book.

Editorial Foreword to the Series

The books in this series have been written for a specific and significantly large readership; namely those who have an interest in, and have as their job the task of, improving the productive output at work. The common theme running through all of the volumes is to present the results of psychological research and principles that are concerned particularly with ways of improving organizational efficiency.

The format of the series, which contains edited, single-authored and multi-authored volumes, helps greatly in this endeavour. Thus, the various aspects of this multi-faceted problem of working efficiency can be addressed in a number of different ways and from different viewpoints. The list of titles already produced or in preparation illustrates this.

This volume, like earlier volumes, shows how psychology has been applied extensively to a rapidly developing and economically critical area. The book covers not only the design of computers, and the psychology of software, but looks at the social and economic implications of computers in general and at specific application to the office, medicine and education. As the lives of all of us are materially affected by the computer, this book is of relevance to anyone with an interest in the significance of psychology for our everyday economic and social lives.

D. J. Oborne
M. M. Gruneberg

Preface

There can be little doubt that computers have affected our lives considerably and that this will continue for many years to come. Almost every month new computer systems arrive on the market to be used in the home, the office, the factory floor, in education, in medicine—indeed in any situation in which information has to be stored, manipulated and recalled. That is, in any situation in which the transactions of normal living take place.

These new computers are becoming increasingly more powerful, smaller in size, transportable and are able to interact not only with their operator but with each other. At this time of writing, there are cheap pocket computers which are capable of performing computations faster and more efficiently than would have been thought possible only a decade or so ago; there exist inexpensive computers, well within the price range of most modern families, that can produce recognizable speech sounds, can display complex patterns on screens, can play sophisticated games such as chess and backgammon with skills that they can be beaten only by Grandmasters; there are slightly more costly computers which are completely portable, can be used anywhere and at any time that the operator wishes, and can retain the stored information without the need for external memory devices—even when the electrical power to the machine is removed. Slightly more expensive, but still within the budget of even the smallest company, are self-contained 'desk-top' computers: systems in their own rights which are capable of transmitting data via a number of electronic systems such as telephone lines or radio transmitters. Then, of course, there are the very expensive, mainframe computers used by large organizations. Certainly, the age of computers has arrived.

The problem that arises from this information technology explosion, however, is that the age has arrived rather too quickly. Individuals are often slow to adapt to new concepts and the concept of information manipulation, with its associated jargon, has often been hard to grasp. It is almost as if history is repeating itself—during the Second World War, for example, the development of technology was so fast that new machines were designed that often required skills quite outside the capabilities of those who were to operate them.

It was at this time that the application of psychological knowledge, coupled

xiii

with knowledge from other areas of human capacities, came to the help of designers. Using the relatively new disciplines of ergonomics, with its grounding in applied psychology; of anthropometrics and biomechanics, with their groundings in applied physiology; etc, the working environment was able to be redesigned to fit the operator's capabilities and expectations.

This book, then, has been written to do the same for the present generation of workers in the information technology world of today—to present the current knowledge of how computers work and can be made to work with human beings. With information of this nature, it should be possible to ensure that future computer purchases are made on the basis of informed knowledge, rather than glossy advertisements.

The book is divided into four parts—the first three reflecting the three main areas that need to be considered when contemplating a computer system.

The first section discusses the impact the computers can have on the social environment—both at a 'macro' (societal) level and at a level related more to the individual and organization. Since the effects can range from acceptance to the total rejection of computers, with all that that entails, questions such as the attitudes of individuals towards computers, the social and cognitive skills needed to operate and to program computers, and the effect that such new technology can have on established working practices are important.

Section II moves away from the social factors relating to computers towards considering the hardware itself; what is actually bought in the first instance. Thus, the three chapters in this section consider the electrical and mechanical devices that are available for putting information into the machine (the input devices—Chapter 4), and those used to present information back to the operator (the output devices—Chapter 5). Because none of this can work in isolation, the computer environment (including such features as the console, seating, lighting, etc) also needs careful consideration (Chapter 6).

In Section III, the same approach is taken, but from the viewpoint of the instructions within the machine that make it work as a computer (the software). This is an area which is only recently receiving interest from an applied psychological viewpoint, which is unfortunate because it is the quality of the software instructions that make computers computers. These features will be considered in Chapter 7, whilst Chapter 8 will discuss the other side of the software coin—the way in which the information needs finally to be displayed to the operator.

All of the applied psychological information relating to computers in general, then, is contained in the first three sections in this book. However, computers are often used not merely as general utility machines, but are employed for specific purposes at work. Frequently, these specific functions bring with themselves special problems, over and above those considered in the first three sections. Also, these specific functions can illustrate well many of the topics discussed within the first three sections.

Section IV, therefore, considers how computers have been applied to specific work areas and the relevant features of their application in the office (Chapter 9), in education (Chapter 10) and in medicine (Chapter 11).

David J. Oborne
Swansea, 1984

CHAPTER 1

Introduction

There can be little doubt that computers provide one of the most potent forces available in modern times. Harnessing their power enables man's relatively limited and fallible capacities for memory, logical decision making, reaction and perception to be extended to almost infinite levels. Millions of complex calculations can be done in mere fractions of the time needed by a human to perform; complex decisions can be made with unerring accuracy; with appropriate sensors minute stimuli can be perceived; and all of this for comparatively little cost. Indeed historians will probably look back on the present era as representing the information revolution. Just as the plough liberated agricultural workers from the drudgery of their work and heralded the agrarian revolution; designing machines which harnessed the power of steam introduced the industrial revolution; so the realization that information can be reduced to just two basic forms ('information' or 'no information'), and the serendipitous discovery of electronic components and circuits that could handle these two states brought about the introduction of the computer and the information revolution.

Despite the tremendous power available from modern computers it should never be forgotten that, with the present state of the art of computer design at least, they can represent only a tool to *extend* man's capacities. Despite the propositions advanced by many science fiction writers of machines which can walk, talk, take independent decisions and, ultimately, control the world, present day computers are really only as good and as efficient as their user. This is because, as will become more apparent throughout this book, the computer and the user represent a very complex closed-loop system; each can only perform to the level allowed by the other. When it is operating, a modern computer cannot do more than the operator and the programmer have envisaged it doing. In the same vein the operator and programmer are limited by the facilities available on the computer, and it is only as computers become

1

more 'powerful' and more facilities become available, that this computer-operator link in the system might be expanded. With an expanding technology, of course, this is likely to happen very quickly and so it is possible that it will be the operator–computer link which will soon represent the greatest limit to the system. Since the most powerful machine is useless without an equally 'powerful' operator, the behaviour of the operator, the quality of the programmer, and the ability of both to perform with the hardware available need to be considered carefully to ensure that the system can operate at its most efficient. It is the purpose of this book to examine the various aspects of the system which can affect this link—particularly from the viewpoint of the operator and of operator behaviour.

PSYCHOLOGY AND ERGONOMICS

The idea of an operator and a computer interacting closely together is embodied in the information technology concept of the 'man–machine system'. From a behavioural standpoint, the scientific investigation of hinderances to the efficient operation of this system has been the province of ergonomics (and its American sister discipline Human Factors).

Ergonomics developed via the interests of a number of different disciplines, primarily during the Second World War (for a more complete discussion of the rise and scope of ergonomics, see Oborne, 1982). It is a field of study which crosses the boundaries of many scientific and professional disciplines and draws on the data, findings, and principles of each. Although its roots are based firmly in the psychological sciences, evidence is also sought in branches of both medicine and engineering in order to attempt to define and to design the physical aspects of the environment to suit the capacities and capabilities of the environment's user. For example the biological sciences provide information about the structure of the body: the operator's physical capabilities and limitations; the body dimensions; how much can be lifted or carried; the dynamics of the seated person, etc. Physiological psychology deals with the functioning of the brain and the nervous system as they determine behaviour; whilst social psychologists supply information relating to the effects that other operators in the environment, and indeed the organization itself, have on the efficiency of the man–machine link. In addition experimental psychologists attempt to understand the basic ways in which the individual uses the body to behave, to perceive, to learn, to remember, to control motor processes, etc., in order to interact efficiently with machines. Finally, physics and engineering provide similar information about the machine and the physical environment with which the operator has to contend.

From these areas, an ergonomist takes and integrates data to maximize the operator's safety, efficiency, and reliability of performance, to make the task easier, and to increase feelings of comfort and satisfaction.

WORK AND PERFORMANCE

The relationship between the work to be performed and the demands of the task on operator performance can be described fairly simply by an inverted-U function as shown in Figure 1.1. Thus when the demands of the environment are particularly low—perhaps the job is boring—or when they are exceptionally high—under conditions of stress—then performance is reduced. Only when the task demands are within a narrow, middle range will performance be optimum.

Although the inverted-U relationship has been discussed so far in terms of the task and environment demands, the actual continuum which underlies the function is that of operator arousal. This concept of arousal refers to the amount of brain activity in the operator and, indeed, is often measured using electroencephalography (EEG). Thus when a person is asleep or drowsy then brain activity or arousal are low; when under stress the arousal is high (this is often accompanied by such physiological reactions as sweating).

The importance of this relationship when considering the effects of the environment lies in the fact that the level of individual arousal is related to the amount of external (and internal) stimulation which a person receives. In this respect the nature of a task is clearly a varying source of stimulation. Thus, during periods of low stimulation, perhaps from a boring job or from environments with little noise or illumination; in situations which are otherwise 'ideal' so that heat and cold receptors are not being stimulated; or when signals from the task are few and far between (such as inspecting objects on an assembly line), because arousal is low performance will also be low. Similarly cases in which the stimulation is too high can cause reduced performance. Too much noise, in environments which are too hot or too cold, with extreme glare levels can all act to increase the operator's arousal levels to produce less than optimum performance.

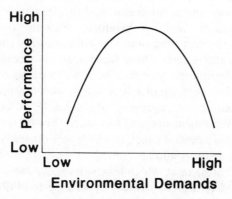

Figure 1.1.   The hypothetical environmental demands/performance relationship.

Unfortunately the inverted-U arousal/performance curve is only a general relationship. Both the shape of the curve and the level of arousal at which performance is optimum depend on characteristics of the operator and the type of stimulation. Personality and intelligence are just two individual characteristics which can alter the relationship. For this reason it is not possible to provide 'tables' of optimum arousal/stimulation levels. All that can be done is to recognize the existence of the relationship and to ensure that the levels of stimulation in the environment are neither too high nor too low for the individuals concerned. If the environment is found to be less than optimum, then steps can be taken either to increase or to reduce the stimulation. For example, Fox (1983) discusses the value of industrial music as a means of increasing arousal for boring, repetitive tasks.

Before leaving the discussion of the arousal/performance relationship, it should be emphasized that the level of stimulation which an operator obtains from the work arises from a number of factors: physical, physiological, social, personal, etc. Each can operate to raise or to lower the overall arousal level. The implication of this is that the value of an otherwise 'ideal' physical environment may be reduced if the operator's arousal is increased or lowered by, say, bad social relationships with colleagues or by worries at home. Of course, such stressors may act detrimentally on one occasion and not on another.

In addition to describing this relationship between work and performance in terms of an arousal model, attempts have also been made to model the effects in terms of 'mental capacity' (for example, Brown and Poulton, 1961; Brown, 1965). In essence this model suggests that an operator brings to a task a limited capacity to perform that task. Provided that the capacity is not exceeded, the task will be executed efficiently. Performance is reduced, however, if the task demands more than the operator is able to give.

The essential value of this model lies in the fact that it suggests that when performing a task some sort of trade-off often takes place between the demands of a task and the environment, and the operator's own abilities. The spare mental capacity model, therefore, suggests that any increased requirements made by less than optimum environments can be compensated by additional operator effort. Thus, when reading a computer display, for example, adverse conditions may well be able to be accommodated by the operator without any performance loss simply because more of the limited capacity store is used up—the operator 'works' harder or 'concentrates' more. If the task and environment demand too much, however, (perhaps increased glare occurs) the spare mental capacity which was otherwise used by the task will be exhausted with resultant reductions in performance. It is likely, therefore, that a difficult task, which leaves less spare mental capacity, will be affected quicker and to a greater extent by adverse conditions than would an easier task.

The implications of this model, therefore, are clear. Operators are able to adapt and to work in less than optimum environments but only at a cost. Provided the environment does not demand more spare mental capacity than the operator is able to give, performance will be maintained. Too much demand, however, will reduce efficiency.

THE MAN-MACHINE SYSTEM

The input of psychology to the efficient interaction with computers arises through various attempts to reduce errors and to maximize safety, efficiency and comfort by adapting the requirements of the computer to the capabilities of the operator. By linking 'man' and 'machine' in this way a relationship is established between these two components so that the computer presents information to the operator via the sensory apparatus (usually by touch, sight or hearing) to which a response is probably given—perhaps to alter the computer's state by pressing a key. For example, a typical computer program might request the operator to type the date. This request is perceived by the operator who presses the appropriate keys. As each key is pressed, the figures appear on the screen to signal to the operator that the next key needs to be pressed. In this way information passes from the computer to the operator and back to the computer in a closed, information-control loop (see Figure 1.2).

Licklider (1960) emphasizes that, when applied to computers at least, this relationship can be described more as a symbiotic than as a 'master–slave' relationship. (Later, in 1965, he referred to it as a 'man–computer partnership'). Thus, he suggests that each of the two components in the system—man and computer—depend on each other to perform well. It is not simply the computer extending the capacities of man; it is that not only does the computer depend on the operator to exist (naturally) but also that, in many respects, man is now unable to be a viable performing entity without the computer's abilities.

Whatever the nature of the relationship it is an unfortunate fact that for a number of reasons the simple loop described above is far more elaborate when it occurs in 'real life'. Firstly, of course, in working environments there are many single loops which are often combined to produce more complex systems. Being composed of groups of different components (both operators and machines), these must be designed to work together. From an ergonomics viewpoint such combinations create many problems: two loops may act efficiently when considered separately, but when combined in a working system they might well act antagonistically owing to unexpected interactions.

The second problem concerns the effect of the environment in which these single, information-control loops operate. As Figure 1.2 illustrates, the physical and social aspects of the environment can affect the efficient operation of these loops. For example, an operator's ability to see a message on a computer screen can be interrupted simply by the sun appearing over a shoulder and producing glare on the screen; noise can interfere with auditory messages; the presence of other people walking or talking nearby can disrupt concentration. Many hundreds of such examples could be adduced to illustrate the fact that the quality of information transmitted from the operator to the computer and back again is mediated by the environment.

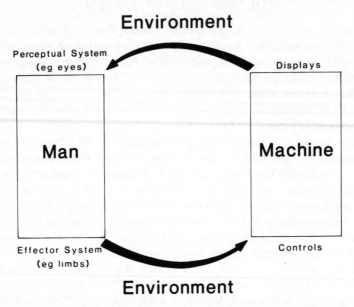

Figure 1.2. The 'man–machine' loop. The machine displays information to the operator who manipulates controls to affect the machine. The environment can interfere with the efficiency of this loop.

Through ergonomics, therefore, the role of psychology at work is to consider all aspects of the man–machine system—beyond simply the 'panel' (Murrell, 1969)—to the total interaction between 'man' and the 'environment'. This is particularly important in the field of computers. As Nickerson (1969) argues, the unique character of man–computer systems, coupled with the increasing heterogeneity of users, ensures that a thorough investigation of this particular system should provide extremely fruitful results. It is for this reason, therefore, that the main impetus of this book will be to consider aspects of this system: the social impact that computers have within an organization, the effects of hardware design (mainly controls and displays) and of software (programming) quality on an operator's performance, and the importance of different aspects of the operator's environment in facilitating or hindering this interaction.

ALLOCATING FUNCTIONS TO HUMANS AND COMPUTERS

In many ways computers and humans are very much alike. Both take in information, process it and, in some way, transmit this processed information to the outside world. The same could be said, of course, for many other objects that exist in the world. A plant takes in information about the state of its world (the temperature, humidity, salinity, etc.), processes it in some way, and then informs the world of its presence (i.e., it outputs information) by moving, growing, etc. A fire can be conceived in very similar ways. By no stretch of the imagination, however, could a plant or a fire be said to function like a human or like a computer. The essential feature of *these* components is the nature and quality of the information that they process and the ways in which they do the processing. Indeed, to be able to interact properly in the system, these two components—man and computer—do need to have relatively common information processing capacities.

As will be shown throughout this book, many of the processes of 'man' and computer are similar in concept although not so similar in function. This being so it is pertinent to ask the question 'What can men and computers do and not do?' before considering how these components can be designed to interact fully. Such a question can also be composed in a slightly different form: 'What kinds of things can and should human operators be doing in the system, and what kinds of things should the computer be doing?' In other words, why and when should a computer system be implemented in an otherwise human domain?

In response to questions such as these, many authors have attempted to compile general lists of operations which are carried out most efficiently by people and by machines (for example, Chapanis, 1960; Murrell, 1971). Taken together these lists suggest that man is a better maker of complex decisions, particularly in cases in which unexpected events may occur; is able to improvise; has a fund of past experience; and is able to interpret complicated forms involving depth, space and pattern. Machines, on the other hand, are highly efficient computing, integrating and differentiating devices; are able to deal with predictable events in a reliable fashion; and are useful in hazardous environments.

Since these lists were produced, and with the evergrowing sophistication of computers, however, a number of other factors have needed to be included in this list of comparisons.

Thus, man has a complex language system which is not entirely verbal in nature; the languages with which the computer is able to communicate, however, are limited. People are mobile and, because of internal homeostatic systems, are adaptable to different environments; computers, on the other hand, presently are static objects and are able to operate only within very well-defined environmental limits of such factors as temperature, humidity and air

cleanliness. Finally, of course, the human body is generally able to replace
worn parts of itself; the present generation of computers are not self-
maintaining.

Computers, on the other hand, have infinite patience and do not have
problems of social interaction. As will be seen in later chapters, these are very
valuable functions when dealing with slow operators or with embarassing
material such as might have to be revealed at a doctor's surgery. Furthermore,
a computer's ability to increase the number of channels for information input
is potentially limitless (limited only by its design). Man, on the other hand, has
a very limited information input system—sometimes limited to only seven or
eight items at a time (see, for example, Miller, 1956).

COMPARING HUMAN AND COMPUTER ABILITIES

Because a symbiotic relationship will work properly only if the two
components are well attuned to the abilities and requirements of each other, it
is useful to compare in more detail both 'man' and 'computer' for a number of
faculties. In this respect it should be remembered that both operate on very
similar principles: information is fed into the system via senses, it is operated
on in the central processing unit, and the transformed data are presented back
to the outside world through effector mechanisms such as arms or printers.
Each of these three components (input, processing, output) are important for
efficient functioning and the efficiency of the whole system is greatly reduced
without any one of them working properly.

Putting information into the central processor

As far as the human operator is concerned, various types of information are
fed into the sensory system through many body receptors. These can be
classified into three groups. The *exteroceptors* receive information about the
state of the world outside of the body and so include the normally recognized
five senses: sight, sound, touch, taste and smell. Using the same terminology,
the *interoceptors* inform the individual about the internal state of the body, for
example, its state of hunger or fullness of the bladder. Finally the
proprioceptors are concerned with motor functions and give information
about the position of the body or parts of the body in space —for example, the
semicircular canals in the ears help to maintain a stable posture.

In whatever form the information takes originally, once it has been
preprocessed at the site of the sense organ it is passed to the brain in a very
similar manner. Small electrical impulses travel along the nervous system as a
series of 'spikes' (so called because they appear as spikes against a background
if an oscilloscope is connected to a live nerve). Variations in the intensity of the

stimulation are represented by corresponding variations in the frequency of the spike activity along the nerve. Thus 'intensity' is converted to 'frequency' by the nervous system, and it is the pattern of these frequencies which is finally analysed by the brain to form some sort of image of the stimulus.

Unfortunately, human information processing is often faulty. Since the final images which we perceive represent only the brain's interpretation of the stimuli initially processed at the periphery—at the eye, the ear, etc.—it is possible to understand how factors such as past experience, the presence of other features in the perceptual world, the individuals's motivation, emotion, etc., can interfere with this analysing process to produce incorrect interpretations of the initial stimuli. Because they have less experience from which they can draw, however, and because they are not affected by such aspects as the social features of the environment, etc., computers are less likely to suffer from such errors in processing perceptual information.

This account of perception, of course, represents an extremely simple description of a very complex and not yet fully understood perceptual system. However, it does help to put into perspective the man–computer comparison with respect to information input. Thus two analysing systems are in operation. The first occurs at the periphery of the body—at the eye, or the ear, or at the computer's electronic or mechanical sensor. The function of these structures is to detect the presence or absence of the stimulus and to convert the energy contained in the stimulus (light, sound, temperature, etc.) into electrical energy of a form which is able to be both transmitted to and analysed by the central processor. (This process is sometimes called reception.) Secondly *perception* takes place centrally by either the brain or the computer program which analyses the pattern of impulses in order to identify the stimulus. To do this the central processing unit compares stimuli in a number of ways: with a 'template' stimulus, with previous stimuli, in association with stimuli from other senses, etc. These processes and their performance will be discussed in more detail in later chapters.

Central processing (cognitive) faculties

Memory

Probably because they have been designed by man, the ways in which computers store their information are well understood. For the purposes of comparing computer and human memory systems, it is not necessary to understand the precise detail of the ways in which the information is stored, although some description is useful.

In essence, information is stored in computers in terms of 'bits'—a bit being either the presence or absence of 'information'. (In computer terms, either a '1' or a '0', or either 'on' or 'off'). These bits are then normally grouped into either 4's, 8's, 16's or 32's to form 'bytes'. Each byte occupies a memory location and the number of bytes that a computer can store is an indication of its memory capacity. Indeed, it has been mainly this aspect of the machine which has formed the major cost of computer systems. Because recent discoveries and inventions have allowed single components to have greatly increased memory capacities, the capital cost of computing equipment has fallen dramatically in recent years. This aspect of the cost/benefit equation will be considered in more detail later.

In some respects the ways that humans and computers store and allocate memory are very similar. Both, for example, store information in a short and a long term memory system. Although there is presently controversy as to the precise mechanisms of these two systems in humans (for example, Gruneberg, 1970, argues that a dichotomous theory of memory in humans is not supported by empirical evidence and that memory should be conceived as a single dimension over time extending from short to long term), there is no doubt that in both computers and humans information is stored in the central processor firstly in some sort of volatile, immediate, 'short-term' memory. This is then stored in a longer term system at a later time. Humans and computers differ, however, in their capacity to *lose* information. In the human central processor, information can be lost at any time for a number of reasons—overloading, interference, decay, etc. Information in the computer memory, however, is stable and, providing an electricity supply is maintained, will not fail unless other information is entered (deliberately or inadvertently) into the memory area.

The techniques adopted by both systems to store the material that would otherwise overload the processor capacity are also similar. Thus, to facilitate memory the human operator uses such aids as books and paper on which to store additional material. The computer's external storage medium is magnetic, in the form of tape or disks. In both cases the storage is done in terms of the language that each uses. For the human this is words or pictures; for the computer this is bits. Since a bit takes up far less physical space than the written word, one advantage that computers have over the human operator is that their total external storage media are less space consuming. For example this book, produced on a word processor (see Chapter 9), takes up magnetic media (disks) which, in total, measure approximately $140 \times 140 \times 6mm$. Unfortunately they can only be read by an appropriately programmed computer.

Differences do exist between the two components' memory systems. Firstly, human memory is largely associative in nature. Information is retained in terms of its association with other stored information. For example, Gruneberg (1978) discusses many mnemonic techniques which can be used to increase the amount of information memorized, all of which are based in some way on 'pegging' the information to be remembered to some other—more easily retained—image. Computer storage, on the other hand, is more literal in character. As was described earlier, information is stored in terms of strings of bits and, as far as the computer is concerned, the contents of one memory cell bears no relation to that of another. Information is, quite literally, entered into and taken from specific memory locations.

Differences exist, too, in the speed of accessing the information within the processor. As Shackel (1980) points out, human central processing is very slow compared with a computer. Thus, whereas computers can presently process about 100 million bits of information each second, using comparable units humans are capable of processing only in the region of 5–50 bits/sec.

In summary, therefore, it appears that with fast technological advances, computers will soon be able to retain far more information than humans. Furthermore, the processing rate in this memory far exceeds the rate capable by man, and storing extra information takes far less physical space than the paper-based system frequently used by human operators. On the other hand, to enable the computer to have such capacity, information needs to be stored in memory in a rigid and structured manner which allows less flexibility for memory strategies and recall than does the human system.

Intellectual processes

Because human reasoning is complex, and is not yet fully understood, a detailed discussion of the processes involved is clearly outside of the remit of this book. What will be instructive, however, is to describe, at a simple level, the basic processes involved in human reasoning to compare them with the current abilities of computers to perform in a similar way.

Using complex cognitive tasks such as medical diagnosis or flying aircraft, much work has been done in the past to determine the various behavioural components involved in processes such as decision making. For example, working on the decision making requirements of U.S. Air Force pilots, Williams and Hopkins (1958) distinguished two main categories of behaviour in decision making: firstly, diagnosis of the state of the system or of the problem, and secondly, selection of appropriate actions. As Vaughn and Mavor (1972) point out, these two categories have stood up quite well to subsequent experimental verification although, since 1958, the majority of research has been directed at elaborating sub-tasks within them. In 1969 Shrenk reviewed and synthesized many of these studies and distilled nine components in the problem diagnosis category and 17 components in the action selection category. He also added a third main category—problem recognition—which is processed before the problem diagnosis phase and which includes four sub-tasks. These sub-tasks, and their suggested relationships, are shown in Figure 1.3. Once again, however, it should be stressed that these are

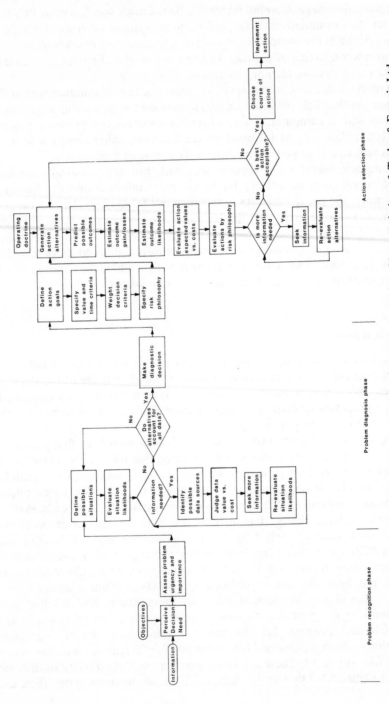

Figure 1.3. Model of decision processes (Shrenk, 1969). Reproduced by permission of Taylor & Francis Ltd.

very much simplifications of the true processes that constitute human problem solving.

As an example of the more complex cognitive processes which occur in humans, many authors (for example De Soto, London and Handel, 1965; Johnson-Laird and Wason, 1977) have argued that an important underlying process is an ability to conjure visual images of the problem to be solved. The power of an image, particularly one that can be modified over time, is that it enables an individual to make predictions about the way that events are likely to go. This appears to be the case particularly for complex problems such as playing chess or navigating ships through difficult waters (Eisenstadt and Kareev, 1977; Oatley, 1977) in which the operator needs to evaluate the outcome of different operations before a decision can be made.

In addition to imagery, of course, memory and learning are other functions underlying the sub-tasks illustrated in Figure 1.3. For example, Newell (1977) has proposed a theory of problem solving which is composed, essentially, of a large associative memory component. Indeed, he suggests that limitations to this memory size pose the main boundaries to our capacity for problem solving. Thus, many of the results of the problem solving subtasks shown in Figure 1.3 need to be stored temporarily and the strategies constantly have to be reorganized and re-evaluated in the light of updated information. This is clearly an area in which modern computers are likely to perform better than the human operator, given their very large and almost infallible memory capabilities.

A third process which underlies efficient problem solving is an ability to reduce the problem to manageable proportions. Hunter (1977) illustrates this well when describing how one mathematician performs very complex mental calculations.

> 'Professor Aitken solves any given numerical problem in a sequence of steps. First he examines the problem and decides the plan or method by which he will calculate the answer; *in doing this, he typically recasts the problem into a form which he can more easily handle.* Then he implements his chosen method and, step by step, generates the answer.'

Clearly, the implication here is that efficient problem solving is largely a function of efficient reorganization of the material so that it can be processed into manageable chunks.

Having considered, at a very basic level, the processes which have been found to underlie and to characterize human problem solving, it is now useful to consider how far computers have reached this goal. In this respect the use of computers to play successfully highly strategic games such as chess can help illustrate the level of their intellectual processing.

The reasons why computers are able to perform well on complex tasks such as chess playing are three-fold: Firstly is the very large, infallible memory that they possess. As Berliner (1977) points out, some chess programs have to evaluate between 5000 and 50,000 possible paths to arrive at the best (i.e. the most cost-effective) move. Clearly, a large memory is required to store the results of such tasks. Secondly is the fact that, despite its apparent complexity to beginners, chess is a game firmly based in simple decision rules of the nature IF...THEN: "If the pawn is moved forward, then it will be taken by the queen; if it is left where it is then it is safe", etc. Such processes form the basis of all decision making in the computer program. These simple 'statements' are combined in complex ways to evaluate, for example, board positions and the consequences of actions. Finally, the computer can perform these computations at high speed. A human operator would be unable to evaluate all possible board positions within the time allocated for a game. On the other hand, of course, it is unlikely that a human operator would *need* to evaluate all possible positions—some would be ridiculous. Furthermore, as discussed earlier, one of the valuable features of human reasoning is the ability to conjure up visual images. With experience, one image can represent a number of different positions so that the evaluation is carried out in a more 'compact' and efficient way.

In summary, therefore, it appears that computers cannot yet perform complex intellectual functions. Certainly they are able to be programmed to perform specific tasks at a level which is, possibly, better than the human operator—particularly when large memory stores are required and fast, structured decisions need to be made. However, as Marr (1979) points out, this performance is simply at the level of mimicry; as yet computers are unable to move outside of the boundaries set by their programmers to perform complex intellectual functions for which they were not originally built.

Language and communication

One aspect of human behaviour which sets man above all other animal species is the development and possesion of a complex language system. We can communicate not only simple desires, needs or warnings (as can other animals via their 'languages') but also very abstract and sophisticated concepts which could not easily be transmitted by such techniques as gesturing. In addition to providing a means of communicating ideas and concepts, however, our language has more subtle qualities—it actually helps to shape our behaviour and our perception of the world and events in it.

Examples of how language usage affects behaviour can be seen in applied settings such as eye witness testimony in the court room. For example, it has long been accepted that 'leading' questions—those which suggest the answer—should not be asked of the witness; the words used can affect the witness' memory of events. Loftus (for example, Loftus, 1975) has further demonstrated that only slight changes in the structure of a sentence can influence a witness's behaviour.

In one experiment Loftus showed people a short film of a car accident and, immediately afterwards, questioned them about what had occurred. She asked groups of subjects exactly the same question except that one group was asked 'Did you see a broken headlight?' whilst the other was asked 'Did you see the broken headlight?' The word *the* implies that there was a broken headlight to be seen, whereas *a* leaves the possibility open. The results showed that people who were asked the questions containing the word 'the' were more likely to report having seen something than those with the questions containing 'a' —whether or not it had actually appeared in the film. The word used, therefore, affected recall.

In a variation of this experiment Loftus demonstrated that the words used can affect other forms of behaviour such as numerical estimation. The question 'About how fast were the two cars going when they smashed into each other?' consistently yielded higher speed estimates than when the word 'smashed' was replaced by 'collided', 'bumped', 'contacted' or 'hit'.

In addition to the actual words used, the structure of the language itself can also affect behaviour, and this needs to be taken into account when considering man–computer interaction. For example, Licklider (1960) points out that

> 'Men naturally speak redundant languages organized around unitary objects and coherent actions and employing twenty to sixty elementary symbols. Computers "naturally" speak non-redundant languages, usually with only two elementary symbols and no inherent appreciation either of unitary objects or of coherent actions.'

By implication, therefore, Licklider reminds us that man's language is complex and adaptable whereas the computer's is simple and rigid. Since some sort of language is necessary for complex behaviour, this suggests that the computer's behavioural repertoire is lacking in at least one important area.

From these examples, therefore, it is clear that human language is far more than simply a means by which two or more people communicate messages or information. Impressions, ideas, feelings and motivations are also communicated by the way that the language is structured, by the tone and intonations of voice, and by the actual words and structures used.

In whatever ways the communication takes place, one important characteristic must exist for efficient communication to occur: both the receiver and transmitter of the message must agree on the ideas being transmitted. Fisher (1978) points out that this agreement does not necessarily have to mean that all participants in the communicative process need to have *identical* understanding of the symbols or thoughts to be transmitted. It is important only that some understanding is common to them all. This implies, therefore, that communication can take place even if both the transmitter and receiver do not 'speak' the same language—as long as the basic ideas are received accurately.

Chapters 7 and 8 will consider in more detail how such pitfalls can, and have been, overcome when designing man–computer languages and communication systems but it is instructive to remember, at this point, that two aspects of communication are important when dealing with man–computer communication. First is the problem faced by the programmer whose task it is to make the computer perform in a particular way; to mould its performance to the task in hand. In this case the problem of language compatibility refers mainly to ensuring that the set of instructions available can be combined into meaningful programs. Secondly are the problems faced by the more naive operator sitting at the computer terminal. Problems here concern more those of ensuring that the questions or information presented to the screen or printer are understandable and unambiguous, and conform as much as possible to 'natural' human language.

In summary, it is apparent that language is an extremely important feature of behaviour. If man–computer communication is to be at all efficient and productive then the language systems used by both need to be compatible and commonly understandable. Since 'man' populated this planet well before computers, and since computers represent only a tool for man's use, it is not unreasonable to expect that the language used by computers should be adapted to the requirements of the human operator. This argument will be extended in Chapter 7.

Outputting information from the central processor

The output devices available to the human operator generally take the form of some sort of movement under muscular control. This is not simply represented by movement of the limbs but includes the mouth and larynx for speech, and what is normally considered to be a sensory system—the eyes. For an ideal 'man'–computer link, of course, so that the output of one component can match the input of the other, these effector mechanisms need to be considered in relation to one of the senses that are available for input to the central processor (the human's brain or the computer's central processing unit). The physical and behavioural aspects of these processes will be discussed in detail in Chapters 5 and 6.

THE BENEFITS AND COSTS OF COMPUTERS

Although it is not particularly the place of psychology to delve deeply into the economic costs and rewards of installing a modern computer system it is, nevertheless, appropriate to consider their cost-effectiveness. Any person within an organization who contemplates replacing all or part of existing practices with a computer of whatever size will probably have to be able to justify the costs in relation to the rewards. This section will consider only very briefly the variables which should be included in the cost–benefit equation. With rapidly reducing costs of computer hardware, with an increasing availability of peripherals and functions able to be performed by smaller and smaller computers, it would not be appropriate for a book of this nature to consider the question in more detail.

The variables which need to be included in each side of the cost–benefit equation are particularly complex, as King and Schrems (1978) point out. They suggest that the benefits of installing such a system may be subsumed under five headings: cost reduction (of printing, space usage, etc.), error reduction, increased flexibility, increased speed of activity, and improvement in management planning or control.

Many of these benefits will be considered in more detail in other chapters in this book. However, it should not be forgotten that such simple headings mask a number of problems of definition when trying to arrive at a quantifiable account of the system benefits. Indeed, because of the considerable inconsistencies and intangible values, many analysts consider the quantification of benefits to be the greatest obstacle to such an analysis. King and Schrems itemize some of the problems, which include difficulties in defining consistent and comparable values to different benefits, measuring the output of individuals in multi-user environments, the values to be placed on aspects such as 'improvements in decision making' or 'enhanced morale', and to what extent trade-offs occur between human and machine operations. Furthermore, many of the overall benefits simply cannot be quantified. As Cunninghame-Greene (1973) asks: 'What economic value are we to ascribe to a probability of better customer service through better stock control by the computer? If one is trying to assess the success of computer applications within hospitals, what value does one attach to the reduction of the average length of a patient's stay by one day, in order to set that off against the cost of the project?'

If assessing the benefits of computers is difficult, counting the cost is just as hard. The cost of the system is not simply represented by the capital cost of the hardware concerned. Indeed, the cost structure of running a computer system has often been likened to a triangle with the obvious hardware costs accounting for only the top portion (like the tip of an iceberg). Depreciation, maintenance, the cost of programs and operator training often comprise the hidden base of the triangle.

King and Schrems also point out that many other pitfalls confront an adequate cost account. These include double counting (including the same cost in two ways), omitting significant costs (for example, electricity, space, etc.), hidden costs, and spillovers (for example, trained personnel subsequently leaving because of their newly aquired, marketable skills).

The costs of a computer system, of course, do not simply end at the amount of money that the organization needs to spend to keep the system operating. Other potential hidden costs, both social and organizational, must be taken into account. Many of the social costs (and benefits) will be discussed in detail in the next chapter but it is interesting to consider here some of the consequences of poor computer design that can lead to hidden costs.

In a study of 254 computer users from two levels of industry (clerks and managers), Eason, Damodoran and Stewart (1975) describe serious consequences of poor computer interface design. The consequences were different for the clerical users than they were for irregular users such as managers. Most of the clerical users had little choice but to accept any inadequacies a system possessed and to compensate for them as best they could. The cost of continued compensation, however, led to a build-up of user frustration—leading to a loss of morale and interest in the work and, possibly, to increased staff-turnover with all of its associated retraining costs.

The occasional users of the computers, however, were much less tolerant of poor systems. They expected a tool which fitted their needs and did not expect to have to modify their behaviour to fit the machine. This led either to non-use or a very limited use of the system (so wasting the resources purchased) or (just as costly) employment of extra personnel to act as human intermediaries between manager and computer.

SUMMARY

This chapter has introduced many of the aspects that need to be considered when comparing human and computer abilities in order to produce circumstances in which these two components may interact most efficiently. The primary message is that it is important to consider the complete environment in which the interactions take place, and the many ways in which aspects of the environment can impede or enhance these interactions.

The remainder of this book will consider these environments. In particular the social environment (Part I), the hardware environment (Part II), the software environment (Part III) and different working environments (Part IV).

PART I

Social Aspects

Whenever a social situation is set up between two or more people, the social bonds are likely to be strengthened the longer that the group has been established. Any intruder into such a situation, any agent—human, mechanical or electronic—which might interfere with established social patterns, is likely to be viewed in an unfriendly light, possibly causing deleterious effects on performance. The extent to which the intruder affects the established working relationships, therefore, will depend on how the intruder is perceived and how it is introduced.

In these terms, of course, the problems faced by an organization which is about to introduce computers to the workplace are no different from those that are experienced when introducing any new technology or different working practices. To provide insight into the ways in which the introduction of computers may affect social practices, therefore, it is instructive to consider how technology *per se* has affected organizations and societies in the past.Understanding these problems may then lead to an understanding of the problems that are likely to be faced when introducing computers, and how they may be overcome. These aspects will be considered in Chapter 2.

The efficiency with which computers are able to be used and the extent to which social relationships are likely to be formed, will also be related strongly to the operators' own abilities—at programming, at typing, at understanding abstract concepts, etc. For this reason, an important aspect of the relevant social environment relates to the ways in which such personnel are selected in the first place—features of their abilities which need to be considered before employment. These aspects will be considered in Chapter 3.

CHAPTER 2

The Impact of Computers on Organizations and Society

The evidence from Chapter 1 provides little doubt that computers can be extremely powerful tools at work. They may not yet have many of the important faculties available to man—flexible decision-making and intelligence, the ability to perceive and to make sense of ambiguous stimuli, fine manual dexterity under the control of a purposive will—but they do effectively have infallible memory abilities which presently rival the capacity of man and they can also perform complex, albeit standard, computational actions at incredible speeds. Furthermore, as will be seen in later chapters, the increased availability of other equipment that can be attached to the computer, such as speech input and output devices, light pens, joysticks and other controls, make it an even more powerful tool at work.

For increased efficiency, however, performance is only one factor—a very important factor—in the equation. As was pointed out in Chapter 1, another major consideration that is likely to ensure an increased reliance on these electronic machines is cost and the cost of associated equipment and programs. In this respect, the great increase in computer usage and sophistication which has occurred over the past decade has been related also to a steady decline in the real cost of computer systems. Indeed, even as this book is being written, the costs of all types of computer systems are falling dramatically.

Given the dramatic reductions in hardware costs and increases in computing 'power', it is not surprising that many large and small organizations have purchased computer systems of one type or another. Indeed Cerullo (1980) has traced the rise in computer purchases from only 50 systems in use in 1953 to a predicted 500,000 + by 1985. These figures do not include over 400,000 minicomputers and an even greater number of microcomputer sales. Such vast numbers of powerful machines cannot help but make an impact on society at large—let alone on the organizations purchasing them. Unfortunately,

21

however, the overall effect of introducing new technology to a working environment may go well beyond those originally envisaged—even to the extent of becoming detrimental to overall performance. This chapter will consider some of these impacts and the extent to which complex technology has affected, and is likely to affect, workers, organizations and societies. Although some of the examples which will be provided may relate more to other technology than to computers, it is argued that appropriate lessons can still be learnt from them about how the introduction of computing machinery may affect social and organizational arrangements.

INTRODUCING TECHNOLOGY

Introducing technology to people at work has always been difficult; the problems certainly did not start with computers. The reason for this often lies in the rationales given for introducing the technology: new machines, techniques or working practices would not be initiated if someone in the organization did not feel that they were justified for economic, organizational or social reasons. They are introduced, therefore, because they *will* affect the organization, and these effects are always likely to have some impact on the organization's level of employment, job characteristics or social interactions. Before considering how computers have affected society, therefore, it is useful to consider how new technology has been accepted in the past. As argued above, these experiences might provide some insight into how computers might or might not be accepted.

When considering the relationship of technology to organizational and worker behaviour, two primary approaches can be discerned that differ in terms of the importance given to the technology. One model, proposed by Woodward and the Tavistock group in Britain and by Walker and Guest and by Sayles in America, treats technology as an important variable that actually helps to shape organizational structure and behaviour. This will be called the 'Tavistock' approach. The other approach, proposed primarily by the Aston group of Pugh, Hickson, Hinnings, MacDonald, Turner and Lupton (1963) downgrades the importance of technology as an agent of organizational change and insists that it is only one of a number of variables that could affect organizational structure. In addition to these two, a third model, the 'socio-technical systems' approach, suggests that all of the factors, technological and social, that can affect organizational effectiveness are important. Although in some organizations some factors will be more evident than others, all need to be considered.

The Tavistock approach

The central theme of the first of these approaches then, (described by Rose, 1978, as the 'technical implications approach') is that technology shapes organizations and that technology and worker behaviour are intimately related. There is no suggestion that technology *directly* influences behaviour; rather only that it operates through the medium of an associated working organization.

Perhaps the earliest, and most well-known, set of studies to illustrate this approach was undertaken by the Tavistock Institute of Human Relations in the late 1940s. This involved investigating the effects of new mining technology on the work behaviour and productivity of coal miners, and it was published initially by Trist and Bamforth in 1951. In essence, the effect of the technology was to alter the working behaviour and productivity of the groups.

With the advent of new mining technology at the turn of this century the old 'hand-got' method of mining, characterized by small working groups (usually pairs) who worked independently of other groups and effectively decided their work goals and pace, was replaced by a new, 'longwall', layout of working. To use this new technology the small, independent workgroups were abolished and the working practice was replaced with a procedure in which larger, less autonomous, groups attacked continuous faces up to two hundred yards long. The new technology available, therefore, had caused a change in organizational structure away from tiny groups of 'all-round' craftsmen into what Trist and Bamforth (1951) described as 'rigidly sequenced work systems, organized on mass production lines'.

Although the technology was introduced to *increase* productivity, the overall result was to produce an average output far below the theoretical potential of the longwall faces. Furthermore, there was an increase in the incidence of maladaptive defence mechanisms such as absenteeism and sickness although, as Rose (1978) points out, these effects were masked to some extent by the general industrial conflict present during the early 1900s. Nevertheless, the studies do suggest that introducing new technology can be counterproductive if it upsets already established practices.

Rice's (1953, 1958) studies of the reorganization of the work structure in the weaving room of an Indian textile mill also demonstrate the importance of task-related social variables in the technology–organization relationship. Although an appropriate machinery layout and work load allocation had been carefully studied by engineers, the mill still failed to attain satisfactory performance levels. Unfortunately, however, although the work required a great deal of co-ordination between individual workers, the groups had been organized in terms of their role-similarity rather than their performance of similar tasks. Rice redesigned the groups by bringing together all workers whose tasks were interdependent and, as a result of the reorganization, he demonstrated that productivity rose from an average of 80% to an average of 95%, with damage dropping from 32% to 20%. The control situation could be seen in the rest of the weaving room where no changes were made; productivity dropped to 70% and finally rose to 80%, while damage remained at an average of 31%. Once again, therefore, the message is clear: simply introducing new working practices without considering the social-organizational implications, can be counterproductive.

Another way in which new technology can have an important effect was demonstrated by Walker and Guest (1952) in America. They investigated the influence of technological factors on work, in particular the effects of social relations in the workplace. Data were obtained from interviews with 180 car workers from 'Plant X' which was newly built in a previously non-industrialized area. The work was mainly machine-paced and repetitive. On the social side, Walker and Guest's results indicated that less than half of the sample experienced frequent social interaction on the job—not so much because of environmental influences such as noise, but because of the plant layout itself. Some workers, however, were able to find opportunities to talk with a few workmates, and these men could be said to belong to teams whose tasks allowed some social cohesion. On these occasions 'members of true teams spoke of their group interaction in positive and cheerful terms'. Once again, therefore, it would appear that technological changes can affect structure by preventing the formation of true work groups and that this 'frustrates the worker's natural urge for social attachments' (Rose, 1978).

Sayles (1958) approached the same question from a slightly different perspective. He set out to examine and to explain the effects of technology on worker behaviour from the starting point that different plants, shops or departments within an organization have varying reputations for being troublesome. He then attempted to demonstrate that such groups (or 'patterns of grievance behaviours') are related to the types of technology employed. In his samples, he isolated four kinds of behaviours: apathetic, erratic, strategic, and conservative, and claimed that actual departments or shop segments which exhibited a given pattern show a 'striking similarity in technological characteristics'. He does recognize, however, that the impact of technology on behaviour is not direct, rather it is a function of the plant structure, a 'product of its inherent ability to function in a certain way'. He further accepts that although technology may influence the patterns of conflict, it cannot initiate it:

> 'The technological factors are really *enabling conditions*. They do not explain what sets off a spate of aggressive activity, what brings it to a halt, and what are the personal motivations involved'.

The picture which is emerging from studies such as these, therefore, is that the introduction of technology can disrupt previously stable working environments, changing organizational structure and worker behaviour. Much of this disruption occurs through the technology causing increased alienation due to workers being unable to control their immediate work processes; to belong to integrated industrial communities. Such alienation, Blauner (1964) suggests, may arise in any of four states: powerlessness, meaninglessness, social isolation, and self-estrangement.

Powerlessness is related to control: 'A person is powerless when he is an object controlled and manipulated by other persons or by an impersonal system (such as technology), and when he cannot assert himself as a subject to change or modify this domination.' Technology, Blauner feels, increases powerlessness alienation by reducing the control that workers have over the degree of pressure exerted, the freedom of physical movement and the freedom to control the quantity of production. Many of these points are illustrated in the studies already discussed.

Meaninglessness refers to a lack of understanding the purpose of both the work and the process. The fact that technology often requires work to be redesigned so that each individual completes only part of the entire process (as in many assembly lines) means that only a few can 'see' the finished product—what the work is all about.

The problem of social alienation has already been discussed with respect to Walker and Guest's work. The introduction of technology can often imply the break-up of established social groups with the result that the normal social interaction does not take place.

Finally, self-estrangement refers to the possibility that a worker may become alienated from himself or herself with respect to the work. It arises mainly if other of the states are also present:

> 'This lack of a present-time involvement means that the work becomes primarily instrumental, a means toward future considerations rather than an end in itself.'

In a comprehensive survey of 100 firms conducted mainly in 1954–5 Woodward (1958) suggests that in addition to affecting worker behaviour, technology also dictates management organization. She reached these conclusions after demonstrating that the wide variety of formal organizations she had studied could only be categorized sensibly according to their technology. Later (1965) she examined variables such as the span of control and the characteristics of the labour force employed at various plants. She reported finding that those firms in which the organizational structure matched the technological requirements tended to be more successful than those in which structure did not (the 'consonance hypothesis'). She proposed the model, therefore (1970), that:

> 'different technologies impose different constraints on individual members of organizations and on the choice of organizational structure'.

Such an effect is created by the impact that technology has on organizational control and mechanisms.

One failing of Woodward's thesis is that the establishment of a relationship (for example, between the level of technology and organizational success or structure) does not, by itself, suggest either a direct causal relationship or the direction in which the association occurs. Thus, it may not necessarily be the case that technology *causes* organizational change, simply that technological changes affect variable 'a' which, in turn affects 'b', which in turn affects the organization. Indeed, Woodward herself began to accept this point when she suggested that technology affects the organization through its impact on control, although the influence of other possible intervening variables such as attitudes, motivations, accident rate, economics, etc., were not considered. Nevertheless it still remains the case that she did demonstrate *some* relationship between the technology level and organizational structure.

Without further evidence the second problem, that the presence of an association does not suggest its direction, is more difficult to resolve. A relationship between, say, reading ability and writing ability does not, by itself, imply that reading ability affects the ability to write, or the converse. Obviously the direction of some associations can be discerned by 'common sense'. For example any association between, say, intelligence and birth order can only be in one direction: birth order can only affect intelligence; one's intelligence cannot affect whether one is born first, second, third, etc.

Woodward's relationship between technology and management structure, however, is not of this nature. It may well be that, through controllability, new technology changes the structure. It may just as easily be argued, however, that changes in management structure affect the way in which work is done, with resultant implications for the degree and type of technology applied.

Woodward's work has also been criticized because of the crudity of her classification of production technology and because of her excessive emphasis on one variable: technology and its relation to organization.

With regard to her classification system, Woodward divided the 100 firms surveyed into three broad classes according to the type of process involved: small batch and unit production, large batch and mass production, and group processes. These three units were then broken down into ten. Unfortunately, however, as Rose (1958) points out, Woodward's conception of technology was not rigorous and does not always refer to the type of technology involved but to a loose classification of 'production system' or of 'system techniques'. It is more a 'developmental theory of industry' rather than a classification of technologies. Because of this, therefore, it is not necessarily unreasonable to expect some relationship between organizational structure and technology *per se*.

The Aston approach

The second criticism of Woodward's work, that of an excessive emphasis on technology as a determinant to the exclusion of other variables, has been advanced mainly by the 'Aston' group of investigators. For example, Pugh *et al.* (1963) argue:

> It is our view that while technology (or any other variable) may well be important, we must investigate much more systematically than has been possible the differences in patterns of values over ranges of associated variables, so that the relative significance of any particular variable or cluster of variables can be more easily assessed.

In a study involving 46 British organizations Hickson, Pugh and Pheysey (1969) failed to replicate Woodward's findings. Their study found few associations between production technology and the organization of work. Indeed their results indicated that differences in organizational structure depend not so much on technology as on the size of the firm. These conclusions have been substantiated by workers such as Child and Mansfield (1972) in Britain and by Hickson *et al.* (1974) for American and Canadian corporations. However, Aldrich (1972) has re-examined many of the original Aston data, only to produce completely different conclusions from the original authors. His analysis suggests that technology is indeed an important independent variable in determining organizational structure—a position which is, of course, more akin to that of Woodward.

Socio-technical systems

At present, the debate concerning the role of technology in organizational behaviour is still very much alive. Nevertheless it is clear that technology does influence worker behaviour and attitudes, and the extent to which this occurs is mediated somewhat by the way in which the technology is introduced. These assertions are included in a more recent concept of the *socio-technical system* (Cooper and Foster, 1971; Pasmore and Sherwood, 1978) in which *all* aspects of the organization—social, technical, organizational—interact to influence behaviour. Altering any one will affect the efficiency of the other. The concept of the socio-technical system, therefore, is similar to the man–machine system concept discussed in the previous chapter.

A theoretical model of how such a system works has been proposed by Whyte (1959) and is shown in Figure 2.1. He takes three concepts: interaction (the social–interpersonal contacts developed at work), activities (the tasks performed), and sentiments (the ways that the individuals feel about the world about them), and suggests that they are mutually dependent, each upon the other two, and any one of which may be modified by environmental forces (for example, technologies).

Although it is difficult to conceive of Whyte's description as a general theory of organizational behaviour, it does provide a graphic illustration of the stresses and problems involved in introducing new technology into the system.

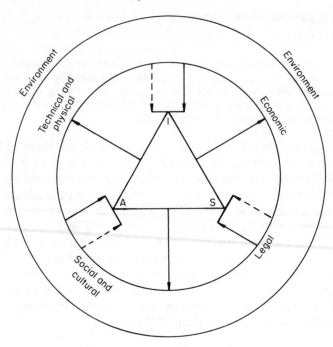

Figure 2.1. The socio-technical system (Whyte, 1959). The diagram represents interaction (I), activity (A), and sentiments (S) in mutual dependence with each other and in relation to the forces of the environment. Environmental forces may have an impact on the social system of any three points. The impact may come directly (solid line) or symbolically (dotted line). The outwardly pointing arrows indicate that the social system has impacts on the environment.

Thus, the technology can have impact on the individual, the organization and even the society, and these will now be considered particularly in relation to the introduction of computers.

ATTITUDES TOWARDS COMPUTERS

From the above discussion it is clear that introducing new technology into the workplace can affect worker behaviour and even organizational structure. However, it is also clear that many of these effects are mediated by the attitudes and the approach taken towards the new technology by both workers and management. Alienation and a loss of individual control play a large part in shaping subsequent behaviour.

Attitudes are an area of study favoured by social scientists for a number of years, and attitude surveys have investigated public response to many issues, both great and small. Unfortunately, however, relatively few have been performed to investigate reaction to computers, despite the ever-increasing role of automation at work. The studies which have been carried out can be divided broadly into two: those which have surveyed general public opinion, and those which have investigated the attitudes of the people who have to use computers at work.

Public opinion

In 1972 a survey was made of some 1030 Canadian households to determine what were the major social concerns about computer uses (see Brune, 1978). Highest in importance was the fear that computers cause unemployment, although the complaint that computers can result in serious errors (particularly in cases involving bills) was placed a close second. Depersonalization, because of unresponsive or poor systems design, was also mentioned by over 60% of the respondents, although this seems to be a question which concerned more the way in which computers are used than one relating to the existence of computers *per se*. The same argument also applies to the fourth and fifth important fears expressed during the survey—both were concerned with privacy and the use to which information stored in computers may be put.

Although this survey was carried out in the early part of the 1970s, when the explosion of home and personal microcomputer sales seen a decade later had not occurred, subsequent surveys of public opinion have produced surprisingly similar trends (e.g. Ahl, 1975). For example, a 1978 American survey of current issues found that 56% of 1508 people sampled believed that in the future, large numbers of people would be displaced by automation and be forced to change jobs. Only 16% disagreed and 36% had no strong opinion about how automation would affect them (American Council of Life Insurance, 1979).

In a survey in New South Wales, Australia, Smith (1981) administered an attitude questionnaire to over 400 people of a wide variety of ages and backgrounds. By a statistical technique known as factor analysis, he was able to extract three common factors of attitudes from the pattern of responses:

The first, most important, factor was negative towards computers and he describes it as an 'apprehension over computerization' construct. The factor contained attitude items which concern mainly the effects of computers on the individual's self image, employment prospects, and privacy. Alienation from computers and anxiety about them is strongly suggested by items such as 'some day... (computers will be) ... running our lives ...'; 'Computers ... know too much'; and 'Computers ... throw us out of work.'

The second factor represented a positive 'acceptance of computers' construct. People who agreed with the items of this factor demonstrated an appreciation of the life enhancement aspects of computers: 'Computers ... make life easier for all'; 'Computers ... trustworthy and secure.'

The third scale again represented a negative affect towards computers, and Smith termed this the 'superiority and threat of computers' perspective: 'Man's freedom ... jeopardized ... increased use of computers'; 'If ... computer ... likely to ... displace workers it should not be introduced.'

From his analysis Smith was also able to differentiate between the respondents in terms of their attitudes towards computers. He produced five such groups:

1 Group 1 (the 'mature age, technical trades' group) were older than the average, were less well-educated, and rarely used computers at work. They held no extreme views about computers in society and felt that computers had a basically positive role in society, although they also have some important negative effects on jobs.
2 Group 2 (the 'computer enthusiast' group) was typified by people who used computers often. The group had a positive attitude towards computers, and strongly rejected all negatively stated items. For this group, computers were definitely good for society and for the individual.
3 Members of group 3 were younger and well-educated. Possibly because they had had some experience of computers and understood their impact, the group had a complex attitude profile which expressed both good and bad aspects of the computer's role in society.
4 Group 4 was a group of people with mixed backgrounds who had rarely used computers. They generally held negative attitudes towards them.
5 Members of group 5 had used the computer less frequently than any of the others. Again, despite the fact that they had the highest education levels, the group attitudes were strongly anti-computer.

Surveys such as these, therefore, suggest that in the minds of the public there is basically a positive to negative continuum towards computers which is relatively independent of age or intelligence. The positive side, emphasized by those who use or who have access to the machines, views computers as being beneficial in many areas of society such as health and education. The negative side, proposed by those who have had little contact with the machines, is concerned about computers and employment, depersonalization, privacy, error and the misuse of information. Whether such a continuum is mirrored in the people who have to use computers at work, however, and to what extent such public attitudes are reflected in such a continuum is another matter.

Worker opinion

Despite the public's fears of automation, it would appear that office workers at least have not been hostile to the introduction of computers, possibly because they have direct experience of their benefits to work (and those who are displaced as a result of the introduction of computers are not surveyed!)

Hardin (1967) reported that in a number of studies conducted in American insurance companies in which computers had been introduced, the computer appeared to have had only a moderate effect on the social work environment and job satisfaction. Furthermore, in answer to the question 'if it would not make any difference in the pay and security of your job, would you like to see your job become more highly automated?', in the six industries that they surveyed Loubser and Fullan (1970) found generally three times as many people welcomed automation as opposed it.

This picture of acceptance of automation by workers is surprising, particularly given the fears expressed by the public. However work by Shepard (1971) may serve to explain at least some of the disparity.

Shepard was interested in alienation amongst workers and compared the attitudes of factory workers with those of clerical workers in organizations such as insurance companies and banks. In the jobs involved, Shepard distinguishes between three production systems: craft (where the worker is basically using skills), mechanized (where the worker simply performs standardized tasks on, for example, the production line), and automated (where a large process is being automatically controlled, and the worker performs monitoring or design functions). Given these definitions, Shepard was able to conclude that alienation in both the factory and office was *reduced* by automation, but (as described in the previous section) not by mechanization. He argued, therefore, that the automated production systems provided greater emphasis on the entire process, more centralization and better integration into the system. This, in turn, usually resulted in a less specialized division of labour, job enlargement, and a great deal of interdependence between jobs.

These findings, in fact, support some produced by Elizur (1970) from a survey of 450 employees of two clerical organizations in Holland. Although before the introduction of the computers many workers reflected the public's fears of unemployment and problems in integrating with computers, after their introduction most employees felt that the work was more varied, interesting, responsible and productive. Furthermore the majority were satisfied with job security, social relations with their colleagues, the work and the organization.

The impression should not be gained, however, that computers are universally accepted by employees. For example, in Elizur's survey the majority of workers were found to be concerned about opportunities for promotion and felt that upward mobility had been decreased as a result of the introduction of computers. Furthermore workers in both organizations disliked the way that the computers had been introduced, with little information or training about the new systems being given. Attitudes, therefore, are formed not simply by the perceived value of the computer system but, as Gotlieb and Borodin (1973) suggest, by 'the organizational structure, the quality of supervision and management, and the manner in which changes are introduced'.

COMPUTER IMPACT ON THE USER

When considering the computer's effects it is, of course, very difficult to consider the worker and the organization who use computers as somehow being independent entities. They are obviously related, so that each of the components (worker, computer, organization) are intimately bound up with each other: what is good or bad for one must be good or bad for the other; the way that the computer affects one must be related to its impact on the other. Nevertheless, it is necessary to treat the two main components (individual and organization) as being separate if only to see how one can possibly provide the optimum conditions for the other's interaction with computers. This section, therefore, will consider how computers affect the individual at work, whereas the next will consider the impact on organizations.

Employment

Employment is possibly the most frequently cited area in which computers are likely to affect individual workers; as the previous section illustrated, most public opinion polls and writers on the topic have expressed concern about the possible serious adverse impacts that computers might have on employment. Indeed one self-appointed U.S. Ad Hoc Committee once advised President Johnson that computers will mean that 'the nation will be thrown into unprecedented economic and social disorder' (Gilchrist, 1980). The pertinent question, therefore, is 'to what extent are such dire predictions, and the fears expressed in many public surveys, justified'"

It is difficult, if not impossible, to obtain an overall view of the impact that the introduction of computers has had on employment statistics; interpretations of the statistics vary. For example, Gotlieb (1980) points to a Canadian report of the impact of computers on employment which drew together 87 papers on the topic, and covered 12 countries. The report's authors quote in extensive detail from 42 of these publications which they regard as particularly important, and present the wide disparity of views in sequence from the most alarming, in that they forecast 'massive unemployment', to the most reassuring. All agree, however, on one trend: the introduction of microelectronic technology, although bringing about increases in unemployment, also created increased productivity.

Although such overall conclusions appear, on the face of it, to be critical of the computer's role in causing unemployment, the effects of even these general conclusions are open to varying interpretations. For example, a number of analysts argue that the introduction of computers will be likely to spur *overall* employment. Thus, Simon (1977) stresses that a cost reduction in any part of the system releases resources that can be employed to increase the output of goods and services elsewhere in the system. Productivity, then, spurs economic growth, which should ultimately spur employment. A similar argument was advanced by Whisler (1970), particularly in situations in which a new system is being installed. Again, rapid increases in sales volume should offset, at least partially, any tendency that the computer may have for displacing personnel.

Green, Coombs and Holroyd (1980) suggest another reason why an overall view of computer impact on employment is not possible. They point out that the many figures which have been produced are, quite simply, predictions of *jobs at risk*—not of unemployment (jobs lost). Before unemployment occurs the workers have to be laid off or made redundant by their employers, and they only become unemployed if there are no other jobs available for them elsewhere in the organization or the 'market place'. A number of factors can intervene to stop *potential* displacement turning into *actual* displacement, and so job closure must be seen to be separate from unemployment.

Simple interpretations of the statistics, therefore, can lead to many pitfalls, as can the actual collection of the statistics. Again, a number of variables may interfere. For example, any employment effects caused by the computer are likely to be a strong function of two variables: the type of organization and the nature of the work done, and the motivation for introducing computers. These variables, of course, are linked: a manufacturing organization may wish to introduce computers to automate the process, perhaps to ensure that material is produced more accurately; a clerically based organization such as a bank, however, is also likely to introduce computers to reduce clerical costs and errors.

Simon (1977) does point out, however, that there is one case in which the organizational and motivational factors may not be directly related: when part of the motivation is to improve the quality of the system's output. In this case, whatever the type of organization, either more staff may be needed to cope with the increased activity or, at the very least, the net reduction in personnel may be smaller than would be estimated solely from the increase in efficiency.

Since the impact of computers on employment is often likely to be industry, or task specific, it is useful to consider the effects on different tasks separately.

In a wide ranging study of 19 large life-insurance companies, Whisler (1970) asked questions concerning the effects of computer systems on the number of personnel employed at clerical, supervisory, and middle- and top-management levels. The data relating to the eight companies which replied are shown in Figure 2.2, from which it is immediately clear that the computer had detrimentally affected the employment prospects of clerical staff. This is possibly because computers had been introduced to take over many of their tasks. Two companies, however, also reported increasing the supervisory and managerial staff (whether this means that two companies had increased staff

Computers at Work

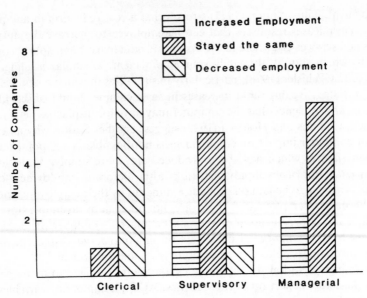

Figure 2.2.   The effects of computers on employment at different organizational levels in insurance companies (Whisler, 1970). Reproduced by permission of Praeger · Publishers.

at both levels, or that two had increased only supervisory and two managerial staff is not clear from Whisler's report). Since there were less clerical staff for these people to supervise, the data in Figure 2.2 suggests that the extra staff were employed to operate the computers themselves.

Whisler also presented his data in terms of the number of departments affected, and these results are shown in Table 2.1. As he points out, presenting the information in this way possibly gives a more accurate picture since it does not mask the effects of the computer that are caused by such organizational

Table 2.1. The effects of computers on employment in departments at different organizational levels within eight life insurance companies (Whisler, 1970). Reproduced by permission of Praeger Publishers.

Organizational level	Number of departments in which employment:		
	Increased	Stayed the same	Decreased
Clerical	7	11	45
Supervisory	8	39	16
Managerial	1	57	5

responses to potential job loss as redeployment. Once again, however, the table illustrates that effects on employment vary consistently with organizational level. In only a small proportion of affected departments did clerical employment remain unaffected; only a few departments showed employment effects at the managerial level.

A second observation to be made from Table 2.1 is that the displacement effects outweigh the addition effects at all levels. This difference is less pronounced at the supervisory level where computer implementation may be taking place. However, as Whisler points out, with time and as the computer is installed and running efficiently, many of these jobs may also be at risk. Furthermore, Whisler's data do not suggest to what extent job change or redeployment had occured as a result of the computer. Thus, it may have been the case that sometimes a person does exactly the same job with the computer as before it was installed. Only the job name may be changed so that what was once classed as a 'clerical' job becomes a 'supervisory' job simply because it deals with computers.

In an attempt to check some of these conclusions, Whisler asked the respondents also to estimate the number of people who would be required to do the *present* job in computerized areas if the computers were to disappear. Overall, an increase in clerical staff of 60% was estimated, with a 9% increase in supervisory and a 2% increase in managerial staff.

Green, Coombs and Holroyd (1980) investigated the effects of computers on employment in a wide range of industries situated in a particular area of Greater Manchester (Tameside). By looking at the number and distribution of employees in different firms in the area, and by interviewing people in these firms, the authors were able to predict the possible direct job risk due to the introduction of microelectronics within the next decade (1990). Their data suggest that only in certain industries was a significant jobs-at-risk problem likely to occur—the main ones being in the engineering, textile, and publishing industries—with about 3% of jobs being at risk. As the authors point out, however, such predictions must be understood in the light of the employment and manufacturing pattern of Tameside; some of the industries had already implemented microelectronic technologies and so would not appear to be badly affected. Also, other places may well be affected in other areas. Nevertheless such data imply that, overall, jobs are likely to be lost as a result of introducing computers—although possibly not at the high level suggested by earlier predictions.

Despite the depressing effect of computers on overall employment, as was suggested earlier it is the case that in some areas the installation of computers is likely to increase employment prospects. Thus, as was seen in Whisler's data, although the proportion of clerical staff was reduced overall, managerial and supervisory staff sometimes increased. One such area is the computer industry itself, in which employment has grown as the demands for computer services have increased. This is so both for industries which produce computer systems, and for departments set up to implement them. Indeed Gilchrist (1980) has estimated that 2–3 million (3%) jobs in America have been created directly for the manufacture and support of computers. Similar trends were reported by Green *et al.* (1980) for manufacturing firms which use microelectronics in their products.

As far as employment is concerned, therefore, computers have been very much the 'curate's egg'—good in parts. Overall they have probably reduced employment *prospects* although, because of processes such as redeployment, they may not necessarily have increased long term unemployment significantly. In specific areas, however, such as manufacturing and clerical work, they have had dramatic negative effects. This may be offset, however, by the jobs created in microelectronic industries and in more supervisory roles.

Job and work characteristics

When discussing the effects of computers on employment, it became apparent that one significant effect has been to change the nature of the jobs that people do. This occurs either by redeployment or because the ways in which they do the job, and some of the skills required, are altered through interacting with the computer (for example, changing from a 'typist' to a 'word processor operator'). Such changes, however, may also occur in other ways; since using the computer system sometimes requires different work strategies, many of the social arangements at work can become disrupted. As an example, Eason (1980) considers this effect from the point of view of managerial roles. Because much of the manager's job is concerned with collecting information from other areas and disseminating this information, the manager's role normally contains a large element of control. After the introduction of computers, however, the need for the manager to act as an information disseminator may be reduced: other members of the organization might also have access to information previously denied them. Similarly, in reducing the manager's information monitoring tasks, the interpersonal contacts previously needed may become less important with, again, a possible change in perceived role.

On the other hand, of course, the information which the manager does collect from the computer is likely to be more structured and complete. It is likely to be richer and the prospects exist for the manager to explore the task more deeply and to examine more possible actions.

For managerial users, therefore, computers can alter their role and increase the effectiveness of the information supplied although, in some cases, they can also reduce managerial control by allowing others to have relevant information. At the same time, however, Kling and Scacchi (1980) also point out that computers can *increase* managerial and supervisory control in some areas, particularly when automated information systems are used to monitor the activities of employees; for example, the quality of their work. Systems of this nature can be found in many computer-using organizations (Kling, 1974) but, as Kling and Scacchi also point out, such uses of computers are not universal. Thus, some types of organizations such as the police, or some types of departments such as accounts, are more likely to use computers for this type of function than are others.

As has been discussed, one effect of new technology on the work force that was found by earlier studies is a tendency to increase feelings of alienation from the task; a feeling that the worker becomes remote from the job and from the product. In view of the fact that computers often enable workers to be removed physically from the main place of work, it could well be anticipated that their introduction would also increase alienation. However Blauner (1964), in his study of a number of industries referred to earlier, found that this was not the case. In the chemical industry, for example, automation actually *reduced* alienation.

Crawley and Spurgeon (1979), however, question Blauner's conclusions. They point out that his data were obtained in cases where 'blue-collar' workers in manual systems performing fragmented work became semi-skilled 'white-collar' workers responsible for the monitoring of complete segments of work. Their jobs, therefore, became more enriched owing to the implementation of automation. This will not necessarily be the case when computers are introduced into 'white-collar' tasks, many of whose workers previously had some sort of control over their task. Indeed, the problem can be exacerbated by the computer. Thus, as Kling and Scacchi (1980) point out, computing specialists and those in managerial roles generally are able to control the periods in which they use computers. Clerical workers on the other hand are constrained in their use of computing systems to data entry and/or retrieval (Mumford and Banks, 1967). The work of clerical workers, then, is generally managed so that they *must* use a computing system as provided; their control over their work patterns is diminished. It still remains possible, therefore, that computers may increase a sense of alienation in some sections of the workforce.

Even for managers, however, all is not well and Eason (1980) adds support to the contention that computers can reduce the control of many individuals. In his survey of eight organizations who had implemented computers he demonstrated that, although computer systems supported the manager by offering an improved view of the task, they also introduced greater sources of constraint; increased workload and workpace together with increased variations in workpace contributed towards negative perceptions of the computer.

Such conclusions are in line with those of Mann and Williams (1962) who reported a study of an office in which many procedures were computerized. They found that there were more deadlines to be met after the computer had been installed than before, and that these deadlines were considered to be more important. They suggest that the imposition of these deadlines reduced job satisfaction and created anxieties. Similar results were also obtained by Whisler (1970) in his study of computer usage in insurance companies.

Despite these points Kling and Scacchi (1980) report studies which have demonstrated that in many cases the computer can enlarge the overall jobs of workers who use the technology. As was discussed earlier, for example, surveys by Elizar (1970) showed that after introducing computers, most employees felt that their work was more varied, interesting, responsible and productive. In addition, computers can provide more efficient information at faster speeds so helping the operator to make more appropriate decisions.

In summary, therefore, it would appear that the introduction of computers and automation is likely to affect the job content and perceptions of individuals differentially. For those who previously had little or no control over their work, computers are likely to reduce alienation and to enlarge the job. Introducing computers is also likely to benefit those who need to supervise and to make decisions based on as complete information as is possible. To those who previously had a measure of job control, however, the introduction of computers can reduce job satisfaction and actually increase alienation. Because of their tireless and demanding qualities, and because they require information to be presented in standardized ways, the pace of work is likely to be increased and the span of individual control reduced.

COMPUTER IMPACT ON THE ORGANIZATION

Despite the fact that the capital costs of computer systems are falling rapidly, it is still the case that they represent a large investment for organizations to make. Costs of implementation, software, maintenance, etc., all serve to remind the finance section that a computer has been purchased. Since one of the main reasons for installing such costly machinery is to increase efficiency, it is not unreasonable to expect them to affect the organizational structure. The interesting question is in what ways this occurs.

Organizational authority and control

It is often said that information is power, and the introduction of a computer system is an occasion where power may be shifted around. For example the value of computers to the power of individual managers and supervisors has already been considered when discussing surveillance. Computers can be used to keep records and accounts of employees' behaviour—both personal and productive. However, the concept of power can also be extended to the organizational structure itself—the way in which an organization behaves (autocratic, democratic, bureaucratic, centralized, decentralized) is a function of where the power lies.

Bjorn-Andersen and Rasmussen (1980) suggest that power can be divided into two aspects. First, structural power, which is related to the organizational hierarchy and the ways in which organizational decisions are taken and control exercised. Second are the behavioural aspects which are more concerned with the individual, and possibilities for shaping individual work environments. This second aspect they further sub-divide into 'discretion' (the power to decide on one's own role and the absence of power being exerted by others) and 'influence' (the power to change the behaviour of someone else).

With regard to the behavioural aspects Kling and Scacchi (1980) point out that it is a relatively common observation that computer-based systems increase the influence of those who have access to the technology and understand it. Such an analysis led Downs (1967) to suggest that those who have command of the system and those who control the information will gain power relative to other staff.

As an example of this effect, Bjorn-Andersen and Pedersen (1977) point to a loss of discretion for all groups of managers as a consequence of the introduction of a production and scheduling system in an electronics company. The organizational hierarchy in each of the three assembly plants studied consisted, in principle, of a plant manager in charge. Underneath was a line hierarchy (work managers, foremen) and three parallel staff functions (production planning, production technique and production control), each of these headed by a section manager. The computer system primarily changed the job content of the production planners who took over a large part of the planning task. One consequence of the introduction of this system was that all groups of managers involved with the system had lost discretion as they were now receiving more 'goals, policies and plans' and worked more with 'rules, procedures and preplanned methods'. Furthermore they were more 'dependent on the work of others' than before, and they felt more 'controlled in their tasks'. Similar conclusions were reached by Stymne (1966) who demonstrated that, after the installation of a computer in an insurance company, the computer department tended to acquire control of a number of different company functions.

Computer automation, therefore, appears to alter patterns of influence and power among key participants in organizations where no such consequences were necessarily intended.

As an example of individual power shifts in other areas, Kraemer and Dutton (1979) investigated the role of automated information systems in altering power relations among key partcipants in American municipal governments. They collected data in 42 cities to investigate alterations attributable to the use of computer-based reports in policy formation and policy making. Data relating to the use of computer-based reports and their roles in influencing policy preferences were collected in interviews with 10–20 key people in each city (such as urban planners, Mayors, chief administrative officers, city council members, etc.). Their results showed that some participants discernably gained or lost power as a result of computer use in each of the cities studied. However, no single type of role ('Mayor', 'planner' etc.) gained or lost power; in different cities different participants gained or lost, although many had their power unaffected. In support of Down's hypothesis, city councillors were most likely to lose (20%) and rarely gained (5%) power. Moreover top-level administrators often gained (27%) and rarely lost (3%) power when there were any shifts at all. Kling and Scacchi (1980) suggest that these data imply that computer-based information *reinforces* the patterns of influence in municipal governments, possibly because it is the top officials who can authorize large expenditures and who will, on the average, ensure that the expensive analyses serve their interests. In this case, then, computers served to make the strong stronger and the weak weaker.

With regard to organizational power the important question is whether the computer facilitates centralization or decentralization.

Whisler (1970) argued strongly that computers are likely to increase the centralization of systems control in organizations:

> They tie together and integrate areas of decision making and control that formerly were relatively independent of one another. ... [They can] monitor, correct, and adjust actions over a much broader area than could any human group. Given the typical pyramidical structures of business organizations, this integration results in shifting system control ... up higher in the organization than where it formerly was located.

In his study of 19 insurance companies Whisler demonstrated definite tendencies towards centralization as a result of the computer implementation, although the pattern was not the same over all companies. In one company, for example, it was reported that a significant percentage of day-to-day administrative responsibilites had been entrusted to the computer applications themselves, whilst another respondent noted that, through computer applications, top administrative officers were able to exert a much broader span of control over the work in their area of responsibilty. At the same time, those organizations who reported less centralization occurring felt that this was due mainly to the fact that the computers had not been installed for long and many people had not realized their full potential. They therefore anticipated an increased tendency to centralization in the future.

A similar type of study carried out on 110 American manufacturing establishments by Blau *et al.* (1976), however, led to completely opposite conclusions. They found that on-site computer use was associated with *decentralization* of operational decisions—primarily in the form of granting autonomy to the plant manager (although no further down the line of hierarchy).

The reason why these two contradictory conclusions are reached probably lies in the types of organizations studied. Thus, Whisler investigated essentially clerical based organizations whereas Blau *et al.*'s organizations were manufacturing based. In this respect findings of Withington (1969) are useful. He examined a number of organizations in both the public and private sectors and concluded that automation, while it may result in centralized data processing, tends to promote decentralization of line responsibilites.

Robey (1981) also questions whether what appears to be decentralization actually is so. He uses an argument advanced by Child (1972) to suggest that decentralization is usually coupled with increased formalization of rules and procedures for job behaviour. Together these elements become the basis for bureaucratic or administrative control of lower levels. Indeed Blau and Schoenherr (1971) have demonstrated that computerization plays a key role in this control strategy. Robey suggests, therefore, that computer systems are likely to be a chief tool in the strategy of administrative control by increasing the formalization of tasks and by monitoring lower decision outcomes:

> 'Thus, what appears to be greater decentralization may simply entail the delegation of more routine decisions whose outcomes are more closely controlled.'

A further explanation for the difference between the two findings can be seen in the results supplied by Blau *et al.* They indicated that the physical location of the computer facilities governs where the decisions are likely to be made: if the computer is central, then centralization is likely to occur; if access to the computer is distributed around the organization, then decentralization will occur. Such conclusions, of course, have implications for the future. The current trend in computers is towards more powerful, individual microcomputers which are cheap enough and small enough to be sited on individuals' desks. Furthermore the software for such machines is becoming more complex and sophisticated in many fields including record keeping and financial modelling. If power resides with the computer, therefore, Whisler's observations of over a decade or so ago of increasing centralization are likely to be overtaken by the development of the machinery. In many respects, therefore, the centralization/decentralization issue is fast becoming sterile.

Planning and decision making

A major aspect of the locus of control discussed above is that of decision making. Quite naturally, planning and decision making are carried out in the control centre of the organization. These activities, however, are not simply individual acts of choosing between a few alternatives; decision making does not generally reside solely in the hands of one or two people as does often the authority of an organization. As Whisler (1970) points out the elements of decision making are frequently carried out by a number of different people in an organization. It involves

> 'the establishment of a goal, definition of problems, collection and consideration of information, drawing up possible alternative courses of action, estimation of the probable outcomes of the various alternatives and, finally, actual commitment to some course of action'.

All of these responsibilities seldom lie with a single individual, they require the integration of a number of people at different levels and with different sorts of jobs. Planning and decision making, therefore, are both social and organizational activities, and computing systems may play a large part in their efficiency.

Scott-Morton and Huff (1980) suggest that the value of computers to organizational planning is a function of three approaches for the gathering, storage, analysis and supply of the information required.

First is a *manual* technique which covers all non-computer methods of formal information handling such as 'talking', 'committee meetings', thinking, etc. Secondly is the use of *management information systems* (MIS) in which the computer is used basically in terms of clerical replacement. MIS includes information gathering, handling and transmission between offices, the maintenance of large information (data) bases, and the maintenance of information files. Thirdly, and more recently, are the *decision support systems* (DSS); computer packages aimed at *assisting* (not replacing) managers in their decision-making tasks. Scott-Morton and Huff emphasize that these modelling tasks are aimed at supplementing managerial decision: 'Neither the manager nor the computer can do as effective a job as the two together.'

Despite the suggestion that computers *can* be used to aid decision making, the question still remains to what extent computers are being used in this respect. Scott-Morton and Huff, for example, suggest that computers have had little impact so far on management for this type of comprehensive planning activity. However they predict that this state of affairs will soon change as more powerful applications arise.

In an attempt to answer questions of this nature Naylor and Schauland (1976) surveyed nearly 2000 corporations to determine the degree to which computer planning models were used and the resources required. Models were being used or developed in 73% of the firms surveyed, and another 15% were planning to develop them. This represents quite an advance in less than a decade since Gershefsi (1970) conducted a similar survey of 63 corporations and found only 20% of his sample who claimed to be using or developing a corporater planning model. Of the firms which did use such models Naylor and Schauland showed that most were using them for financial applications (cash flow analysis, financial forecasting, balance sheet projections, etc.) although, interestingly, the models were generally used for most of Scott-

Morton and Huff's stages of planning: evaluating alternative policies (79%), providing financial projections (75%), and for facilitating long-term (73%) and short-term (56%) planning.

Despite encouraging results of this nature, other evidence suggests that the overtly expressed uses of computers to aid decision-making have not actually been implemented to the same extent. Thus Greenberger, Crenson and Crissey (1976) investigated uses to which computer-based modelling systems were used by public agencies. Contrary to expectations they found that policy makers' choices were rarely influenced directly by such analyses. Indeed it was often found that the main use to which the results were put was to generate support for policies already decided in advance. When results were influential it was often the computer modelling expert who was called in to help to make the decisions, rather than the results themselves. Whisler (1970), in his study of insurance companies, also found similar trends in that computers were used to strengthen the hands of the decision makers.

Further problems confronting those who argue for computers as aids to decision making arise from the lack of flexibility that often has to be incorporated into the models to be manageable. For example, Bjorn-Andersen (1979) has described three applications where small- to medium-sized computers were installed to carry out functions normally done by middle managers. The first was for inventory and marketing analyses in a plant in the United Kingdom, the second for scheduling production in a radio factory, and the third for patient scheduling in a British hospital. In all three cases the results were unsatisfactory, and the hospital system was abandoned because it failed to respond to the basic needs of the doctors and patients. Difficulties arose because the systems were too inflexible to meet new demands. Bad weather accompanied by unexpectedly heavy snow falls led to transportation problems which disrupted the inventory planning, whilst changes in the taxation system resulting from new regulations in the European Common Market made the radio marketing program obsolete. As Gotlieb (1980) points out, human managers have no difficulty in dealing with such emergencies, but the computers are limited by an inability to deal with a problem when the context changes. Once again the need to design systems to take account of the user is emphasized.

As far as the computer's role in decison-making and planning is concerned, however, all is not bad. For example, Greenberger *et al.* emphasized the increased social relations that are involved in the development of models. It may be, therefore, that better decisions are reached due to stronger social and organizational links being forged.

Kling (1978), in his study of the use of automated information systems in 42 American cities, found that in 35% of the cities the computer reports generated were generally used to enhance the decisions made. He also found that in the more highly automated cities, policy makers were far more likely to report clearer perceptions and surprises gleaned from reports based on automatic analyses. However, he also found that policy makers in highly automated cities were more likely to use the same reports to legitimize their personal perceptions and gain publicity for their preferred programmes. He interprets these findings to suggest that computer-based analyses are a social resource used by the decision makers in the same way that they use any other social resource. They do not alter the policy making style of political bodies but are appropriated and adopted by policy makers to *their* styles of organizational work.

In summary, therefore, it would appear that the effects of computers on organizations are variable and depend largely on the type of organization and the abilities, wishes and desires of the people they contain. Colton (1979) has summarized the situation thus:

> Students of technology and society have largely abandoned the view that computers and their technologies will impinge directly on institutions and organizations causing dramatic collisions and changes of direction. Computer technology does not create social forces or trends; rather, the application and the use of new technologies are strongly influenced by political forces and social values. ... Nevertheless technology may well support or enhance established trends or directions of change. They may make powerful people more powerful, and established practices more set.

SUMMARY

Whatever the size of an organization, computers are likely to be introduced for one reason only—it is thought that the cost of introducing them will be offset by the benefits that they promise to bring for accuracy, productivity, etc. Thus, they are introduced to affect the organization. Because of this, introducing computers into previously established working systems will be bound to affect the existing social structure at all levels, from small groups to the full organization.

How much of an effect computers are likely to have can perhaps be predicted by considering the results of introducing new technology to established working groups in the past. Thus, this chapter has shown that if the new technology disrupts the existing social patterns and alters the nature of the work, with resultant changes in perceived roles, then problems might well occur.

In addition to altering individual groups' practices, however, it has also been demonstrated that new technology, particularly computer technology, can affect the organizational structure. Depending on the nature of the task performed by the organization, power-shifts towards or away from centralization often results—although the power generally shifts to those people within the organization who operate and use the computer.

Finally, this chapter also considered the ways in which computers are viewed both by the general public and by workers who have to interact with the machines. In this respect it was shown that whereas public attitudes are generally unfavourable towards computers within organizations, such attitudes are not necessarily reflected within workforces. One of the reasons for this might possibly reside in the perceived effects of computers on unemployment. Whereas, again, the public attitude suggests that computers increase unemployment, when the statistics are examined closely it would appear that such fears are not necessarily grounded in fact. Certainly, the introduction of computers can have detrimental effects on employment in specific forms of work—particularly clerical—but their *overall* effects might, in some cases, be to increase employment owing both to increased organizational productivity and to the fact that personnel are required to operate them.

CHAPTER 3

Computer Personnel

The previous chapter considered the impact that computers, automation and advanced technology have on the efficiency of individuals and groups at work. In this chapter the system will be considered from the point of view simply of the people who work with computers: how satisfied are they with their jobs, what interests and values do computer personnel have, what skills are required of them, and is it possible to predict operator success? Questions such as these have more than simply 'academic' value; they have implications for the success of the whole system. For example, job dissatisfaction can lead to increased absenteeism and turnover with adverse implications for retraining costs. Similar consequences can obviously accrue from selecting individuals who are not suitable for the task, either because of a lack of interest or aptitude.

Before considering the psychological aspects of these questions, however, it is useful to ask 'Who uses computers?, and 'Whose behaviour should we be investigating?' Smith (1980) divides users into three broad categories: end-, mid-, and system support-users. The end-user may be defined as the consumer of computer services which are provided by the other two: for example, data processor operators, clerks, managers, etc. Although these are the people who have the ability to 'make or break' the computer system, to use it efficiently or inefficiently, very little research has been performed directly to investigate their abilities or requirements, apart from the ergonomic studies which will be considered later in Part II and some studies of the application of computers discussed in Part IV. Most of the information relating to this group concerns the nature of the effects of the computer on such aspects as employment prospects and opinions, as discussed in the last chapter.

Smith's second group of computer users, mid-users, includes the people whose task is to ensure that a particular computer application is successful. In more recent years their job has become known as 'software engineering'; they are the programmers who design the instructions to make the computer system operate in a particular way.

46

Finally, the system support-users' task is to maintain the complete system and to ensure that it functions efficiently. They are sometimes known as 'systems analysts' and they perform both administrative and operational functions. They need to understand the technology involved, the range of software available as well as many organizational aspects.

Most of the work available relating to satisfaction, interests and aptitudes of computer personnel concern members of these last two groups.

SATISFACTION FROM COMPUTERS

The factors which act for or against satisfaction at work are far too numerous and their effects far too complex to be considered in detail here. Nevertheless there are some quite well documented effects of dissatisfaction at work, and these include influences on job performance, absenteeism, turnover, and physical well-being.

Prior to the mid 1950s it was generally assumed that a favourable attitude towards the job was necessary for high performance and productivity. For example, the Human Relations movement of industrial relations argued that, under friendly supervision, the individual increases productivity as a consequence of increased satisfaction. However, a number of reviews of the relationship between job satisfaction and productivity have cast serious doubts on the assumption that any relationship exists between the two factors (for example, Brayfield and Crockett, 1955; Vroom, 1964).

Although there is little evidence of a link between overall productivity and satisfaction at work there is a relationship, albeit small, between dissatisfaction and absenteeism (for example, Porter and Steers, 1973; Vroom, 1964). The effects of absence, of course, are to disrupt work schedules and, possibly, to require the organization to employ more staff to cover for 'missing' employees. Indeed, Mirvis and Lawler (1977) have estimated that, in a bank which they were studying, the cost to the bank was over 60 dollars for each absence.

Whereas absence causes temporary disruption to the work process, if an employee leaves the job entirely this can also disrupt many of the social relationships which work groups set up both amongst themselves and within the organization. In addition, of course, there are often further costs involved including advertising for replacements, payment of selection staff, and retraining. Indeed, owing to the high costs of training and the specialized nature of the personnel involved, the impact for the computer industry of the significant relationship between dissatisfaction and turnover which has been demonstrated by many studies (for example, Porter and Steers, 1973; Porter *et al.*, 1974; Bartol, 1977) is likely to be particularly high. As Awad (1977b) argues, without long term employee commitment to the system's development, using computers can create costly chaos rather than the economic efficiency that they are designed to produce. Nevertheless, there is a positive side to having some turnover in an organization. Thus, as Woodruff (1980a) and Gruneberg and Oborne (1982) point out, some turnover may be thought to be a 'healthy thing' since it can help to remove 'deadwood' and bring 'new blood' into the workforce.

Several studies have been carried out to investigate factors that affect the turnover of computer personnel and, whilst each offers a different cause, they all agree that the turnover in data processing staff resulting from voluntary resignations is excessively high. For example, Thompson (1969) found that the average-sized firm experiences 30–40% turnover per year, although Willoughby (1977) does point out that such figures should be considered in relation also to the general state of the economy and to the supply-and-demand for computer systems prevailing at the time. Thompson concluded that the main reasons for turnover were a lack of internal opportunities for promotion, regular involvement with routine tasks, limited participation in task-related decisions and inadequate fringe benefits. From the point of view of satisfaction, in a survey of computer personnel Awad (1977a) reported that only 2% cent of the programmers and 6% of the analysts were satisfied with their job in any way.

Unfortunately the published studies which are concerned with the work satisfaction of computer personnel are few and poorly reported. Many have used 'home-made' self-report job satisfaction questionnaires which fail to meet even the minimal psychometric standards, whilst others fail to report statistical measures other than simple averages. Scientific assessment of these studies, therefore, is extremely difficult and only information of a qualitative, descriptive nature is available.

In his study of computer personnel, Awad (1977a,b) presented 50 business programmers and 36 system analysts with the Minnesota Job Description Questionnaire that measures aspects of a job which a person finds reinforcing. From the data he extracted nine important dimensions which showed some differences between the programmers and analysts. Thus, the analysts scored significantly higher than the programmers on the dimensions of ability utilization ('I could do something which makes use of my abilities'), authority ('I could tell people what to do'), compensation ('My pay would compare well with that of other workers'), creativity ('I could try out some of my own ideas'), recognition ('I could get recognition for the work I do'), responsibility ('I could make decisions on my own'), social status ('I could be "somebody" in the community'), supervision–human relations ('My boss would back up his men'), and variety ('I could do something different every day'). Systems analysts, therefore, are satisfied by autonomy, responsibility and the authority that their position (as described earlier by Smith) carries.

Couger and Zawacki (1978) used a complex 'Job Diagnostic Survey', containing 94 questions, and administered it to more than 1600 data processing personnel in 25 organizations. Again, their report is devoid of much quantitative information but one interesting finding concerns a variable which they define as 'social need' (the need to interact with others). Whereas the average score on this variable for 'other professionals' was 5.48, for data processing personnel the score was lower at 4.19 (suggesting a lower social need) and from personnel in five of the organizations the score dropped to 2.2. Whilst no statistical information regarding the significance of the differences is given, the results do *suggest* that the programmers and analysts surveyed wish for less cohesive professional structure than many others. As the authors point out, these results throw some doubt on the benefits of the widely accepted 'programming team' concept. Indeed a similar type of study performed by Woodruff (1980b) supports this less-than-extraverted view of data processing personnel. He measured the personality of over 200 people and demonstrated (unfortunately again without statistical reinforcement) that data processing males possess a 'much higher' need for endurance, achievement, cognitive structure and avoidance from harm, and 'noticeably lower' needs for aggression and social recognition than do males in the general population. Similar trends were observed for female personnel.

COMPUTER PERSONNEL INTERESTS AND VALUES

One way of ensuring that personnel are as happy and satisfied with their work as is possible is first to determine which attributes of the job appeal to potential applicants. Thus, in many respects, the sketchy information about the personalities and satisfaction of computer personnel discussed above may also be related to any research data concerning their reported vocational interests. Following this line of thinking, then, it might be suggested that successful computer personnel should be less extraverted, more ready to work individually and enjoy autonomy and responsibility.

Another approach to the question of sensibly matching potential personnel to the jobs to be performed is to consider the *interests* (rather than the personalities) of potential applicants and to ensure that they match those of 'succesful' computer personnel. In this respect, for example, Tiffin and Phelan (1953) have shown that turnover tends to decrease as the amount of interest in the job increases. The majority of the work in this area has been reported by Perry (Perry, 1967; Perry and Cannon, 1967, 1968) using the Strong Vocational Interest Blank (SVIB).

The SVIB is a device which has received considerable research attention over the years and attempts to identify different vocational interests amongst the members of different occupations. It accomplishes this by providing an index of the similarity between a person's interests and the interests of successful men and women in a wide range of occupations. The Blank appears to the respondent as a long list of 400 concepts (100 occupations, 36 school subjects,

49 recreation activities, 48 other activities, 47 types of people, etc.) and they are asked to indicate, in different ways, those aspects which they like or dislike. (For comprehensive details of the history, application and interpretation of the SVIB, see Campbell, 1971.)

Scoring the responses is a very complex procedure, as is interpreting the results which arise. In relation to the present discussion, however, one of the most useful aspects of the Blank is that it allows a trained interpreter to compare the vocational interests expressed by the respondent with those obtained from members in specified occupations. This is done by building a 'profile' of the respondent's scores and comparing them with the scores produced by members of particular occupations. The SVIB is designed so that members of these criterion groups would produce an average score of 50 points on their own scale, and so it is possible to relate the respondent's interests to those of the different groups.

In addition to the comparisons with specific occupational groups, the most recent version of the manual for the SVIB (Campbell and Hansen, 1981) groups occupations into six types, based on Holland's theory of vocational choice (1973). These six types are related both to types of people and the jobs that they might take: 'realistic', 'investigative', 'artistic', 'social', 'enterprising', and 'conventional'.

Much of the definitive work on the interests of computer programmers has been performed by Perry and Cannon. They produced profiles of 1192 male (Perry and Cannon, 1967) and 293 female (Perry and Cannon, 1968) computer programmers from 130 organizations in America. The two profiles obtained are shown in Figure 3.1, and the bars represent the middle third range of scores for each occupation obtained from the 'man-in-general' group.

Although there are many complex interpretations and implications of Figure 3.1, a few are more obvious. Firstly, as shown by the two profiles, the interests expressed by the two samples are fairly similar. However, male programmers score higher overall on occupations in group III (technical supervision) and lower overall on groups II (physical science) and VI (aesthetic–cultural) occupations than do women. Secondly computer programmers have particular affinities to certain occupations. Thus peaks occur with such occupations as chemists (male and female), engineers (male and female), librarian (female), musician-performer (female) and senior Certified Public Accountants (male and female).

The pattern of interests obtained by Perry and Cannon also allow some comparisons to be made between programmers and the 'man-in-general' samples. Thus, programmers were more interested in problem and puzzle solving activities. This was not limited simply to mental problems, as represented by a strong interest in all forms of mathematics, but extended to the mechanical area. Programmers also showed some liking for research activities, but no more than people in most of the sciences themselves.

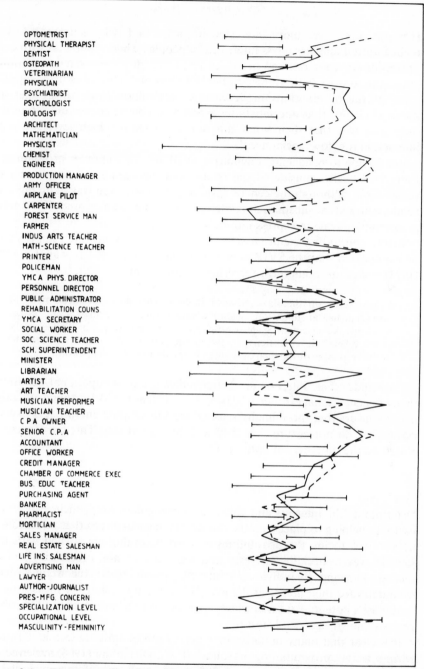

Figure 3.1. The Strong Vocational Interest Blank (SVIB) profile for male (- - -) and female (——) computer programmers (Perry and Cannon, 1968). Copyright 1968 by the American Psychological Association. Reprinted by permission of the author.

However, they were more interested in varied and risky activities, disliked regimentation and were 'less interested in people'. Thus, compared with other professionals, they disliked activities involving close personal interaction—preferring to work with 'things' rather than 'people'. This, of course, supports some of the observations made earlier, particularly those of Couger and Zawacki (1978), that one satisfying aspect that computer personnel found of their jobs was that their work did not often require high levels of social interaction (i.e. low 'social need').

In addition to producing a definitive SVIB key for computer programmers, Perry (1967) also considered the relationship between SVIB scores and job satisfaction. Although the general level of job satisfaction was quite high, the results showed a substantial tendency for those who scored low on the programming scale to express more dissatisfaction.

Before concluding the discussion of computer personnel interests, it should be emphasized that the SVIB does not *predict* abilities in any way. Campbell (1971) makes this point most forcefully, arguing that:

> A high score on the Basic Science Interest scale does not mean that the individual has an illustrious scientific career ahead ... a high score on the Academic Achievement Scale is no guarantee of intellectual brilliance ... the scores reflect the consistency between the individuals' responses and the modal responses of the men or women in the designated occupation.

He concludes that 'interests are better indicators of occupational persistence than of occupational excellence'. Using keys such as the SVIB, therefore, might help to ensure that those finally selected are job satisfied and are less likely to leave; they do not ensure that they will do a good job. This burden can be placed on the shoulders of aptitude tests.

APTITUDE TESTING

Determining the interests and values of a particular group, then, can be very useful in helping to place suitable candidates in occupations that relate to their needs, to reducing the possibilities of their becoming dissatisfied with their job. However, because interests and abilities are not necessarily strongly related, knowing an individual's interests has no real value when selecting candidates for their *ability* at the job. This can only be done by measuring the candidate's potential at tasks which are thought to be important to the job—a process known as aptitude testing.

It is clear that many organizations place faith in aptitude testing, certainly when selecting programming personnel. Thus, Dickmann (1966) surveyed 483 U.S. firms and found that about 70% used some sort of test, and often a combination of tests. Furthermore there appears to be little doubt that, from a financial point of view, aptitude testing is cost effective. Using economic models, for example, Schmidt *et al*. (1979) estimated that the impact of using valid aptitude tests for selecting computer programmers for (a) the (U.S.) Federal government and (b) the (U.S.) national economy would be to save hundreds of millions of dollars each year owing to increased productivity. However, it is important to realize that these assessments were made not empirically but according to economic models.

It is important, also, to note the stress made on the word 'valid' when considering the conclusions of Schmidt *et al*.'s analysis. A psychometric test is only valid to the extent that it predicts accurately what it is meant to predict. Not all aptitude tests pass this criterion.

There are two ways in which a test can be validated—either *predictively* or *concurrently*. A test is validated predictively by correlating the scores obtained by a group of people before they start their training with their actual performance later. Concurrent validity, on the other hand, involves determining the degree to which test scores obtained by people actually working vary in relation to their ability. Although measures of this type of validation are easier to obtain (for example, measuring concurrent validity does not need a long time commitment) they do not necessarily produce the full information that is required for an aptitude test that is to be used for predictive functions.

With some occupations it should not be difficult to develop a valid test. For example, if someone applies for the job of a typist, the interviewer can conveniently include a test of the candidate's skill by dictating a letter and can make a judgement on the results. Such a test of the candidate's abilities, with allowance made for the stress of the circumstances, is likely to be quite useful for predicting future performance. However, it is not so easy a task to devise appropriately valid and reliable tests for more complex occupations such as computer programmers or analysts. (Reliability is another important index of a test and indicates the extent to which the test produces similar results from the same individual, or group of individuals, on different occasions.)

A number of aptitude tests are available to help in the selection of computer personnel and these have been summarized well by Dickmann (1971) and by Bloom (1980). In essence these tests can be divided into two groups: tests to select computer operators (data processors, console operators), and tests for computer programmers.

Tests for computer operators

Dickmann (1971) argues that the requirements of this type of personnel can be deduced, generally, from observation: for example, finger dexterity, perceptual speed, accuracy and eye–hand coordination for those whose task it will be to enter data at the keyboard. However, evidence exists which suggests that some of these criteria may not prove to be entirely valid in a predictive form. For example, Flanagan, Fivars and Tuska (1959) compared typing speed (in words per minute) at the end of various typing courses with the speed test scores obtained before the course. They found predictive correlation coefficients of approximately 0.5 (in other words, only about 25% (0.5^2) of the factors influencing the scores at the end of the course could be said to be due to the factors measured before the course). Cleaver and O'Connor (1982) found similarly low predictive correlations between finger dexterity and subsequent gross typing speeds (about 0.4). However, they did find that the ability (speed and accuracy) of typing three random characters at a time correlated quite highly (up to 0.75) with subsequent typing ability. Another factor that appears to provide fairly valid predictors of typing speed is that of choice reaction time (that is, when subjects are required to respond quickly to one of a number of possible stimuli) (Leonard and Carpenter, 1964).

In addition to typing skills, of course, other features of computer operators' jobs may need to be taken into account. For example, physical fitness might be an important factor to consider for computer-room staff, particularly if the job requires extensive time on the feet or handling heavy equipment and runs of paper.

Tests for computer programmers

It is in this area that most work has been carried out, although only two tests (the IBM Programmer Aptitude Test and the Computer Programmer Aptitude Battery) have stood the test of time and empirical investigations. As far as programmers are concerned, two aspects of performance are important: first predicting success in training and second success on the job once trained.

IBM Programmer Aptitude Test

This is possibly the most well-known test, having been developed in the mid 1950s. Indeed, in his 1966 survey of aptitude test usage, Dickmann showed that nearly 60% of the firms questioned used this test when selecting their programming staff. Since the first version appeared, a number of generations of this test have been published, although they are essentially similar in form.

The test is a 'pencil-and-paper' test of reasoning ability, and takes about an hour to administer. It is broken down into three timed parts, and the test is scored simply by summing the correct answers for all three parts and subtracting one-quarter the number of wrong ones.

Part I (10 minutes) deals with *letter series* in which the examinee is given a series of letters that follow a certain rule and is asked to predict the next letter in the sequence. For example, the series 'a c e g i' should be followed by 'k' since the series consists of alternate letters of the alphabet.

Part II (15 minutes) is similar to part I but deals with *figure series*. Each of the 40 problems provides a series of four figures on the left hand side of the page and five on the right. The four figures on the left make a series and the examinee's task is to determine which of the five on the right completes the series.

Part III (*arithmetic reasoning*—30 minutes) presents 25 mathematical problems, posed in English but having to be solved by translation into algebraic form, such as: 'How many apples can be bought for 60 cents at the rate of 3 for 10 cents?'

Much of the validation work on this test has concerned a revised version—the Revised Programmers Aptitude Test (RPAT)—although Dickmann (1971) reports that the RPAT and the published Programmers Aptitude Test correlate very highly together (0.81) indicating strongly that they are measuring similar abilities.

Studies of the predictive validity of the PAT and the RPAT have produced conflicting results. For example, the authors of the test, McNamara and Hughes, obtained a correlation of 0.44 for scores on the RPAT with job performance for 41 programmers (1961). Other independent studies, however, have not produced such high figures. For example, Mazlack (1978, 1980) obtained correlations only in the region of 0.2–0.3 when comparing PAT scores with computer students' exam successes. Reinsdedt (1967) found only very low correlations between test score and subsequent supervisory ratings. In respect to this latter study, however, Bloom (1980) questions the use of supervisory rankings as a measure of a person's programming skills, since many other employment factors (perseverance, motivation, personality) could possibly colour the evaluation. Other studies have obtained negative correlations between RPAT scores and subsequent ability, suggesting that if these corporations were using the RPAT as a primary selection method they would be giving preference to candidates who would be *un*successful in their organization.

The position with regards the RPAT and PAT as predictors of programming success, therefore, is unclear, particularly since very highly significant correlations have been obtained in some organizations. The only sensible conclusion to be reached is that the test should be used selectively and should not be automatically employed. It may be, for example, that programming is not a homogeneous task requiring the same skills for all tasks or for all organizations. Thus testing an individual's mathematical or visual reasoning ability might be appropriate in some cases but not in others.

Computer Programmer Aptitude Battery (CPAB)

The CPAB was first published in 1964 and revised in 1974. It was designed after having considered the programming task which led the author to produce a list of aptitude and mental ability items that were likely to be involved

(Palormo, 1974). These covered those already in the PAT (letter series and reasoning) as well as 'verbal meaning', 'number series', 'number ability', 'ingenuity', and 'diagramming'. These were finally reduced to five, time, sub-tests:

1 *Verbal meaning* (8 minutes)—a vocabulary test involving finding synonyms to words from data processing and related fields.
2 *Reasoning* (20 minutes)—translating word problems algebraically into mathematical notation.
3 *Letter series* (10 minutes)—determining the pattern in a sequence of letters and finding the next letter in the series.
4 *Number ability* (6 minutes)—quickly estimating rough answers to computations without the aid of paper and pencil.
5 *Diagramming* (35 minutes)—filling in blank sections of flow charts solving a variety of stated problems.

In the test manual Palormo reports that the reliability of the test is very good (0.95 for the overall test battery). However, Bloom (1980) points out that this figure was obtained using the original seven-part experimental version and a different population. The manual discusses ten studies which have been carried out to validate the scales against various measures of programmer success. Four deal with success in training (with reported correlations of between 0.3 and 0.7) and six with job performance (a mixture of predictive and concurrent validations in the much lower range of 0.02 to 0.6).

There have been very few other independent validatory studies of this test. Bell (1976) did relate test scores to programming ability (he used the ability to spot and remove mistakes—bugs—in programs) and produced a wide range of correlations (from 0.02 to 0.51) for the different sub-tests and aspects of the task. Unfortunately, however, he used only 11 subjects which is a sample size that is so low that it makes any firm conclusions extremely suspect. Nevertheless, it does *suggest* that the CPAB is useful for predicting ability at some tasks (highest correlations were all obtained with the spotting of syntactic errors (using the correct language codes) than with the others). Exceptionally low, non-significant, correlations were obtained with spotting semantic errors (when syntactically correct expressions are in the wrong place).

In addition to the standard population norms, the 1974 manual also contains data relating scores to such demographic variables as applicant status, age, sex, education level and ethnic background. In this latter respect it appears that the CPAB possibly discriminates against non-whites and a separate norm table for 'non-whites' is provided.

SUMMARY

This chapter has considered some of the important factors from the viewpoint of ensuring that appropriate computer personnel are employed and that they remain satisfied with their jobs. In this respect, emphasis has been placed on matching the requirements of the jobs with the interests and abilities of prospective personnel. Thus, it was demonstrated that satisfaction or dissatisfaction with jobs relating to computers arises as much from the organizational structure as from the job itself. Many computer personnel are generally highly skilled and features such as promotion prospects and management participation play important roles in their perceived satisfaction.

With regard to the interests and personalities of computer personnel, the scanty data available suggest that computer programmers are more introverted and prefer to work more independently than members of most other groups. They are more interested in problems and problem solving activities, and tend to dislike 'regimentation'.

Finally, the chapter considered some of the measures presently available to investigate the aptitude of potential programmers. Although tests such as the IBM Programmer Aptitude Test and the Computer Programmer Aptitude Battery are available, more validatory research is required before they can be said to be generally applicable.

PART II

Hardware

One of the initial pieces of 'computer jargon' that the novice computer user has to overcome is the distinction between computer 'hardware' and 'software'. These two terms are used very glibly by those 'in-the-know' but, because they are not immediately meaningful, they can be confusing to newcomers to the subject.

Quite simply, the hardware refers to the aspects of the computer system that can be seen: the mechanical, electrical and electronic components of the system. They are, literally, hard. They are produced by normal industrial processes; some pieces of hardware can hurt anyone who knocks against them, etc. The software, on the other hand, cannot be seen. It comprises, essentially, the computer programs—the ideas, concepts, languages which instruct the computer and make it operate in the ways desired by the operator. It is soft and flexible. The software can be altered and its features changed simply by varying the form or the ideas contained in the instructions. (A third jargon term, firmware, has also entered the computer language. This refers to the hardware on which the software is placed—disks, cassettes, etc.).

Since they both have different problems with respect to the interaction with users this distinction between the components and the ideas will be continued to be made in this book, although it is recognized that the two must also interact for the computer to work properly. The three chapters in this part (Part II), therefore, will deal with the hardware aspects of computer systems; the two chapters contained in Part III will consider important aspects of the 'software interface' between the computer and both the operator and the programmer.

The electrical, electronic and mechanical components which make up the computer hardware are clearly the most important aspects of the whole computer system. Without them no computations or operations could be performed on any information. However, even with a limited number of components, there is an almost limitless number of ways in which they can be put together to form the system. Indeed, this is evidenced by the large number of computers, systems and peripherals presently available on the market. Clearly some of these arrangements are likely to be more appropriate than others for the efficiency of the man–machine system, and it will be the purpose of the following three chapters to consider the most appropriate hardware designs from the point of view of the 'man' in the system: the user. Thus, the next chapter will discuss hardware aspects associated with the process of putting information *into* the computer: keyboards, speech, lightpens, joysticks, etc. Chapter 5 will perform the same function for the hardware used by the system to display information back from the computer to the operator: visual displays, printers, speech, etc. Naturally, some of the problems encountered will be common to both input and output. For example, speech synthesis: the problems of breaking speech down into simple 'pulses' able to be understood and operated on by the computer (i.e. input problems) have many aspects in common with problems of composing speech from simple pulses which arise from the computer (i.e. output problems). Nevertheless other features (such as speech production and recognition) are different enough to enable the similar processes to be considered in two separate chapters. The final chapter in Part II, Chapter 6, will consider how the computer system is inserted, physically, into the working place; aspects of the operator's seating design, the physical environment, etc.

Finally, it is important to realize that, from the above synopsis of the chapters in this Part, there is to be no discussion of the hardware aspects of the computer's 'brain'—the central processing unit (cpu). Although it is essentially this component which distinguishes a small, desk microcomputer from a large, 'mainframe' computer (and thus creates the differences in the computer power and facilities offered) the problems of cpu design and use are essentially those of the computer scientist and engineer. They only become problems which are of interest to the behavioural scientist when they interact with the user (and the abilities that the user supplies) to perform the appropriate tasks. Those occasions when this occurs will be considered in the relevant chapters in Part III (software).

CHAPTER 4

Input Hardware

In the man-machine system conception of the world, aspects of the machine which enable information to be transmitted from the operator to the computer need to act as efficient extensions of the operator's own effector (output) mechanisms. Thus, they have to perform as effective extensions of the fingers, the arms, the feet, the mouth and perhaps even the eyes. Whatever system the operator chooses for conveying information from 'within' himself or herself to the computer requires a compatible and comparable computer input system to allow efficient information transfer. To take an extreme example: say the operator was able only to speak to the machine—that is to use the voice to pass information from the brain—then the computer would be useless if it did not posess an input device capable of recognizing and decoding the auditory information. Say, then, that such a device was present; the efficiency of the information transmission would then depend on how compatible this device was with the operator's own voice and ideas. If, for example, it 'insisted' that the operator only used an extremely limited vocabulary—say a dozen or so 'key' words—then the system efficiency would be limited to the information that could be conveyed in those dozen words. Similarly reduced efficiency would be likely to occur if other restrictions were put on the operator—to speak with or without an accent; at a particular pace; with a particular syntax; in a particular acoustic environment, etc. Only when input devices are built to match the operator's abilities and *natural* behaviours will it be likely that the information transmission will be optimum.

All of the input devices used in computer systems are based, essentially, on switches. This is obvious since the computer itself works only on the presence or absence of an electric signal—in information terms, on 1's or 0's. All of the information flowing from the human operator, therefore, needs to be reduced to the simple 1:0, on:off type through switches which can be mechanical, electrical or electronic in nature. When information is presented in this way it is said to have been *digitized*.

61

The main ways in which information can be passed (input) to the computer are via one of three of the operator's effector systems: limb movement and touch (usually using the hands or fingers), speech, and eye movement. These will be considered separately in more detail below.

HAND AND FINGER INPUT DEVICES

The types of devices which can be subsumed under this heading fall basically into two: those which allow continuous movement—say moving a spot on the screen or recording information from a moving strip—and those which only allow the discrete, on/off, form of information. These latter types of input devices comprise those which operate on a switch principle, for example, keyboards, touch sensitive switches and lightpens (switches operated by light). Of course, the information presented to the computer using continuous controls (joysticks, rollerballs and scanners) must also be converted into a digital, on/off, format, but this is generally done either by the computer itself or by some piece of electronic equipment placed between the input device and the computer (an analogue to digital, A–D, converter).

Before discussing the design and operation of specific types of hand/finger controls, it is useful to consider some of the features which could limit their effectiveness.

General aspects of hand and finger controls

Moving the control

The operation of these types of controls arises essentially as a result of the operator's movements—in this case by contracting muscles in the arms, hands and fingers. It is important, therefore, to understand how the muscles are made to operate if appropriate controls are going to be designed.

The ability of a limb to control movement depends on three main aspects: firstly, the number of muscles which are brought into play, secondly the quality of the feedback (from hearing, sight and the touch and stretch sensors in the skin and muscles), and thirdly the type of action required.

Muscles are only ever able to contract and all of our movement occurs as a result of muscles contracting in an antagonistic fashion. The number of actively contracting muscle fibres determine how much power is developed during the period of contraction. For example, to maintain pressure on a pen to write requires appropriate muscles to be under tension (contraction) continuously by varying amounts (although, as Grandjean, 1980 a,b, argues, with slow or maintained muscular contractions, different muscle fibres are successively brought into active contraction). Pressing a button, on the other hand, requires essentially only one contraction of the appropriate muscles in the finger, wrist, forearm, etc.

Whatever type of operation is performed, the degree of accuracy attained would be very low if the operator was not fed back with information concerning how the movement was progressing. This obviously occurs from aspects of the tasks which involve perception: operators are generally able to see or hear the results of their actions. However, there is also an additional sensory system operating within the muscles and tendons themselves which conveys information regarding the extent to which these structures are being stretched. This is known as the kinaesthetic system and is part of a general 'position in space' sensory system which we have, known as the proprioceptive system (see Oborne, 1982).

The receptors embedded in structures such as muscles and which comprise this system provide the operator with some idea of where the body or the limbs are positioned in space—without necessarily having to use the eyes. For example, by integrating the information obtained from the biceps and triceps in the arm, an operator can tell by how much the arm is extended. With further information from the biceps' and triceps' tendons and from the shoulder muscles, an operator should be able to tell by how much the arm is having to be supported—in other words its position with respect to the horizontal.

The proprioceptive system also plays a major role during training skilled behaviour, since much of the development of complex motor skills depends on the efficient feedback mechanisms. For example, in a skill such as typing, the feedback obtained from kinaesthetic receptors in the fingers, arms, shoulder muscles and joints allows the operator to be able to sense where the fingers ought to be placed without any conscious placement. In addition, the efficient use of the kinaesthetic system (in other words when fully skilled) enables the operator to sense when a limb is incorrectly positioned and to move it rapidly to the correct location. Typists, for example, often 'know' that a wrong key has been struck without having to look at what has been printed.

In addition to the quality of information that is fed back to the operator, another limiting factor for movement is muscular fatigue. It can often be avoided, however, or at least the time before its onset reduced, if the manner in which it arises is understood. Then working conditions can be designed to avoid the factors which induce it.

For a muscle to contract (that is, to do work) an extremely complicated chemical reaction is set up in the muscle itself. Described in its simplest form, the energy for the contraction is supplied by the breakdown of a chemical in the muscles called adenosine triphosphate (ATP) to adenosine diphosphate (ADP). However, the ADP must be 'regenerated' to ATP before further contraction can take place, and the energy for this reversing action is provided by the breakdown of glycogen.

Unfortunately, a by-product of the glycogen breakdown is a substance called lactic acid which quickly accumulates in the muscles causing the pain so well associated with muscular fatigue. This is removed by a reaction with oxygen and is converted into carbon dioxide and water. The transport of the oxygen and these waste products is undertaken by the blood system. So, the importance of understanding the mechanisms which cause fatigue lies in the fact that the oxygen supplied by the blood, and the blood itself, are the sole agents for either reducing the level of fatigue or for increasing the time before fatigue sets in. Conditions need to be designed, therefore, in which the flow of blood to the muscles is maximal.

In relation to muscular fatigue, when considering the type of work which a muscle has to do a clear distinction must be made between types of work—that is between *static* and *dynamic* work. This distinction is normally made in terms of whether or not motion accompanies the muscular tension. The work is said to be static if no motion occurs, for example when holding a weight in the palm of the hand with the arm outstretched or maintaining an erect posture. If the arm moves up and down, however, or the body is made to bend forward, then the muscles are said to be doing dynamic work.

The importance of this distinction rests in the fact that, when doing dynamic work, blood flow is increased simply as a result of the pumping action set up by the muscles. Blood is pumped through the blood vessels which supply the muscles, so aiding the breakdown of lactic acid and removing the waste products. As long as the supplies of blood and oxygen can be maintained in sufficient quantities, therefore, and are not exceeded by the production of lactic acid, muscular fatigue is likely to be kept at bay.

A further implication of this distinction between static and dynamic work is that the amount of fatigue experienced is likely to occur as a function of the type of task performed and control used. Different muscles will be doing static and dynamic work. For example, the muscles in an author's fingers rapidly moving the pen over the page are doing dynamic work. However the shoulder, upper arm and wrist muscles are likely to be doing more static work, having to maintain the hand and fingers in the correct position on the page. An artist's shoulder and arm muscles, however, although still having to position the hand holding a brush in the correct place, may well be doing more dynamic work when, say, sketching.

With regard to hand actions, this variation in work with types of control operation can also be considered in terms of the nature of the manipulative task to be performed; most tasks can be placed along a continuum of 'gripping' to 'non-gripping' activities. Clearly the more that a task involves gripping, the more muscles are likely to be involved. In gripping tasks the fingers and parts of the palm form a closed chain and act in opposition to each other to exert compressive forces on the object being gripped. In non-gripping actions the forces are exerted either through the whole hand or through the fingertips in an open chain.

In addition to the amount to which the fingers are closed, Oborne (1982) suggests that a second manipulative dimension can be added which relates to the degree of hand/object contact. From such a two-dimensional classification it is possible to determine which dimensions are required for any particular type of control and which types of control are likely to cause fatigue.

Movements required for different controls

As is evidently clear from the preceding discussion the nature of the movement required when putting information into the computer from a keyboard is characterized by an 'open chain' approach, with the hand having little contact with the control. The operation is performed using more of a 'pointing' movement which has a ballistic nature (Chambers and Stockbridge, 1970). Essentially, therefore, the problems facing the operator are considerations of speed and accuracy: to place the fingers accurately over the appropriate keys, and to strike the keys as quickly as possible. The muscles involved include those in the shoulder, arm and wrist, in addition to the muscles needed to operate the appropriate fingers.

The operations that are required when using input controls such as lightpens, however, are different. These involve rather more hand–object contact, particularly because more than one finger holds and operates the control. Thus, more muscles are employed and, because of the nature of the controlling task, they are maintained under tension for longer. This inevitably will lead to more static load and to a higher risk of muscle fatigue. On the other hand, of course, controls such as light pens are likely to be used for shorter periods of time than are, say, keyboards.

A further biomechanical problem associated with input controls occurs when the controls have to be positioned or operated at some distance from the body. Since increased stability occurs the nearer to the body an operation is carried out, it follows that operations such as touching a lightpen to a screen at arm's length may be less accurately performed than pressing a key on a keyboard near to the operator. The reason for this is two-fold. Firstly, as the arm is extended the forces placed on the shoulder muscles are increased because the centre of gravity of the hand–arm complex moves away from the body. More work will be required from the muscles, therefore, to maintain a stable position—to counteract the force of gravity. This was demonstrated well by Mead and Sampson (1972) who measured hand steadiness whilst subjects performed various types of movements. The amount of tremor was considerably reduced, and thus accuracy increased, when subjects made ballistic-like 'in–out' movements than when they were required to move a stylus 'up–down'. Secondly, as the arm is extended the wrist orientation has to change so that, for example, a pen can make contact with a screen. This means that the degree of finger–pen contact tends to be reduced—unless the operator takes specific steps to counteract this tendency. Doing so, of course, will increase the amount of static load on the finger muscles.

In summary, therefore, it is clear that different input devices are likely to require different forms of control movements from the operator. Keyboards, for example, operate using essentially a ballistic-like, open-chain movement, and most static load is likely to occur in the muscles which have to maintain the position of the hand over the keyboard. At the other end of the scale, controls such as lightpens require a gripping type of operation so making the muscles in particular fingers work harder. Furthermore, they are generally used away from the body so increasing problems of stability. In addition to these considerations of differences between control operations, it is also the case that even the same type of control may require different types of operations on different occasions—for example, a lightpen can be used to point at a place on the screen or it can be used as a continuous control to 'draw' on the screen. In this respect, Mead and Sampson's results suggest that a ballistic type of operation in which, for example, the operator simply points at choices on the screen will be performed more accurately than an operation involving moving a lightpen over the screen to draw a picture.

Problems affecting operator control

Gloves and protective clothes

Although gloves are designed to protect the operator's hands they may have a number of undesirable consequences, particularly in relation to the ability to manipulate and to obtain feedback from a control. As an example, the normal sensation of 'grip' probably results from the pressure perceived when the flexed fingers around the gripped object press against each other. Between the fingers are located nerve endings which provide the operator with feedback about the degree of closure of the hand (Tichauer, 1978). If the working glove happens to be too thick in these regions, high pressures can be generated between the fingers before the hand is firmly closed around an object such as a pen, which may result in an insecure grasp. Furthermore, a thick glove can also obstruct the fingers from wrapping around the pen sufficiently for a firm grip. On the other hand, an operator who is aware of these problems may grip the control unnecessarily tightly and firmly so increasing fatigue in the finger and other muscles.

After carrying out a series of experiments to determine the degree to which gloves interfere with control manipulation and operation speed, Bradley (1969) concluded that the efficiency with which instrument controls may be operated by a gloved hand depends on the glove characteristics, the physical characteristics of the control, and the type of control operation. Specifically, snugness of fit and resistance to slipping were shown to be the two most important glove parameters, and under some circumstances a snug glove which did not slip over the controls actually improved performance. In many circumstances, however, gloves are worn for protection against injury to the flesh and then snugness and even resistance to slipping may be absent. In such cases, therefore, the size of the controls would have to be increased to allow adequate manipulation, and the control might be textured to reduce the possibility of slipping.

In addition to interfering with grip, gloves can often impede the perception of any coded texture differences on various controls. Such texture differences cause different pressure patterns on the observer's skin and it is these which could be occluded by the gloves. Indeed, Taylor and Berman (1982) demonstrated that the reduction in tactility as a result of wearing gloves is a more important factor in causing performance reductions than reduced mobility.

Of course, the interference with control manipulation may not rest simply with gloves as being the sole culprit. As was discussed earlier, efficient hand control operation requires the integrated activity of all of the muscles and joints from at least the shoulder to the finger. Any protective clothing which interferes with this activity is also likely to interfere with control manipulation. This was demonstrated well by Pierce (1963) who measured the effect that full-pressure suits (used, for example, by astronauts) have on dexterity and tool manipulation. His results demonstrated severe reductions both in the ability to perform dexterous tasks and to exert forces, even when the suit was not pressurized. Whereas the first of these two effects is quite predictable given that the suit included gloves, the second (force reduction) does illustrate the restrictive nature of many types of protective clothing.

The presence of vibration

Vibration is a stimulus which occurs to a greater or lesser extent in most environments. However, its effects on control manipulability are likely to occur only in environments in which the levels of vibration are severe enough to cause the arm or hand to move in ways not desired by the operator. The ways in which vibration causes these effects, and the variables which act for or against them, are too complex to be described here (see, for example, Oborne, 1983). However, it is important to realize that they act in such a way as to convert a simple task, for example positioning a control, into one in which the operator has essentially to maintain a stable position—i.e. a tracking task.

Two aspects of the operator's immediate workplace can exacerbate this problem: firstly the presence of backrests, and secondly seat belts. Both are designed to provide the operator with support and protection. However, both have the effect of making the operator come into contact more with the vibrating environment (the seat) and, since motor performance is related very strongly to the level of vibration reaching the appropriate limb, this is likely to increase the problem.

Two studies serve to illustrate this point. Firstly, Rowlands (1977) measured the amount of vibration transmitted through the body by placing acceleration sensing devices at the seat and shoulders of a seated operator. His results indicated significant increases in vibration transmitted to the shoulders when the operator sat with the back against the backrest, than in a 'back-off' position. This vibration problem, of course, is exacerbated if the operator is also wearing a safety harness—perhaps in an attempt to increase stability. The effect of the harness will be to pull the operator back into the seat and so increase the level of vibration transmitted to the shoulder. That this will then have a detrimental effect on motor control was demonstrated clearly by Lovesey (1971) when he asked subjects to perform a tracking task both with and without a seat harness.

Although backrests and seat belts are likely to increase the problems of motor control in a vibrating environment, some evidence exists which suggests that seat armrests have some beneficial effect. Thus, Torle (1965) tested three subjects on a tracking task using a 'small', a 'large' or no armrest (unfortunately dimensions were not provided). His results demonstrated some improvement in tracking ability using the armrest, although he observed no difference between the types of armrest used. The armrest improvement increased with increasing vibration intensity. Unfortunately, it is not possible to deduce from the experimental report whether the improvement was due to increased total body stability created by the armrests, or simply to forearm or elbow stability.

Vibration is not only an important problem when considering its effects on the muscles of the arms and hands for controlling mechanical devices. It can also detrimentally affect our ability to speak and to see—two systems which, as will be considered later in this chapter, can be used quite efficiently to input data to the computer.

Speaking is a complex action which involves forcing air from the lungs through the larynx to make the vocal folds vibrate. Precise control of the air movement, then, is most important to efficient voice production. Unfortunately, however, a severely vibrating environment can interfere with the muscular control of the ribs and diaphragm causing a loss of control over the lung movements. In very severe environments this can often be exacerbated by body organs buffeting the diaphragm.

With regard to the optical system, it is obvious that the eyes move in the head and are under the control of muscles which attach them to their sockets. Under vibrating conditions the eyes can move in unpredictable and often uncontrollable ways. These movements can occur in two ways: firstly the movement of the eyes relative to the head, and secondly the eyes themselves may resonate. Oborne (1983) discusses in detail the effects that this may have on visual ability and control.

Comparing devices

Before considering in detail the design of different hand/finger input devices, it is appropriate to discuss their relative efficiency—both in terms of speed and ease of use—and their accuracy. Unfortunately, however, very few comparative studies have been performed to investigate this question. Those that have been reported have generally been restricted in their application and have considered simply the relative efficiencies of different controls for the simple task of selecting an item from a screen. This might be used, for example, when the computer program presents to the operator a 'menu' list of options from which one is selected.

Earl and Goff (1965) compared two ways of entering information to perform this type of task. Subjects were asked either to type in the selected item using a conventional keyboard or to point to and to sweep a pen over the required item. This second method, then, is analogous to pointing a light pen at the appropriate point on a screen. Their results indicated that the keyboard was clearly a slower method for entering this type of data, even for experienced typists. More importantly, however, they also demonstrated that nearly 700% more errors were made using the keyboard than the pointing method.

The advantages of pointing devices to the keyboard were supported and slightly extended by Goodwin (1975) who used a different type of task. Instead of having to input words or phrases, subjects were asked to position a cursor at a particular point on the screen using either the keyboard keys or one of two pointing controls—a lightpen or a lightgun (this latter control was essentially a lightpen modified for easier use with a handle and activated using a trigger). For all types of task the subjects were able to position the cursor faster with the lightpen and lightgun than with the keyboard.

Unfortunately Goodwin did not report the types of errors made using the different controls, although she does point out that the relative speed disadvantage of the keyboard probably lies in the type of task needed to be performed by the operator. Thus with the lightpen the observer simply needed to locate the item and point to it. With the keyboard, however, the observer had additionally to locate the cursor to determine which direction it needed to take (and thus the keys which were used).

Using a sample size of only five subjects Card *et al.* (1978) considered the relative efficiency of keyboards, joysticks and the 'mouse' (a type of free ball control). Both the mouse and the joystick are continuous controls which can be moved in any direction. The keyboard keys, however, are discrete controls—different cursor positions being indicated by different keys.

Both in terms of reduced error rate and the time taken to make the positioning, the mouse type of control was shown to be most efficient and the keyboard keys were the least efficient. Interestingly, the experiment used two types of keyboard key arrangement. In the first the keys used to change the cursor direction were arranged in a diamond pattern (holding down a key caused it to repeat the movement). The second arrangement used text keys to move the cursor in large steps such as a word, a paragraph, or a line, in addition to being able to move it by one character. Whereas the two keyboard arrangements produced little difference in the times taken to perform the task, more errors were produced using the single cursor control keys.

In summary, therefore, it appears that the few published studies which have compared the efficiency of control types have consistently indicated keyboard controls to take longer and to be more prone to errors, when the task is one of inputting discrete pieces of information. Continuous positioning devices are the most efficient, although no study has been performed to compare a screen based pointing control such as a lightpen with a keyboard based pointing control like the 'mouse'. Since a screen based control presents more compatibility with the task (i.e. to move the cursor), however, and since fewer head movements from keyboard to screen are required, it is likely that the lightpen would be more efficient.

Finally, it should be pointed out that none of these studies has investigated either operator preference or the effect of the type of task to be performed. Thus, as Goodwin (1975) suggests, both of these variables may play important parts in affecting conclusions about relative efficiency. For tasks in which a keyboard must be used fairly continuously (for data entry or for editing (changing) a display, for example) an experienced operator may prefer to use keys for cursor positioning rather than to interrupt the task to manipulate a separate device such as a lightpen. Indeed, Goodwin observed that operators often *prefer* to use both types of control to position a cursor:

> The operator tends to move the cursor sequentially from one entry field to the next using tab and carriage return keys, as one would using a conventional typewriter. However, as soon as it becomes necessary to move the cursor backward to correct an earlier entry, for example, the operator uses the lightgun. ... Poor performance using the keyboard does not mean that cursor positioning keys should be eliminated. Rather, the present results confirm that a lightpen or lightgun can be a useful addition to the display–keyboard combination.

DISCRETE ENTRY DEVICES

Keyboards

Possibly one of the most common methods of presenting information into a computer is via keyboards—groups of on/off push buttons which are used either in combination or separately to compose information. When discussing their design, therefore, the design and arrangements of the keys—both as individual components and as groups—need to be considered. As will become apparent in this discussion, alterations in the arrangement, the number or even simply the physical characteristics of the keys can affect the operator's speed and accuracy, and changes in efficiency can obviously affect the worker's and the organization's productivity.

Anthropometric considerations

Quite obviously the design and arrangement of the keys on a keyboard need, literally, to 'fit' the operator using them: keys which are too small may cause difficulty in locating and hitting them accurately; keys that are too large might produce a keyboard which itself is large and needs more wrist or arm movements than are ideal. Similarly the spacing between keys is important: if the keys are separated too much the keyboard will be too big; with the spacing too small there is a danger of hitting more than one key at once.

The question of the size of the keyboard keys is clearly related to two aspects: the size of the finger that is to operate the key and the type of keyboard and arrangement of the keys being considered. For example, an important dimension to be considered for keys on an alphanumeric (typewriter) type of keyboard is the distance between the keys. Thus, it is important to ensure that if, for example, 'G' is to be struck then neither 'F' on the left nor 'H' on the right is pressed by mistake. Suitable interkey spacing is also important on keyboards such as chord keyboards (which will be discussed later) that require more than one key to be pressed at the same time. In these cases, the keys must be positioned so that the fingers can easily span them to activate relevant key combinations. On specialized keyboards which use only a few keys, however, it may be the physical dimensions of the keys themselves which are important.

As an indication of the importance of ensuring that the key size is optimum, Deininger (1960) reports a study which included button size as one of the variables used to investigate different keyboard arrangements. By increasing the dimensions of a square button from 9.5 to 17.4 mm, he was able to show a reduction in keying times from 6.35 to 5.83 seconds, and reduced errors from 7.1 to 1.3%.

For use when designing key sizes and spacings to fit the operator's hand, Garrett (1971) provides a number of anthropometric dimensions for different parts of the adult human hand. His data suggest that the average breadth of the top of the finger joints is approximately 1.7 cm for males and 1.5 cm for females. Ninety per cent of the male population falls in a range 1.6–1.9 cm, and of the female population 1.3–1.6 cm. Naturally, the width of this joint is not the same as that of the fingertip, since fingers tend to taper, but data such as these are presently the nearest available. Provided the separation between keys is greater than these dimensions, therefore, it should ensure that keys will not be pressed in error simply because the finger 'spreads out' over more than one key. However, for keyboards which have only a few, widely separated, keys the important dimension is the breadth of the key itself. In these cases it is unlikely that keying errors will occur because two keys are pressed at once.

Problems still exist with such keyboards, however, and these relate to the optimum finger spread. In such cases the important dimensions to consider are clearly the distances between keys and the distances of the keys from a point on the keyboard on which the wrist is rested.

Unfortunately, the established literature is poor in providing such data. Garrett's data, for example, concern primarily the dimensions of parts of the flat, outstretched hand—a posture which is not ideal for operating such a keyboard efficiently and without fatigue. In these circumstances the dimensions of the relaxed hand are more important and it is here that data are sadly lacking. Garrett does provide some data concerning angles involved in the relaxed hand—particularly at the joints of each finger—but, without additional information regarding the lengths of different finger segments it is not possible to calculate, for example, the distance of the tip of the relaxed thumb to its base. Similar problems are apparent with respect to the interkey positions. Although Garrett's data include fingertip to fingertip dimensions, these are for the outstretched and not for the relaxed hand. Unfortunately, therefore, some more basic anthropometric data are required before such keyboards can be designed effectively.

Hand and finger dimensions and forces

The important considerations in this respect are the ways in which the fingers operate to depress the keys, and the muscular loads placed on the fingers which might cause fatigue.

With respect to muscular fatigue the important design consideration relates to the amount of resistance incorporated into the key. In this respect key resistance performs two functions: first, it provides the operator with kinaesthetic feedback relating to the extent to which a key has been pressed, and second, if force is required to depress the key key resistance can prevent accidental operation of a key.

With regard to the force able to be exerted, the first question to be answered is to what extent the musculature of the hand limits the ability of the fingers to exert force. In this context Alden, Daniels and Kanarick (1972) report a study performed by Haaland et al. (1963) in which the maximum pushing force for each finger of the adult male hand was measured. As can be seen from Table 4.1, quite wide variations occur over the five fingers, and Haaland et al. attribute this to differences in the finger musculature. Furthermore, they observe that individuals whose fingers bend back when pushing perpendicularly could not apply as much pushing force as those whose fingers remain rigid.

Of course, the maximum force able to be pushed is not necessarily going to be the ideal force required for a keyboard. The question thus becomes one of, up to this maximum—the maximum for the little finger, that is—what is the *optimum* force for maximum speed and minimum fatigue?

Table 4.1. Maximum Finger Pushing Force (grams) (Haaland *et al.*, 1963).

	Finger				
	Thumb	Index	Middle	Ring	Little
Mean	1055	684	627	513	342
Range	855–1226	485–884	485–741	342–627	171–542

In his investigation of different key arrangements, Deininger (1960) found that varying the key force from 3.5 to 14.1 oz (100 to 403 grams) or varying the maximum displacement from 0.03 to 0.19 inches (0.08 to 0.48 cm) produced insignificant differences in his subjects' keying performances. However, later reports from the subjects indicated a general preference for the light touch keys and a definite dislike for the keys requiring greater displacement. Unfortunatley, however, as Alden, Daniels and Kanarick (1972) point out, many of Deininger's results are questionable given his lack of experimental controls. Nevertheless the subjective reports have some value and the results do relate favourably to other studies in the area.

For example, Bergenthal (1971) reports a study in which 60 subjects were required to push buttons having a range of forces from 3 to 48oz. (86–1371

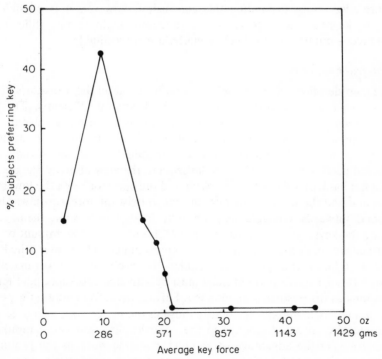

Figure 4.1.   The preferred forces of pushbuttons (adapted from Bergenthal, 1971).

grams). His results, shown in Figure 4.1, illustrate the variation in preference with button resistance. Clearly, the buttons having a force of about 9.5oz. were preferred by the highest proportion of the subjects; indeed, no subjects preferred buttons with a force higher than 23–25 oz. It must be remembered, however, that Bergenthal's study was performed with subjects pressing the buttons sequentially with a 'stiff' finger. As will be emphasized later, typing (alphanumeric input) is not performed in this way and so it is likely that lower key forces would be preferred for continuous keying using all fingers.

A further example of the importance of ensuring optimum switch force can be seen in a study by Droege and Hill (1961). They compared the efficiency of over 500 subjects using manual and electric typewriters, in which the main design differences between the two types of machine lies in the key resistance: the manual typewriter keys have higher resistance as a result of the system of levers connecting the key to the typeface, rather than the connection being made by an electric solenoid (or, with microprocessor operated keyboards, no mechanical links at all). The authors measured both the speed and accuracy of their subjects and demonstrated, on average, a performance improvement of nearly 10 words per minute using the electric typewriter, with an average of two fewer errors. Both of these differences were statistically significant. Clearly, therefore, variations in key resistance can have important implications for performance. Notwithstanding this conclusion, however, it is possible that different keyboard arrangements and functions might require different key resistances—but data regarding this matter are not available.

Hand-arm biomechanics

These considerations concern the workload imposed on the operator's fingers, hands, arms, and shoulders to operate the keyboard efficiently. The main aspects, then, relate to the keying task and the muscle loads engendered.

Most standard keyboards are operated with all of the keys facing the operator in a line at right angles to the operator's direction. Although the keyboard itself may be tilted to the horizontal, the view afforded the operator is of a flat bank of keys. At such a keyboard the operator (with the lower arms horizontal and the upper arms vertical) has to twist the forearms inwards and the hand outwards to enable the palm to be flat downwards and the fingers to operate the keys. Indeed, as Kroemer (1972) points out, the amount of twist required (protination) is near to the anatomical limits. (The reader is invited to adopt this hand–arm posture to realize the problem.) Unfortunately, to perform this act the forearm muscles must be activated and kept under tension for as long as the posture is maintained. Furthermore, to maintain the posture other antagonistic muscles (primarily those in the upper arm) also need to be contracted by an equal amount in the opposite direction (supination)—but without having the advantage of as much dynamic work as the protinating forearm muscles. Under these circumstances, fatigue frequently results.

To relieve some of the tension from these muscles, both Kroemer (1972) and Ferguson and Duncan (1974) suggest that the operator performs frequent postural changes by lifting the elbow at the same time outwards and forwards. This, naturally, affects the shoulder and neck muscles and can lead to further fatigue, as Lundervold (1958) has demonstrated. Furthermore the increased separation between the elbows means that the forearms must turn further inwards across the front of the body, which increases the amount of twist at the wrist.

Of course, the major biomechanical problems involved in keyboard operation do not end simply with the arm and shoulder muscles. They must include the fingers which have to operate the keys. Again, as Kroemer (1972) emphasizes, the finger extensor and flexor muscles are also closely associated with the protination and supination muscles in the arm. The problems of fatigue in the finger muscles, therefore, are superimposed on the muscular problems arising from the standardized flat keyboard.

Duncan and Ferguson (1974) and Ferguson and Duncan (1974) provide detailed descriptions of the physical ill-effects that such forced postures can produce. Their investigations produced clinical evidence of finger, wrist and shoulder aching with keyboard operators. Furthermore, Osanai (1968) gives evidence of neck, shoulder, arm, hand and back pains which appear to be caused by repetitive quick motions of the hand and fingers as well as by the static muscular tension required to sustain the working posture.

In an attempt to determine the ideal angles of the hands and forearm for typing, Kroemer (1972) reports a study which he performed in 1964. Each of 38 female subjects sat with their forearms at 90° to the vertical upper arm. The subjects then laterally elevated (i.e. lifted upwards and outwards) the upper arm by 15, 45 or 90° with, at each position, the most comfortable palm angle being recorded. Kroemer's data are shown in Figure 4.2, and are compared with the angles required when using the standard, flat keyboard. As can be seen, the protination angles forced on the operator who uses a flat keyboard are widely variant to the optimum angles—particularly at lower angles of forearm lifting.

The finger motions required by different keyboard arrangements are, naturally, specific to the key arrangements used. With respect to the most frequently used keyboard (the QWERTY arrangement of characters), however, Ferguson and Duncan (1974) have demonstrated a slightly higher frequency of keying activity by the left hand compared with the right. Thus, for typists 54% of the keyboard load was on the left hand, whereas for telegraphists the proportion fell slightly to 51%. This was because telegraphic keyboards use more keys on the right to control functions such as 'carriage return', 'line feed', etc. This point is emphasized since computer keyboards also often use such additional control keys.

When the actual finger motions were analysed, however, wide variations in

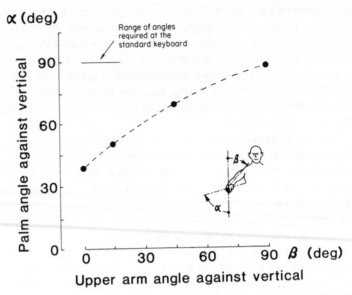

Figure 4.2.   Optimum wrist and arm angles for comfortable operation (Kroemer, 1972). Reproduced by permission of the Human Factors Society).

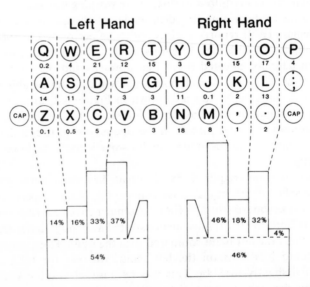

Figure 4.3.   Distribution of finger strokes of each hand on individual keys using the QWERTY keyboard (Ferguson and Duncan, 1974). The figures below each key represent the percentage of times the key was pressed when the particular hand was used.

finger load were found as shown in Figure 4.3. From this figure it is clear that the loads placed on the fingers do not bear any relation to the relative strengths of the fingers. Certainly, in teleprinter operations the ring and little fingers appear overloaded. Considering the data on finger strength discussed earlier, it might well be expected that fatigue will vary as a function of the finger being used. Indeed, this has been demonstrated by Haaland (1962) (cited in Alden *et al.*, 1972). He verified that the thumb is most resistant to fatigue and that susceptibility to fatigue increases as one moves progressively from the index finger to the little finger. The angle at which force was applied to the keyboard was also a factor, lateral force (which is a direction in which the little finger often has to move) resulting in more rapid fatigue than downward force.

Behavioural considerations

Efficient typewriting using a full-sized keyboard is an example of a very high-speed performance task. Thus, Fox and Stansfield (1964) have shown that skilled typists (i.e. those having an overall typing speed of at least 80 words per minute) using alternate hands typed at an average rate of one keystroke every 110 msec. Some could even type as fast as one keystroke every 80 msec. Rumelhart and Norman (1982) suggest that these very high speeds can occur because skilled typists carry out many actions at once. Typing is a task which has cognitive, physical and physiological components; it includes linguistic as well as manual skills. Skilled typists, then, have to develop special abilities for transforming visual input into finger movements; for coding and organizing the information that is seen or heard into meaningful units which are capable of making the fingers, hands and arms operate effectively.

Analyses of the actual finger motions that occur during typing have only been able to be made relatively recently with the advantage of high speed filming techniques. Rumelhart and Norman (1982) present data which illustrate the parallel nature of typing skill, in that typists appear to perform a series of finger movements simultaneously. Examples of these movements are shown in Figure 4.4, which illustrates the ten finger positions, in steps of four 'time units', when typing the words *very well*. At time 0, all of the fingers are resting on the 'home' (middle row) keys. At time 3, however, not only is the left index finger falling in readiness to strike the *v* key, but the right index finger has moved up towards the top row in readiness to strike the *y* of 'very' in three letters' time! Clearly, typing involves a great deal of anticipation, with fingers often hovering over the keys that are to be struck next by particular fingers.

Even such simple finger analyses, then, suggest that typing is not a sequential act, with each key being sought out and pressed as the letters occur in the words to be typed. Rather, the typist 'looks ahead' and appears to type in 'chunks' of text. The question then needs to be asked how this is done. A number of studies have considered this question—particularly in respect

Computers at Work

Figure 4.4. Hand and finger positions recorded at time intervals while the words *very well* are being typed (Rumelhart and Norman, 1982). Each frame displays the patterns approximately four time units after the previous frame. The star indicates an actual key press. Reproduced by permission of Ablex Publishing.

to the processes that occur between viewing the copy to be typed and executing the keystrokes. The general findings to have emerged from these studies is that typists process the material that they read or hear on the basis of meaningful linguistic units. Further, the basic unit of processing is the word—not smaller units such as syllables or larger units such as many words (Schoonard and Boies, 1975). Just how many words are important is a question which is not easy to answer. However, Shaffer (1976) suggests that preview of at least two words is necessary for fast typists to attain normal speeds.

The basis for statements of this nature arise from studies which have considered how typing speed varies with the nature of the text being typed. For example, Thomas and Jones (1970) showed that typing speed is slowed down by removing the spaces between words and by decreasing the amount of structure in the material. Similarly, Lee (1972) demonstrated the superiority of grouping digits into fours for keying performance over presenting simply a list of 12 digits. As further evidence of the need for grouping, a study by Hershman and Hillix (1965) indicated that being able to preview letters, to the point of a word boundary, aids performance. However, additional amounts of preview do not help to increase performance. It would appear, therefore, that typists try to input information into meaningful chunks.

On the basis of their experiments, and as a result of showing that the interkey interval is smaller for the intraword strokes than for the interword strokes, Thomas and Jones (1970) have presented a model of typing behaviour. This model, which is shown in Figure 4.5, suggests that two processes occur when text is being converted into type. Depending on the type of material, these processes will occur sequentially or in parallel.

The model first proposes a store (the visual information store—VIS) which receives information from the text in an unspecified manner and simply stores it until it is required. This information is scanned by one of two scanners, depending on how much redundancy there is in the text. If the redundancy is high, the phrase (P) scan component transforms the letters into groups of

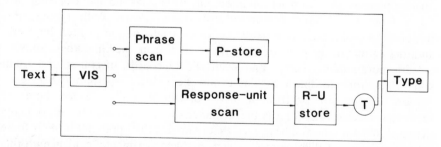

Figure 4.5.   Model of typewriting behaviour (Thomas and Jones, 1970). The large box represents the typist. Reproduced by permission of the Experimental Psychology Society.

particular size and transfers them to the P-store. The information in the P-store is then scanned by the response-unit (R-U) scanner which transfers letters in smaller groups from the P-store to the R-U store. If the redundancy in the text is low, however, the R-U scanner operates directly on the VIS transferring letters in the smaller groups. Finally, there is a translator (T) which converts the information in the R-U store, letter by letter, each into a series of motor actions ending in a key press. The phrase scanner, then, can be thought of as the component which defines the 'unit of thought'; the response-unit scanner defines the well-practised response patterns.

The components of this model are similar to those of a model for short term memory proposed by Sperling (1967).

Although the natural grouping for alphabetic text appears to be related to words—it is appropriate to question what is the optimum number of characters for grouping numeric text. Thus, if it can be arranged that the phrase scanner is, itself, made redundant (or less used) then keying speed might be increased. Significant speed increases might also be produced if the keyboard grouping can be made compatible with the R-U scanner and translator.

A number of studies have been performed in this area which suggest that the optimum group size is about three or four digits (for example, Conrad, 1960; Severin and Rigby, 1963; Thorpe and Rowland, 1965). Klemmer (1969) has reviewed many of these studies and also reports the results of some studies of his own which support this 'natural' grouping.

Gradually, therefore, a 'picture' is being built up of the behavioural components important in skilled typing and thus important in keyboard design. The model proposed by Thomas and Jones, however, is very much an 'open-loop' model—i.e. information passes, essentially, in one way only: from the eye to the finger. There is no suggestion of the role of feedback from either the finger or from the typed text to the operator.

As discussed earlier, feedback provides important information regarding the performance of a skill. It enables a self-correcting, 'closed-loop' system to operate by providing information about any deviations the operator may have taken from the desired performance (Adams, 1971). With typing, this feedback information arises from the visual (sight of the printed line) and auditory (sound of the printing action) as well as from the kinaesthetic senses.

With more modern electric and electronic keyboards, of course, the visual and/or auditory feedback available may be reduced—perhaps because of reduced display size or from a drive for quieter offices. Since these are important mechanisms for the performance of high speed motor movements (Keele, 1968) it might well be argued that removing their presence is likely to be to the detriment of the operator. The available experimental evidence on this topic, however, has shown only small decrements in performance as a result of removing auditory feedback. For example, Diehl and Seibel (1962) reported a small, although statistically significant, decrease in the performance of experienced typists when normal typing sounds were masked with extraneous noise. However, Pollard and Cooper (1979) suggest that these decrements may have arisen from the noise which was used to mask the auditory feedback also masking the operator's 'inner speech'. Furthermore, other experimenters such as Deininger (1960) and Klemmer (1971) (who used keypads rather than typewriters) have demonstrated no significant improvements in either keying speed or error reduction when using auditory feedback with signalling tones. Pollard and Cooper (1979), after obtaining similarly negative influences, suggest that the 'naturally occuring sounds of operation and the tactile and kinaesthetic sensations experienced during keying provide adequate feedback and eliminate the need for additional, electronically generated feedback'.

The importance of visual and auditory feedback to skilled performance is demonstrated, however, in the issue of keypressing training. Fleishman and Rich (1963) have suggested that there is a transition from visual feedback dependence to a reliance on kinaesthetic feedback whilst acquiring a complex psychomotor skill. West (1967) applied this line of reasoning to the acquisition of typing skills. His results showed an increase in kinaesthetic dependence from the begining to the intermediate levels of proficiency and then no change through to the expert level. Furthermore, performance with kinaesthetic feedback only was always worse when feedback occurred in all of the possible senses.

With regard to the value of kinaesthetic feedback itself, many studies have investigated this question by reducing, removing or manipulating the quality of the cues. Keele (1968) has reviewed many of these studies and concludes that kinaesthesis is a necessary feedback mechanism for such high speed performance tasks as finger tapping, tracking, and reaction time. Unfortunately, however, none of the studies considered typing directly but tapping and fast reactions must be considered to be important components of such a skill (Flanagan, Fivars and Tuska, 1959).

It would appear, therefore, that typing performance is very much a closed-loop system. Although kinaesthesis is the most important, although not the only, feedback mechanism for successful performance of the skill, in the early stages of learning vision is more important. Once the keyboard arrangement and the R-U and Translation units have been learned well enough, however, vision gives way to kinaesthesis.

It should not be forgotten, however, that one essential feature of Adams' (1971) conception of a closed-loop system is the use of feedback for error detection—to compare the returned information with an idealized 'template'. For this purpose, it appears that *both* vision and kinaesthesis are used. For example, Long (1976) showed that skilled typists were able to correct fewer errors when their copy was obscured than under normal conditions (55% vs. 71%). Clearly, therefore, vision is important to error detection although errors were still able to be detected. However, as Rabbit (1978) points out, this may have been because the typists might have detected many of their errors by watching their hands in peripheral vision rather than by using kinaesthetic feedback alone. Nevertheless, in an experiment of his own, Rabbit demonstrated that, even with both keyboard and copy masked, typists were still able to recognize that errors had occurred—with better accuracy than Long's 'keyboard only' subjects. Kinaesthetic feedback, therefore, is clearly as important in error detection as it is in accurate finger placement.

In summary, therefore, the behavioural considerations suggest firstly that skilled typists and keyboard operators transform the material-to-be-typed into keystrokes in terms of specific 'phrase' chunks. With such chunks of information, typewriting speed can be increased as a result of anticipatory finger movements. For alphabetic text these chunks are about 2–3 words long; for numeric material they are 3–4 characters long. Secondly, the role of feedback in such performance cannot be overstated. Certainly kinaesthetic feedback is the most used channel although, during training, it is superseded by vision. The roles of vision and audition at high skill levels are not so clear— although they have a value for error detection.

Keyboard design

Having considered the human operators' requirements for keyboards, it is appropriate to question how these requirements can be incorporated into efficient keyboard design. In this respect the anthropometric and biomechanical considerations influence the physical size and shape of keyboards; the behavioural considerations will relate to the ways in which the keys are arranged on the board.

In essence three types of board can be produced. Firstly, *alphanumeric keyboards* contain alphabetic, punctuation and numeric keys. These are used, primarily, for processing text. Secondly, *keypads* contain only the numeric keys with associated function keys (plus, minus, etc.) for keying in numeric data. Finally, the *chord* keyboards are used to input both alphabetic and numeric information. Their characteristic lies in the fact that each letter or number is 'composed' by pressing groups of keys—rather than separate keys as with the alphanumeric boards and keypads.

The physical dimensions of alphanumeric and numeric keyboards are clearly determined by the dimensions and arrangements of the keys which they contain. In this respect, the anthropometric dimensions of the fingers and hands discussed earlier are important. So, too, are the ways in which the keys need to be pressed—sequentially or in combination. This, then, determines the minimal interkey spacing.

With respect to keyboard angle, or tilt, both Alden *et al.* (1972) and Cooper (1976) point out that there is a relatively small literature on the question of typing performance as a function of the keyboard tilt. Furthermore, the few studies that are available suggest that, provided the board does not deviate too far from the optimum tilt, performance is not greatly disrupted. For example, Alden *et al.* report a study by Galitz (1965) who investigated the effect of a computer keyboard tilt on typing performance. He used slopes of 9°, 21° and 33° to the horizontal, and found no significant performance differences between them. However, his subjects did appear to prefer the 21° slope. This 'idealized' slope of about 20° is substantiated in a study performed by Scales and Chapanis (1954). They used keyboard slopes of between 0 and 40° to the horizontal, and their subjects were asked to perform a task of keying ten-character alphanumeric characters. Although no significant differences were obtained in either typing speed or errors, the 'operator preference data' suggested that some slope was desirable. Half of the preferences occurred between 15° and 25°.

With regard to numeric, as opposed to alphanumeric, keying Alden *et al.* point to studies performed by Creamer and Trumbo (1960). They used a keytapping task in which subjects were required to tap keys in a particular sequence, alternating fingers and hands. Five tilt angles were used (0, 22, 44, 66, and 88°). Although the maximum number of errors were made at O°, the variation in errors after 22° was only very slight. Using an actual number keying task (telephone numbers) Cooper (1976) again showed that the 'best' keypad angle appears to be around 25° to the horizontal, since this produced least keying time and fewest errors. However he also points out that his data indicate that the effect of a deviation either way from this angle was quite small.

In summary, therefore, the optimum keyboard angle appears to lie between 20 and 30° to the horizontal.

As an extension of the idea of tilting the keyboard, and taking account of the biomechanical data regarding the ways in which the wrist and forearm have to be extended during typing, Kroemer (1972) describes a new type of alphanumeric keyboard (called the K-board) which is split at the centre and hinged backwards at angles of either 30 or 50°—each half being operated by each hand. The main feature of the K-board is that the keys are arranged in straight columns (rather than offset as on a conventional board) and in curved rows. The space bars, one for each sectional keyboard, are bent from the inside of the keyboard to below the bottom row (see Figure 4.6). Such an arrangement reduces the tendency to ulnar deviation described above as noted by Ferguson and Duncan (1974) and prevents operating the wrists in the 'abnormal' (protinating) posture. Kroemer (1965) reports that normal keyboard tilts of 15° proved significantly slower and more fatiguing than the experimental K-board. With regard to the K-board itself, Kroemer (1972) reports an investigation in which four angular tilts (0, 30, 60 and 90°) were used. Inclinations of 30 or 60° produced significantly faster and less fatiguing stroking performance than either the 0 or 90° inclinations.

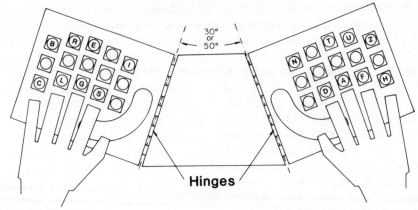

Figure 4.6.   The design of the K-board (Kroemer, 1972). Reproduced by permission of the Human Factors Society.

Arranging the keys on a keyboard will clearly be related to the type of information needed to be input to the system. In this respect the key arrangement for alphabetic text must be distinguished from that for numeric input.

Alphabetic keyboards

The normal typewriter keyboard (often called the QWERTY board because these letters occur at the beginning of the top line) has been in existence since before the beginning of this century. It was designed by C. L. Sholes and his colleagues in 1874 (patented in 1878) to conform to the mechanical constraints of contemporary typewriters. The problem which they faced was that typists were able to press keys at a rate which was faster than the machines, with their mechanical links and reliance on gravity to return the keyhead, were able to respond. The resulting key jamming was overcome by the apparently haphazard arrangement of the letters shown earlier in Figure 4.3. The QWERTY board, therefore, was designed originally to *slow down* typists.

Various authors have suggested different reasons why the QWERTY arrangement as such was developed. Norman and Fisher (1982), for example, suggest that the arrangement is such that the keys are typed successively as far apart on the keyboard as possible, so that the type bars will approach each other at a relatively sharp angle with minimum chances of jamming. Hackmeister (1979) supports this argument but adds one further observation: the top row contains all of the letters in the word 'typewriter', and it was Sholes who designed the first 'Typewriting Machine'!

Regarding how the arrangement slows typists down, Martin (1972) argues that the arrangement is such that the letter most likely to be typed next is obscured by the operator's hand. Biegel (1934), however, argues that the board produces less efficient performance because of both anthropometric, biomechanical and perceptual factors. Thus:

1 The ring (third) finger and little fingers have to be stretched when moving from the home keys to the third and fourth rows. This reduces the strength of the stroke and leads to the edge of the finger-tip rather than the centre being used to hit the keys.
2 The division of the keys into vertical 'strips' for the different fingers is made parallel but oblique. This means that the strips for the fingers of the right hand present the same shape as those for the left—despite the fact that the hands are not congruent, but are inverse images of each other.
3 Tracks from the home keys are difficult to follow so that often the wrong key is struck.

One positive feature of the QWERTY board suggested by a number of authors, however, (for example, Kinkead, 1975; Cakir, Hart and Stewart, 1980; Noyes, 1983a) is the workload that it places on each hand—rather than on each finger. Thus, when typing English text almost all keystrokes alternate from one hand to the other. Noyes (1983a), for example, argues that common letter sequences typed on the QWERTY board involve either alternate hands being used, the whole hand being moved over the keyboard, or non-adjacent fingers being moved sequentially. This is likely, then, to increase the proportion of dynamic work done and to reduce muscular fatigue.

Despite this positive aspect of the QWERTY arrangement, and despite (or possibly because of) the fact that many millions of typewriters have been produced using the arrangement, a number of attempts at producing alternative keyboard arrangements have been proposed. All of the new arrangements are based on the frequencies that letters and letter pairs occur in the English language. The two which have captured most experimental time are the Dvorak and the Alphabetic board.

The Dvorak board (patented by A. Dvorak in 1932) was produced as a result of a decade of physiological and language research. The main principles behind the arrangement are as follows:

1 Layout is arranged on the basis of the frequency of usage of letters and the frequency of letter patterns and sequences in the English language.
2 All vowels and most used consonants are on the second (or 'home') row, so that something like 70% of common words are typed on this row alone.
3 Faster operation is possible by tapping with fingers on alternate hands (particularly the most used index fingers) than by repetitive tapping with one finger. Since the probability of vowels and consonants alternating is very high, all vowels are typed with the left hand and frequent (home row) consonants with the right hand.
4 Finger travel and consequent fatigue are thus greatly reduced.

Using these principles, the arrangement shown in Figure 4.7 was produced which, Dvorak claims, provides a more even distribution of finger movements and a bias towards the right hand. This is also shown in Figure 4.7 (compare these figures with the finger analyses for the QWERTY board shown in Figure 4.3). Dvorak also claimed that this arrangement reduces the between-rows movement by 90%, and allows 35% of all words normally used to be typed on the middle row.

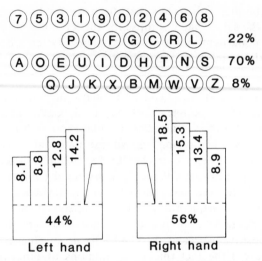

Figure 4.7.   The Dvorak keyboard layout and workload distribution in typing English text. The row figures relate to the proportion of times the keys in each row are used.

Controversy presently exists as to the relative merits of the QWERTY and the Dvorak boards. For example, a U.S. government sponsored study in 1956 demonstrated little difference between the advantages of each arrangement (Alden et al., 1976). Martin (1972), however, discusses (unreported) novice training experiments carried out in Great Britain which demonstrated a 10% saving in training time using the Dvorak board. Furthermore, Dunn (1971) argues that the Dvorak board is superior in terms of ease of learning, reduced likelihood of error and fatigue, and increased speed of entry.

In the alphabetic board, keys are arranged as the name suggests: from A to Z. These boards are seen on many machines, for example, stock quotation machines (Michaels, 1971). The argument behind the use of this arrangement is, quite simply, that an alphabetical ordering of the keys makes logical sense, particularly to inexperienced typists who presently need to spend considerable time learning the QWERTY arrangement.

Despite the apparent logic of using an alphabetically arranged board Norman and Fisher (1982) point out that the available studies do not support the view that inexperienced typists find the alphabetic board easier to use. Indeed both Hirsch (1970) and Michaels (1971) have shown that for semi-skilled typists, keying rates and error correction are better using the QWERTY board, and the performance on the two boards is essentially the same for novices. Norman and Fisher have also shown that typing speed is faster with the QWERTY board.

Norman and Fisher (1982) suggest two reasons for these apparently paradoxical findings: firstly, an experimental one in that it is difficult to find subjects who have not had some exposure to the QWERTY arrangement; and secondly, the alphabetic keyboard, although logically superior, still requires considerable visual search and mental processing (to remember, for example, that 'm' appears after 'k'). At the novice stage at least, therefore, all keyboard layouts are equivalent. Once the skill has been learned, of course, as discussed earlier, visual feedback gives way to kinaesthetic feedback, so that the different board arrangements are likely to be equally efficient.

In summary, therefore, it would appear that, from the point of view of key arrangement alone, it makes little difference which type of board is used. Since the high cost of converting machines and of retraining typists to use the alternative boards are likely to ensure the continuation of the QWERTY arrangement, more valuable time could possibly be spent in redesigning the physical arrangement of the board, along the lines suggested earlier, to make it fit more the anthropometric and biomechanical properties of the user.

Before concluding the discussion of alphabetic input, one final point should be emphasized. All of the discussion so far has centered around the arrangement for entering Roman characters into the computer (Cakir, Hart and Stewart, 1980, describe some experimental boards for Spanish and German languages). However, as Chapanis (1974) points out, there are number of different languages and forms of script, and the problems outlined above are increased markedly when languages which do not use the Roman alphabet are considered—such as Japanese which uses between 2000 and 4000 characters. To this end Brown (1974) describes the development of a Japanese card punch machine which, as with the Dvorak concept, puts the most frequently used characters an a special high-usage region of the board. For example, about 70% of ordinary Japanese can be written with 600 of the most frequently used characters. Grouping these characters decreased the search time and the average distance needed to be reached when keying in ordinary text. Using these principles Brown was able to show that skilled Japanese operators could key about the same average number of words per minute, and almost as accurately, as skilled American card-punch operators working in English.

Numeric keyboards

Fewer studies have been performed to determine the optimum arrangement of the numeric keys (0-9) than the alphabetic keys—possibly because, with only ten keys, there are fewer sensible arrangements that can be accommodated.

A number of these arrangements were investigated by Deininger (1960) in his study of pushbutton telephone sets. Four designs, shown in Figure 4.8, were

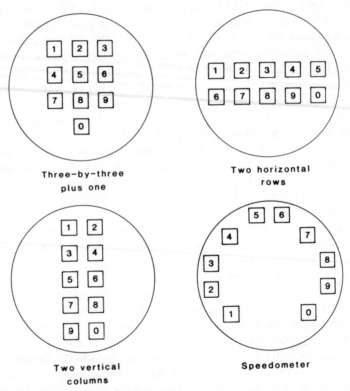

Figure 4.8.   Four efficient numeric key arrangements found by Denninger (1960).

shown to be roughly equally acceptable on criteria such as keying time, errors and 'votes' for and against. For 'engineering' reasons, however, Deininger suggests either arrangement 1 or 2 is used for telephones. Indeed, the 'standard' telephone arrangement has now become that shown in arrangement 1; i.e. a $3 + 3 + 3 + 1$ matrix starting with 1, 2, 3 on the top row and ending with 0 below the third row.

Although this arrangement has become standard for telephone keypads, it is not that currently used for numerical input on keyboards such as calculators. This is normally the reverse of the telephone arrangement, the keys on the 3 + 3 + 3 + 1 matrix having the order 7,8,9: 4,5,6: 1,2,3: and 0.

Conrad and Hull (1968) compared the keying efficiency of these two types of arrangement. No significant differences were obtained in terms of the speed of data entry but they did find that significantly fewer errors (6.4% versus 8.2%) were made using the telephone keypad (1,2,3: 4,5,6: etc.) than with the calculator pad arrangement (7,8,9: 4,5,6: etc.).

Chord keyboards

Before concluding the discussion of keyboards, it is important to consider whether ways other than single keys might be more appropriate for entering alphanumeric data. Minor and Revesman (1962) compared the effectiveness of four different ways of inputting numerical data (a 10 key keyboard, as on hand calculators; a 10 × 10 matrix keyboard; a 10-lever device; and a 10 rotary knob device). They demonstrated a 50% increase in input time and almost 600% increase in errors for the 'worst' over the 'best' device. Clearly, then, some types of devices lend themselves to more effective use than do others.

In the search for improved ways of keying data, particularly alphabetic data, the possibility of reducing the number of keys by requiring the operator to press more than one key at once has often been suggested. Such key arrangements are called *chord keyboards* and they appear in many different forms. Some are operated by one hand only (usually with five keys—one for each finger), whilst others are operated by both hands (with 10 keys). (Litterick, 1981, describes some of these boards, and Noyes, 1983b, describes the history and development of chord keying.) Some boards require combinations of keys to be pressed to form different letters whereas others, usually the larger boards, also enable words or parts of words to be formed. By pressing combinations of keys, then, a large number of characters can be formed; in fact with N keys ($2^N - 1$) sensible combinations can be made (one combination—no keys pressed—is not sensible in this context). Furthermore, with appropriate logic systems, even more than the ($2^N - 1$) combinations can be attained—for example, using one key as a 'control' key.

The main impetus to reduce the number of keys arises, clearly, from a wish to reduce the amount of time that fingers travel over the keyboard and the possibility of errors being made. Thus, Fitts (1954) has shown that the difficulty of making small hand movements is determined largely by the extent to which the hand has to move and the size of the target. If the fingers are hovering over chord keys (as they appear to do during 'normal' typing), the argument goes, the time take to form characters and the number of errors should both be reduced.

Unfortunately, the little evidence available does not support this argument fully. For example, both Ratz and Ritchie (1961) and Seibel (1962) required subjects to react quickly to combinations of lights by pressing the corresponding keys place under the fingers. Between the best and the worst of the 31 possible chord combinations, increases in reaction time of about 70 ms were recorded whilst the error rate increased by about 400%. Not surprisingly, the fastest time and the fewest errors were recorded when only one stimulus light needed to be reacted to—a situation which is similar to, although given the evidence of Rumelhart and Norman (1982) referred to earlier not the same as, typewriting.

Very few experiments have been performed to compare directly keying performance using a typewriter and a keyboard. As Conrad and Longman (1965) point out, this is probably because of difficulties in obtaining matched groups of subjects and being able to train them for very long periods of time using the same instructor.

Bowen and Guiness (1965) compared performance on a semi-automatic mail-sorting task using either a typewriter, a small (12 key) chord board, or a large (24 key) chord board. Both chord boards resulted in higher numbers of items being sorted correctly per minute than the typewriter, with the small board proving superior. McCormick (1976) attributes this observation to the fact that the small keyboard did not require such difficult finger patterns as the large board.

The superiority of chord keyboards over typewriters has also been established by Conrad and Longman (1965) who, like Bowen and Guiness, used a letter-sorting task. However, they continued the experiment for nearly a month. Their subjects used either a two-handed, 10-key chord board (with some associated control keys) or a typewriter. Their results suggested that subjects trained on the chord board learned the key arrangement quicker than those on the typewriter (with an average of 12.5 days as opposed to 20.5 days) and, once learned, operated the machine faster. It should be pointed out, however, that most of the letter and number sequences used by Conrad and Longman were postcodes—apparently random pairs of letters and numbers. Whether or not the typewriter would maintain its inferiority with recognizable chunks of English is an unanswered question.

Finally, the impression should not be gained that chord keyboards will automatically be more efficient than standard keyboards. Thus, as McCormick has pointed out, much is likely to depend on the combinations of keys needed to be pressed to produce particular letters. In this respect Seibel's (1962) data are important in showing how different combinations of keys can lead to varying keying times and errors. Furthermore, the time required to learn particular key combinations is bound to be a strong function of the ease of remembering the logical arrangement of the keys to be used and this is determined by the quality of the system used to code combinations of keystrokes (Seibel, 1964).

Touch displays

The amount of space which has been devoted to discussing keyboards for entering information into a computer reflects the importance of these devices. However, the computer is a very powerful piece of equipment and really should be treated much more than a simple typewriter. As such, with appropriate programs, it has the ability to allow other, more complex, input devices to be used—provided, as discussed earlier, the information is input in a manner which can be broken down to 'ons' or 'offs'; 1's or 0's.

A touch display allows the user to input information to the machine simply by touching an appropriate part of the screen or some representation of the screen. In this way the computer screen becomes, essentially, a bidirectional instrument in that it both presents information to and receives information from the operator. A touch display, therefore, combines the functions of keyboard and display.

Using appropriate software, different parts of the screen can represent different responses as different displays are presented to the operator. For example, a screen may first present a list of actions available to the operator, who choses a particular action by touching—say the centre of the screen. The centre of the screen for the next display, however, may represent a totally different type of choice.

Screen-based touch displays are essentially transparent masks which are fitted over the display screen and have a number of 'touch sensitive' points or areas. These are generally labelled on the screen and the operator touches the label. The resultant signal is transmitted to the computer in the same way as a signal from a key depression on a standard keyboard is transmitted. *Remote* touch displays operate on the same principle but do not cover the screen. They often take the form of a separate desk-top board (Ritchie and Turner (1975), Johnson (1967) and Bird (1977) describe a number of different forms of touch displays).

Both Hopkin (1971) and McEwing (1977) discuss the advantages of screen-based displays, which can be summarized thus:

1 *They are easy to use.* As argued above such displays present a direct, 1:1, relationship between the information presented to the operator and the response required. Indeed, the two are the same. Being easy to use, training time is likely to be reduced (Usher, 1982) so that the need for careful selection of operators is also reduced.

2 *They are fast to use.* In a small pilot study, McEwing compared the speed of inputting information using typewriters and touch displays. Touch displays took about one-third of the time taken when using typewriters. In addition, using air traffic controllers, Hopkin (1971) demonstrated that touch wire displays proved to be significantly faster than conventional keyboards for entering both single characters and groups of characters. McEwing further

suggests that, since arranging data into groups for entry will obviously enable higher operation speeds to be attained, the flexibility of touch displays makes them superior even to specially designed function keyboards.

3 *They minimize errors.* Because they limit the choices available to the operator and because of the close proximity of the responses to the choices, touch displays minimize the occurence of keying errors. Again, Hopkin's (1971) study with air traffic controllers demonstrated that both error detection and correction were significantly faster with touch displays than with a conventional keyboard.

4 *They are flexible.* Because touch displays are under software control they are extremely flexible, both in the variety of ways in which sequences can be arranged and in the comparative ease with which modifications and additions to sequences can be made. The same visual display unit, therefore, can present many different forms of response alternatives.

5 *Operator reaction is generally favourable.* Usher (1982), for example, describes an experiment carried out to compare the efficiency of a touch sensitive screen with a conventional keypad. Nearly five times as many subjects preferred the touch display to the keypad as vice-versa and, for emergency operation, this ratio doubled. Hopkin (1971) also reports that 'operators enjoyed using the touch display and immediately formed favourable attitudes towards it'.

Against these advantages, however, Pfauth and Priest (1981) suggest a number of disadvantages of touch displays. These include an initial high cost for the system, increased programmer time, reduced flexibility for some types of input, the possibility of screen glare affecting response accuracy, physical fatigue from reaching to the screen, and the finger and hand blocking the operator's line of sight to important areas of the screen.

As described above, an alternative type of touch pad available to designers is one which is (topographically) associated with, but not actually situated on, the screen. The advantage of this type of touch display, of course, is its increased mobility. Like a remote keyboard it can be moved around to suit the posture of the operator. For example, as Bird (1977) and Pfauth and Priest (1981) emphasize, continuous pointing to a vertical, or near vertical, screen is likely over time to cause fatigue. Thus the optimum angles of the surface for vision and for touching may not be the same. Also, Pfauth and Priest's argument against touch displays—that in the act of touching the screen, the fingers or part of the hand may obscure the rest of the display—is reduced with an 'off-display' touch panel that is mounted on a desk surface below the screen. Unfortunately, of course, although it is biomechanically more convenient, such a display lacks the immediate visual feedback on finger position in relation to the displayed information. Operators, therefore, have to translate information presented from the screen in the vertical plane to responses made somewhere else in the horizontal plane.

Despite these disadvantages Hopkin (1971) also reports a study in which performance on a touch-wire display was compared with that on a 'remote labelled keyboard' (this is different from a typewriter). Using these two variations of the touch input concept, Hopkin reported no significant differences between the devices. Furthermore, when subjects trained on one type of device were asked to transfer to the other, complete transfer of training resulted; the subjects showed no marked preference for either device.

The lack of any performance difference between the two forms of device, however, was not substantiated in a study reported by Whitfield *et al.* (1979). They used two types of task which differed, effectively, in terms of the amount of information presented to the operator on the screen. In terms of the times taken to select the information correctly, the screen-based input device was consistently faster than the off-screen, horizontal, touch pad. However, as the authors point out, the average speed difference was less than one second which, although being statistically significant, may not be significant in practice.

In summary, therefore, it would appear that when relatively few alternatives need to be selected, or when data can be arranged into logical groups, computer generated and analysed touch displays are both efficient and are acceptable to operators. They do have their disadvantages, however, mainly from the point of view of the operator's posture required to operate them. This, coupled with any costs involved in tailoring the displays to match particular screens, may suggest that a remote, 'off-screen', touch pad might be better—despite the fact that some display–response compatibility is lost.

Other types of discrete entry devices

Lightpens

Like touch displays, lightpens are fully interactive control devices. They can be used effectively to position the cursor on the screen or to select responses from a 'menu' displayed to the operator. The user simply touches the appropriate part of the screen with the 'pen' and, through the photosensitive diode situated in the end of the pen, the computer is able to compute the pen's position on the screen. The operation of the pen, therefore, is very similar to that of the finger on a touch display.

Unfortunately, little research appears to have been carried out to investigate either the design or the efficiency of this type of control. As discussed earlier, Goodwin (1975) demonstrated that for selecting particular words or characters from a text display as, for example, in text editing, a lightpen appears to be much faster than using keyboard cursor controls. However, Morrill, Goodwin and Smith (1968) demonstrated a slight advantage of the keyboard over the lightpen when presenting instructions to subjects during a computer-aided instruction study.

If the task requires the operator to mix modes of data entry, however (say to type using the keyboard but, on occasions, to use a lightpen to respond to questions) then using the lightpen can be quite detrimental (Earl and Goff, 1965). Thus the operator needs to stop using the keyboard, reorientate the hands (to pick up and to operate the lightpen), and then return to using the keyboard.

Although little information is available for designing the pen itself, it should be possible to predict some of the problems which constant users of lightpens might face—in particular those to do with muscular fatigue in both the arm and the wrist. Thus, as was discussed earlier, as the arm is extended the prehensile grip of the hand on the pen varies so that higher forces are required to maintain the pen support. Secondly, continuous working of the hand both away from the body and high up causes the upper arm and shoulder muscles to be under static muscular load. Thirdly, the distribution of the pen's weight is important to ensure that undue forces are not placed on the wrist. A 'heavy' cable connecting the end of the pen to the computer, which is needed to transmit information from the pen to the computer, *could* detrimentally affect the weight distribution and thus increase the static muscular load on the wrist. Finally, when operating any pen, the forces acting on the pen itself are in an opposite direction to the direction in which the pen is pointing, i.e. from the screen towards the operator. This being so, to stop the fingers slipping down to the tip of the pen, the operator has to grip hard with the fingers. Any design which will increase the finger/pen resistance, such as using a non-slippery surface or by putting grooves *around* the barrel (i.e. in an opposite direction to the direction of slipping) will help to reduce the amount of grip required and thus the amount of static load.

Bar code scanners

These are devices which both look and operate very much like lightpens. However they are not used interactively with the computer screen, rather the scanner is passed over alternate black and white bars, the composition of which contain the information to be input. Although the movement is continuous they are described as discrete entry devices because the input takes the form of on/off; black or white. The information to be input is previously coded in the form of the black bar thickness and frequency (a wide black bar represents a '1'—on—and a narrow one represents a '0'—off). The operator's task, then, is to run the pen along the bar code, in either direction, and the pen (which includes a light source and detector) is able to input information to the computer. In some installations, the pen remains still and the operator has to pass the code over it.

As with lightpens, little work has been published that considers the appropriate design and operating characteristics of a bar code reading system.

However, the increased use of such devices in all aspects of work seem to attest to their perceived usefulness. Gilchrest and Shenkin (1981), for example, have plotted the rise of scanners in U.S. supermarkets from six in 1974 to nearly 4000 in 1981, with a predicted 10,000 to 12,000 in use in 1984. They report that the obvious savings for one large U.S. supermarket chain through using bar code scanners arose in the following way: 37% increased checker productivity; 21% easier cash register checking and balancing; 21% automatic produce weighing and pricing; and 14% eliminating pricing, reading or keying errors. It is not certain, however, from their figures, whether the increased productivity arose from the reduced keying errors, etc., or whether it occurred because data entry using a scanner is faster.

As far as the operator is concerned, bar scanners have a major advantage over lightpens—their operating postures are not constrained by the computer system itself. Thus, the arm and hand does not need to be maintained under static load to enable the pen to touch the screen. The code on the product can be read at any angle desired by the operator. However, Wilson and Grey (1983) point out that the fixed 'pen' system of scanners, in which the material to be read is passed over the scanner, can create postural difficulties for the operator. In their study of supermarket scanners, they demonstrated that the fixed nature of the device and the amount of reach required created problems for operators with smaller stature. As will be discussed in Chapter 6, however, these are problems associated with the workplace rather than with the device itself.

CONTINUOUS ENTRY DEVICES

Continuous entry devices allow the operator to vary the amount of information being put into the computer. Thus, rather than the information being transmitted in digital, on/off, form a control such as a joystick produces a continually varying (analogue) signal to the computer which has to be converted to its digital state before the computer is able to use the information.

The important differences between discrete and continuous controls do not simply end with the necessity or otherwise of changing the form of the incoming signal. From the operator's viewpoint two other aspects of the control are important. These are the control display–ratio and the control resistance.

The control–display ratio describes the relationship between the movement of the two components and has implications for the sensitivity of the system. A small movement of the control which is associated with a large display 'deflection' means that the operator has to deal with a highly sensitive system; as with a 'hair trigger' on a gun a small movement produces a large response. At the other end of the continuum lies the low sensitivity system in which a large control movement is required to produce a small movement on the display. The ratio between the control and display movements is, naturally, called the control–display ratio and is an index of the system sensitivity.

The ideal ratio for any particular control–display system depends entirely on the system's requirements and properties, and so no general formulae exist to help the designer to decide the appropriate ratio to use. However the optimum ratio for any system can be determined experimentally, as was demonstrated by Jenkins and Connor (1949).

Whenever a continuous control is used, the operator effectively performs two types of movement. The first is a relatively crude, gross motor movement to position the control in the vicinity of the final setting. Jenkins and Connor describe this as the 'travel phase'. Second there appears a much finer movement, the 'adjustment phase', in which the operator regulates the motor control to bring about the final control setting. The optimum control–display ratio, Jenkins and Connor argue, will be when both of these movements occur in the shortest time.

The control resistance has important implications for the amount of feedback which the operator receives and this relates to the 'feel' of the control (Burrows, 1965). In the majority of cases when continuous settings are being made, some inbuilt resistance in the control is desirable since it allows the operator to make settings with a certain degree of precision. In addition, resistance will often help to guard against accidentally operating the control. If too much resistance is incorporated into the control, however, or resistance of the wrong type, performance may be reduced and the operator could experience fatigue. Understanding the nature of different types of resistance, therefore, should make it possible to choose or to design controls which have resistance characteristics which will minimize any possible negative effects, while at the same time maximizing performance.

Control resistance takes four main forms, and their advantages and disadvantages are shown in Table 4.2 (from Oborne, 1982). From this table it appears that, for continuous controls, elastic or viscous resistance will allow greater precision owing to the nature of the kinaesthetic feedback provided.

Levers and joysticks

The difference between a lever and a joystick is simply that joysticks operate in two dimensions whereas levers only operate in one. For this reason, joysticks are used more often for cursor positioning tasks. Because they are used in situations in which precision adjustments are made, it is desirable that only the hand and fingers are used since these muscles are more densely supplied with nerves than in, for example, the arm. For this reason joysticks are generally smaller than levers. To aid precision they should have resistance in all directions with, perhaps, a return to centre position if the hand is removed.

Table 4.2. The characteristics of static and coulomb, elastic, viscous and inertial control resistances (After Oborne, 1983)

Type of resistance	Example of incidence	Characteristics	Advantages	Disadvantages
Static and coulomb	1. On/off switch 2. A 'stuck' control	The resistance is maximal at the start of the movement, but falls considerably with further force, i.e. the control slips	Reduced chance of accidental activation	Little precision control once the control has begun to move
Elastic	Spring-loaded control	Resistance is proportional to control displacement	1. Kinaesthetic cues may be maximally effective 2. Control returns to null position	Because control returns to neutral, operator's limb needs to be constantly active
Viscous	Plunger	Resistance is proportional to the velocity of the control movement	1. Good control precision— particularly rate of movement 2. Reduced chance of accidental operation 3. Operator can remove limb and control remains in position	
Inertia	Large crank	Resistance is caused by the mass of the control	1. Allows smooth movement 2. Reduced chance of accidental operation due to high force required	1. May cause operator fatigue 2. Does not allow precise movement because of danger of overshooting

Morgan *et al.* (1963) further suggest that the joystick should be designed to enable the operator to rest the wrist while making the movements, and that the pivot point should be positioned under the point at which the wrist is rested. However, as discussed earlier, the value of resting the wrists while making adjustment movements may be severely reduced if the joystick is to be used under vibrating conditions.

Few data are available to guide the designer in choosing the optimum dimensions for joystick handles, perhaps because the important consideration relates more to the extent to which the display alters in relation to the control movement. In this respect Jenkins and Karr (1954) suggest that the lowest ratio that can be considered optimal is about 2.5:1. That is, the tip of the joystick should move 2.5 times as fast as the cursor. The lengths of the stick that they used (up to 72cm) and the fact that the control was able to be moved only in one direction, however, suggests that they were discussing more the use of levers than the normally understood joystick.

The roller ball and mouse

As the name suggests, 'roller balls' are spherically shaped objects which the operator can rotate in any direction. Their distinctive characteristic is that they rotate within a socket; thus they are fixed pieces of equipment. On the other hand, the 'mouse', although it operates in a similar fashion to the 'roller ball' is not fixed; the operator is able to move it around, much like a pen is moved around paper to form characters. In most other aspects, however, the two devices are similar.

As discussed earlier, Card *et al.* (1978) demonstrated the superiority of these input devices over the conventional keyboard when used to move a cursor around the screen. Despite their apparent superiority in this type of situation, however, little research appears to have been carried out to determine their optimum parameters.

Roller balls can be manipulated in a number of ways. Thus, as Jackson (1982) illustrates, the fingers can be placed on the surface and moved, so drawing the ball surface along in continuous contact, or the ball can be flicked into ballistic motion by the fingers, with further flicks for additional motion. Friction pressure is then used to halt the ball abruptly. The palm of the hand can also be used in the same manner as the fingers.

From these descriptions of the operation of this type of device, it would appear that an important parameter in the ball design is the amount of surface area which is exposed to the operator. This, of course, is a function of the ball diameter, and it determines the extent to which displacement can occur without repositioning, for example, the fingers. The size of the ball is also related to the friction and inertia that it presents to the operator; these will increase with ball dimensions. Unfortunately, information is not available on performance sensitivity to such variables as inertia and friction, although Bahrick (1957) has suggested that operators quickly learn the physical 'feel' of a control. They balance its friction and inertia against the amount that they want it to move, and gauge their manual input by this 'feeling'. The result is that each control movement takes roughly similar times to accomplish. In a study performed in 1963, Rogers used a 3.5 inch (8.75 cm) ball to determine the optimum velocity at which the ball could travel for correct placement of the cursor on the screen. From his results, he recommended a maximum surface velocity of 28 inches/sec (0.71 m/sec). When considering these recommendations it is important to remember that the velocities used by his subjects were related to the distance of the target from the cursor. Thus an inertial system which allowed this velocity would produce fastest and most accurate responses.

SPEECH INPUT

To a person who knew nothing of how computers operate on the information that is presented to them—how it needs to be in the form of 1's and 0's, ons and offs, and how it needs to be presented under very controlled conditions—it might well appear that speech would be the most obvious way of communicating with computers. Historically, speech has dominated the human scene as a basis for immediate, person to person communication; communicating through the written word is generally used only when a permanent record is required or when communicating over long distances. Neither of these two conditions apply to human–computer interaction.

Unfortunately, however, speech input is not as simple as it may at first seem. Acoustic stimuli are not produced in a form which is readily understood by computers. Some very complex mathematical and electronic processes are required to convert the continually varying analogue signals into a digital form which is able to be interpreted by the computer. Despite these problems, however, some limited speech input devices are presently available and, doubtless, full speech interaction will eventually occur. It is important, therefore, to consider the behavioural and physiological aspects which relate to these devices. Many of these points can be introduced by first considering the advantages and disadvantages of speech input.

Advantages and disadvantages of speech input

The advantages

The first, and possibly the most important, advantage of using speech for input is that it is *natural*. Speech is the means by which we generally communicate with one another and it allows us to be freer and more forceful in our communication of ideas. We are able to use contextual, situational and all manner of linguistic and paralinguistic cues such as voice tone, rhythm, the rise and fall of pitch, pauses, and emphasis to impart information in various ways. The same words can appear to produce dominating, friendly, submissive, questioning, bored or interesting messages simply by varying some of these aspects of speech. Many of these cues are missing in written communication, and have to be inferred from punctuation and other marks.

Hill (1979) also points to the reduced amount of work required when using speech as further evidence of the natural nature of this means of communication:

> Grammatical rules of all kinds may be broken with impunity in speech to give a stream of language that would be incomprehensible in written form. ... Thus the planning load for speech communication is less, ... for ideas can be added to and expanded as required, unlike a written document which must anticipate and deal with all questions and obscurities that may arise whoever reads the document, whenever they read it, and under whatever circumstances, without all the additional resources available to the orator.

This point, then, leads to a second advantage of speech—that of its immediacy in allowing feedback both of the words said and of the ideas being communicated.

As was emphasized earlier, feedback is an important aspect for the efficient performance of any skilled behaviour. When typing, for example, it is only when typists are able to improve the nature and quality of feedback which they receive that they are able to increase significantly their performance. Communicating complex ideas is just as much a skill as typing and it, too, requires adequate feedback. Speech produces this, both because the words uttered are heard immediately by the speaker and in the same mode (acoustic) as they were produced, and because the listener often produces feedback (gestures or further speech) to indicate that the message has been received and the quality of the understanding. Again, Hill (1979) emphasizes the importance of feedback for speech communication:

> Without feedback, speech must put on some of the formal trappings of written language, which explains the difference in character between a lecture and a seminar—the lecture is formal, often read in fact, because there is no feedback. The seminar is much closer to conversation, allowing interaction and feedback, so that the constraints of language may be relaxed, short cuts taken, and the communication experience greatly improved.

From a behavioural viewpoint, then, these points suggest the importance of speech as a communication device with computers: speech is natural, convenient and immediate. It enables ideas to be transmitted and received with less effort and with greater efficiency than other forms such as writing.

The effect of these points was demonstrated well in a simple experiment by

Ochsman and Chapanis (1974). They asked pairs of subjects to solve 'credible real-life problems' using one of ten particular communication modes: (1) Typewriting only; (2) Handwriting only; (3) Handwriting and typewriting; (4) Typewriting and video; (5) Handwriting and video; (6) Voice only; (7) Voice and typewriting; (8) Voice and handwriting; (9) Voice and video—i.e. closed-circuit television; (10) 'Communication rich'—i.e. handwriting, typewriting, voice, direct vision and closed-circuit television.

When Ochsman and Chapanis analysed their data, they found large differences between the performances of subjects who had communicated using some form of speech as compared with those who had used 'hard copy' such as hand- or type-writing. Thus, as Figure 4.9 illustrates, subjects using voice solved their problems consistently faster than those who were forced to use the written word. This cannot simply be put down to the argument that it takes longer physically to write a message than to say it, since the data shown in Figure 4.9 also indicate that it took slightly longer for the 'voice only' subjects to solve their problems than the 'voice and typewriting' subjects. Interestingly, too, the data indicate no time differences between using handwriting and typewriting. Finally, there is no evidence to suggest that the addition of a video channel had any significant effects on communication times. Conclusions of this nature have been supported by an experiment performed by Gould (1982). When he asked subjects to compose letters either by writing or by speaking, the spoken letters took only 35–75% of the time that writing did.

A further analysis of these data, reported by Chapanis *et al.* (1977), however, suggest additional, more qualitative differences between the behaviours of subjects using the different modes. Thus, although oral modes were faster the messages sent were more wordy. More messages, sentences, words and unique words were passed by the 'talkers' than by the 'writers'. The different modes, therefore, altered quite significantly the behaviour of the communicators. Whether these alterations are 'good' or 'bad' is a matter which can only be assessed with regard to specific situations.

In addition to its advantages of being natural, speech has a number of other practical advantages.

Firstly, as will be discussed in more detail later, because it *is* natural the time required to train operators to use speech input devices is likely to be far shorter than that for other devices such as keyboards. Secondly, speech input devices do not need to be adapted to the physical capacities of the human operator as, for example, keyboards need to be designed to anthropometric requirements. Indeed, the physical spaces required by speech input devices are far smaller than for other devices such as keyboards. Furthermore, by not having to use valuable limbs to operate the computer, speech leaves the human body to be free for other activities, so providing an extra channel for multi-modal communication.

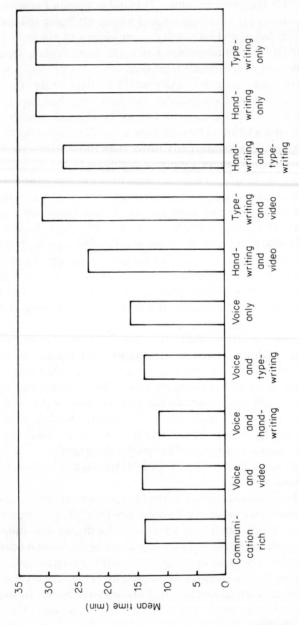

Figure 4.9. Effects of communication modes on the time taken to solve problems. With permission from Ochsman and Chapanis, 1974. Copyright: Academic Press Inc. (London) Ltd.

A third benefit of speech input devices relates to the fact that acoustic stimuli are omnidirectional. Provided the information is able to be received accurately by a microphone, the operator does not have to adopt a fixed position, for example facing the computer. This point, clearly, is related to the fact that speech frees the user's limbs enabling more complex activities, perhaps remote from the computer, to be undertaken.

The possibility of remote input, of course, can be extended using speech since the now standard and international telephone system was designed specifically to allow spoken messages to be communicated over great distances. As Sharp and Waterworth (1982) point out effective speech input devices linked to telephones would provide people with access to many useful information services which are unable to be connected to present telephone systems—every telephone user, therefore, would be a potential computer user.

Finally, the advantages of speech input devices to many physically handicapped operators (other than those with speech or hearing difficulties) should be obvious. Speech does not require either visual feedback or the movement of limbs other than the operation of the vocal apparatus. Blind or paraplegic operators, therefore, should benefit greatly from any implementation of these devices.

The disadvantages

Despite the obvious advantages of speech input, they also have disadvantages—not the least being that no means have yet been found to produce devices which can recognize natural, continuous speech as opposed to a limited vocabulary of words. This has meant that present speech input devices are used either to command the computer using one- or two-word commands, or to produce very basic and stilted communication.The reasons for this are many and, as will be discussed later, revolve primarily around the complexities of both the ways in which we produce speech sounds and the languages which we use to interpret the sounds. Thus, although they may say the same words, because of factors such as accents, emphases, physical differences and even environmental differences, different speakers are unlikely to produce the same sounds for the computer to interpret. This point will be considered below when discussing speech production. Furthermore, even if the same words, parts of words or sounds are produced, their positions within words or sentences can impart different meanings which, with our knowledge of linguistic rules, we are able to interpret. Without very complex programming, however, computers are unable to make sensible interpretations of the sounds being produced. Again, these points will be discussed further later.

In addition to these complex engineering and linguistic problems which mitigate against speech input devices, however, there are others.

Firstly speech, by its very nature, tends to make factors such as privacy very difficult. As Turn (1974) pointed out, speech communications can be overheard directly by others in the vicinity, or by using acoustic pickup devices. Hence, another dimension would be introduced to the security problems already evident when using computers. Secondly, speech is a transitory and volatile medium. It does not leave an easy-to-perceive hard copy of the transactions. Acoustic tape-recordings could be made but these are troublesome to consult. Thirdly, the quality of speech as an input medium is likely to be subject to environmental noises which occur naturally such as other operators speaking or other machines being operated. The speech input device needs to be able to filter out these other noises and to take account of only the speech intended. This is likely to be particularly difficult with respect to other operators talking in the vicinity—perhaps communicating with other machines. The problem, of course, does not occur with the keyboard—only one operator generally uses it at a time.

Whilst considering the effects of the environment it is well to realize that the environment can also affect the quality of the speaker's own voice. Stress, for example, can alter the voice characteristics, sometimes dramatically. In addition severe vibration levels can cause difficulties in breathing control for speaking if, for example, the diaphragm is being buffeted by internal body organs.

A final point, although not *against* speech input devices, does call into question the necessity of having a fully natural speech communication mode. Thus, Kelly and Chapanis (1977) found that pairs of subjects undertaking problem solving tasks did no worse when restricted to a vocabulary of 300 words than did those working without restriction. It would appear, therefore, that a full and natural vocabulary may not be so necessary for useful input.

Despite these points, however, speech is likely to be an important input medium of the future because of the advantages and flexibility that it gives to the computer designer.

Speech recognition systems

Although any discussion of speech and word recognition systems is likely to be rendered out of date before many years have passed, it is instructive to consider how the technology has advanced.

Welch (1980) suggests that practical word and speech recognition systems can be considered to lie along a continuum. At one end are devices which have a limited vocabulary and recognize only single words. Near the other end of the development spectrum are so-called speech understanding systems which attempt to interpret sentences in which the words are run together, as in natural speech. Unfortunately, because of many of the problems which will be outlined later, the present technology has not allowed the production of efficient voice recognition systems beyond only the most crude word or phrase recognizers. The 'Holy Grail' of computer peripheral designers, full and automatic speech recognition, is still elusive.

Word recogniton

Using computers to identify single words, or sentences and phrases which have the words separated by significant pauses, has been achieved by many people (both Atal, 1976, and Rosenberg, 1976, review the computer problems; Martin, 1976, discusses many of the earlier studies of word recognition system design). With regard to the human input into the system, Welch (1980) considers two important aspects of the design: first, whether the words are isolated or are able to be connected in some way—perhaps by shorter and less frequent pauses; secondly, whether the recognition is speaker-dependent or operates effectively with any speaker.

Isolated word recognition systems typically require the pauses between words to be longer than 100 msec to prevent them being confused with other pauses within words or with the 'stop consonants' b, d, g, p, t, k. These are sounds which are generated by stopping the flow of air and then suddenly releasing it. Such systems also require the co-operation of the speaker since they typically have a limited vocabulary from which to recognize the words.

Connected speech recognition systems, on the other hand, are capable of recognizing individual words within strings of words although the words, not separated by pauses, are run together. In this case the system's problem clearly is to determine where one word ends and another begins, and the acoustic patterns of words exhibit much greater variability depending on the context in which they are spoken. Thus the vocabulary available needs to be much greater, and this brings concomitant problems of programming and increasing system complexity. Although such systems still operate, albeit on a restricted number of words, they do provide faster data entry and are more natural to use.

One way of reducing the possible confusability between words, of course, is to restrict the number of people with whom the system will operate. This reduces the variability both in the use and in the presentation of the words. *Speaker-dependent systems,* then, solve the problem of wide variations in speech among individuals by requiring that each user 'train' the system to recognize his or her voice by repeating all of the words in the vocabulary one or more times before using the system. While the training requirements can be a nuisance, it does result in a system which accepts any variant in pronunciation.

Finally, *speaker-independent* or 'universal' systems attempt to accommodate a wide range of speaking characteristics without training by the individual user. Welch (1980), however, points out that such systems are generally less accurate, operate with smaller vocabularies than speaker-dependent systems and, in practice, may not work for all speakers.

Speech understanding systems

At the other end of the continuum are the speech understanding systems which, in addition to the problems encountered with connected word recognition systems have the additional requirement that they must perform accurately even when the utterance is not quite grammatical or well-formed, and in the presence of speech-like noise (for example, babbles, mumbles, coughs). As Reddy (1976) points out, the requirement is somewhat relaxed by the concession that what matters in the end is not the recognition of each and every word in the utterance but rather the meaning and intent of the message. Thus, in addition to the problems encountered with connected automatic word recognition systems of determining when a word begins and ends, speech recognition systems also have to keep track of the context of the conversation in order that any ambiguities that arise can be resolved *in the context of that conversation*. It is for these reasons that the 'present' state of speech recognition input devices primarily revolve around the recognition of words from a specific vocabulary which are input in a specified way, although both Reddy (1976) and Hill (1977) do describe how systems are being developed which, eventually, should reach the Holy Grail.

Speech analysis

Since such a wide variation in sounds can be produced both by different speakers and by the same speaker on different occasions, the next aspect to be considered is the ways in which they are analysed. This will be done from two viewpoints: physical and behavioural. Thus, the physical analysis is used to break up the speech sounds into their component parts for input to the computer. Behavioural (linguistic) analyses can then be used via the computer's program in an attempt to reconstitute the sounds to understand both the words and of the messages.

Physical analysis

The invention of the sound spectrograph apparatus in the early 1940s represented an important breakthrough in speech research because it allowed a convenient representation of the way the speech sounds (spectrum) vary with time. Essentially, the speech is passed through a network of electronic filters, each of which allow through only a narrow frequency band. The output voltage from each filter is a representation of the intensity at that frequency and, classically, determines the brightness of a small light, which in turn leaves a trace on a moving belt of phosphor. Thus a graphical representation of the frequency content of a speech sound is produced on the vertical scale, with brightness representing intensity. Time is represented along the horizontal scale. More modern analysing equipment, of course, employ computers.

At any one instant a 'vertical cross-section' can be taken of the spectrograph to indicate how the different tones vary in intensity. Both of these forms of analysis then—the spectrograph and the 'amplitude section'—can be used to define and to measure the speech sounds. It is these two ways of analysing the sounds that are used to transform speech sounds into computer-meaningful input.

Unfortunately analysis of speech sounds based solely on the physical analysis of the frequency components within the sound can lead to misleading information. This is because whereas words spoken in isolation are characterized by relatively stable auditory patterns, the same words in conversational speech are not. Articulation is not nearly so precise and the acoustic structure of a word may vary substantially in relation to other words in the message. This is known as 'phonological variation' and has been studied in detail by Oshika *et al.* (1975). They suggest that '... much of this variation is governed by phonological environments, such as the influence of surrounding vowels or consonants or stress patterns'. As will be discussed later, the problem becomes acute when the behaviour of the speaker is considered in terms of where he or she segments words and phrases.

Linguistic analysis

Unfortunately, difficult as it is, ensuring that the speech is transformed accurately into machine-readable forms is only the beginning in the process of producing speech recognition systems. The physical analysis can be conceived of as being at an analogous level simply to perceiving characters on a printed page—not even recognizing that they are letters and certainly not being able to read and understand the printed words. Hill (1977) further suggests that the problem is even more complex than that which faces the reader in this analogy. In addition to the character recognition and understanding aspect, speech has the additional problem that the characters are not discrete entities as are, for example, letters on a page. Because speech symbols interact and overlap, the coding that has to occur bears no simple one-to-one relationship between the sound and the character.

At this point in the discussion, the input to the computer is solely in terms of the characteristics of the tones which comprise the speech. Before the computer program can act on these data in any meaningful way, they have to be combined into the basic 'blocks' of human speech sounds—phonemes.

These are the smallest distinguishably different sounds that are produced by the human vocal apparatus. Two sounds are placed in the same phonemic category if they never can be used to distinguish between two words in the language. The different sounds falling in one phoneme category are termed allophones of phonemes.

Understanding and being able to define the phonemic basis of a language is crucial for efficient speech recognition input devices. As Broad (1972) points out, attempts at such systems which have used only acoustic data without reference to these physiological and behavioural categories have been severely limited in their performance. Indeed, he argues that a number of phonetic characteristics must be taken into account, including the relations between the continuous physical events of speech and phonetic units, the organization of phonetic units into higher-ordered sets as specified by the phonological structures of given dialects, and the rules by which strings of phonological units make up words and phrases.

Once some kind of phonetic description of the speech has been input to the computer, there are syntactic, semantic and pragmatic rules that must be obeyed before any level of understanding can occur. These rules, then, need to be taken into account in the computer program.

Syntactic rules relate to the arrangement of 'symbols' (phonemes in this case) to form words and of words to form phrases and sentences. The semantic type of rule is concerned with meanings in a dictionary sense; that is, given the sentences, the imposition of structure to produce 'meaningful' messages. The pragmatic knowledge takes account of particular experiences, culture and situations - of speakers and listeners and may vary from individual to individual. A detailed consideration of these categories of rules is well outside of the boundaries of this book but can be found in many texts which deal with lingusitic analysis.

In addition to this form of linguistic analysis, Hill (1977) points out that there is another behavioural means by which we analyse speech for our understanding. This is done by analysing the sounds 'segmentally' and 'suprasegmentally'.

Segmental cues relate to a differentiation between the phonemes. Thus we recognize what is being said as a result of the ways in which the phonemes are put together; each phoneme being considered in the context of neighbouring 'symbols'.

Suprasegmental cues, on the other hand, take account of other aspects of the acoustic waveform reaching the ear. Aspects such as rhythm, intonation and stress, although they may involve the same acoustic parameters at a segmental level, provide additional information about what is being said. Such cues give information about higher level constructs in the syntactical domain, such as syllable, word and phrase structure, and also give cues as to meaning. Suprasegmental cues are used, therefore, to distinguish *im*port from im*port* or to distinguish between dialectic words. They also give information at another level since they allow possible inferences to be made as to the speaker's state of mind, health, attitude, etc. Of course, at this point, we reach the domain of the pragmatic levels of analysis.

All of these behavioural aspects, then, need to be incorporated into the computer program to enable it to understand the speech in the same way that we do 'naturally'. It is not surprising, therefore, that true automatic speech recognition systems still have far to go.

Speaking behaviour

Having discussed how speech might be able to be input to machines, and how machines might interpret the speech, one final consideration is how we speak—not from a physical/physiological viewpoint but from the viewpoint of the patterns of behaviour which generate the message. This is an extremely important consideration if the requirements of the speech input device are to be designed to match the behaviour of the operator.

The importance of idiosyncratic variables such as dialect, experience, etc., has already been discussed. However, these further aspects also need to be viewed in terms of speaking behaviour—speed, accuracy and segmentation.

With regard to speed, Bezdel (1970) demonstrated that the average rate of uttering words, separated by gaps of silence, was approximately 80 words per minute. However this transmission rate halved when voice feedback was used for correction of errors. Zagoruiko and Tambovtsev (1982) performed a similar experiment (using Russian text) but analysed their data in terms of phonemes/minute transmitted under different reading conditions (ranging from reading text unprepared to having previously prepared the text). Their results, shown in Figure 4.10, illustrate the advantages of having prepared text in advance. They also demonstrated quite large sex differences in reading speed, with females reading consistently faster. Unfortunately, since no variability scores are presented in their report it is not possible to determine the significance of the difference between the sexes' scores (indeed the authors point out that variability between the operators was high, so possibly reducing the statistical significance).

Zagoruiko and Tambovtsev also considered how fatigue affects these transmission rates. In a separate experiment they asked subjects to read aloud continuously for several hours with only short breaks. Individual subjects' work periods stopped when they decided that they had had enough. Although Zagoruiko and Tambovtsev's data were only preliminary and thus incomplete, they do illustrate that operators are able to continue speaking for quite long periods before fatigue affects performance detrimentally. On the basis of their data, they divided the performance periods into three 'bands'. The first (start) period lasts for about 15-20 minutes after the beginning of work. It is

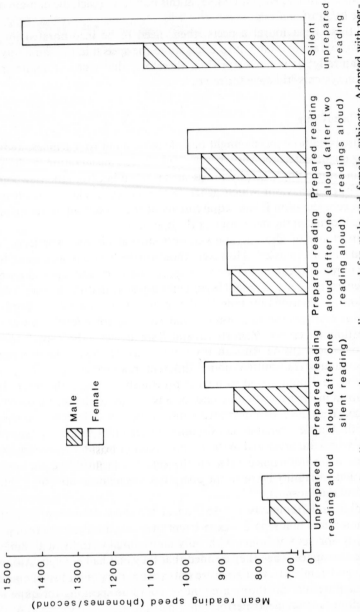

Figure 4.10. Effect of reading preparation on reading speed for male and female subjects. Adapted with permission from Zagoruiko and Tambovtsev, 1982. Copyright: Academic Press Inc. (London) Ltd.

characterized by fairly efficient reading: 'The speed is not high; intelligibility is good; reliability is high, but there are some mistakes'. In the second (middle) period, which extends between 15–20 minutes to 2–3 hours after the beginning, performance improves considerably: 'Optimum reading with high speed; intelligibility and reliability are high'. Finally, after 3–4 hours of work, the last stage is reached with fatigue becoming evident: 'The speed drops strongly; intelligibility and reliability worsen rapidly'.

Clearly, therefore, these (descriptive) data suggest that speaking behaviour can go on for quite some considerable time before performance is reduced.

In addition to speed, accuracy is an important consideration for efficient transmission of communication. However, the available data suggest that the problem is very small—certainly less than with other means of inputting data such as keystrokes. Thus Zagoruiko and Tambovtsev suggest error rates of about 0.2% whilst Bezdel suggested 0.1%. In this case no differences were shown by Zagoruiko and Tambovtsev to occur between the sexes.

Finally, the question needs to be asked to what extent using speech affects the *quality* of the message transmitted—i.e. the operator's behaviour with respect to the ability for transmitting concepts. Thus it has already been pointed out that Chapanis *et al.* (1977) demonstrated significant differences in the types of language used when problems were solved using speech or written text. Speech was characterized by more messages, sentences, words, unique words and higher transmission rates.

Despite evidence of this nature, however, Gould (1982) showed no *qualitative* differences between letters composed using a dictation machine when compared with those composed by writing. Certainly the dictated letters were composed quicker (taking only 35–75% of the time) but the quality of the letters were judged to be equally good. More will be said about text composition using computers in Chapter 9.

Segmentation refers to the ways in which we break up speech to produce separate sounds. Unfortunately for speech recognition systems, fluent speech is not reliably separated by pauses and so they do not exist in the speech wave as discrete and separate events. The fact that words in fluent speech are not separated by pauses is reflected in the principle of *geminate reduction*, which holds that 'two identical consonants reduce to one across a syllable, morpheme or word boundary' (Oshika et al., 1975). For example, whenever two nasals occur at a word boundary, a single nasal murmur is likely to occur. In combinations such as 'some more' there is no point at which a word-final or word-initial sound (m) can be identified in the speech wave. Of course, the effect does not occur only with nasal sounds; similar geminate reduction can be seen in 'that train', 'half fast', 'real love', etc. Because the physical signal is continuous across word boundaries, a particular word sequence can often be meaningfully segmented in more than one way. For example, 'that drain' or 'that rain', 'half assed', 'reel of', etc. Indeed, most spoken sequences of two or more words can be segmented in more than one way, although the unintended segmentation may not always make sense.

Unless one is listening to an unfamiliar language, it is difficult to appreciate that individual words are decoded from a continuous signal. As Cole and Jakimik (1978) point out, however, it is possible to construct English sentences that listeners have great difficulty in segmenting into words. The most famous example is the nursery rhyme 'Mares eat oats and does eat oats and little lambs eat ivy.'

The problem involved with segmentation, then, is that the listener forces his or her own interpretation of what is heard, and not necessarily what may have been intended by the speaker. Computers, being less flexible machines, are unable to perform the linguistic relevant analyses to overcome these segmentation problems.

Training

Although speech is an appropriate input channel, and although spoken messages can be transmitted at quite high rates, the previous sections have demonstrated that speech recognition systems for continuous, unbroken speech are still a long way off. The best that has been produced so far are systems which recognize only broken, continuous speech. This, of course, is not 'natural' behaviour and so some type of training might be required to enable the operator to fit the constraints of the system. This is particularly important if speech input devices are to be used by relatively unskilled personnel such as the general public, who may have to use speech input devices connected to telephones. The matter also has importance since Martin and Welch (1980) have demonstrated that performance itself tends to decrease when the operator loses confidence in the recognition system.

In terms of the time likely to be taken to train operators, Cochran, Riley and Stewart (1980) suggest that at least two weeks of training with a system is necessary for maximal performance:

> People are not accustomed to exercising strict control over voice patterns. As a result numerous misinterpretations and outright rejections are made by the device at first. Although this can be frustrating, it can be minimized by preparation of the operator.

In terms of training schedules, three types have been evaluated: random, blocked and sequential. Connolly (1977) has suggested that there is advantage in randomizing the order of repetitions during training (rather than presenting them in blocks or in a repeated sequence) since this will achieve the wide variety of sounds required by most tasks, and will maintain operator concentration over the training period. De George (1981), working on speech verification, compared blocked (repetitive) with sequential training but found that any difference between the two in subsequent performance was only slight. Finally, Sharp and Waterworth (1982) compared all three types of training schedule and found that the method used had no differential effect at all. Performance was better, however, when the device was used immediately after training as opposed to 24 hours later.

Speech recognition devices

Despite the difficulties clearly encountered in designing useful speech *understanding* systems, quite efficient speech *recognition* systems operating on a limited vocabulary have been in operation for a number of years. As a conclusion to the discussion of speech as an input device, therefore, some of the tasks for which these systems can be used will be considered.

Martin (1976) divides the applications into three areas: quality control and inspection; automated materials handling; and direct voice input to computers. Included with this list, of course, should be voice recognition for security purposes.

In most quality control and inspection tasks, the operator's eyes and/or hands are often occupied in the task itself—handling material, watching items pass on a conveyor, etc. The advantages of a voice input system over other, more traditional, means of recording information, then, is that it releases the hands and eyes to perform their main function. The inspection information, verbally entered into the system, can provide status reports and can also be transmitted directly to the computer. In his article, Martin describes the systems which have been in operation for some time at four different organizations and concludes that these systems have produced increased operator productivity and have provided considerably reduced response time to customers.

Automated materials handling using voice inputs have also been in operation for some time. Voice coding of materials for distribution to different parts of the organization can produce high accuracy rates and often need to involve only a single operator where, in the past, at least two would be required: one to identify the material and its destination and the other to key in the information.

A similar use of voice input devices, this time in the design of electronic circuit boards, has been described by Cochran, Riley and Stewart (1980). They measured the times taken to input, and to check the input accuracy of, lists of components and connections in the circuit board and demonstrated that the operators took approximately 400 minutes to input the information using the normal keyboard but only 200 minutes using voice. Similar reductions in error rate were also recorded.

Finally, voice input has obvious applications for direct computer control. Indeed, Martin describes examples of the use in programming the computer. Mountford and North (1980) also describe an experiment in which pilots used voice or keyboard input to perform a radio channel changing task, which is an analogous task to both the inspection and the materials handling operations described earlier; that is, using the voice to command the computer to choose between a limited number of options (in the present experiment, the pilots chose between five discrete entries).

An interesting feature of this study was that the pilots also had to perform a compensatory tracking task using a joystick (to keep an otherwise moving spot stationary). Their results clearly demonstrated that having to use the keyboard to input data caused significant decrements in performance of the tracking task. The voice entry method, however, produced no significant decrements in performance. The implications of this result, then, are that the keyboard input required more from the operator than did the voice entry. Such an explanation is embodied in the concept of 'spare mental capacity' discussed in Chapter 1. Thus, carrying out the primary, tracking, task required a certain amount of the operator's 'mental capacity', leaving some spare for other, secondary, tasks. In this experiment, then, the primary voice input task did not require all of the spare mental capacity and so both tasks were performed efficiently. When a keying task was used as the primary task, however, more capacity was consumed than the operator had to spare—with the result that performance was reduced when the secondary task was introduced. Such observations serve to remind, therefore, that although a task may be able to be performed accurately under 'ideal' conditions, if it demands too much from the operator performance will fall when conditions become bad.

Finally, with regard to using voice input for security purposes, Flanagan (1976) points out that the task can really be conceived of as two tasks: speaker verification or identification. In the first of these (verification) the speaker enters a verification claim and speaks a pre-arranged verification phrase. The computer's task is then to compare the voice sample with data which it already posesses in order to decide whether or not to accept the individual. The task of identification, however, involves no claimed identity from the caller who essentially asks the question 'Who am I?' The machine needs to examine its library of information and attempt to match this with the information received via the voice input. Its task, then, is to produce as close a match as possible. The identification problem, therefore, is likely to be less simple to solve and to lead to more machine errors than is the verification task.

Flanagan also describes a series of experiments performed to compare the efficiency of a computer and a number of human operators in voice verification tasks. Whereas the computer rejected only one 'customer' and accepted only one 'imposter', the human operators erred by rejecting four 'customers' and accepting four 'imposters'. Of more interest for security purposes, however, is the question of how well the system can be 'fooled' by an experienced mimic. Under these conditions the computer accepted the mimic 'imposter' four times. The human operators, however, were fooled 22 times.

In summary, therefore, it is apparent that voice entry methods can have significant advantages for both system effectiveness and operator satisfaction. However, owing to the very complex problems both of producing a system which will *recognize* 'natural' speech and of programming the computer to *understand* the message, most practical applications of speech input presently remain at the level of entering discrete pieces of information.

OPTICAL INPUT DEVICES

After the discussion of speech as an input device, the advantages of using eye movements should be clear. Thus, in addition to speed, the main adavantages of speech was that it should require no 'translation' from what occurs naturally during cognitive processes such as reading—that is 'inner speech' (Poulton, 1977)—into the commands needed to control other effector mechanisms such as the hands or fingers. Furthermore it releases the already overburdened motor system for other activities.

The optical system provides similar advantages. Many data input tasks require the operator first to locate the information to be entered—say in a 'menu' of choice on the screen, or an object to be tracked across the screen. Using manual controls this information has to be 'translated' into the movements required to operate the control. If the data could be input directly at the first (optical) stage in this process, increased speed and reduced errors are likely to result.

There are a number of ways by which eye movement data, after suitable electronic conversion, could be recorded for computer input, but they all can be classified, essentially, into two types: electrophysiological (which records the movements of the muscles which control the eye) and photoelectric reflection (which records movements in reflected light from the eye). These are discussed in detail by Young and Sheena (1975).

There is a small but steady difference in electric potential between the cornea and retina (in the region of 10–30 mV). This sets up an electrical field in the tissues surrounding the eye and can be recorded with electrodes placed anywhere on the head—although the nearer the eye they are placed, the better is the signal. Typically, paired electrodes are placed above and below the eyes for vertical movement, and on each side of the eye for horizontal movement. Integrating the output from these two pairs, then, enables the movements of the eye in any direction to be recorded.

Unfortunately, however, such techniques (known as electro-oculography or EOG) suffer from two major drawbacks as far as their practical use for computer input is concerned. Firstly, the electrodes need to be fixed securely to reduce the effect of skin movement; secondly, the recordings are often subjected to physiological and electrical 'noise'.

More popular, are the reflective techniques which work because the cornea, being shiny and convex, is able to reflect a point source of light back to some electronic sensor. This allows motion in both the horizontal and vertical plane to be recorded. Furthermore, if the spot is reflected into a small TV camera, the image can be mixed electronically with that from a second camera viewing the scene that the subject is looking at. This type of apparatus, described by Mackworth and Mackworth in 1958 and subsequently developed to very high levels of technological sophistication, allows not only the eye movements to be recorded, but also the movements in relation to the scene being observed.

Eye movements

The eyes are clearly not fixed in the skull but are able to move by the action of six muscles that attach them to the orbit (eye socket) in the skull. Indeed, the proprioceptive feedback that arises from these muscles helps a person to maintain the head in a stable position. When the head changes position, feedback from the vestibular apparatus in the ear produces a reflex action of these eye muscles so that the eye moves in an opposite direction to that of the head. For example, flexing the neck back so that the face points upwards causes the eyes to rotate down; the eyeballs, then, 'gravitate' to the '*status quo*'.

Benson and Barnes (1978) and Barnes, Benson and Prior (1978) have suggested that this statokinetic reflex (Alpern, 1972) is composed, essentially, of two reflex systems. First, a retinal reflex (which operates with low frequency head movements) uses information gained from the moving image on the retina to maintain a stable image by moving the eye. The second system (which operates if the head is moving faster—say in a moving vehicle) uses the information gained from the vestibular apparatus to infer head position and again maintain a stationary image by inducing compensatory eye movements.

Maintaining a stable image

If eye movements are to be used to input information into the computer, it is important that we should be able accurately both to point the eyes at the target and to maintain the target position. Unfortunately, however, whereas the first can be accomplished with some success, it is impossible to maintain the eyes perfectly motionless. During even the steadiest of fixations the eyes are constantly making extremely fine movements known collectively as '*physiological nystagmus*'. In essence, three types of movements comprise this physiological nystagmus (Alpern, 1972): (i) slow drifts occurring in an amplitude range of about 5 minutes of arc having an average velocity of 1 minute per second; (ii) rapid flicks of the eyes (or saccades) having larger amplitude (1–20 minutes of arc) and velocity (10 degrees per second); and (iii) high frequency tremors of about 17 seconds of arc.

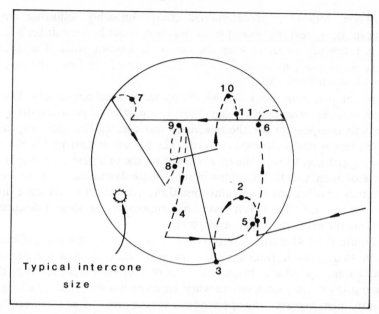

Typical intercone size

Figure 4.11. Movement of the image of a point object on the retina (Ditchburn, 1955). The large circle has a radius of 5 minutes of arc. Slow drifts are represented by the dotted lines and saccades by the solid lines. The numbers indicate the order in which movements were made. Reproduced by permission of Taylor & Francis Ltd.

The effects of these movements on fixation have been illustrated well by Ditchburn (1955) and are shown in Figure 4.11. The large circle has a radius of about 5 minutes of arc; the numbered dots indicate the order in which movements are made and are spaced at equal time intervals of 0.2 seconds. As can be seen, the slower and smaller drifts (dotted lines) are frequently compensated for by the faster and more direct saccades (continuous lines).

Following a moving object

Although it is difficult to maintain a motionless optical system, using appropriate electronics in the interface between the eye and the computer many of the drift and less intense saccadic movements can be filtered out to ensure that relatively accurate and stable data entry occurs. The problems facing designers using eye movements to track a moving object, however, are different.

In essence, an operator may be required to track an object in one of two ways: by pursuit or by compensation. In pursuit tracking, the operator's task is to move the controls so that the object (usually a spot on an oscilloscope) follows a predetermined course (possibly following another moving spot). A 'real-life' example, in this case, could be a car driver's task of moving a steering wheel to keep the car on a winding road. The operator corrects errors then, by comparing the movement of the 'spot'(the car) with that of a standard (the road).

In the compensatory tracking task the operator 'sees' only errors. The task is to maintain an otherwise moving 'spot' in a particular position—to use the controls to compensate for the machine's movement. The spot only moves when the task is not performed correctly. The car driver's attempt to maintain a steady speed (i.e. to keep the speedometer needle in a particular place) is an example of such a task. Variations in the vehicle dynamics, the road incline, the weather or other environmental conditions may all act to influence the car speed and so make the driver have to compensate for these influences by controlling the accelerator and other pedals.

As Poulton (1974) argues, compensatory tracking is clearly more difficult to perform than pursuit tracking. An operator tracking in a compensatory manner cannot see what is being done, nor predict what is meant to be done; the operator can only compensate when an error has occurred. Tracking in a pursuit manner, however, the operator can see the movements produced by the track program, in addition to seeing the effects of the control movements.

Whatever type of tracking is being performed, however, the operator's task is generally one of moving the eyes to maintain a stable image on the central part of the retina where vision is most acute. However, because the eyes do not move smoothly, but in saccadic jerks, this is not easy to do.

Robinson (1965) asked subjects to maintain fixation on a spot moving with an unpredictable (but constant) velocity in an unpredictable direction. Since the subject was able to see the spot, this was an example of pursuit tracking; it is also an example of the type of task likely to face, say, a combat pilot attempting to shoot down an enemy aeroplane.

Figure 4.12 shows typical responses of the eyes to four different velocities (the dotted lines indicate the target 'position'; the continuous lines the eye movements.) Clearly, the optic system experiences some time lag before operating (typically about 150 msec), due both to the observer's reaction time and the inertia of the eye muscles. The pursuit movement then appears to be characterized by two types of movement until the target is 'caught'. These are saccadic jerks (the vertical movements) and slower, constant velocity tracking movements. Alpern (1972) describes these second movements as 'pursuit' or 'smooth' movements.

Figure 4.12 also illustrates that the amount and number of saccadic movements also varies with target velocity. Indeed, in some cases there is velocity overshoot in the early part of the movement before the eyes and the target match. Thus, at 5° per second there appears quite a lot of overshoot; at 15° per second there is little. At 20° per second, however, it would appear that

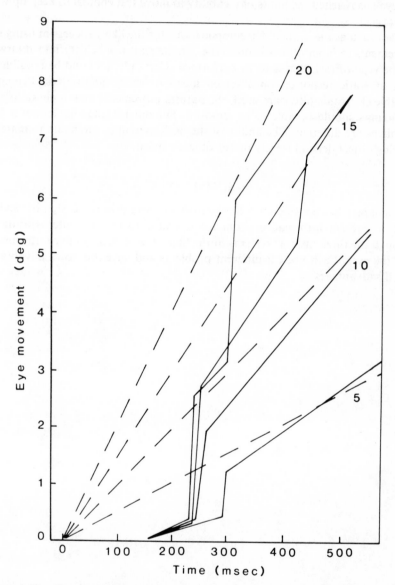

Figure 4.12. Eye movement responses to smooth target motions of constant velocities of 5, 10, 15 and 20 degrees a second (Robinson, 1965). The dotted lines through the origin represent the target position, the other lines the eye position. Reproduced by permission of the Physiological Society.

the eye has reached the limits of its ability to move fast enough to keep up with the target.

Data such as these, then, have implications for the likely success of using eye movements to input information to the computer; it will be determined largely by the type of task that is to be performed. Certainly it should be possible to look at static responses on a screen menu to chose alternatives. Provided suitable electronic filters are used, the natural movements due to physiological nystagmus should be able to be removed. For pursuit tracking, however, the problems are different. The ability of the optic system to catch and to match a moving object depend largely on the object's speed.

SUMMARY

This chapter has considered the principles important in the design of devices used to present information from the operator to the computer—primarily through the three 'motor' systems of the finger/hand/arm complex, the larynx and the eyes. Each present different problems and have their own advantages and disadvantages.

CHAPTER 5

Output Hardware

In Chapter 4 emphasis was laid entirely on ways of putting data into the computer. This chapter will deal exclusively with the transmission of information in the opposite direction—from the computer to the operator. Its purpose, then, will be to consider how the operator's appropriate sensory systems function, and how the output from the computer can be designed to fit their requirements.

As with the case of input devices, the primary sensory systems used to perceive information transmitted from a computer are vision, hearing and touch. The order of importance of these systems, however, is almost an exact reverse of that for inputting information to the computer. Thus, most of the information produced by computers is *seen*—either on the screen or on paper. Secondly, with the increased popularity of speech input, auditory outputs of synthesized speech are becoming more frequent. Finally, there are specialized outputs which stimulate our senses of touch; Braille is an example of these.

VISUAL OUTPUT DEVICES

Two main types of device fall into this category: computer screens (often called visual display units or visual display terminals—VDUs or VDTs), and printers. In each case the digital information from the computer is converted into analogue signals which take the form of recognizable characters that form a particular language. As will be shown later, the quality of these characters, the extent to which they are recognizable and are distinguishable from one another, plays a large part in determining whether or not they are read properly. In addition, other aspects peculiar to the hardware (the screen or printer) such as the brightness, and size of the characters and background can influence perception and recognition. These aspect will be discussed in detail later. However, before the manner of their effects can be understood at any more than a superficial level, it is important to understand how the visual system operates—how we receive information and how we interpret it in the process known as perception. It should then be possible to ensure that the way in which the computer presents information to the operator is compatible with what the operator both wants and is able to cope with.

The Visual system

Of all the senses, vision has probably been the most thoroughly studied. It is also, perhaps, the system which is most overloaded at work. In essence it consists of two eyes, to each of which is connected an optic nerve. The nerves from each eye meet at the optic chiasma at the base of the brain, where parts of each nerve cross over to terminate in the visual cortex on the opposite side of the brain to the eye from which it originated. In fact fibres from the left-hand side of each eye terminate in the left visual cortex, and fibres from the right-hand side of each eye terminate in the right visual cortex. The result of this arrangement is that information in the right half of our visual field, which falls on the left half of each eye, is more likely to be processed by the left hemisphere of the brain. Information in the left visual field, however, is processed in the right hemisphere. Since both sides of the brain receive information from both eyes, a more coherent representation of the world can be produced.

With regard to the eyes themselves perhaps the easiest way to understand their structure is to compare them with a camera (although the comparison should not be taken too literally.) A controlled amount of light enters the eye through the pupil (aperture), the diameter of which is regulated by the coloured portion—the iris (stop). It is then bent and focussed by the lens, to fall on to the retina which acts as a photosensitive layer. This works in the fashion of a complex photo-diode to convert luminous energy to electrical energy. It is made up of three types of neurones, the most important being on the outside surface which contains two different types of neurones called the rods and cones (so-called because of their shapes). These are the main receptor cells in the eye and perform different functions, primarily in the perception of light and dark and of colour.

The rods function mainly when the ambient illumination is relatively low, for example, at night. They are used essentially for differentiating between shades of grey and black. The cones, however, function at higher illumination levels (such as in normal daylight) and their primary function is to differentiate between colours. The two receptor types also have different sensitivities to the various wavelengths of visible light. Thus the rods are most sensitive in the greenish part of the spectrum and are relatively insensitive to red light. The cones, however, are more sensitive to the yellowish part of the spectrum.

Vision in the light by means of the cone mechanism is called 'photopic vision' while vision in the dark by means of the rods is called 'scotopic vision'.

Hopkinson and Collins (1970) suggest that moonlight can be taken as the upper limit of scotopic vision; the test is whether or not colours can be recognized. Twilight vision is called 'mesopic vision' and its effects on visual perception are difficult to define in precise terms, but lie between the true scotopic and true photopic characteristics (Palmer, 1960). The relationships of these levels of vision, and average illumination levels of various objects, are illustrated in Figure 5.1. Definitions and explanations of the lighting units used will be given in Chapter 6.

These rods and cones are not distributed evenly about the retina and this has important implications for accurate perception of characters. The cones, the receptor cells used mainly for 'normal' vision, are more numerous around the central part of the retina (known as the *fovea*), wheareas the rods predominate away from the centre and towards the periphery of the retina (i.e. parafoveally) (see Figure 5.2). Since the cones are the main receptors for differentiating between colours and are used in normal vision, therefore, for maximum perception it is important that the information is presented centrally

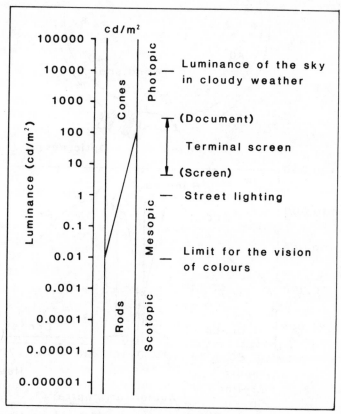

Figure 5.1. The luminance scale.

to the eye rather than to the periphery. Of course, the eyes are able to move to focus an object at the centre but, before they can do so, the object has to be perceived. Because of the reduced number of cones at the periphery, stationary objects are less likely to be perceived if their images fall here.

This is not the case, however, if the object is either moving or is viewed in

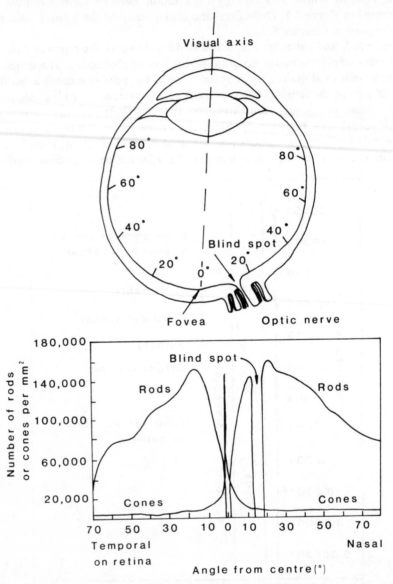

Figure 5.2.   Variation in the density of rods and cones at different parts of the retina.

dim light. Under these conditions the rods are more efficient and, since these are more numerous at the periphery of the retina, it is here that the image should fall.

As an example of the superiority of the centre of the retina for accurate perception, Timmers, Van Nes and Blommaert (1980) presented short (three-lettered) words to different parts of the retina under different letter-background contrast conditions. Their results, shown in Figure 5.3, indicate

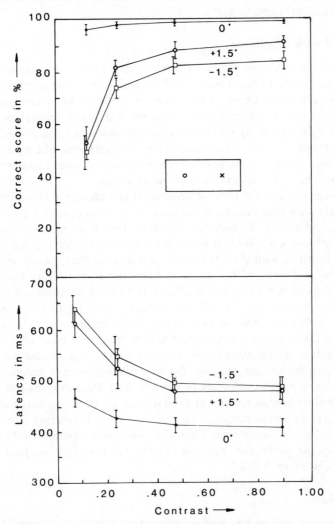

Figure 5.3. Effect on recognition of presenting words to different parts of the retina and using different contrasts (Timmers, Van Nes and Blommaert, 1980). Reproduced by permission of Taylor & Francis Ltd.

that, both for recognition accuracy and speed, words presented to the central part of the retina were consistently perceived better than when presented further from the centre. The difference in superiority was greater when the contrast was poor than when it was high. The small insert in Figure 5.3 provides an indication of how far apart on the retina the two curves represent. Thus, if this book is held at about the normal reading distance (approximately 38 cm) and the eye is fixated on the 'O', then the ' × ' is stimulating retinal cells at about the same distance from the fovea as the words used in the experiment (i.e. with a visual angle of 1.5°).

Light and dark adaptation

Because of the two types of receptors in the retina (the rods and the cones) the human eye is able to function over an extremely wide range of illumination levels. As discussed above, cone vision provides acute vision at daytime (photopic) levels of illumination, wheareas rod vision allows for the high degree of light sensitivity that is essential for seeing at night and in low light levels (scotopic vision). With increasing or decreasing illumination levels experienced in, say, moving from outdoors into a darkened computer room or vice versa, there will always be a point at which one set of photoreceptors ceases to operate and the other takes over. If this change in illumination levels is relatively slow then adaptation to dark or light conditions is fairly smooth. However, with fast illumination changes the well-known experience of temporary blindness results. It is for this reason that when moving from pitch darkness to bright sunlight it is sensible first to wear dark glasses to enable the rods to be used less and the cones to become adapted. Once the eyes have become adapted they can function efficiently within a new range of intensities.

Because the cones are relatively fast-reacting, their light adaptation is often complete within a minute or two. Rods, however, are much slower in their action and dark adaptation may take half an hour or even longer, depending on the previous illumination levels. For this reason, and because the rods and cones are sensitive to different wavelengths (see Figure 5.4), coloured goggles are often worn by people having to work in dark environments (for example, radar operators or maintenance people) for some time before entering the dark room. Red is the colour normally used because it has a wavelength to which the rods are relatively insensitive. Thus the cones may operate fairly normally during daylight while the rods are able to become dark adapted (see, for example, Cushman, 1980).

Colour vision

A quick glance around any modern workplace will illustrate immediately the importance of colour. It is often used to help an operator to distinguish between different parts of the workplace, types of files, action requirements,

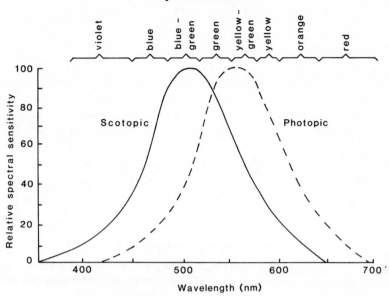

Figure 5.4. Sensitivity of the eyes for lights of different wavelengths (hues) during scotopic and photopic vision.

etc., and is becoming more and more important as a component of visual display layout.

Strictly defined, colour consists of 'characteristics of light other than spatial and temporal inhomogeneities' (Judd, 1951). However, a definition of this nature fails to rule out the effects of brightness differences; and so if two stimuli look different because one is brighter than the other (even if both appear 'white') then there would be, by definition, a colour difference between them. This, of course, is not the normal understanding of the word 'colour'; the sensations normally described as 'red' or 'green' or 'yellow', etc. These sensations, in fact, relate to the *'hue'* and arise as a result of the eyes receiving different wavelengths of light. These sources can be reflections from a coloured surface or they might arise from a coloured light source.

The normal eye is able to sense light in the spectrum having wavelengths of between about 400 and 700 nanometers (1 nm = 10^{-9} m). To these different wavelengths we attach various colour names, with the shorter wavelengths (around 450 nm) being described as 'blue' and the longer wavelengths (around 650 nm) as 'red'. Figure 5.5 shows the results of a classical colour naming experiment performed by Boynton and Gordon (1965). Their subjects were instructed to judge spectral hues, one stimulus at a time, and to name the colour which they saw using either one (for example, 'red') or two (for example,'bluish-green') colour names. From their results they were able to produce the curves shown in Figure 5.5 which indicate, effectively, the

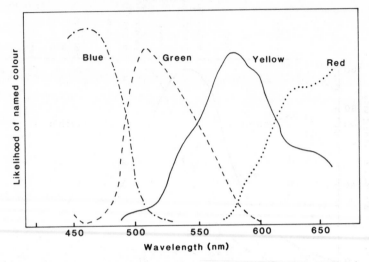

Figure 5.5. Appearance of lights having different wavelengths obtained using a colour-matching technique (Boynton and Gordon, 1965). Reproduced by permission of the Optical Society of America.

composition of the hue arising from any particular wavelength in terms of the primary colours 'blue', 'green', 'yellow' and 'red'.

The important dimensions of colour, however, do not end simply with hue. The saturation and luminance of the wavelengths contained in the light also have important implications for the quality of the colour experienced. The dimension of luminance is possibly easiest to understand and refers to the amount of light reflected into the eye. At one extreme the stimulus will be barely visible, at the other it will appear almost painfully bright. The dimension of saturation, however, is less easy to conceptualize. It refers, essentially, to the amount of white light (that is all of the wavelengths of visible light) contained in the light perceived. It is an index, therefore, of the 'purity' of the hue.

These three attributes are depicted in the colour cone shown in Figure 5.6. In this cone hue is indicated by the position around the circumference; saturation by the position on the radius; and luminance by the vertical axis. This last dimension extends from black at the bottom to white at the top of the axis. Any colour, then, can be described by its position in the cone, and this is the basis of the Munsell Colour System (1929) which is still used today to define colours. It is important to notice that since the system is cone (rather than cylindrical) shaped, the number of possible colours having different saturations and hues reduce as the luminance increases or decreases. Thus, our ability to discriminate colours is at a maximum under 'optimal' luminance conditions, but as the luminance increases or decreases the number of colours

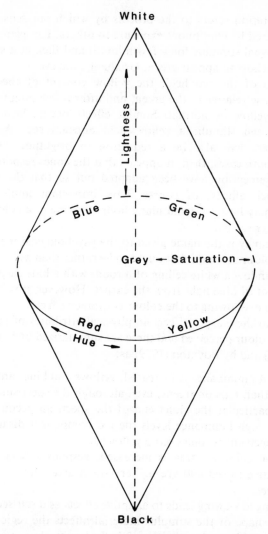

Figure 5.6. The colour cone. Hue is shown on the circumference, lightness on the vertical and saturation on the radius from circumference to the centre.

which we can perceive becomes smaller. This has obvious implications for any computer display which uses colours, say to define areas of messages.

Although the impression has so far been given that colour sensation depends on purely physical parameters, this is not strictly correct. Our cones in the retina and our interpretive mechanisms in the brain do sometimes cause the colour sensations to appear other than they actually are. Two phenomena are particularly important here: colour adaptation and colour constancy.

Colour adaptation refers to the process by which our sensations of some colours are altered by continuous exposure to others. For example, looking at a bright, red visual stimulus for a few minutes and then at a yellow stimulus will cause the yellow to appear green. Gradually, the eye will recover from the adaptive effects of the red field; the yellow content of the test field will gradually increase relative to the green, and after a few minutes the field will again appear yellow as normal. Similar effects occur through continuous exposure to green stimuli: a yellow field appears red. Along with this adaptation, there will also be a reduction in brightness and changes in saturation. In both cases, then, it appears that the cones responsible for either red or green perception have been adapted out so that the other becomes prominent. Such effects, of course, have important implications for an operator who may have to spend many hours looking at a coloured (green or amber) computer screen.

Colour constancy is the name given to the psychological mechanism which makes us see colour as we think it ought to be rather than as it is. For example, near a sunlit window a white ceiling of a room with a blue carpet will actually reflect quite a lot of blue light from the carpet. However, it will look the same white colour all over owing to the colour constancy effect.

In addition to these aspects, certain physical attributes of the stimulus can also affect the colour perceived and these are summarized by both Hurvich and Jameson (1957) and by Boynton (1979) as:

1 *Luminance*. As luminance is increased, yellows and blues are more likely to be reported than reds or greens, even although the spectrum itself may not change. In particular the violet end of the spectrum becomes less reddish until at very high luminance levels the red component disappears; the red end of the spectrum becomes more yellowish.

2 *Area*. As the coloured area is increased, responses of yellow and blue increase relative to red and green. Very small areas, however, produce the converse effect.

3 *Time*. Prolonged viewing leads to adaptive effects as discussed already.

4 *Shape*. The shape of the stimulus material affects the region of the retina stimulated and this can have a powerful effect on the hue experienced. Other things being equal, increasing eccentricity of the stimulus relative to the point of fixation leads to a relative ascendence of yellow and blue responses and a reduction of red and green ones. Yellow sensations tend to be replaced by white ones when the stimulus is perceived in the far periphery of the visual field.

Colour vision theories

Having discussed some of the phenomena associated with perceiving colour phenomena which often have important implications for the use of colour in computer displays—it is now appropriate to consider some of the theories relating to how we perceive and distinguish the colours. In essence, two main theories predominate (the trichromatic theory and the opponent-process theory) but, because both fit the evidence available in some but not all cases, neither theory has yet been universally adopted.

The *trichromatic* theory was first proposed by Helmholtz in 1851 as an extension of an idea originally put forward by Thomas Young in 1801. The Young–Helmholtz theory maintains that there are three receptor mechanisms in the retina (that is, three types of cones) which, when stimulated, give rise to the sensations of red, green and blue. Each receptor is subjected to maximum stimulation by a particular wavelength and to a lesser extent by wavelengths immediately adjacent on the spectrum. However, such adjacent wavelengths also stimulate the other two receptors and so 'mixed' colours result.

Some evidence is available to support the suggestion of three retinal receptor types. Thus, as Morgan (1965) points out, by choosing a wavelength somewhere in the blue region of the spectrum, another somewhere in the green, and a third in the red region, and by varying the mixture of the three, one can match the hue of any colour seen by man. When all three receptors are stimulated equally, then a sensation of white light results. Unfortunately, however, the theory tends not to be supported so well when some of the colour phenomena described above are considered. Thus, it does not explain why, after adapting to a red light an observer will later have a green sensation when looking at yellow, and vice versa. Nor does it explain why, as stimulus size is decreased, discrimination between yellow and blue hues becomes progressively worse than that between red and green; and it does not explain why the hues drop out in pairs in instances of colour defective sight.

In an attempt to adapt the trichromatic theory to one which takes more account of the subjective nature of colour experience, Hering (1834–1918) developed an *opponent-process* theory of colour vision. He was concerned to explain, for example, why we never see reddish-greens or yellowish-blues and speculated that this might be because the visual system might be capable of generating signals of two kinds, depending on wavelength. Like the trichromatic theory, the opponent-process theory also assumes three sets of cones but, in this case, one set consists of luminosity receptors which function only on the black–white continuum. Of the other two colour receptors, one provides the basis for yellow and blue perception, the other for red and green. The important aspect of the theory is that each of the two aspects of each receptor opposes the action of the other so that a 'bipolar' retinal cell is postulated. Thus, a yellow receptor would oppose the influence of the blue receptor and the red would oppose the influence of the green receptor in some final common path upon which the two members of each pair would converge. Such a suggestion would explain, for example, both the colour adaptation phenomena and how many types of colour vision deficiencies occur. Boynton

(1971, 1979) has recently extended this theory to produce an 'opponent-colour' model of colour vision. This explains the process in more quantitative terms than that postulated originally and appears to fit many of the data relating to the present state of both physiological and psychological knowledge of colour perception.

Colour deficiency

Before concluding a discussion of the nature of colour reception and perception, it is appropriate to consider those members of the population who are deficient in their colour discrimination. These people, who represent about 6% of the males and 0.5% of the females in any population (Morgan, 1965) may experience difficulty at work, particularly if colour is used in displays.

Colour deficient people (note that the term 'colour blindness' is a misnomer—very few people are actually blind to colour) may be classified in a number of ways. The most common is on the basis of an ability to discriminate between the colours red, green and blue. Normal people are able to discriminate all three colours, hence they are called *trichromats*. The most common type of colour-blind individual is the *dichromat*—this person might confuse red with green or yellow with blue (red–green 'blind' individuals are considerably more common than yellow–blue individuals). The relatively rare person who is totally 'colour-blind' (0.003%) sees only white, black and shades of grey. Such a person is described as a *monochromat*.

The presence of 'colour-blindness' may be fairly simply determined using cards which make up the Ishihara colour test. Each card, which needs to be presented under standardized conditions, contains a number of different coloured dots, some of which form a pattern—either a number or a wavy line. Because of the inability to discriminate particular colours the 'colour-blind' individual has difficulty in perceiving these patterns and the deficiency can be demonstrated by an inability either to name the number or (for illiterate subjects) to trace the wavy line. Although the test appears simple to administer, it must be emphasized that it produces valid and reliable results only in the hands of a skilled tester and under controlled lighting conditions.

Visual acuity

Before considering design aspects of visual displays, it is appropriate to turn to the topic of visual acuity. This refers to the process by which we are able to see details of a display, such as characters in prose or points on a graph. Many aspects of displaying information require this ability—to register the fact that a very slowly moving character on the screen has in fact moved; to detect differences in the positions of two characters; to recognize the presence of an object in the visual field; to localize and to distinguish between two objects close in space, etc. The three types of acuity most commonly recognized are line acuity (the ability to see very fine lines of known thickness), space acuity (the ability to see characters or lines as being separate or, in other words, the ability to see a space between them), and vernier acuity (the ability to detect a discontinuity in a line when one part of the line is slightly displaced) (Murrell, 1971).

In essence three factors are important in determining the degree of acuity under any given condition. First is the size of the pupil—acuity is fairly linearly related to pupillary diameter down to a value of about 1 mm. High ambient illumination levels and some drugs, however, may cause the pupil to be constricted and this could be an important factor for the efficient viewing of displays which require high levels of acuity. A second factor is the light intensity being reflected from the object (its luminance). An object which is too fine to be seen at all in low illumination may become clearly visible when illumination is increased. (As was mentioned above, however, too high a level of illumination is likely to cause the pupil to become constricted so reducing acuity). Over the range of illumination levels normally found, acuity varies linearly with a logarithmic increase in illumination between a visual angle (that is, the angle subtended by the object at the eye) of about 0.2–1.5 minutes of arc. Finally, and within limits, acuity is related to the time allowed to view the object so that a reduced exposure time reduces acuity. The exposure times experienced in normal work, however, are usually above those needed for this to be a problem (above 200 msec at normal daylight levels of illumination).

One fairly simple way of measuring an operator's visual acuity is to use the chart employed by opticians which consists of letters arranged in rows, each row consisting of letters of a different size. This is known as the Snellen chart and is usually used at either of the standard distances of 6 metres or 20 feet. The largest letter, at the top of the chart, is usually of such a size that it could be read by a person of normal acuity at a distance ten times that of the standard, that is, at 60 m or 200 ft. If the person being tested can see nothing more than this top letter, then the acuity is described as being 6/60 or 20/200 because the vision is so poor that detail which a person with normal vision can see at 60 m (or 200 ft) can be seen only at 6 m (or 200 ft)—i.e. the observer's vision is only 6/60ths as 'good' as a normal person's.

Age and visual performance

The question of acuity becomes particularly important when considering how our visual senses fare as we become older. Computers in various situations are used by a cross-section of the working population from the young to the old. Unfortunately, from a fairly young age (some writers, such as Cakir, Hart and Stewart, 1980, suggest from about age 10) all visual functions are subject to deterioration. We are normally able to compensate for such losses, however, since increasing experience and familiarity with a given object means that we require less information for the purposes of recognition. Nevertheless, as was explained in Chapter 1, such compensation might well bring with it further costs to overall efficiency.

A number of experimenters have investigated the course of visual depreciation with age (for example, Fortuin, 1963; Blackwell and Blackwell, 1971) and have demonstrated that some of this reduction can be offset by increased luminance of the object. As Weale (1963) demonstrated, this is because of factors such as a yellowing of the lens which means that the amount of light reaching the retina of a 60-year old person is about one-third that reaching the retina of a 20-year old person. Thus Bodmann (1962), for example, compared the visual performances of a 20–30 age group with a 50–60 age group. He found that the performance of relatively simple tasks achieved by the older subjects with illumination levels of 100–400 lux were matched by the younger ones in an illumination of only 2–5 lux. Unfortunately, simply increasing the amount of illumination may not be enough to reduce the natural aging effects on performance.

Data such as these, therefore, imply that careful attention has to be paid to the design of visual tasks in order to take account of the variations in visual abilities among different age groups. In many visual tasks involving reading printed text, it might be possible to raise the general level of illumination of the material to be read (although even this practice might have some difficulties since sensitivity to glare also increases with age due to changes that take place in the eye which results in more light being scattered in the optic media— Hopkinson and Collins, 1970). When the material is presented on a visual display screen, however, the solution is not so simple. The level of illumination can be increased within only a relatively small range of values without 'burning' the screen. Furthermore, if the overall illumination is increased by shining light onto the screen this will have the effect of reducing the object's contrast with its background (since the background illumination will also be increased) and might also cause glare (see Chapter 6).

A further problem of decreased visual function with age relates to our ability to focus on objects at different distances—accommodation. This is normally performed by the ciliary muscles in the eye contracting and changing the lens shape. With age the functioning of these muscles may deteriorate, with the result that the nearest point to which the eye can be sharply focussed (the 'near point') moves further from the eye (that is, we become longsighted). In addition, the speed of accommodation decreases with age, a problem that is particularly important when, for example, typing text at a computer keyboard. Thus, the eyes often have to move between the material on the manuscript to the VDU screen and, if these are at different distances from the eye, the eyes need to accommodate rapidly if blurred images are not to result.

These problems are not entirely insoluble, however, since the aging effects

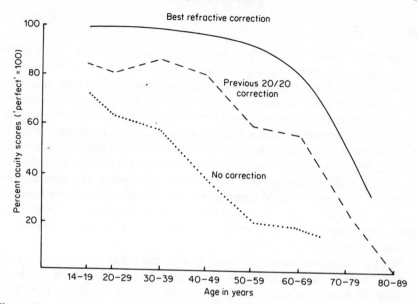

Figure 5.7. Relationship between age and visual acuity, and the effect of using corrective spectacles.

can be ameliorated using appropriate spectacles. Figure 5.7 illustrates the change in visual acuity for a group of 696 people of different ages. Some members of this group were non-spectacle wearers, some wore their normal spectacles, whilst others were provided with the best possible spectacle correction just prior to the test. As the figure shows, it is possible to correct for the reduction in visual acuity in the range 60–69 years to a level that is higher even than for the 20–29 year age group who did not wear spectacles.

VISUAL DISPLAY UNITS

Possibly because, along with the keyboards, they are the aspects of computer hardware which are most obvious to the operator, visual display units have received a great deal of research attention. This has ranged from the design of the characters presented on the screen, through the appearance of the screen itself (its colour, brightness, contrast, etc.), to any possible health hazards that may be caused by continuous operation of cathode ray tubes. However, before discussing various aspects of human interaction with visual display units (sometimes called visual display terminals or VDTs), it is useful to consider briefly how they operate. It should then be easier to understand how the human operator can interact with them.

VDU operation

The operating principles of VDUs have not changed significantly since the times of early television sets. Indeed, both have as their basic mechanism the cathode ray tube. This is essentially an evacuated glass tube containing a 'gun' at one end and a phosphor coated 'screen' at the other. The purpose of the gun is to fire a stream of electrons at the phosphorized screen, which interact with the phosphor material in such a way as to cause it to glow at each point of impact. An observer viewing the face of the screen will perceive, at each point, a bright spot of light which dims as soon as the beam has moved. Indeed, since the glow does disappear as soon as the beam has passed, the screen needs continually to be refreshed in order to present a stable, flicker free image to the operator. The speed with which this happens is called the 'refresh' or 'regeneration' rate and this is also determined by the way in which the beam of electrons is moved over the screen.

When the scanning control circuitry sweeps the electron beam across the surface of the CRT screen, the character images are 'written' on the screen by switching the beam 'on' and 'off' as it travels through its scanning pattern. These scanning lines are generally made horizontally, as on a television, and it is the density of these lines which determines the resolution of the display and thus the size and clarity of the characters. Jones (1976) and Cakir, Hart and Stewart (1980) describe the various ways in which scan lines are produced on the screen and the ways by which distortion due to the screen curvature is eliminated. Gould (1968) presents data on the refresh rates of a number of types of terminals.

The colour of a VDU screen is determined by the type of phosphor used of which there are approximately 50 different types, each designated by a 'P' number. Most produce light with wavelengths in the region 450–550 nm, and the more common types are provided in texts such as by Cakir, Hart and Stewart (1980).

Finally, there are basically two methods by which the character images can be generated on the screen: stroke and dot matrix generation. (Two others, facsimile and Lissajous generations, are rarely used, but are discussed by Cakir, Hart and stewart, 1980).

Using the technique of stroke generation, the character shapes are composed of sequences of horizontal, vertical or diagonal straight-line segments or 'strokes'. Each character image occupies a rectangle or cell, and the electron beam is switched 'on' and 'off' as directed by the character shape.

The most commonly used procedure for text processing on VDUs, however, is the dot matrix method. Using this method each character is composed of a series of bright dots (sometimes called 'pixels'), the required dot positions for each character being stored in a dot matrix memory in the computer. The resolution of the matrix is defined by the number of horizontal and vertical dots—usually 5 × 7 or 7 × 9—and the character is written to the screen in a 'sliced' form. Thus the tops of all characters in the line are written first, followed by successive horizontal slices until the bottoms are reached some seven or so lines later. This is different, of course, from the stroke method whereby the whole of a character is written before passing on to the next. More will be said later about the readability of these different types of character presentation.

In addition to characters presented on a cathode ray tube screen, of course, many modern computers use displays which are composed of crystals that glow when a current is passed though them. These are called liquid crystal displays (LCD) or light emitting diode (LED) displays.

Light emitting diodes are semiconductor crystals that discharge light when an electric current is passed through them. They are robust and very bright, but consume a great deal of current which is a disadvantage when using battery powered machines. LCDs, on the other hand, require very little power. They do not glow as LEDs but operate on the principle that when a current is passed through the liquid 'sandwich' the molecules vary their orientation so allowing less light to pass through the transparent electrodes and producing a black appearance. To be seen, therefore, LCDs require ambient light. In more recent years multicoloured LCDs have been produced (Matsumoto, 1977).

Visual display units and the user

The discussion so far has provided details of the basic physical requirements of both the visual display unit and the person who has to operate it. It is now appropriate to consider how these two components are likely to interact when they have to perform together. Thus, the discussion will turn to the design and operation of VDUs from the viewpoint of a user's behaviour. Three aspects will be considered: firstly the user's needs with respect to the physical characteristics of the display—its brightness, colour, etc.; secondly the needs from the point of view of the information displayed—in a sense the 'software' aspects; thirdly, the question of any potential health hazard which might arise from continuously interacting with the display.

Physical aspects of the display

Illumination and luminance

From the earlier discussion of the way that the eye operates, and from our own experience, it is obvious that we can only see objects when light enters the eye, either directly from the object or reflected from it. The light which falls on an object is termed the illumination, whilst that which enters the eye from an object is known as the luminance. (Brightness is the term used to define the subjective experience of luminance.)

As was discussed earlier, the eye responds differently under different levels of illumination, allowing us to be able to see within a large range of luminance levels from 3^{-5} to 3^8 candelas per square metre. At low illumination levels, the rods in the retina are most responsive, thus allowing scotopic vision. As the luminance rises above about 3 cd m^{-2}, however, the cones become more stimulated, allowing coloured, photopic vision.

Despite the fact that we are able to perceive objects over a wide range of luminances, however, it is clear that some illumination levels are more ideal for working than are others. To investigate the effects of illumination level Gilbert and Hopkinson (1949) asked subjects to read various letters on a Snellen chart lit with different levels of illumination ranging from 0.1 to 100 lumens ft^{-2} (1.076–1076 lux).

The results showed that the acuity of subjects with 'normal' vision increased with increasing illumination, although the increased advantage tended to level out above about 10 lumens ft^{-2} (107.6 lux). Children with 'subnormal' vision, however, did not demonstrate this levelling off, even up to an illumination level of 100 lumens ft^{-2} (1076 lux). Hopkinson and Collins (1970) suggest that these data confirm the generally held opinion that people with poor eyesight benefit more from increased levels of lighting than do people with normal sight.

With regard to the levels of illumination required for 'normal' reading, there appears to be very little data available, although the Illuminating Engineering Society (1977) recommend a value of 300 lux for reading surfaces in libraries. In an early study, Tinker (1939) compared performance on the Chapman–Cook Speed of Reading Test at six different illumination levels. The test required subjects to cross out words that spoil the meaning of the text printed in.10-point characters and, in contradiction to the IES recommendations, the experimental results showed no improvement in performance with levels above 8 lux. It must be remembered, however, that visual performance decreases with age and so any general illumination levels set should be able to be used by all ages of operators.

With regard to the luminance of visual display units, Gould (1968) points out that the amount of light reflected from the usual paper pages which people read these days under ambient house and office illumination is around 160 cd m^{-2}. He, therefore, suggests that this level may be used as an estimate for the recommended luminance for symbols on VDUs. Comparing the specifications of different VDUs at the time of his survey, Gould considered that most fell within this loose specification. More recently Läubli, Hünting and Grandjean (1981) have measured the luminances arising from terminals in more modern offices and recorded average (median) luminance of 163 cd m^{-2} on terminals used for data-entry, and 108 cd m^{-2} on 'conversational' terminals. (The main difference between the two types of terminals was in the task performed: with data entry terminals the operator had to keep moving the eyes from the terminal to the source document on which the data were recorded, and back

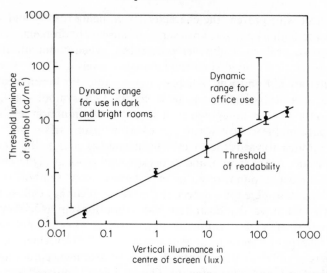

Figure 5.8. Suggested ranges of display luminances in different environments (Schmidtke, 1980). Reproduced by permission of Taylor & Francis Ltd.

again. Conversational terminal use, however, was typified by the operator interacting only with the screen.)

Schmidtke (1980) points out that the range of display luminances is a function also of the overall illumination levels in which the screen is to be used. Thus in a normal office environment having illumination levels of between 100 and 1000 lux, a range of symbol luminances between 10 and 150 cd m^{-2} would be required. In much darker environments, for example in military operations control rooms, however, the range must be able to be extended downwards or else the symbols will appear too bright. On the basis of his own experiments he suggests a range of 0.2 to 200 cd m^{-2}. The data from which these suggestions were made are shown in Figure 5.8.

Finally, as Schmidtke points out, the symbol luminance is controlled by a potentiometer. If its control resistance characteristics are linear, a small deflection of the potentiometer will brighten the screen to such an extent that the operator's adaptation level may be disturbed if the display is used under dark conditions. He suggests, therefore, that a non-linear control resistance is used as the dimmer. The same control deflection will then lead to a small increase of symbol luminance under dark conditions, with larger increases under daylight conditions.

Contrast

Coupled with overall luminance is the factor of luminance contrast between the characters on the display and the background. If the contrast is too low, then the effect is to prevent the characters from being readily and accurately identified. Too high a contrast, however, can cause glare problems.

The contrast problem is further exacerbated when a dot matrix type of character generation is used since the luminance levels of the dots comprising the character are not uniform. Whereas, for example, the luminance from any one of the characters on this page is constant, a symbol (or light spot) produced on a VDU is composed of a spread of illumination levels with the brightest part in the centre where the electron beam strikes and gradually becoming dimmer towards the edges. This means, of course, that the contrast between the edge of the symbol and its background is not as high as between its centre and the background, resulting in a slightly 'hazy' symbol. Fellmann *et al.* (1982) have considered this aspect of contrast (which they call 'sharpness of characters') and have demonstrated wide variations in efficiency between different makes of VDUs. Unfortunately, however, they do not relate their measured 'sharpness' levels to operator performance. Nevertheless, the study of the effects of different VDU contrasts on both reading accuracy and latency already discussed and illustrated in Figure 5.3. (Timmers, Van Nes and Blommaert, 1980) demonstrate the importance of ensuring that the contrast between the characters and the background is at an optimum. Furthermore, to overcome the slight blurring effect from dot matrix displays, Gould (1968) suggests both reducing the level of ambient illumination (and thus the amount of illumination reflected from the background) and adding a darkened filter to the screen.

The question whether light symbols should be viewed against a dark background (positive contrast), or vice versa (negative contrast), has been posed recently by a number of investigators. The evidence which has emerged appears to demonstrate, fairly conclusively, that performance is increased using the *negative* contrast (dark symbols against a light background) technique. For example, Bauer and Cavonius (1980) found that changing the contrast from the normal positive contrast to negative (by setting the letters to be as dark as possible and increasing the background illumination), the success rate for recognizing nonsense words increased by 23%, and the speed of recognition increased by 8%. Radl (1980) suggests that the reason for the negative contrast advantage lies in the type of task which a VDU operator has to perform: to move the eyes from the VDU to a printed sheet which, itself, is negatively contrasted (i.e. black letters on white paper); the screen and data sheet, therefore, appear the same. Furthermore, having a light background reduces the possibility of glaring reflections on the screen which might mask the displayed symbols (see Chapter 6).

Resolution

As was discussed earlier, the usual way of producing characters on the VDU screen is to build them up as a sequence of bright dots caused by the electron beam being successively switched on and off as it scans the screen from top to bottom. Each character, then, is composed of a number of scan lines and the size and definition of the character (the resolution) will be related to the number of scan lines used. In this respect, an important parameter involved in perceiving an object accurately is its size or, more accurately, the size of its image on the retina. For this reason the minimum acceptable character size for VDUs has been determined by some experimenters in terms of both the number of raster lines and the visual angle (i.e. the angle subtended at the eye by the object). Essentially, the research has indicated that about ten raster lines per character height are needed for accurate detection of individual characters, and somewhat fewer are needed to detect words.

Elias, Snadowski and Rizy (1965) reported fairly good performance with alphanumeric symbols composed of as few as 5 lines per character, although reading speed increased progressively from 5 to 11 lines. These figures, however, are averaged over all alphanumeric characters—the authors also found quite high variability in performance with different characters. For example, when using 4 scan lines approximately 90% of the subjects recognized the letter 'L' correctly wheareas only about 30% recognized the number '8'.

Hemingway and Erickson (1969) discuss a number of studies which have investigated the effects of resolution on recognizing geometric symbols. From such data, they conclude that about 10 lines per symbol are required for good (80%) identification with about 12 lines being required for 90% identification, although the results of their own study showed that at least 8 raster lines and a visual angle of at least 10 minutes of arc are required per geometric symbol. With an average viewing distance of 66 cm (Grandjean *et al.*, 1982) this would imply a minimum character height of about 2 mm. This is sightly smaller than one suggested by Giddings (1972) of approximately 4 cm for words and 4.6 cm for digits. Hemingway and Erickson have produced a family of curves relating lines per symbol and the angle needed to be subtended at the eye for 80, 90 and 95% correct detection (see Figure 5.9).

Flicker and regeneration

As discussed previously, when the electron beam has passed a particular spot on the screen the glow of the phosphor declines and, unless it is regenerated on the next scan, it will disappear. If the regeneration rate is too slow, therefore, characters will appear to flicker and this could cause operator fatigue and even, as will be discussed later, other physiological reactions such as epilepsy. In a survey of VDU users, for example, Stammerjohn, Smith and Cohen (1981) found that 68% of the operators complained of flicker from the screens. To ensure that this does not happen, relevant data regarding an observer's ability to perceive flicker is important.

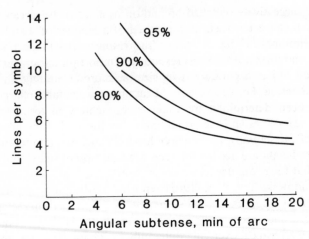

Figure 5.9. Relationship between the number of VDU raster lines and the angle between the lines subtended at the eye for 80, 90 and 95% correct detection (Hemmingway and Erickson, 1969). Reproduced by permission of the Human Factors Society.

If a light is repeatedly turned on and off at a fairly slow rate, then it appears to flicker. As the frequency of reversals is increased, however, there comes a point at which the flickering appears to stop and the light appears to fuse. This point is known as the critical fusion frequency (c.f.f.). To ensure that the characters do not appear to flicker, therefore, it is important that the screen regeneration rate is faster than cff.

A great deal of experimental literature has been built up regarding the parameters of cff (see, for example, Brown, 1965; Hopkinson and Collins, 1970; Riggs, 1972). They can be summarized as follows

1 cff increases linearly with the logarithm of illumination intensity over a wide range of intensities of the light stimulus (this is the so-called Ferry–Porter Law, see Kelly, 1961). Gould (1968) suggests that this relationship implies that for large homogeneous fields, an increase in luminance from about 10–100 mL (32–320 cd m^{-2}) requires an increase in display regeneration rate of about 15 Hz.

2 When the brightnesses of the stimulus and the surrounding area are the same, cff is at its highest. It reduces as they separate in intensity.

3 At very small visual angles, the cff increases linearly with the logarithm of the area of the stimulus.

4 cff is relatively independent of wavelength.

5 cff decreases during dark adaptation.

6 There is wide individual variability in cff, but individuals are fairly consistent within themselves.

7 cff is relatively independent of practice.

Because it depends on so many variables, it is not possible to state precise regeneration rates to ensure that flicker is overcome. However, Gould (1968) suggests that the normal electric mains regeneration rates that are used (50 Hz in the U.K, 60 Hz in the U.S.A.) are probably sufficient to prevent the perception of disturbing flicker. Furthermore, if screen phosphors having longer persistence are used, the regeneration rate can be reduced.

Colour

With advancing technology the use of coloured symbols on VDU screens is now a viable proposition. This can be brought about either by using different phosphors or by placing filters over a monochromatic ('black and white') screen. This section will discuss only the use of colour for character presentation and the screen background. The use of colour for highlighting, coding or making specific parts of the displayed information more interesting will be considered later when discussing the 'software' aspects of visual display units.

The importance of considering the use of different colours for displaying the information can be seen if the spectral sensitivity curves for light- and dark-adapted eyes, as was shown in Figure 5.4, are inspected. Thus, if the luminances of the colours are kept constant, the light-adapted eye is more sensitive to wavelengths which produce a greenish-yellow sensation than they are, say, to the reds. The sensitivity curve for the dark-adapted eye, however, shifts down the wavelengths to peak in the blue–green area. Since our visual ability is a function of the eyes' sensitivity, it would appear sensible to display colours which fall in the region of maximum sensitivity.

Possibly because the use of colour in VDU displays is quite a recent advance, little published work is presently available to suggest which colours should be used. Using 30 subjects, Radl (1980) conducted an experiment to investigate operator performance and preference for different coloured phosphors and filters: white (monochrome), green, two types of orange and three types of yellows. His results indicate that both performance (a letter transcribing task) and preference were maximum for the yellow phosphors. Of the yellows, the true yellow phosphor produced maximum performance and preference, although a monochrome screen with a yellow filter was nearly as 'good'. The reason for this discrepancy is probably related to the luminances of the screen: whereas the yellow phosphor transformed the full energy of the electron beam into the yellow colour, the yellow filter is likely to have removed some of the luminous energy.

Radl also considered the combined effects of different coloured characters and backgrounds. Using five character colours (red, blue, green, yellow and violet) and seven background 'colours' (red, blue, green, yellow, violet, grey, and grey with 'noise'), he showed that the different colour combinations produced combined error rates (wrongly named colour and character not detected) which varied between 4% and 95%. As is shown in Figure 5.10, not unreasonably the maximum error rates occurred when the character and background colours had wavelengths close to each other (for example, violet on blue, yellow on green). This is in line with the results of experimenters, such as McLean (1965) and Ohlsson, Nilsson and Rönnbert (1981) for example, who have shown that legibility and text scanning speed increase with increasing colour contrast. However, Radl's results also showed that *minimum* overall error was obtained when coloured characters were presented on a *grey* background.

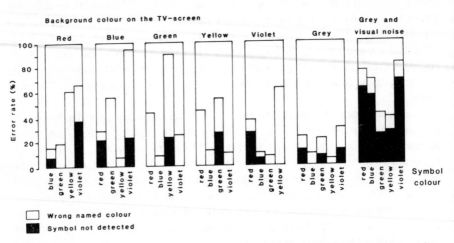

Figure 5.10. Error rate for the different VDU symbol/background colour combinations (Radl, 1980). Reproduced by permission of Taylor & Francis Ltd.

Aspects of the software

In addition to discussing the hardware aspects of visual display design, it is also important to consider the actual characters which are displayed and the ways in which these characters are produced. For example, if a raster generation method is used the display resolution is likely to influence the size and typography of the displayed characters. This is also likely to have implications for whether or not characters should be presented in lower case and whether lower case characters should be produced with their descenders. This section, then, will consider these 'hardware' aspects of the display design: the design of appropriate letter case and shape and of other display aspects such as the cursor. It will be left until Chapter 8 to consider how the software should be written to arrange and lay out groups of characters on the screen.

Upper or lower case characters

When alphabetic information is displayed, irrespective of its size it can be presented in capitals, lower case letters or a combination of both. The different modes, of course, affect both the character outline and distinctiveness, and the amount of space between the lines. Furthermore, the presence of ascenders and descenders on certain lower case letters (for example, the top parts of 'b', 'd' or the bottom parts of 'g', 'y') has two design implications. Firstly, the main body of both the particular letters and the letters without such ascenders or descenders need to be smaller than the same letters printed all in upper case. Secondly, when ascenders and descenders are used the space available between lines of text is variable. Thus, Foster and Bruce (1982) point out that, wheareas there will always be three blank lines between the bottom of one capital letter and the top of another using the 'Viewdata' system, for lower-case letters the number of lines varies from five (no descender over no ascender) to one (descender over ascender). For these reasons it is important to consider the question of character case for ease and speed of reading on a display.

Most of the work in this area has been carried out using printed material— usually for the newspaper industry. For example, in 1946 Paterson and Tinker investigated the relative values of upper and lower case letters in newspaper headlines. They presented their subjects with one headline at a time for a limited period and measured the number of words read in the time available. At normal reading distance, their results indicated that on average more words were read when using lower case letters than when using headlines printed in upper case in the same type face and point size (in this case 24-point Cheltenham Extra condensed). These results were replicated by Poulton (1967) who showed a 9% advantage in reading ability of lower case over upper case headlines. A similar advantage was obtained by mixing upper and lower case letters, although they were not read any more reliably than headlines printed entirely in lower case. Poulton and Brown (1968) and Poulton (1969a) have also demonstrated a lower case advantage, as did Fox (1963) who compared reading speeds and comprehension using 'gothic elite' (capitals) and 'standard elite' (lower case) typefaces. Interestingly, however, this advantage occurred only when the standard elite text was read before the gothic elite text. When the results from the other group of subjects (those who read the gothic text before the standard) were added to the data, no case advantage was observed.

Paterson and Tinker (1940) and Poulton (1969b) have suggested that the reason for any superiority of mixed over upper case letters probably lies in the shape of the envelope surrounding the whole word as presented (rather than the individual letters). Words presented in capitals do not have any distinctive shape since all the letters are the same height. The shapes of various lower case words, however, are more likely to be different because of the ascenders and descenders on different letters. For example, the shape of the envelope enclosing the word *dog* is different from that enclosing the word *cat* owing to the extensions of the *d* and *g* in dog and the *c* and *t* in *cat*. The envelopes around DOG and CAT, however, are not greatly different, and this lack of distinctive shapes between different words in capitals means that the reader has to examine some of the intermediate letters to identify the words, so increasing reading time.

An explanation for the lower case advantage couched in terms of distinctive shapes has been challenged, however, by Phillips (1979)—at least when a search task is employed. He compared subjects' abilities in searching for place names on a map when the names were typed all in lower case, in lower case but with the initial letter a capital, all in upper case, and in smaller sized upper case with the initial letter larger. His results demonstrated that names set entirely in lower case took significantly longer to find than names in the other conditions; the shortest time was taken for names in capitals with the larger initial letter. On the basis of his results, Phillips suggests that, for search tasks at least, the important aspect of the word is not the overall shape but the initial letter and, by making this distinctive, the word should be found more quickly.

Finally, another exception to the lower case advantage findings should be mentioned. Foster and Bruce (1982) asked subjects to read aloud text composed of 'nonsense' phrases written either in lower case with upper case initial letters of sentences, or all in upper case. Their data showed no significant advantage of lower over upper case letters, although there was a slight trend towards faster mixed case reading. It is likely, however, that their task—reading aloud—may have reduced any advantage that the lower case arrangement presents. Thus the experiments described so far have asked subjects either to read to themselves or to read for comprehension. Silent reading can be performed much quicker than reading out loud since the processes involved in translating the cognitive stimuli into vocal responses are not required. Thus, although perhaps lower case letters and words may be perceived and 'registered' quicker, it is possible that the speed advantage gained is reduced if a vocal response is required.

In summary, therefore, it would appear that for general comprehension and reading, text composed in both upper and lower case letters (as in this book) is superior both for speed and accuracy of reading. The advantage is reduced, however, when the task includes components of search and reading aloud.

Character shape and design

The question of the shape of displayed characters concerns not only whether or not they are in upper or lower case, but also how they are created (stroke or dot matrix) and the ways in which the dots and segments making up the character are put together.

With regard to dot matrix displays, Vartabedian (1971) reported a study in which he compared the speed of subject's recognition and the numbers of errors made for different CRT displays. In essence, two forms of displays were used—four types of dot matrix and two types of stroke display. The dot matrix display took the form either of a 5 × 7 matrix, using circular or elongated 'dots', or a 7 × 9 matrix, using circular or slanting 'dots'. The stroke displays were either upright or slanted.

The results indicated, fairly conclusively, that the 7 × 9 circular dots produced fewer errors and faster reaction times than did the other forms. Whereas the 5 × 9 circular dots produced roughly similar numbers of errors to the 7 × 9 matrix, the characters took rather longer to recognize. The two slanted displays (7 × 9 elongated and stroke) produced a higher proportion of errors and slower reaction time than their upright counterparts. Finally, Vartabedian also demonstrated that elongating the 'dot' also affected legibility.

On the basis of this work Vartabedian (1973) produced a set of alphanumeric characters for a 7 × 9 dot display. A similar matrix was used by Huddleston (1974), although his display was composed of square rather than circular dots. In addition Maddox, Burnette and Gutman (1977) have produced recommendations for a 5 × 7 dot matrix display.

Pastoor, Schwarz and Beldie (1983) considered the efficiency of larger dot matrices, including 9 × 11 and 11 × 15. Their results demonstrated greater efficiency with both the 9 × 11 and the 11 × 15 matrices, although the difference in both performance and suitability ratings between the two were not significant. On the basis of these data, since the 9 × 11 matrix requires less room than one which is 11 × 15, the authors suggest that a 9 × 11 matrix should be used.

Another dimension of character shape relates to the height:width ratio of the character. In this respect, Beldie, Pastoor and Schwarz (1983) demonstrated that character sets which are composed of variable width characters—as in proportional spacing, for example—produced faster reading times and fewer errors than fixed width character sets. They explain these findings in terms of the word-shape hypothesis described above.

Like dot matrix displays, the important criteria governing the shape of liquid crystal and light emitting diode displays concern the size, alignment and number of 'segments' which make up the character. In this respect, alphanumeric characters are generally composed of seven segments (two at each side, one at the top, one in the middle and one at the bottom of a rectangular shape), and the character is produced by 'illuminating' different segments (for example, the top and two right side segments produce a '7'; the top, top right, middle, bottom left, and bottom produce a '2').

Unfortunately, the available evidence suggests that seven-segment displays using either LCDs or LEDs produce worse performance in subjects (more errors—usually errors of confusion—and slower reading) than both conventional (printed) characters (Plath, 1970) and dot matrix produced characters (Orth, Weckerle and Wendt, 1976). Ellis and Hill (1978), however, have demonstrated that such conclusions apply only when the reader is placed under time stress. Where time is not critical, reading segmented numbers is as efficient as reading conventional ones. Furthermore, even with time stressed reading, appropriate training was able to overcome difficulties in reading segmented numbers. Without the opportunity for continued practice, however, the skills acquired were reduced significantly within a month.

Van Nes and Bouma (1979, 1980) have suggested that the inferiority of seven-segment characters is likely to be caused by the design of the segments themselves. On the basis of their own experiments they suggest that:

1 The smaller the number of segments from which a digit is built up, the better it will be recognized. For example, the number 1 (which is composed of two segments) is recognized more quickly than 9 (which is composed of 6 segments).
2 The probability of confusing two different numbers decreases as the difference between the number of segments which make up the two numbers is increased.
3 Not all segments appear to be equally important for perception.

Using these suggestions and data from their own experiments, they have produced a new set of segmented numbers which have variable segment thickness. As can be seen in Figure 5.11, the top and right hand segments of a seven-segment number are about two-thirds the thickness of the other four segments. The authors do emphasize, however, that these new designs are still at the experimental stage.

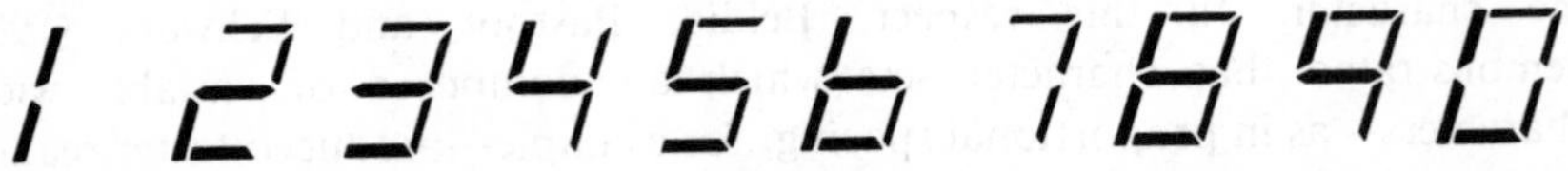

Figure 5.11. Proposed designs of seven-segment numbers based on analyses of confusion errors (Van Nes and Bouma, 1980). Reproduced by permission of the Human Factors Society.

The Cursor

The cursor is a very important aspect of a visual display since it often performs two major functions: first, it acts in the same manner as the carriage position on a conventional typewriter and indicates where the next character is to be placed. Second, it directs the operator's attention to specific parts or features of the display. Its twin roles, therefore, are first as an information presenter and second as an attention seeker.

Cakir, Hart and Stewart (1980) suggest that cursor types can be divided into three categories, defined by the effect that they have on the character which they are meant to be indicating. They describe these categories as 'superimposing', 'replacing' and 'enhancing'. *Superimposing* cursors do not affect the character at all; the cursor, for example a box, simply adds to the character. A *replacing* cursor is one that actually replaces the character, although it perhaps alternates with the character. Finally, an *enhancing* cursor highlights the character in some way, perhaps by intensifying the character or by colouring it.

Unfortunately, there is very little work in the published literature to guide the design of cursors—either to choose between the types outlined above or to determine their parameters (size, speed of flashing, brightness, shape, etc.). However, it is well known that we orientate our eyes towards a novel stimulus and so a flashing cursor is likely to prove most effective for the attention seeking aspects of its task. With regard to the frequency of flashing, Cakir, Hart and Stewart suggest that a blink rate between 3 and 5 Hz minimizes both search and tracking times. Although it may be effective as an attention seeker, however, a flashing cursor can be distracting to the operator when, say, simply typing data from the keyboard (particularly if the operator has to think whilst doing so—for example, when composing text). For this reason they suggest that facilities should be provided for turning off the blinking cursor to provide a steady symbol.

Possible health consequences of using visual display units

In recent years, with the increased used of computer controlled displays in industry, offices and the home, fears have arisen concerning possible risks to health from continued use of VDUs. As will be shown in this discussion and in later chapters, however, fears of direct health hazards are groundless. Any hazards to health, either physical or psychological, which can be linked to computer terminal use arise not from the terminal itself but from poor interactions between its facilities and the user's requirements. Such 'health' aspects as possible increased frequencies of postural complaints and increased complaints of social isolation and stress will be considered in the next chapter. This section will deal exclusively with possible complaints that could be laid at the door of the display itself—particularly radiation hazards, visual fatigue and epileptic experiences.

Radiation

For a VDU to operate it must produce a considerable amount of radiated energy—otherwise we would be unable to see the characters on the screen. This type of radiation, however, (electromagnetic radiation in the visible spectrum) is quite safe; what many operators fear is the possibility of other radiation wavelengths being produced by the cathode ray tube—radiation that is unable to be perceived through our normal, biological sensors.

In essence, radiation takes two forms; ionising and non-ionizing. Ionizing radiation (of the x-ray type) is generated whenever the field of electrons surrounding the nucleus of an atom is disturbed to such an extent that at least one of the nuclear electrons is excited enough to make it migrate from a lower to a higher energy state and back again. It is this type of radiation that can cause genetic damage. Any thermionic type of valve or similar device which operates with a voltage greater than about 5 kilovolts *could* produce such radiation, but both Cakir, Hart and Stewart, (1980) and Grandjean (1980) suggest that much higher voltages (of at least 35 kV) are required before occupational exposure levels are reached. Furthermore, much of the radiation produced by conventional screens operating with voltages in the region of 18 kV is often absorbed by the glass of the cathode ray tube.

Non-ionizing radiation, on the other hand, has wavelengths which occur just outside of the range of visible radiation—primarily in the infra red and ultra violet ranges—and, if it occurs at all, is likely to result from the excitation of the screen phosphor. Although intense doses of these wavelengths could cause damage to the skin or eyes, very few screen phosphors overlap into the infra red region and most of the small quantities of ultra violet radiation that are produced are trapped by the glass screen (Cakir, Hart and Stewart, 1980).

All of the evidence that is available, therefore, strongly suggests that the levels of both ionizing and non-ionizing radiation produced by commercial cathode ray tubes fall far short of any levels set for occupational exposure to such radiation. Indeed, in measurements of ionizing radiation from a number of terminals, Terrana, Merluzzi and Giudici (1980) have demonstrated that the levels produced are often no higher than the normal background radiation to which we are constantly exposed. (See also, Grandjean, 1980; Cakir, Hart and Stewart, 1980.)

Visual strain and fatigue

In addition to radiation fears, one further VDU-related health problem has received quite a lot of attention. This concerns the results of over-using the visual system to cause fatigue and strain. With this hazard at least, the available research certainly suggests that some problems might exist.

Although asthenopia (eye strain, eye fatigue) has been studied by many different investigators around the world at both a theoretical and a clinical level, in terms of understanding the specific physiological mechanisms involved there is still much to be learned. Many of the reasons for this dearth of understanding stems from the lack of any valid and reliable measuring techniques. Thus, Hopkinson and Collins (1970) suggest that 'Over a period of activity by many research workers, of whom some have spent years of concentrated effort in the search for a fully valid and sensitive practical method of testing for visual fatigue ... nothing has emerged which seems to be a substitute for direct subjective assessment of the situation'. These subjective techniques revolve around symptom checklists and rating scales (Dainoff, 1982).

Dainoff presents a comprehensive and recent review of studies investigating the effects of both short and prolonged use of VDUs on visual fatigue. As Table 5.1 shows, all of the studies report significant fatiguing effects, although it should be pointed out that many of the earlier studies lacked good control groups against which the results could be compared (groups of equivalent workers who did *not* use VDUs), and some of the more recent studies simply

Table 5.1. Summary of studies showing visual problems of workers who use VDUs (adapted from Dainoff, 1982). Reproduced by permission of Taylor & Francis Ltd.

Name	Proportion (%) complaining	Types of workers and comments
Hultgren & Knave (1973)	47	VDT operators No control group
Gunnarsson & Osterberg (1977)	46	" "
Gunnarsson & Soderberg (1979)	62	Newspaper compositors
	83	VDU users in office
Technical University Berlin (in Cakir et al., 1980)	85	Workers on incentive schedules
	68	" " "
Rey & Meyer (1980)	75	VDT operators (50% in control group)
Shipley et al. (1980)	61	Newspaper workers
Ghiringhelli (1980)	50	VDT operators
Coe et al. (1980)	51	VDT operators—analysis made in terms of type of *task*
Läubli et al. (1981)	50-70	VDT operators—analysis made in terms of type of *complaint*
Dainoff et al. (1981)	45	Clerical workers with varying VDT experience
Smith et al. (1981)		Investigated effects of VDUs on mood as well as eye strain.
Mourant et al. (1981)		Compared fatigue from VDU use with fatigue from using normal writing

asked operators what effects they *felt* VDUs had (this is not the same as asking what effects they actually had). The misleading conclusions that could be reached using poor experimental controls can be seen, for example, in the study of Rey and Meyer (1980). Thus, 75% of the operators sampled (computer personnel in a Swiss watch-makers) felt that they experienced visual fatigue after working. Although this is a high figure, it needs to be compared with the other data produced by Rey and Meyer that 50% of the control group (other workers such as watch-makers, engravers who also had to perform 'close' work) also reported visual fatigue. Despite the fact that the difference between the two figures (75% and 50%) is significant, this study does remind us that any visual fatigue experienced is not necessarily due entirely to working with VDUs.

The nature of the complaint

Läubli, Hünting and Grandjean (1981) asked a number of VDU operators to provide details of the visual impairments that they felt were caused by VDU operation. From the responses they were able to extract two eye impairment factors as shown in Table 5.2. Thus the major group is composed of a 'discomfort' dimension, whereas the minor group of factors comprises, essentially, a visual impairment dimension.

Comparing clerical and professional VDU users with non-users, Smith *et al.* (1980) observed that the clerical VDU users complained mainly of visual fatigue, and of musculo-skeletal and emotional problems (in 1981 they reported differences in psychological mood state). In the professional group the three significantly different symptoms were eye strain, irritability and burning eyes.

Table 5.2. Factor analysis of eye impairments of VDU users (Läubli, Hünting and Grandjean, 1981). Reproduced by permission of Taylor & Francis Ltd.

Factor	Proportion of variance	Name	Symptoms
1	81	Visual discomfort	Pains Burning Fatigue Shooting pain Headaches
2	19	Visual impairment	Blurring of near sight Flicker vision Blurring of far sight Double images

The effects of the task

Dainoff (1982) provides an excellent description of some of the work in this area. In particular he describes an extensive series of studies carried out in New Zealand by Coe *et al.* (1980) who sampled nearly 400 employees from 19 different firms. Of these, 257 were VDU users and 124 were controls. The authors divided the type of work that they did into four categories. Firstly, *input* work was characterized by high rates of data entry in which the eyes were directed primarily at the copy and keyboard. Secondly, *creative* work was mainly tasks such as programming the computer. Thirdly, *editing* tasks, although similar to the creative tasks in that both required continual feedback between display and copy, required more intensive physical use of the workplace. Finally, *question and answer* was highly screen interactive and involved a great deal of dialogue between the screen and keyboard.

In the study both personal health and environmental conditions were investigated. The personal health component involved a questionnaire, a visual function test and a physical examination of the outside of the eye. They also separated the visual strain symptoms into two categories—fatigue-like effects and irritant-like effects. The environmental component of the analysis consisted of anthropometric measurements of desk/chair/terminal dimensions, illumination and luminance assessment and temperature and relative humidity.

When the data were analysed according to the type of symptom, a significant difference was obtained between the VDU users and the controls (50 vs 33%), but only for the *fatigue-like* symptoms. The creative group reported fewer symptoms than any other of the groups. Furthermore full-time operators were significantly more likely to report asthenopic complaints (both fatigue and irritation) than were part-time operators.

This task duration effect has also been reported by other investigators. For example, Rey and Meyer (1980), in their study of VDU users in a Swiss watch-making factory, found that VDU operators who worked 6–9 hours per day at their terminals were significantly more likely to have visual complaints (73%) than those who used their terminals for less than four hours per day. These patterns of complaints appeared to be the same for both young and old operators. Ghiringhelli (1980) also found that complaints of eye irritations increased for workers who used terminals for more than three hours per day, and they were significantly greater than for control (clerical) workers.

One reason for the relationship between eye strain complaints and the type of task probably lies with the amount of work which the eye muscles are called upon to do—particularly the ciliary muscles which control the lens shape. As was explained earlier, to perceive near and far objects, the lens shape constantly has to be altered to focus the image on the retina—a process known as accommodation. For practical purposes all objects further than 6 metres away from the normal eye are sharply in focus and the nearer the object is to the eye the greater is the amount of muscular effort required to maintain the correct lens curvature. With 'normal' visual work, then, the ciliary muscles are continually varying in the level of contraction and, because they are performing dynamic work, are able to pump blood to maintain their oxygen supply, etc. For the type of work normally done at a computer terminal, however, this does not necessarily happen. The copy and the screen are generally placed close to each other and the operator's eyes rarely have a chance to vary the accommodation level from one which requires the ciliary muscles to be under constant static load. This argument is supported by findings of Starr, Thompson and Shute (1982) who showed that if operators wear correctly prescribed glasses, the incidence of complaints from VDU users is no greater than those from other workers.

Effects of environmental conditions and the display type

In their study which investigated the symptoms of asthenopia, Läubli, Hünting and Grandjean (1981) also considered how different aspects of the display affected these complaints. In particular, they considered the effects of luminance contrasts between the screen and the surround (arising from, say, windows and reflections off the copy), the presence of screen reflections and the quality of the displayed characters.

With regard to contrast, their data suggest that it is the high contrast displays which cause more eye complaints to occur. Indeed, significantly larger numbers of members of the high contrast group reported that the complaints continued after work and even until the next morning. In addition, the extent of reflections off the screen correlated well with operator annoyance, although there was no relationship between the measured luminance of the reflections and actual eye complaints.

With regard to the characters themselves, the authors measured the extent to which the character luminances oscillated in brightness. Complaints of eye irritations were more frequent from the operators who had used displays with strongly oscillating luminances, and observations of red eyes, although not significantly higher in the high oscillation group, were reported more often. Character luminance oscillation was also related to performance—with high oscillation leading to reduced visual acuity.

VDUs and photosensitive epilepsy

One final medical aspect of VDU use that needs to be considered is its potential for inducing minor epileptic seizures. A small proportion of the population (estimated to be about 1 in 10,000—Jeavons and Harding, 1975) suffer recurrent convulsions in the presence of flickering light stimuli and, of course, the most common 'natural' cause of such stimuli at work is likely to be the VDU. The probability of an adult VDU operator reacting to the screen in this way, however, is likely to be much less than the 1 in 10,000 since the age distribution of patients who complain of these seizures is markedly skewed towards the age of puberty (Harding, 1979).

Using complex striped patterns to affect the brain's responses (measured by electroencephalography—EEG), Wilkins (1978) was able to determine aspects of the display which were likely to trigger an epileptic onset, without actually inducing seizures in his patients. His results suggest that the primary correlate of such seizures is the number and intensity of retinal cells stimulated. In particular his data suggest that the epileptogenic attributes of VDU screens can be reduced firstly by reducing the area of the retina stimulated. This can be achieved by using a small screen, by displaying light characters on a dark background, by limiting the amount of text on the screen, and by seating the operator further from the screen.

Secondly the tendency can be reduced by reducing the overall luminance of the display, perhaps by the observer wearing dark glasses. (Wilkins notes that this is quite common among TV studio managers who have to watch TV displays for long periods.) However the glasses would have to have a transmission rate of only 10% or so to be effective.

Finally, work by Wilkins, Darby and Binnie (1979) suggests that reducing the screen–surround contrast will also reduce the potential for seizures. Thus, with a contrast ratio of 0.2 the probability of seizures was about 25% of that when the ratio was 0.3. It should be remembered that high contrast was also shown to be a factor in inducing eye strain.

In summary, therefore, this section has demonstrated that, under certain conditions, continued VDU use can have detrimental effects on the visual health of operators. However, it is apparent that, apart from the effect of the quality of the displayed characters as shown by Läubli and his colleagues, most of the effects can be placed at the door not of the computer terminal itself but of the environmental and task conditions. The position of the operator, the screen and the copy; the amount of display–surround contrast; the duration of the task, etc. all contribute to the incidence of complaints. These aspects will be considered in more detail in the next chapter.

PRINTERS AND PRINTING

Although one generally thinks of visual display units as being the primary means by which information is presented to the operator, the role of printers should not be forgotten. These machines provide the 'hard-copy' of output from the computer; they allow material to be produced which is not lost when the machine is switched off. Furthermore, the material that is produced can be filed away and read in its final format at a later date by anyone without the need for a fairly costly machine—it does not need further formatting by the computer program.

For written information to be communicated efficiently, the message needs not only to be read (and interpreted) correctly but absorbed in the shortest time possible. Fast reading is necessary from the point of view of economy of time and, perhaps more importantly, it ensures that our long term storage memory capacities are not overloaded. For example, the longer that a reader needs to decipher a word or a symbol on a page (perhaps because of poor handwriting or because the material is the fifth carbon copy or the ribbon has run faint on the printer), the slower will be the rate of comprehension. Furthermore, it seems likely that such factors play quite a large part in determining whether the material will be read at all (McLaughlin, 1966).

Although there are a number of ways of making a permanent impression on a sheet of paper, the majority of printers sold take one or other of two forms: either the character is composed of a series of 'dots' in much the same way as the characters on many VDU screens (because all of the dots form a block, such printers are often called 'dot matrix' printers), or it is formed by striking a template of the letter against a ribbon and on to the paper. This second type, of course, uses the same procedure for creating characters as the typewriter— the only difference is the increase in printing speed of modern machines. This is generally accomplished because, instead of having separate keys for each character, each with its own inertia, all of the characters are pressed onto the same structure—sometimes on a spherical 'golfball' but more frequently on a circular 'daisywheel' (so-called because the character spokes produce the appearance of the petals of a daisy).

Despite the importance of printing as a means of presenting computer information, there has been very little research dealing with the design of such machines—particularly the characteristics of the 'typefaces'—from the point of view of the user's needs. The information that is available generally has to be distilled from data produced in other areas, such as ergonomic aspects of newspaper typefaces or the design of matrix characters for VDUs. Whereas such data can provide pointers as to the appropriate design parameters for printers, they cannot be taken as wholly valid for this particular situation.

With regard to the design of matrix printer heads, then, the available evidence from VDU character design suggests, not unreasonably, that the more dense is the matrix (for example 9×9 rather than 7×5), the more efficient will be the character produced—both for reading speed and accuracy. With a fixed matrix size, however, one aspect that does require consideration is whether or not the lower case letters have 'true' descenders (i.e. that the lower parts of letters such as 'p' or 'q' descend below the print line). These are generally not present on 'cheaper' matrix printers, since a larger matrix is needed (at least an extra two lines) to produce the descenders. Although no experimental data are available to determine the cost in reading efficiency of characters not having true descenders, it is likely that they will be less easily read since the shape of characters without descenders needs to be different from that normally expected—to fit into the matrix the main body of the character has to become more 'squashed' in order to accept the descender.

With regard to printed material formed by printers that strike the whole character on the paper, for example daisywheels, more design evidence is available. As far as type size is concerned, for example, much of the evidence arises from studies performed within the newspaper industry—they have to capture their readers' attention very quickly.

Using two measures of readability, the amount read and the degree of comprehension, Burt (1959) compared the readability of passages composed of different sizes of Times Roman print (designed in 1932) ranging from 8 to 14 point. (Type size is conventionally specified in terms of the height of a line of print, the unit being the 'point' which is 0.0138 inches—about ⅓ mm high). Unfortunately he did not provide any data to support his claim, but was able to state that the 10 point prose was the most legible. Most subjects found the 9 point print equally as legible as the 10 point, while older people often did best with 11 or even 12 point. These results were replicated by Poulton (1969) when he asked housewives to search for particular words in lists of ingredients printed in 10, 7.5, 6 and 4 point lower-case type. Although the implications of data such as these are that the larger the typeface the better, such a conclusion should not be taken to extreme. Thus, as the typeface becomes larger, for a specific line length the number of characters and words that can be fitted on to the line is reduced. If the number is reduced by too much, the natural 'flow' of reading (which will be discussed in detail in Chapter 8), is likely to be lost. The optimum typesize, then, will depend as much on the size of paper and the message to be transmitted as on the person who is to read it.

Deciding on the appropriate type size, etc., is only part of the battle of designing a printed page for easy reading and comprehension. The layout of the page, the use of paragraph indentations, the number of columns, etc., all play an important part in producing an aesthetic as well as a readable print-out. Poulton, Warren and Bond (1970) provide an interesting summary of the appropriate points that need consideration, and Oborne (1980) has discussed many of them in greater depth.

SYNTHESIZED SPEECH OUTPUT DEVICES

The value of using speech to interact with computers was considered in the last chapter. Thus, speech was seen to be a more 'natural' means of communicating and, provided efficient speech recognition (or, more precisely, word recognition) systems could be devised, spoken input is performed more efficiently and accurately than input from devices such as keyboards.

Many of the advantages of using speech input also apply to speech output.

Again, speech is natural, it releases otherwise overburdened communication channels (in this case the eyes rather than the limbs), we can speak and understand messages faster than we can read them, etc. In addition, as Turn (1974) points out, perception of the spoken message does not depend on the receiver actually facing and looking at the transmitter—the human listener can be some distance from the computer, behind a barrier or even in motion. Furthermore, any number of listeners can receive the spoken message from the computer simultaneously—although this might present problems in cases of security.

Because the basic signals of both speech input and output are the same—speech—the problems that arise in producing efficient systems are also likely to be similar. Thus, one needs to understand how speech is produced and analysed in order that the listener (be it human or computer) can 'understand' the meaning of the speaker's message (be it computer or human produced). For this reason, many of the basic details concerning speech synthesis by machine have already been discussed in the previous chapter. However, the process of designing machines that produce speech able to be understood by humans also has some problems which are different from the man–computer direction of the speech interaction process. These deal primarily with the ways in which we process speech sounds and the ways in which computers are able to generate them.

The mechanisms of hearing

If the eye can be likened to a camera, the ear can be thought to perform like a microphone. The main job of both is to convert the sounds which they receive in the form of air pressure waves into electrical patterns, which are then recognized by a decoding apparatus. However, unlike the eye which functions in a superior way to the camera, in many respects the human ear is inferior to the sophisticated modern microphones which are available today.

The ear itself is composed of three recognizable sections: the outer ear, the middle ear, and the inner ear. What most of us commonly call the 'ear' is to the anatomist the pinna of the outer ear, which in animals like the dog or cat can be moved in different directions to help 'collect' sound waves. In humans, however, the pinna is a less effective sound trapper. The outer ear also consists of a eustachian tube which runs inwards from the pinna and is terminated at the eardrum (the tympanic membrane). It is through these parts of the external ear that sounds are conducted to the middle ear and then to the inner ear.

The middle ear performs two main functions: to transmit sound waves and to protect the inner ear. Sound wave transmission is carried out by three small bones, the malleus, the incus and the stapes, which are collectively called the ossicular chain. They are so arranged that they span across the middle ear and connect the eardrum to a thin 'oval window' on the other side. For this part of the ear to function properly, it is important that the air pressure in the middle ear remains the same as that in the environment and this is achieved by a tube (the eustachian tube) which connects the inner ear to the back of the throat. However, sudden changes in air pressure can close the eustachian tube thus creating pressure differences between the middle ear and the outside atmosphere. The effect of this may be to cause the excrutiating pain experienced by some air travellers, or even permanant damage to the ear.

The outer and middle ear appear to have the function not only of transmitting sound to the inner ear, but also of protecting it from having to operate on sound pressure levels which are outside of its capacity. Kryter (1970) points to three ways in which this can occur. First, the action of the eustachian tube may prevent pressure waves which have fast (less than 20 msec) rise times (the time taken for the sound pressure level to reach its maximum intensity) being transmitted to the inner ear. (Events such as explosions can easily produce sounds with such fast rise times.) Second, if high intensity pressure waves are experienced, small muscles in the middle ear can contract to stiffen the ossicular chain and attenuate the sound. Third, the mass and stiffness of the ossicular chain are such as to prevent the transmission of a pressure wave with extremely fast rise times (of less than 20 microseconds).

The inner ear performs two separate functions. The first concerns the process of hearing and the second (which is not important in the present discussion) the maintenance of posture. The primary receptor organ for hearing is the cochlea, which derives its name from its coiled structure, similar to the shape of a snail's shell. It tapers slightly along its length, with the broader end incorporating the oval window of the inner ear, and it is filled with fluid. Running the length of the cochlea is a membrane (the basilar membrane) which acts in a similar way to the ribbon in an old carbon ribbon microphone.

Oborne (1982) points out that opinions differ as to the precise mechanism of hearing. However, a simple model would suggest that the sound pressure waves are transmitted as vibrations across the inner ear from the eardrum to the oval window by the action of the ossicular chain. These in turn set up hydrostatic travelling waves along the cochlea and basilar membrane, which cause the membrane to vibrate and its covering of hairs to be compressed. The tonal sensation of pitch is produced because different parts of the membrane are sensitive to different frequencies. High frequency sounds are perceived at the base of the basilar membrane, whereas the apex is sensitive to low frequency sounds, while loudness is discriminated by the extent to which the hairs are compressed.

Understanding speech

When discussing the ways in which computers are able to recognize words in the last chapter, it became clear that the processing which occurs was essentially that of 'template matching'—comparing the frequencies and frequency distributions of the incoming signal with a set of previously stored information. If the distribution shape of the word input to the computer matched that of one already in the memory store (or at least fell within a predefined band of acceptable error), then the word was recognized.

Cole and Jakimik (1978), however, suggest strongly that for fluent speech at least such a pattern-matching process cannot occur as far as human perception of speech is concerned. The structure and complexity of the stimulus rules this out; no two utterances are ever the same, no two vowel tracts will produce the same sounds and, even when the same monosyllabic word is repeated by the same speaker, small differences in the microstructure of the acoustic signal can always be observed. This is particularly so when 'natural', fluent speech is concerned. However, they do accept that a form of pattern-matching might occur for words spoken in *isolation*. When someone is asked to read aloud a series of words, he or she articulates each of the words in a fairly precise manner so that they exhibit a great deal of stability at the acoustic/phonetic level.

As far as fluent speech is concerned other cues need to be used for us to be able to decode the utterances at an acoustic level into meaningful messages. These cues (or 'perceptual anchors', as Cole and Jakimik call them) are contained in the message itself and relate to the positions of different words in the message and the nature of the syllables from which the words are composed. On the basis of these two categories of information, Cole and Jakimik propose a model of fluent speech understanding which suggests both serial and parallel processing.

The basic means by which we understand spoken communications were described as early as the beginning of this century by a hitherto unkown psychologist named Bagley. As Cole and Rudnicky (1983) point out, research which has been performed subsequent to his monograph published in 1900 has really only served to extend slightly some of his findings or to allow his conclusions to be reiterated with more conviction because they were obtained using more reliable equipment (such as computers).

With regard to the importance of word position, in his pioneering work Bagley found that words heard in a sentence context are recognized more accurately than words presented in isolation. Words occurring later in a sentence are less important to the message than those occurring earlier. In this respect, the measure of 'importance' was taken as the likelihood that a mispronounced word would be noted when speaking a message back. The argument is advanced, therefore, that if a word is not important to an understanding of the message it will be 'automatically' restored to its correct pronunciation on hearing the message—the mispronounced important words, however, will be noted.

The importance of the earlier words in a sentence probably arises from two aspects of their position. Firstly, the first words in a sentence are likely to set the meaning of the sentence. This is known as 'semantic priming'. Secondly, once the meaning of the sentence has been established, the later words will generally be fairly predictable. Such an assertion was demonstrated by Marslen-Wilson and Welsh (1978) who found that subjects who shadowed (i.e. read aloud with) speech that contained occasional mispronunciations were more likely to restore mispronounced words to their original form when they were able to be predicted from prior context. Furthermore, Miller (1962) suggests that, in addition to reducing the variety of competing alternative words, the sentence context also helps us to organize the flow of sound into decision units larger than individual words. Thus perceptual decisions about what we are hearing can be made at a 'slower and more comfortable rate'.

In addition to the words used and their positions, the sounds comprising the words also play a similarly large part in the decoding process. It is particularly these aspects which Cole and Jakimik (1978) refer to as 'perceptual anchors' which determine how the word is to be recognized. They suggest that these features provide the most direct and reliable indication of the identity of the words; play a major role in guiding the listener in the segmentation process; and provide information about syllable stress within a word *in addition* to the syllable stress that is carried by the vowel. These anchors, then, are very important.

One of the major types of perceptual anchor is whether the sound occurs at the beginning or at the end of a word. As was shown to be the case with word positions, it appears that importance is given to the *initial* syllables in a word. Thus Bagley found that fewer 'restorations' occurred when words were composed of mutilated syllables occurring at the beginning than at the end of words. These findings have been supported on numerous later occasions (Cole, Jakimik and Cooper, 1978; Cole and Jakimik, 1978; Marslen-Wilson and Welsh, 1978). These results are in a similar vein to those of Cooper, Egido and Paccia (1978) who showed that speakers are careful to articulate a consonant segment at the beginning but not at the end of a word.

Another feature of the way in which a word is heard, of course, concerns the stresses that are placed on different parts. Stresses generally suggest importance and the syllables stressed in a word are more likely to be taken note of than are syllables which are not so stressed. This was shown in an experiment by Cole and Jakimik (1978) who mutilated different syllables in words—both stressed and unstressed. Their results showed a very strong effect, with mispronunciations being detected almost twice as frequently when the altered segment occurred in the stressed syllable.

Finally, the actual consonants used are important. Thus, Cole and Jakimik demonstrated that stop consonants (i.e. those which are produced with the total occlusion of the oral cavity, such as 'b', 'd', 'g', 'p', 't' and 'k') enjoy a special status as perceptual anchors in fluent speech. They are separated from preceding segments by a period of relative silence, so that the silence itself cues the listener that a stop consonant is about to occur (Umeda, 1977). Mispronouncing these consonants is also quickly and readily perceived. Cole and Jakimik's results suggest that at least 75% of mispronunciations of, say, 'b' to 'p', or 't' to 'd' were detected.

On the basis of results of this nature Cole and Jakimik (1978) propose a model of word recognition which is essentially both a serial and a parallel process. First, both words in an utterance and the syllables in the word are recognized in a strictly serial fashion. Each component is processed word by word and syllable by syllable. Because words are recognized in order, however, it means that one word's recognition automatically directs the listener's attention to the segmentation of the immediately following word. Secondly, there is a corresponding parallel process since a word is also specified by prior context. Thus, they suggest that a word's recognition also occurs at the *same time* as it is being input, so that recognition carries with it a knowledge of the constraints to be placed on other words in the sequence. In essence, of course, this is both a 'feedback' and a 'feedforward' hypothesis. A number of experiments that they performed support the basic contentions of this model.

In summary, therefore, it appears that decoding fluent speech (as opposed to isolated words) is a very complex and interactive process. Cues are taken from the words themselves and from their position in the speech and also from the sounds which make up the words. As Cole and Jakimik (1978) conclude, there is a considerable amount of active comprehension involved in word recognition: 'It is not only what we hear that tells us what we know; what we know tells us what we hear.' The problem for the designer of a synthesized speech output system, then, is to ensure that the computer's words are presented in such a way that the human listener is able to extract this information from them.

Grammatical rules

Ensuring that the words 'spoken' by the computer are able to be deciphered is only part of the problem of building an efficient speech output system. Although the words themselves may be crystal clear, a message may still not be accepted or understood, the meaning may be lost or forgotten, if the words are not arranged in some sort of correct order—if they do not conform at least to some sort of 'natural' language rules.

A simple example will explain the importance of this distinction. Take the two sentences:

(i) They are eating apples
(ii) They are eating apples

Both have the same words; if they were heard, the sounds would be decoded in the same way. However, they may not *mean* the same since each sentence can be interpreted in one of two ways:

First, 'What type of apples are they?': They / are eating apples
Second, 'What are those people doing?': They are / eating apples.

This simple demonstration, then, illustrates the distinction between decoding speech at a 'sound' level and at a meaning level. The sound level of decoding is directly observable and so is often called 'surface structure'. The level of meaning, however—the 'deep structure'—depends on having a knowledge of the language and rules which are stored in memory. This is not directly observable and has to be inferred from behaviour. It can also lead to many ambiguities and misunderstandings, as the example showed.

Deep structured language is generated from the surface structures using a set of rules called the syntax. It is these rules which allow us to produce an almost infinite number of phrases and sentences from a finite number of words and, moreover, produce them in a 'correct' fashion. Essentially, there are two aspects of English syntax: sequencing rules and hierarchical structures—the former being linguistic rules used to define speech acts, the latter being more 'behavioural' rules used to produce speech acts.

Sequencing rules are, essentially, the rules for generating sentences which are formally taught at school. They are the rules which state that a sentence must normally have within it a noun phrase and a verb phrase; that an adjective precedes a noun and an adverb a verb, etc. Using such sequencing rules we are able to realize that wheareas the noun phrase 'the big boy' is correct (because the noun follows the adjective which follows the article), the same words in another order—'the boy big'—is not. Such rules help us to realize errors in speech because they present simple formulae for generating the speech parts. For example:

Noun phrase = Article + Adjective + Noun

where *article* = 'a', 'an', 'the'
adjective = 'old','young,'helpful','tall', etc.
noun = 'boy', girl', 'man', 'dog', 'house', 'sand', etc.

Unfortunately, however, the rules as they stand do not provide a full definition of the permissible combinations of article, adjective and noun. For example, 'a old girl' is not permissible because of another speech rule which states that an adjective or noun beginning with a vowel (or, sometimes, 'h') should have 'an' as the indefinite article rather than 'a'. Furthermore, even some permissible combinations do not produce 'sensible' phrases. For example, it is quite proper to say 'the young sand', but it is not immediately meaningful. Finally, sequential rules do not help us to decide between the two interpretations of the ambiguous 'eating apples' phrase described earlier.

Because such sequential rules of grammar are used primarily to define the structure of a sentence and do not adequately describe its meaning, a number of linguists interested in the behavioural aspects of language (for example, Chomsky, 1957; Gleason, 1961; Miller, 1962) have analysed language more as a hierarchical structure. The essential feature of this type of analysis is that it relates more to the way that we use language in everyday speech than does the sequential system.

Take the sentence 'the typist strikes the keys'. If one were to show this sentence to an adult English speaker and ask him or her to indicate its chief parts, the division would probably occur between the two phrases *the typist* and *strikes the keys*. Within the context of the sentence, dividing the sentence between '*the typist strikes*' and '*the keys*' would not convey the intended meaning.

That a sentence often 'cracks' into appropriate major sub-parts appears to be a universal aspect of every speaker's feeling for his or her own language. It is also the basis for a hierarchical form of analysing grammar called 'constituent analysis' which divides a sentence into varying numbers of intermediate structural levels, depending on the complexity of the sentence.

Take, for example, the sentence 'the boy hit the ball'. This can be divided first into a noun phrase (the boy) and a verb phrase (hit the ball). The noun phrase can be further divide into an article (the) and noun (boy). The verb phrase, on the other hand, can be divided into a verb (hit) and another noun phrase (the ball). Again, this second noun phrase can be divided into an article (the) and noun (ball). Figure 5.12 shows how this hierarchical, branching structure can be formed and illustrates how the same sentence can be considered at different levels of analysis. Any two words that are joined at a node belong to a common constituent at a particular level of analysis. Using this type of analysis, then, we can differentiate between the sentence which answers the question 'What fruit are they eating?' and that which asks 'What type of apples are they?'.

A full discussion of the properties of this concept of grammar is given by authors such as Chomsky (1957) and Gleason (1961). However, in summary, it is important to realize that such structures allow us to understand how we can derive and analyse different sentences from the same words. Furthermore, as

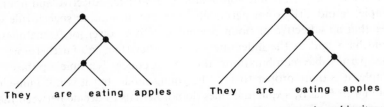

Figure 5.12.   The use of grammatical rules to reduce syntactic ambiguity.

Miller (1962) has shown, these different forms of sentences will be understood and remembered differently. Indeed, he has argued that sentences are not just arbitrary chains of vocal responses but, as has already been shown, they have a complex inner structure of their own:

> 'How we perceive them, understand them, and remember them depends upon what we decide about their structure. Just as we induce a three-dimensional space underlying the two-dimensional pattern on the retina, so we must induce a syntactic structure underlying the linear string sounds in a sentence.'

Interacting with speech synthesizers

Because of the difficulty in designing computer outputs that will 'speak' in a natural language, as with speech input devices the uses to which speech output devices are put generally are those which require only a limited vocabulary (around 200 words). This is certainly not enough to allow the machine either to carry out 'intelligent' conversations (if the appropriate programs were available) or even to generate unique sentences directed to specific actions. At present, all that is possible is to produce a finite number of word strings for actions such as warnings, instructions and the like.

The lack of a comprehensive vocabulary, however, does not present a major obstacle when using speech for output. As Kelly and Chapanis (1977) and Michaelis *et al.* (1977) have demonstrated, even highly restricted vocabularies, *if properly chosen*, can be just as efficient as unrestricted vocabularies. Michaelis (1980) further suggests that there is some evidence that, when compared with unrestricted dialogue, a well-chosen restricted vocabulary can actually improve user efficiency. On the basis of word usage in laboratory studies in which subjects had to interact using limited vocabularies, Michaelis *et al.* (1977) have produced a list of about 200 general English words that is useful for any application.

Although a restricted vocabulary can be used quite effectively, however, synthesized speech still is not natural speech and lacks many of the cues discussed earlier from which we extract much of the meaning—cues such as stress, intonation, accent, etc. With regard to intonation, however, Michaelis (1980) reports that by varying the length of time between words he was able to 'convey enough of a hint of inflection for your ears to fill in the rest'. Although this report was not supported by any statement of the success of the approach, the conclusions might have been expected given an interaction between timing and intonation in natural speech (Pike, 1972).

One further consideration which is important to the success of a synthesized speech system is the *type* of voice that is to be used. In this respect, attempts have been made to relate judged preference of voices to an ascribed personality of the speaker (Cox and Cooper, 1981). In one experiment subjects ranked several voices for preference and on 28 personality dimensions. On analysis, the personality ratings were combined to form two main factors—'agreeableness' and 'assertiveness'. The results demonstrated that agreeableness was the most important factor in determining the acceptability of the speaker (as a telephone announcer), and was reflected in high scores on the 'likeable', 'good natured', 'warmth' and 'popularity' scales. Assertiveness, on the other hand, which was indicated by high scores on the 'dominance', 'ambition' and 'strength' scales, was not so important an attribute. With regard to this factor a difference emerged in terms of the ratings given to male and female speakers. Male speakers were rated lower for exhibiting the assertiveness whereas female speakers were rated higher.

For many of these reasons, much of the empirical data relating to performance using synthesized speech suggests that recognition and memory for the spoken messages is lower than with natural speech. For example, Pisoni (1981) found that when isolated synthetic and natural words were presented, response times for synthetic words and non-words were approximately 140 msec slower than for their natural counterparts. Pisoni and Hunnicutt (1981) report that when subjects were asked to recall the gist of simple stories, recall for the synthetically spoken stories was poorer than for those spoken in a natural voice. Luce, Feustel and Pisoni (1983) suggest that many of these difficulties arise as a result of the synthesized speech placing increased processing demands on our short-term memory capacities.

Finally, the message itself obviously needs to be considered—in terms both of the speed of presentation and the words which it contains. With regard to speed of presentation, Cox (1982) reports studies in which strings of digits 'spoken' in synthesized speech were read to subjects. The data suggest that memory performance could be improved considerably by increasing the duration of pauses between sub-groups of digits within the string. Indeed, he suggests that pauses of about one second should suffice.

With regard to the message content Simpson and Hart (1977) have shown that, for two-word warning messages, response time to the messages was shorter and intelligibility was higher when additional (redundant) words were included in the message to enhance contextual meaning. These findings were later replicated by Simpson and Williams (1980). Although such findings are clearly in line with the behavioural evidence, discussed earlier, that we decode words and sentences largely according to context, it should not be forgotten that adding extra words to the message will increase the time taken for the message to be given. The fact that overall response was reduced suggests that the average word processing time was quite significantly reduced when the messages had contextual meaning.

Simpson and Williams also considered the effect that an alerting tone had on response to these synthesized warning messages. Under normal circumstances, an alerting signal considerably reduces reaction time. However, the authors found that under these conditions overall response time was increased. Again, an explanation lies in the time needed to process both the signal (1 second) and message. Whereas the use of redundant contextual words helped to reduce the average word processing time, the alerting signal had no such effect. On the basis of these results, the authors suggest that if a warning message is used, then a redundant verbal word such as 'warning' or 'caution' is used as an alerting signal before the message.

SUMMARY

This chapter has considered two communication channels through which information from the computer can be conveyed to the operator—the eyes and the ears.

Visual presentation occurs primarily via visual display units and printers. In each case, it was shown that careful attention to the design of the different aspects of these hardware components—the characters, the presentation rate, the illumination, etc., is required in order to present the information in the most efficient manner.

With regard to auditory presentation through synthetic speech, it was demonstrated that, although it is possible to design machines that produce recognizable speech sounds and constructions, the complexities of natural language make it very difficult to produce an 'intelligent' speech producer. What is feasible, however, and what has been used to good effect, is speech output using a restricted vocabulary.

CHAPTER 6

The Computer Environment

The two previous chapters have discussed many of the important aspects of designing a computer system so that information can be passed to and from the operator in an efficient manner, without too many errors or causing too much fatigue. For this to happen, the information needs to be presented in a form that is able to be perceived and understood readily by the receiver—that is the operator when information is passed from the computer, and the computer when the operator is producing the information. Only when this 'man'-machine link is working effectively, when the computer 'understands' the operator and the operator 'understands' the computer's response, is the productive relationship between the two components likely to be at a maximum.

This point, of course, was made originally in Chapter 1 when the symbiotic relationship between people and their working situation was discussed in more detail. However, further reference to Figure 1.1 reveals another possible factor that could affect the efficiency of this link. This is the environment in which the interaction takes place and this can appear as physical or social features. These two aspects of the environment can take a number of different forms. Thus, the physical environment includes the working area itself (often called the 'workplace' or 'workstation'), the maintainance of posture through adequate seating, the presence or absence of noise, glare, etc., and the quality of such aspects as the thermal environment. The social environment includes all of those aspects which affect our relationships with other people: satisfaction with the job, the setting up of territories and groups, the need for social space, etc. Any or all of these environmental factors can contribute to produce adverse working conditions which are likely to affect both a person's arousal level and the level of spare mental capacity. As was discussed in Chapter 1, either increasing arousal or reducing spare mental capacity can have detrimental effects on overall performance.

This chapter, then, will consider these physical and social aspects of the environment, the ways in which they can affect the symbiotic relationship and thus the efficient operation of computer systems.

THE USE OF SPACE

The space surrounding the computer working place is extremely important from the viewpoints of both physically restricting the operator's movements and interfering with feelings of well-being. Thus, three features will be considered in detail. Firstly the design of the computer workstation, secondly the design and use of seating—which can affect mobility, and thirdly the effects that space can have on our social behaviour and overall performance.

THE COMPUTER WORKSTATION

Two important considerations need to be taken into account when designing a computer operator's immediate working area. These are firstly, that the operator should actually 'fit' into the area available and physically be able to operate whatever input devices are to be used (for example, to reach and manipulate the keyboard, the screen, or some other peripheral device such as a joystick or lightpen). This clearly has implications for the man–machine side of the system. Secondly, the operator needs to be able to perceive the computer output (usually to see information on the screen but also, perhaps, to hear synthesized speech). In this case adverse aspects of the immediate physical environment (such as glare or excessive noise) are likely to affect the machine-man link.

Anthropometry and the workstation

As far as the first of these considerations is concerned, that the machine is designed in such a way that the operator is able to 'fit' into it, the important considerations revolve around the structure of the body in terms of the dimensions of various important body parts (the arms, legs, trunk, etc.). This area of study is known as anthropometrics, the term being derived from two Greek words: *anthropo(s)*, meaning human, and *metricos*, meaning of, or pertaining to, measurement. With its closely related field of biomechanics, (the study of mechanical properties of the body) anthropometry deals with measuring the physical features and functions of the body, including linear dimensions, weight, volume, range of movements, etc.

The importance of considering the physical fit between the operator and the environment relates mainly to its effects on muscles over long periods of use. A poor 'fit', one in which the body's dimensions do not relate to those of the system, is likely to make the operator adopt a posture which is not one that would be taken through choice. Arms and hands may have to be operated closer to the body than is ideal; the spine may have to be bent; the legs may not fit under the desk or the feet touch the ground, etc. Under these conditions the muscles are likely to be under increased static load. That is they have to maintain tension without the adequate blood and oxygen supply that arises normally with dynamic work (see the discussion of muscular fatigue in Chapter 4). It may be remembered that some of these considerations were discussed in Chapter 4 with the studies of keyboard design and shape. Thus, a flat keyboard forces the operator to adopt unnatural hand, wrist and arm positions that can rapidly lead to muscular fatigue.

Many examples of the effects of such constrained workstation postures abound. For example, Hünting, Läubli and Grändjean (1981) report results of questionnaire surveys and observations from nearly 300 workers using different types of office environments, including computer terminals. Some of their results are illustrated in Figure 6.1, from which it can be seen that postural complaints increased significantly in those workers who had to adopt unvarying, constrained postures at computer terminals (i.e. the data-entry and conversational terminals). The complaints were fewer for typists and traditional office workers. Interestingly, too, those workers at the data-entry terminals, who used only one hand to enter numbers on the keyboard, reported significantly more postural complaints than did those at conversational terminals who used both hands to input alphanumeric data.

In addition to muscular and postural problems, a poor fit between the operator and system can also lead to circulatory problems. Thus, Pottier, Dubreuil and Mond (1969) have demonstrated that prolonged sitting (for longer than 60 minutes) produces swelling in the lower legs of all sitters, which is caused by an increase in hydrostatic pressure in the veins and by compression of the thighs causing an obstruction in the returned blood flow. Stranden *et al.* (1983) have suggested that a 'footstool' which incorporates a pivot to allow a 'treadle' action might reduce the amount of swelling.

Clearly, therefore, it is important to design the workstation to fit around the operator and, to do this, appropriate anthropometric data are required. Until relatively recently, however, the main source of anthropometric data has been from military settings. This has possibly arisen for two reasons. First, large numbers of subjects need to be measured to obtain representative dimensions of a particular body part for a population. Military scientists have at their 'disposal' many thousands of available men and women, particularly during wartime. Second, the development of faster fighting machines which need to carry more complex equipment has meant that space available for the operator is increasingly at a premium. The need, therefore, effectively to build a machine around a single operator whilst, at the same time, to build for a number of different operators, has meant that appropriate anthropometric data has become a very valuable commodity. In addition, of course, anthropometric data have been needed for the design of efficient clothing for use in a number of different theatres of war.

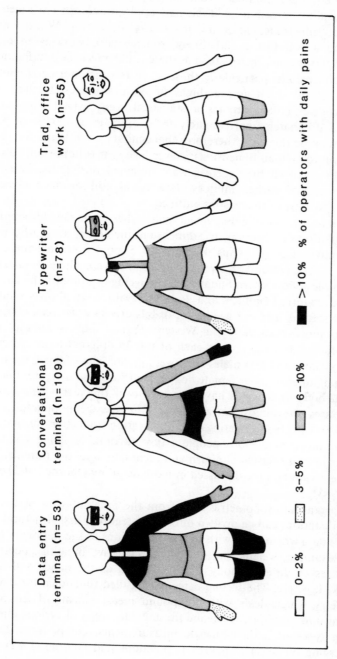

Data entry terminal (n=53)

Conversational terminal (n=109)

Typewriter (n=78)

Trad, office work (n=55)

☐ 0–2%   ▨ 3–5%   ▧ 6–10%   ■ >10%   % of operators with daily pains

Figure 6.1.   Reported incidence of daily body and eye pain in four different office jobs (Hünting, Läubli and Grandjean, 1981). Reproduced by permission of Taylor & Francis Ltd.

Computers at Work

Unfortunately, data obtained from military personnel are likely to give slightly misleading information if civilian applications are envisaged. For example, conscripts measured during or just after the Second World War may not have had a full diet or are likely to have been working in difficult surroundings. Over time, factors such as these could affect the development of some body dimensions, particularly those of parts which normally contain a fair amount of fat (such as the thighs or buttocks). Despite these fears, however, Kroemer (1983) reports a statistical study which suggests that military data do match approximately 99% of male and 94% of female civilians. It may be the case, therefore, that military data could give a good approximation to civilian dimensions. Nevertheless, it is important to realize that the data reported by Kroemer were obtained during the late 1960s. Unrestricted use of earlier military data could still produce misleading information for some of the reasons outlined.

In addition to the type of employment many other factors are also known to affect a population's anthropometric dimensions including, obviously, age and even the country of origin. Thus, Roberts (1975) points out that the average male height of the Central African Pigmy tribes is 144 cm whereas males of the Northern Nitoles of Southern Sudan have an average stature of 183 cm. Even in the same country, Guillien and Rebiffé (1980) have shown significant variations in stature. The average height of bus drivers in Eastern France was about 2 cm more than those in Western France. Sex is another major influencing factor. For example in each of the 34 different hand dimensions measured by Garrett (1971) males sizes were greater than female sizes. With pregnancy a number of other female body dimensions also increase. Finally, it appears that body dimensions have increased over the years. Thus Kroemer (1983) discusses the almost linear increase in average population stature between 1920 and 1980, relating the observation to better nutrition and hygiene. As more and more people enjoy favourable living conditions, however, the increase should diminish and eventually level out (Stoudt, 1978). Many of these variables are discussed in more detail by Oborne (1982) and by Kroemer (1983).

The important anthropometric data from the point of view of designing efficient workstations can be divided into two categories: first structural (often called static) data which deals with simple dimensions of the stationary human being—for example, weight, stature, and the lengths, breadths, depths and circumferences of different body structures such as the hands and fingers, arms, trunk, legs, etc. The second category is called functional (or dynamic) anthropometry which deals with compound measurements of the moving human being—for example, reach and the angular ranges of various joints.

For both types of anthropometric measurements, comparative data are slowly emerging on selected civilian populations and Oborne (1982) details some of the more easily available reports. A collection of papers edited by Easterby, Kroemer and Chaffin (1982) also provide useful civilian data. For complete data sets, however, Damon, Stoudt and McFarland (1971) have collated and tabulated the results of most studies reported before the end of the 1960s. Although most of these data are from military populations, bearing in mind Kroemer's arguments of a reasonable fit between military and civilian data, they can be useful to have in the absence of appropriate civilian data. Regarding functional anthropometry, the most simple forms of such data are tables which indicate the ranges of motion of individual body articulations. In this respect the definitive study remains that of Dempster (1955).

Before discussing how such data can be used to design appropriate workstations, one important consideration is to decide in which form the data should be applied. For example, if overall stature is to be used it soon becomes apparent, when simply looking at representatives of a population, that there is a wide range of statures. To be able to use the data effectively, some statistical analysis needs to be performed on it—usually to produce an idea of the average dimension and an index of its variability within the population. Often, however, such measures are of little use: take, for example, the height of a desk. If it was designed to such a height that a person having an 'average' lower leg length would fit into it then, by definition, only half of the population (those with lower legs of average length or less) would fit. The desk height, then, needs to be designed to be *larger* than the average appropriate dimension. On the other hand, when dealing with a dimension such as reach, the distance employed needs to be *smaller* than the average reach of a population. If it were larger than average then, again by definition, the smaller 50% of the population would be unable to reach.

Just how much larger or smaller than average a particular dimension needs to be depends on the importance and function of the feature being designed. For example, a joystick is useless if it is placed outside of the user's reach and so the reach dimension in this case would need to be related to the reach of the *smallest* member of a particular user population. At the other extreme, and taking a military example, an escape hatch in a submarine would need to be large enough to allow all (100%) of the users through (with their clothes) in an emergency. Other dimensions, however, may not be so critical. For example, as long as adjustable chairs are available, a desk height does not need to be large enough to accommodate all users' heights and so could possibly be designed to accommodate, say, 90 or 95%. For these reasons it is important also to have details of the variability of the various body structures in addition to the 'average'. For most purposes, a range of dimensions from the 5th to the 95th percentile (that is, from a dimension representing the smaller 5% to one which represents 95% of the population) is generally acceptable. Kroemer (1983) provides a useful summary of the problems of using anthropometric statistics, whilst Grieve and Pheasant (1983) provide more detailed statistical information.

A further problem with the over-use of simple averages as statistical indicators should be pointed out. This is the fallacy of the 'average person'.

Because the dimensions of various body parts are not related in a constant ratio, it is not possible accurately to describe the dimensions of one part by reference to another. Thus, it is not possible to say, for example, that because a person has an average height he or she will also have an average arm length. Robinette and McConville (1981) have demonstrated this fact both statistically and by practical example and, as long ago as 1952, Daniels demonstrated the fallacy of this 'average man' concept. He considered the dimensions of 1055 subjects who had an average stature and found that only 302 (29%) also had an average chest girth, 143 (14%) had average chest girth and sleeve length, etc. Indeed when only six body dimensions were added to the equation he found only six of the original sample were 'average' in all six dimensions. (It should be noted that Daniels, conservatively, defined 'average' as falling in the central 25% of the dimension distribution. Had he taken a true average of mean $\pm$ 0 s.d., the proportion that is average in all dimensions would have been much smaller.)

Finally, when considering the anthropometric requirements for computer systems, it is as well to remember that the work that is done at a computer is not necessarily always that of communicating with the machine via a keyboard and screen, speech, or any other device. Often, computers break down and under such circumstances have to be maintained or mended. This means that other workers, in this case maintenance personnel, have to be able to operate on (rather than with) the machine—and often inside of it. With the increasing trends towards miniaturization the problem of the maintenance worker's accessibility to the machine or to the component in question becomes of paramount importance. This applies equally well to large, mainframe computer systems into which the operator might need to climb or to crouch behind as to small microcomputers into which the operator may need to manipulate the hands or fingers. At both extremes, and in all cases in between, efficiency is likely to be reduced if insufficient consideration is given to the anthropometric dimensions of the appropriate body or limb, plus any associated protective clothing such as gloves or overalls.

Vision and the workstation

Although the preceding discussion of anthropometric requirements might at first appear to be stating the obvious, as will be demonstrated it is often the case that they are overlooked with the result that fatigue and postural problems beset the operators who have to work constantly with computer systems. The same is true for visual features of the work: it is obviously important to ensure that the operator is able actually to *see* the computer keyboard, the screen, etc. However, simple observation of any computer workplace will show that even this basic requirement is often violated. The visibility requirements of an operator are often hindered in either or both of two ways: first, if the overall illumination level is too low to be able to see the material accurately, or too high that glare results—the implications of this will be discussed later; second, if the lines of sight are obstructed by other equipment, peripherals, paper, etc. or even by other operators—this is clearly a problem which relates to the placement of the various components which go to make up the computer workstation.

Finally, it should be pointed out that rather than designing a workstation to provide for maximum visibility, it may be more sensible sometimes to ensure that visibility is obscured, perhaps be erecting screens or arranging the computer station in appropriate ways. This is particularly so in two cases: first, when requirments for privacy override visibility considerations (privacy, in this case, might imply personal privacy or privacy regarding the computer material); second, to shield an operator from too high a glare source which might otherwise impair visual performance.

As was apparent when discussing some of the visual fatigue symptoms often experienced after using VDUs, ensuring that all parts of the system are visible is not the only visual feature that needs to be considered. Thus, the previous chapter discussed the role of accommodation during vision, the process by which the lens curvature is varied to allow a clear image to fall on the retina. Clearly, if various pieces of material that have to be read—for example, the keyboard, copy, the screen, etc.—are placed at different distances from the eyes, the ciliary muscles in the eyes will have an increased workload which, over time, is likely to lead to 'visual fatigue'. This, taken with the observation that the eyes themselves have to converge by varying amounts to view objects at different distances, implies that the visibility requirements also include the need to consider how far material that has to be read should be placed from the operator.

Workstation dimensions

The foregoing discussion has highlighted the need to design the workstation to fit the user, both in terms of the user's body and visual abilities. It is now appropriate to consider the dimensions themselves: the dimensions which are important and the ranges of measurements that need to be applied.

Before discussing relevant dimensions, it is useful to consider the workplace dimensions that are currently in use. During their study of postural complaints referred to earlier, Hünting, Läubli and Grandjean (1981) measured various dimensions of different types of workstations. For each of the four office environments that they studied (data-entry, conversational, typing and general) most of the dimensions were very similar. Thus, the tables used in each of the workplaces were generally about the same height above the floor (70–76 cm), as were the keyboards from the floor (78–84 cm), seat heights (49–

51 cm) and keyboards above the seat height (28–33 cm). This similarity between the dimensions of the furniture used for different tasks suggests that designers had considered that one set of dimensions would suffice for all types of office task. That this was patently not the case was demonstrated by the varying severity of complaints between tasks that was described earlier.

When similar measurements were taken for the visual distances required (to the screen, typed text or source documents), however, the position was not the same. As is shown in Table 6.1, operators were required to read the material at different distances. Again, given the differing frequencies of visual complaints illustrated earlier in Figure 6.1 and discussed in the previous chapter, these data reinforce the need to consider carefully the visual aspects of workstation design.

When the authors considered the relationship between the workplace dimensions and the various complaints, they found that the lower the table and keyboards were above the floor, the more frequently were pains in the shoulder, neck and arms indicated. They suggest that this was due to the absence, in most cases, of a document holder which meant that the source documents were further from the eyes: 'the higher the documents, then the better is the posture of head and trunk, and the fewer are the complaints'. In addition, the terminal (data-entry and conversational) operators reported more pains in the hands and arms when the keyboards were higher than about 7–8 cm above the table.

When considering the design of keyboards in Chapter 4, it will be remembered that the keyboard *shape* was discussed as a source of efficiency loss owing to the operator having to adopt an 'unatural' hand–wrist–arm posture. The appropriate keyboard shape, of course, cannot be divorced from the overall postures adopted by the operator, and Hünting and his colleagues

Table 6.1. Average distances (cm) measured between operators and their visual material (Hünting, Läubli and Grandjean, 1981). Reproduced by permission of Taylor & Francis Ltd.

	Average distance (cm)	
	To terminal or text	To documents
Data entry terminals	58	48
Conversational terminals (moveable keyboard & screen)	62	47
Conversational terminal (fixed keyboard & screen)	43	53
Typing	47	57
Traditional office work	47	52

also considered this aspect in their study. They recorded the amount of ulnar abduction of operators' hands (that is, bending the forearm into the body and the hand away) using different keyboards. Their results, shown in Figure 6.2, indicate a sharp rise in pain complaints with abductions greater than about 20°.

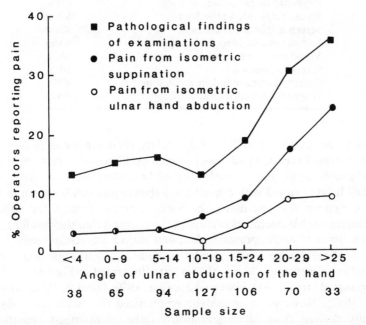

Figure 6.2.   Relationship of reported pain with the extent of ulnar abduction of the hand (Hünting, Läubli and Grandjean, 1981). Reproduced by permission of Taylor & Francis Ltd.

When considering the relationship between posture and complaints, it is also appropriate to consider the 'natural' behaviour of operators. In this respect Hünting and his collegaues observed how their operators rested their hands and arms on the desk and the ways in which they arranged their work to enable then to see all relevant material. Those operators who frequently rested their hands and arms on the desk also reported fewer arm, neck and shoulder complaints. Furthermore, higher complaints were reported by those who had to turn the head and neck more frequently.

In a comprehensive series of experiments designed to consider the optimal dimensions of computer workstations, Grandjean *et al.* (1982) asked 30 subjects to work at a workstation which had a number of adjustable features including the keyboard height, screen height above the floor and table, screen distance and inclination, etc. The overall preferred dimensions for each of

Table 6.2. Preferred workstation dimensions obtained
by Grandjean *et al.* (1982). Reproduced by permission
of Taylor & Francis Ltd.

Dimension	
Keyboard height above the floor	77cm
Screen height above the floor	109cm
Screen height above the table	32cm
Screen distance from table edge	65cm
Visual distance to screen	66cm
Screen inclination	90°
Source–document holder inclination	49°
Height of seat surface above floor	47cm

these variables are shown in Table 6.2. Clearly, these are averaged dimensions and, as discussed earlier, should not be taken as the actual levels to be designed for *every* dimension. For example, the authors illustrate how the preferred keyboard heights varied with overall body stature and this is shown in Figure 6.3. For reasons such as these, the authors argue strongly for adjustable workstations so that operators can adopt the postures that they prefer.

On the basis of anthropometric data and various suggestions such as those outlined above, some recommendations have arisen regarding idealized workstation dimensions. Many of these are illustrated in Figures 6.4 and 6.5 (amalgamated from Cakir, Hart and Stewart, 1980; Dainoff, 1982; Grandjean *et al.*, 1982). However, it should be emphasized that such dimensions are generally derived from static situations, rather than measurements taken

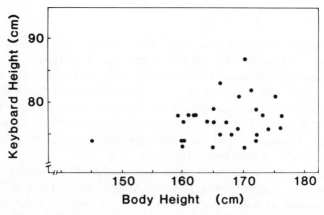

Figure 6.3. Relationship between body height and preferred keyboard height (Grandjean *et al.*, 1982). Reproduced by permission of Taylor & Francis Ltd.

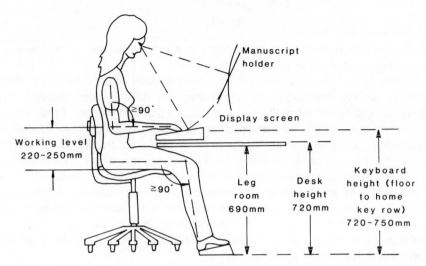

Figure 6.4. Some relevant workstation dimensions (adapted from Cakir, Hart and Stewart, 1980).

during normal work. In this respect, Grandjean, Hünting and Piedermann (1983) report that measurements taken from operators a few days *after* they had set their workplace dimensions often differed significantly from their initial 'preferred' settings.

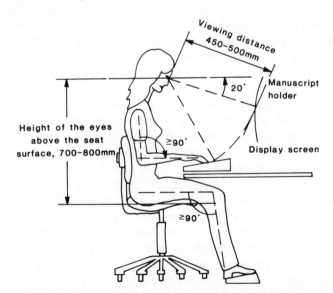

Figure 6.5. Some relevant workstation dimensions for viewing the copy and screen (adapted from Cakir, Hart and Stewart, 1980).

SEATING

In the preceding discussion the seating was often referred to as being an important feature of the operator's environment in that it plays a large part in determining posture. The seat is generally an integral part of the workstation and the various dimensions that are appropriate for a standing operator are likely to be different from those that a seated operator requires. Many of the considerations relating to seating, then, concern the dimensions needed to function at a particular workstation. Thus the chair height, for example, should be adjusted so as to enable the arms to be approximately horizontal; the height of any arm rests need to be related to the height of the underside of the desk, etc. In addition to such workstation-related dimensions, however, an adequate seat design also needs to take account of the sitter's dimensions and behaviour. For this reason the orthopaedic and muscular aspects of maintaining a seated posture need to be considered, in addition to the behavioural features of the sitter.

Orthopaedic aspects of sitting

When seated the primary support structures of the body are the spine, pelvis, legs and feet. Possibly the most important of these is the spine which is composed of 33 vertebrae. For convenience of description these are divided into four areas that roughly correspond to the shape of the spine: the topmost seven _cervical_, the twelve _thoracic_ and five _lumbar_ vertebrae, followed by five fused _sacral_ and four fused _cocygeal_ vertebrae. From the point of view of seating design, the orientation of the lumbar and sacral vertebrae are important since it is these vertebrae and their respective intervertebral discs and muscles which take most of the spinal load of a seated person.

Since it is reasonable to assume that a curved spinal shape has evolved to be one which is most efficient at withstanding these loads, it is also reasonable to suggest that an efficient seat should support the spinal shape and should not unduly alter it for long periods. The orthopaedic aspects of seat design, then, essentially revolve around considerations of spinal shape whilst sitting.

Keegan and Radke (1964) used X-rays to view the shape of the spine whilst in a relaxed position with the person lying on one side (this, they suggest, produces the 'natural' spinal shape) and in various seated postures. Their results suggest that the sitting posture which produces the nearest approximation to the 'normal' lumbar shape is one in which the trunk–thigh angle is about 115° and the lumbar part of the spine is supported with a backrest. A forward posture, adopted by many keyboard operators, caused the normally forwards-bent lumbar area to be straightened, with associated alterations to the thoracic and cervical areas causing a 'hunchback' posture. The implications of such a posture are dealt with in detail by Mandal (1981).

As Grandjean (1973) points out, this trend can be arrested by providing support to the upper edge of the pelvis since, in a hunched posture, the pelvis would make a backwards rotation.

Andersson (1980) reports a series of studies which investigated the effects of lumbar support and backrest inclination on the pressures exerted on the intervertebral discs between the vertebrae. His results, shown in Figure 6.6, emphasize the need for maximum lumbar support during sitting and, again, suggest that a backrest inclination of at least 115° produces minimal pressure to deform the spine.

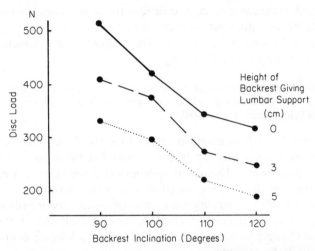

Figure 6.6. Relationship between disc pressure and backrest inclination with different levels of lumbar support. With permission from Andersson, 1980. Copyright: Academic Press Inc. (London) Ltd.

Evidence from orthopaedic studies, therefore, attests to the need for a backrest to support the lumbar area and to stabilize the pelvic backwards rotation. As to the angle of this backrest, one resulting in a trunk–thigh angle of 115° would seem to be appropriate.

Muscular aspects of sitting

Because vertebrae are kept in position by muscles and tendons, any alteration to a 'natural' spinal shape will produce corresponding stresses on the spinal musculature. These increases in muscle activity can be demonstrated and measured by recording the electrical potentials produced by the different muscles (a process known as electromyography or EMG).

Again, the studies which have been performed in this area support the orthopeadic data in that they suggest strongly the need for a suitable backrest, which is inclined at an angle greater than 110°. For example, Andersson (1980) reports data relating to the muscular activity obtained from the lumbar and thoracic regions whilst sitting in chairs with different backrest sizes and inclinations. Whereas the size of the backrest had only a minor influence of muscle activity, the effect of inclination was quite considerable, with an inclination of 110° producing only 25% of the muscle activity that was caused by one of 80° (i.e. leaning forward by 10°).

An interesting use of muscle recording data was made by Mandal (1976, 1981) to suggest that working chairs should be tilted forwards. He measured the extent of muscle elongation of sitters in various chairs with both forwards and backwards tilting seat pans, and demonstrated less muscle elongation and a more even pressure distribution over the seat using a forward-tilting (by 15°) rather than a backward-tilting seat. He supports these conclusions with observations of people actually sitting:

> 'That this position really is one of the most frequently used can quite clearly be seen as only the front part of the seat covers of old office chairs is worn; the rear part being almost untouched'.

His suggestion for a forward-tilting seat alone should be treated with some caution, however, since this can help to destabilize the body and increase its tendency to slip forward. The use of appropriate covering or shapes, however, could alleviate this drawback (Corlett *et al.*, 1983). Nevertheless, Grandjean (1973) reports studies to suggest that although such forward-tilting seats do reduce the amounts of pressure exerted on the seat itself and on the backrest, they induced changes in the spinal shape with the back being maintained in a straighter and flatter attitude.

Behavioural aspects of sitting

Whilst discussing the muscular aspects of seating, it became apparent that it is important to consider the behaviours that a sitter adopts. For example, Mandal's observations that the front edge of a seat often assumes importance for seated workers illustrates the value of examining behaviour under natural settings. Similarly, Grandjean *et al.*'s observations (1982) that people adopt different postures at a computer workstation and that these can create different types of pain complaints provides an example of the ways in which individual behaviour can interact with the environment to affect the efficiency of a design.

It is important to consider seating behaviour, then, since different behavioural interactions with the environment can lead to variations in operator performance. When relating behaviour to efficiency, however, it is important the right type of behaviour is considered and it is at this point that that a subtle change in criterion should be noted as far as seats and seat design are concerned. Thus, in the discussions in previous chapters the measures of efficiency have been couched, essentially, in terms of the speed and accuracy of the operator's response, and the ability to cope with and to respond to incoming information. Fatigue and poor anthropometric fit have been emphasized as contributing factors which can help towards reducing performance effectiveness. In seating, however, the criterion is expressed more in terms of a reduction in fatigue and excessive pressure on parts of the body— particularly the spinal column. Increases in muscular fatigue help to reduce comfort and so, in terms of the discussion in Chapter 1, increase arousal and reduce the amount of the available 'spare mental capacity'. Reduced comfort, then, leads eventually to reduced performance.

The primary criterion for seating, then, is comfort. However this is a concept which is very difficult both to define and to measure: we know when we are comfortable but often cannot explain why. Indeed, the definition of comfort might better be couched in terms of discomfort. As an analogy Branton (1972) uses the definition of health: it is only possible to state that a person is healthy by virtue of the fact that there is no sign of an illness. By itself, health is not a provable commodity. Branton further suggests that the absence of discomfort does not mean the presence of a positive feeling but merely the presence of no feeling at all:

'There appears to be no continuum of feelings, from maximum pleasure to maximum pain, along which a momentary state of feelings might be placed, but there appears to be a continuum from a point of indifference, or absence of discomfort, to another point of intolerance, or unbearable pain'.

Such an argument suggests, therefore, that the ideal state is one in which a person loses all awareness of the surroundings; of the seat and of the posture. When in this condition a person is able to give undivided attention to the task in hand.

The important question now becomes one of how can a seat induce discomfort? Mention has already been made of the longer-term muscular and orthopaedic problems that can arise from sitting in a seat which induces an unnatural posture but, in the shorter term, problems arise as a result of compression of the flesh on parts of the body.

When sitting in a seat without back or arm support, contact with the seat is made essentially only by two rounded bones at the bottom of the pelvis called the ischial tuberosities. Although this part of the buttocks is covered with relatively little flesh, because of the pressures placed on this area by the sitting person the blood supply to the buttocks can still be restricted. Indeed Dempsy (1963) has pointed out that the human body supports approximately 75% of the total body weight on 25 cm^2 of the ischial tuberosities and the underlying flesh. He also suggests that this load is sufficient to produce 'compression fatigue' which varies with the compressive load of the body and the duration of loading.

'In physiological terms, compression fatigue is the reduction of blood circulation through the capillaries, which affects the local nerve endings and results in sensations of ache, numbness and pain.'

Over long periods blood circulation to the capillaries in the buttocks is also reduced if the body is unable to move at regular intervals. If it is confined in a relatively fixed seating position for more than about four hours, the physiological functions that control the flow of body fluids slow down. This action, coupled with continuous pressure loading on the flesh, accelerates the rate of compression fatigue. However, the fatigue can be delayed by periodic movements of all of the major body segments, and this results in changes in the loading conditions and allows muscular expansion and contraction for adaptation to new weight conditions.

The behavioural 'symptoms' of impending compression fatigue, then, are movements of the body to vary the pressure distributions over the buttocks and thighs, that is, fidgeting. Indeed Branton and Grayson (1967) used these movements as an index of seat comfort. They recorded the changes in sitting posture (fidgets) of 18 subjects during a 5 hour train journey while sitting in one of two types of seats. On the basis of the significant increase in the number of fidgets produced in one seat over the other, the authors were able to recommend which seat should be adopted for use.

Any summary of these three considerations (orthopaedic and muscular on the one hand, and behavioural on the other) must lead to antagonistic requirements for seating design. Thus the orthopaedic and muscular considerations suggest strongly that the sitter should be supported as much as possible; that the intervertebral discs and muscles should be constrained in order that the pressures that they experience and work that they need to do to support a particular posture should not be excessive. Indeed, simple observation shows that, in these terms, sitters often actively seek body stability by crossing the legs or resting the arms on a table. The behavioural evidence, however, suggests that the seat should allow the sitter to move body parts; that the sitter often needs to fidget to reduce compression fatigue. Unfortunately, a seat which allows movement is unlikely to be one which provides a great deal of support.

To accommodate these two requirements, Branton (1966) has formulated a theory of postural homeostasis. Homeostasis is a concept which is widely understood in physiology and concerns the self-regulation of body functions. A common example is body temperature regulation: if the body temperature rises sweat is produced which, when it evaporates, has a cooling effect. If the body becomes cold, however, the blood is routed away from the skin to warmer, central parts of the body.

One of the characteristics of such homeostatic activities is that they a.e autonomic; they are not under deliberate, conscious control and awareness only comes with drastic changes of conditions—and then only after the event has occurred. Branton argues that postural activity falls within the same category of autonomic regulation. Postural homeostasis is a process by which the sitter strikes a compromise between needs for stability and variety, so that sitting behaviour will be characterized by cycles of both inactivity and activity. An efficient and comfortable seat, therefore, needs to be able to accommodate these homeostatic requirements and allow the sitter both stability and flexibility.

Dimensions for work seats

From the orthopaedic, muscular, behavioural and anthropometric data that are available, a number of suggestions can be made for the design of work seats. It must be stressed, however, that the dimensions apply only to the 'average' use of a seat—for sitting in and for doing work such as typing. Work seats for specific activities, or for tasks in abnormal environments (for example, with high levels of vibration) will require other considerations. Furthermore, it should be pointed out that the data provided below represent an amalgam of research data derived by a number of different investigators using different types of subjects (for example, male, female; paid, unpaid), sitting for differing lengths of time and performing different types of task. As Grandjean (1973) illustrates, this produces quite a wide variation in design proposals.

Seat height (43–50 cm)

The height is adjusted correctly when the sitter's thighs are horizontal, the lower legs vertical and the feet supported either by the floor or a foot rest. Because the soft undersides of the thighs are not suitable for sustained compression—caused particularly by the front edge of the seat pan—the limiting case of a seat without a foot rest is that of the short-legged person who would be prevented from resting the feet on the floor.

Many authors recommend that working chairs should be made to allow the height to be adjusted to accommodate the wide range of workers who may have to use them. With such chairs the presence of an adjustable foot rest is also strongly recommended.

Seat width (43–45 cm)

In this case the largest person needs to be accommodated. Since the appropriate dimension is the hip width, and since major sex differences occur in this dimension, the limiting case should be the upper range of a female sitter.

Seat depth (35-40 cm)

At work it is particularly important to ensure that the seat is not so deep that the back cannot effectively use the backrest.

Seat angle (3° backwards-tilting–15° forwards-tilting)

This is the angle between the seat pan and the horizontal. The difference in recommendations reflects two design philosophies. The first (backwards-tilting) suggests that the seat pan angle should help the body to fall back into the backrest for lumbar support. The forwards-tilting angle reflects Mandal's suggestion that people working at a desk tend to lean forward and sit at the edge of the chair.

Backrest height and width (12-35 cm above seat, compressed if appropriate)

In order that the sacrum and fleshy parts of the buttocks which protrude behind a sitter can be accommodated, while at the same time allowing the lumbar region to fit firmly into the backrest, many authors suggest that the backrest should have an open area or should recede just above the seat pan. A space of at least 12.5-20 cm is required to accommodate the buttocks in this way.

Backrest shape and angle (103-112°)

Much has already been made of the need for a backrest to allow the lumbar muscles to relax when necessary. For this reason, it is appropriate that the shape of the rest should be such as to fit the lumbar area well. Both the orthopaedic and muscular evidence provided earlier suggest a seat–backrest angle of about 110° is appropriate. Grandjean (1973), however, argues that the backrest should be variable, both in height and in angle as is seen with many typists' chairs. This would then accommodate all shapes and preferred postures.

Cushioning and upholstery

Cushioning performs two important functions. First, it helps to distribute the pressures on the ischial tuberosities and the buttocks caused by the sitter's weight. This was demonstrated well by Diebschlag and Muller-Limroth (1980) who measured the pressure distributions under the buttocks when sitting on hard and soft upholstery. Secondly, cushioning helps the body to adopt a stable posture. To this end the body will be able to 'sink' into the cushioning which then supports it. In this respect, however, Branton (1966) raises a warning against the cushioning being too soft:

> A state can easily be reached when cushioning, while relieving pressure, deprives the body structure of support altogether and greatly increases instability. The body then 'flounders about' in the soft mass of the ... chair and only the feet rest on firm ground. Too springy a seat would therefore not allow proper rest, but may indeed be tiring because increased internal work is needed to maintain any posture.

Kroemer and Robinette (1968) agree with Branton's position and also caution that soft upholstery will allow the buttocks and thighs to sink deeply into the cushioning. If this occurs all areas of the body that come into contact with the seat will be fully compressed, offering little chance for the sitter to adjust position to gain relief from pressure. In addition, the body often 'floats' on soft upholstery, again causing the posture to have to be stabilized by muscle contraction.

With regard to the seat covering, the important aspects are its ability to dissipate the heat and moisture generated from the sitting body (which will, in turn, be related to the type of thermal environment in which the sitter is sitting), and its ability to resist the natural forward slipping movement that Branton and Grayson (1966) recorded over time. For both of these criteria, adequate thermal and mechanical techniques exist to allow appropriate measurements to be made.

THE SOCIAL USE OF SPACE

So far, the emphasis has been placed on the use of space and area for physical requirements: to reach, to see, to relax in, etc. However it is important to remember that the area in which an operator works is also likely to contain other operators with whom interactions often take place. These, more social, relationships can also affect performance. Thus, the physical arrangements of both operators and the equipment that they operate may inhibit or facilitate these interactions and can have important implications for overall performance.

The social use of space is an extremely important aspect of a person's interaction with the environment, but is an area which appears to have been neglected by many designers. Many of the relevant research reports, for example, are to be found buried in the social psychological literature. Thus, despite the fact that the operator's environment includes other men and women, little attention has been given to the influence of social environmental parameters on performance, safety or comfort at work. This section will discuss below two important aspects of the social space requirements, personal space and territoriality, and will then consider how they may be taken account of at work.

Personal space

Personal space has been defined as an area with invisible boundaries
surrounding a person's body into which 'intruders' should not enter (Sommer,
1969). In essence the space can be considered as being composed as a series of
concentric 'globes' centered on the individual, each globe defining an area in
which various types of social interaction can take place.

Much of the early and basic work defining these space zones was performed
by Hall who was interested in the work of animal ethologists who observed the
various distances that animals maintain from one another in different
circumstances. (Indeed we use spatial metaphors in normal speech; thus we
talk about a person being 'distant', or two people being 'close' to each other.)
Hall expanded these ideas and observations and hypothesized four spatial
zones in humans used to regulate social interaction: intimate (up to 45 cm),
personal (between 45 and 120 cm), social (between 1 and 3.5 m) and public
(greater than 3.5 m) distance (see Hall, 1976). Each of these zones can be
further divided into a 'near' and a 'far' phase. However, the boundaries of
these zones are not necessarily constant, either between people or within a
person on different occasions; they often fluctuate for a number of different
reasons. The main point for the present discussion lies in the observation that
only certain classes of people are allowed to enter each space area. The
behaviour of a person whose space is violated may change considerably if the
'wrong' person infringes the 'wrong' zone.

Many variables affect the distances of these personal space zones and
include personality, sex, age, culture and the status of the individuals
concerned (see, for example, Evans and Howard, 1973). Thus some evidence is
available to suggest that extraverts have smaller personal space zones (that is,
they allow people to be closer) than introverts (Patterson and Sechrest, 1970).
With regard to sex, females have smaller zones of personal space, and hence
can tolerate closer interpersonal contacts, than males (Liebman, 1970). One
striking difference between the sexes is in the positions which each adopts;
research on attraction indicates that males prefer to position themselves *across
from* liked others, whereas females prefer to position themselves *adjacent* to
liked others (Byrne, Baskett and Hodges, 1971).

Very little work has been reported which explores the developmental aspects
of personal space, although Willis (1966) has demonstrated that people of
roughly the same age approach one another more closely than those who are
older. Differences in age, however, are often confounded with differences in
status and we treat people having higher status differently, to the extent of
interacting with them at greater distances. Correspondingly, those people of
higher status who wish to convey a friendly impression or a positive attitude
choose smaller interpersonal distances than neutral or unfriendly
communicators (Patterson and Sechrest, 1970).

Finally, clear differences may be observed in the spatial behaviour of members of different cultures. For example, Hall (1976) observed that Germans have a larger area of personal space and are less flexible than Americans in their spatial behaviour. Latins, French and particularly Arabs, on the other hand, were found to have smaller personal space zones than Americans.

Implications of invasion

When a stranger violates a person's space (that is, enters a particular zone not normally reserved for that person or for that type of person) then a complex number of reactions can occur which might include discomfort, tension, increased arousal and flight from the situation.

In a working environment, flight would be seen as an extreme reaction to invasions of personal space. However, less extreme reactions can still be exhibited—particularly in terms of increased levels of arousal. McBride, King and James (1965), for example, found that subjects' arousal (measured by skin resistance, GSR) increased for male subjects at close interpersonal distances, particularly when the males were interacting with a female invader. Similarly, Seguin (1967) reported increases in respiratory rate when subjects were closely approached by another person.

Other, less extreme, reactions were recorded by Patterson, Mullans and Romano (1971) who described both 'leaning away' and 'blocking out' responses, both of which were designed to 'exclude' the intruder. These responses increased in frequency as the intruder was seated closer to the victim. Mahoney (1974), although failing to replicate this study in terms of the moving responses, reported that subjects tended to 'freeze up' as a response to an invader.

Finally, invasions of personal space for longer durations can be considered to be symptoms of overcrowding, and a number of studies have demonstrated the detrimental effects of such conditions for the health of a population. For example, Lundberg (1976) measured the level of catecholamine (a pharmacological stress indicator) in the urine of selected passengers both before and after crowded or empty train journeys. Significant increases were obtained in the crowded conditions. D'Atri (1975) has also reported some moderate, positive correlations between the density of living quarters in a prison setting and high blood pressures for prison inmates.

With regard to the effects that these increases in arousal may have on performance, Evans (1978) suggests that most experimenters have found little or no effect on simple tasks. This is, of course, consistent both with the arousal–performance and the spare-mental-capacity models. More complex tasks, however, are affected. For example, Evans and Howard (1973) found that when subjects had to process information at slow and moderate rates of input, no effects were evident from space invasions. On the other hand, at high rates of signal input, there was a marked drop in performance as interpersonal distance was reduced. These findings were replicated, essentially, by Evans (1975). Furthermore, he found that in a dual-task situation, crowded subjects made significantly more errors than uncrowded controls on the secondary task, but not on the primary task.

Territoriality

The concept of territoriality is one which is widely understood in the animal world but has only been considered comparatively recently in relation to humans. Like personal space, it is a concept which invokes social, unwritten rules of space behaviour, with infringement of these rules causing discomfort and/or other behavioural reactions. It differs from personal space, however, in that one's territory does not have to move around with oneself, it can have fixed markers which have to be quite perceptible to others (animals often use scent).

Although different societies and political systems have different rules governing territoriality, there appears to exist a commonly shared distinction between territory which is private and that which is public. A private territory, for example a house or the space around a desk, may be occupied or owned *in absentia* by a single person who has authority to decide who may and who may not enter it. Public territory (for example, stairs, streets, public workplaces) is accessible to many diverse persons and cannot be owned by a single person. Nevertheless, as Fried and DeFazio (1974) and Oborne and Heath (1979) have argued, territories which are otherwise public, such as seats in public transport and libraries, may be converted to temporary private territories using such markers as coats, bags and books. Indeed, Fried and DeFazio suggest that certain implicit 'byelaws' exist with respect to privatized public territory. First the owner cannot be challenged or deprived of their territory except under very special circumstances such as high density. Second there should be very little verbal interaction between territory holders. These rules, of course, are very powerful. Taking a coat placed on a seat as an example, a passenger wishing to sit at the seat either must ask for the marker to be moved (thus contravening the second rule) or move it himself or herself, which contravenes other social rules.

The implications of these social space requirements for design are very important. Thus, as Oborne and Heath (1979) point out:

> No matter how well the physical environment has been designed to match man's behaviour ... social constraints may intervene to reduce the efficiency of the system. Thus the value of the perfect seat (in terms of comfort and reduced backache) may be reduced if it is placed so close to another that the two occupants' personal space requirements are infringed. A well designed

seminar or boardroom (in terms of noise level, temperature, ventilation, etc.) may be rendered ineffective if the seating arrangements are such that (a) the occupants are unable to mark their territories (for example, not enough desk space is provided to 'spread out' their papers), or (b) no account is taken of personal space requirements, with the result that the participants may tend to 'withdraw' into themselves to maintain 'distance'.

Landscaped offices

One practical suggestion to the problem of accommodating the space requirements that people have is to allow them to arrange the workplace as they wish. Individual territories can thus be set up as required so that infringements of personal space do not occur. This arrangement of both people and equipment in a more free way is embodied in the 'landscaped office' concept, said to have been proposed originally by West German furniture manufacturers, Ebhard and Wolfgang Schnelle, in the early 1960's (Brookes, 1972).

The important feature of the landscaped office lies in its lack of boundaries. Whereas a conventional office system might take the form of a floor which has been further subdivided into smaller offices by fixed walls and doors, a landscaped office will use the same floor space but the different work groups are scattered around without being restricted by walls or right angles. The geometry of the workspace is supposed to reflect the pattern of work processes and is arranged by the individuals rather than being imposed by a rectilinear plan.

The spatial needs of privacy and territory are meant to be accommodated by providing low, moveable screens and allowing the users, within limits, to arrange desks, chairs, bookcase, etc. (boundaries) as they see fit. Furthermore, it allows workgroups to adjust work areas to the changing needs of the business. Brookes and Kaplan (1972) also point out that for the concept to work properly all staff should participate—not just the clerical workers and a few supervisors. In this way the office emphasizes the social cohesion and group cohesiveness of the workforce.

The few controlled studies which have been carried out to investigate these claims do not lead to any firm conclusions. Brookes (1972) has reviewed the literature and concludes that information flow between workgroups might well improve in a landscaped office. So too does a perception of group cohesiveness. Furthermore the employees prefer the brighter, more colourful and friendlier design that such an office provides.

On the negative side, however, this type of office produces a greater loss of privacy, an increase in distractions and interruptions (see Nemecek and Grandjean, 1973) and, paradoxically, a perceived loss of control of the spaces around the workplaces. In terms of the loss of privacy, this occurs both at a visual and at an acoustic level.Thus, as Parsons (1976) points out: 'In the open-plan office, even with head height partitions, everyone can see whether or not someone is at work, present or absent, writing a report or reading the newspaper, thinking or catching forty winks, typing or with feet on desk. Everyone can see who is talking (directly) with whom.' The effect of a lack of acoustic privacy will be discussed later, but it includes both the direct effect that noise can have on the perception of speech, as well as the indirect effect that the perception of other people's speech can have on security.

Finally, it is interesting to note that employees in landscaped offices often perceive not only a loss of privacy but a loss of control around their space area. It appears, therefore, that allowing an employee to have physical control over the size and arrangement of the immediate workplace is not enough to overcome the problems posed by social space requirements. The employees must actually feel that they have control. Thus, whereas the landscaped office concept allows physical control, the lack of privacy which it engenders does not allow subjective control.

LIGHTING CONDITIONS

The visual system is possibly the most overloaded of an operator's sensory systems at work. At computer workstations an operator needs to be able to see the source documents, the display, the input devices, the output from printers, etc. Unfortunately, however, ensuring adequate types and levels of lighting is not necessarily a simple matter; as will become apparent it is not the case that simply increasing the illumination *level*, for example, will increase performance. This might happen, but only to a point: too much light can be as bad as, and sometimes worse than, too little light; light of the wrong colour or quality can sometimes be worse than low levels of 'good' quality illumination; light shining in the wrong place or creating poor contrast between the object and its background can often cause performance and comfort to be reduced by dramatic levels. All of these features need to be taken into account before the illumination levels of the workplace can be said to be appropriate.

Some definitions

Before discussing the effects of different types of illumination on performance and comfort, it is appropriate to consider how the various parameters of light are defined and can be measured.

Light can be conceived as fluctuating energy which reaches the eye, and the defining parameters of light are its intensity (the level of energy) and wavelength. Although the wavelength represents the speed at which the light fluctuates, it is actually measured in terms of the distance between two peaks of the fluctuating energy (rather like the distance between two waves on the sea). The wavelength units are nanometers (1 nm = 10^{-9}, or one-billionth, of a metre). As was discussed in Chapter 5, visible light is simply a form of radiation having a wavelength between 380 and 780 nm, and the eye discriminates between different wavelengths in this range by the sensation of colour.

The intensity aspects of light are rather complicated since light is often perceived not from the original light source but is reflected off various surfaces. (That these words can be read is due to the fact that different light levels are being reflected from the page into the eye, the light originating either from a light bulb or from the sun.)

Illumination or illuminance

The intensity of a light source is expressed in terms of the amount of luminous flux (energy) which it generates. Just as the power of a car is expressed in relation to the power likely to be produced by a 'standard' horse (horsepower), the luminous flux produced by a light source is measured by comparing it with the flux produced by burning a standard candle of a specified material and weight. This candle is said to produce one candle power (or 1 candela, 1 cd) of energy.

Although flux so far has been used effectively as a synonym for energy, strictly speaking it refers to the rate at which the energy is produced and is measured in 'lumens'. Indeed, because a spherical light source, say, is emitting light in all directions, 1 candela is also defined as 1 lumen per steradian (i.e. the rate of flux produced per solid angle of the body).

As energy radiates from a source it spreads out and loses its intensity as it travels through a dense medium such as air, water or glass and the amount of energy lost is inversely related to the square of the distance travelled (this is known as the inverse square law). Thus the level of illumination which falls on a surface will be lower than that which originated from the light source and, because of the diffusive nature of the medium through which it is travelling, will spread over the surface. Illumination, therefore, is defined in terms of the rate of flux (lumens) produced and the surface area over which it spreads (that is, lumens per square foot or lumens per square metre).

Unfortunately, the amount of flux being emitted from a source is not the only measure of the illumination of a surface. In addition to the inverse square law, there exists another law of illumination—the cosine law—which states that the illumination of any surface varies with the cosine of the angle of incidence of the surface to the direction of light. This means, then, that illumination is also a function of the angle of the light source to the surface being viewed. This is important for two reasons. First the efficiency of a light source can be varied by altering its angle of incidence to the surface—for example, by raising it or lowering it. Second, the light that falls on a surface only rarely, and under specific conditions, arises *solely* from a single source.

Most frequently it will arise both as direct illumination *and* as reflections from other surfaces—walls, ceilings, other objects, etc. These, themselves, can be conceived of as being individual light sources and the efficiency of each as a light source will depend on the angle at which they reflect light onto the surface.

In any environment, therefore, the amount of light falling on a surface will depend on a number of factors. These are the luminous intensities of the light sources, the distances of the sources from the surface, the angles of the sources to the surface and the number of original and reflecting sources in the immediate environment.

Luminance

Although a particular light level may fall on a body, this is not to say that the observer will 'see' that level since different bodies absorb and reflect different amounts and qualities of light, depending on their surface characteristics. For example, a highly polished surface may reflect around 90% of the light energy falling on it, whereas a dull, matt surface might reflect only about 10% of the light. In this case the term used to define the amount of light reflected from the surface of the body is its luminance and this is equal, simply, to the amount of light falling on the body multiplied by the proportion of light which the body reflects (its reflectance). Unfortunately for the novice illumination engineer, however, there are a multitude of terms to define luminance. It can be expressed either in terms of the luminous intensity per unit area (candelas per square metre), or in terms of the 'equivalent illumination' (equivalent lux), or apostilbs (asb), or in foot Lamberts (ft-L). The modern standard is to express it in terms of the candela per square metre, but a number of conversion tables exist to relate the various measures (see, for example, Megaw and Bellamy, 1983).

Brightness and retinal illuminance

The luminance qualities of an object, however, will only be perceived by an observer after the light has stimulated the retinal cells and the information passed to the optic cortex in the brain. At this point the concept of the body's brightness is invoked, which is the subjective aspect of its luminance. However, it is sometimes necessary to talk about the retinal illuminance when considering the response of the visual system to light. This is because the brightness of any image depends on the diameter of the limiting aperture of the image-forming device. In the eye this is set by the diameter of the pupil and retinal illuminance is measured in trolands (td). One troland is equal to the retinal illuminance obtained by looking through an artificial pupil having an area of 1 mm^2 at a matt surface whose luminance is 1 cd m^{-2}.

The relationship between these definitions can perhaps be explained by reference to Figure 6.7. Thus a source (for example, a light bulb) illuminates a body. The level of illumination or illuminance is likely to be measured in units such as lumens per square metre (lm m^{-2}). This is likely not to be the only source of light falling on the surface, however, and the total surface illuminance will depend also on the distances of the light sources and their

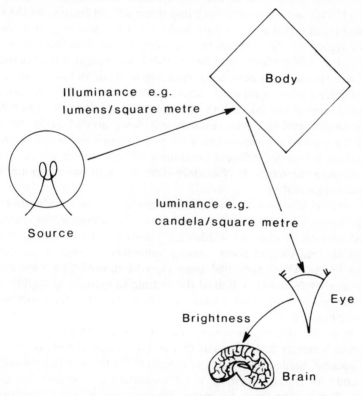

Figure 6.7. Relationship between illumination, luminance and brightness.

angles to the surface. The surface of this body reflects the total light to the eye of the observer, the intensity being determined by the surface reflectance and being measured in many units such as the candela per square metre (cd m^{-2}). The observer then reports the body's brightness, the intensity of the report being determined by the amount of retinal illuminance allowed by the pupil and the subjective experiences of the observer. These experiences, being subjective, are likely to depend on many factors including past experience and the brightness of other bodies in the visual field.

Lighting and behaviour

Most of the important information regarding the relationship between illumination quality and performance has been discussed already in Chapter 5 when considering the way that the visual system operates. However, it is appropriate to recap some of the material here. Thus, for any one viewer, performance is a function, primarily, of the overall illumination levels, the size of the object being viewed and the contrast between the object and its surround. This latter aspect is very important since it introduces the topic of glare and the effects that it can have both on comfort and on performance.

With regard to the relationship between overall illumination levels and performance, Gilbert and Hopkinson (1949) demonstrated that performance (visual acuity) reaches a peak at illumination levels of 10 lumens/sq ft (0.9 lm m^{-2}). Subjects with visual deficiencies, however, required much higher levels of illumination. A similar finding, that increased lighting will be of value only until a certain level has been reached, was demonstrated by Smith and Rea (1979). They asked subjects to check a list of 20 numbers for agreement with a comparison list under different conditions of task luminance (i.e. the light reflected from the page). Performance increased with luminance up to 10 cd m^{-2}, but not thereafter.

The relationship between overall illuminance and more subjective factors such as comfort presents similar conclusions. For example, Saunders (1969) allowed subjects to adapt to windowless rooms lit only by ceiling lamps and then asked them to read from a book. Subsequent ratings of the quality of illumination to which they had been exposed showed that with increasing illuminance levels, subjects judged the lighting to increase in quality until, at about 800 lm m^{-2}, no further value was shown to result from increasing the levels (see Figure 6.8).

As far as the size of the object (i.e. the task) is concerned, Gilbert and Hopkinson's results demonstrated that as the objects (letters on the Snellen chart) became smaller, more light was required for them to be read accurately. In its code for interior lighting, the Illuminating Engineering Society (IES) suggests illumination levels for many different types of work interiors which are related to the type of work carried out. Overall, seven levels are suggested, as shown in Table 6.3. The code suggests, however, that before deciding on an appropriate illumination level for the task in hand, four important questions should be asked:

1 Are the reflectances or contrast unusually low (for example, having to pick out dark objects from a dark, matt background)?
2 Will errors have serious consequences?
3 Is the task of short duration?,
4 Is the area windowless?

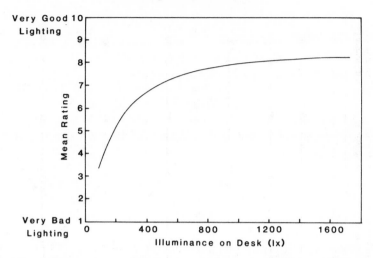

Figure 6.8. Quality of the lighting in a windowless office at different desk illuminations (Saunders, 1969). Reproduced by permission of the Chartered Institution of Building Services.

On the basis of answers to these questions, an appropriate illuminance level can be chosen as indicated in Table 6.3.

The contrast of the object refers simply to the relationship of the object luminance to its surround. It is a measure, then, of how well the object 'stands out'. Without contrast an object cannot be seen, and this applies equally to such stimuli as words on the printed page or on a visual display, to a large machine in a dimly lit room, or to a well-camouflaged soldier or to insects.

The normal way to express contrast is in terms of a ratio between the luminance difference of the object and its surround to the surround luminance. So, an object which is illuminated by 100 units of light placed on a background of 10 units will have a contrast ratio of $(100 - 10)/10 = 9$, as will a 10-unit object place on a 1-unit background.

Unfortunately, however, as Hopkinson and Collins (1970) point out the visual behaviour of the observer also needs to be taken into account when determining contrast relationships. For example, whereas two light meters may register 100 and 10 units in one case and 10 and 1 units in another, and so 'deduce' that the contrast ratios in the two cases are the same, an observer's perceptual system is likely to treat the two sets of stimuli differently because of a phenomenon known as brightness constancy.

To explain this phenomenon, suppose that an observer is looking at two different flat surfaces—one grey and one white—which are so illuminated to ensure that the *luminances* arising from them are equal. Since the stimulus received by the retinal cells is related to the luminance of the surface, and since

Table 6.3. A flow chart for modifying standard service illuminances for unusual conditions. (After IES Code, 1977)

Task group and typical task or interior	Standard service illuminance (lx)	Are reflectances or contrasts unusually low?	Will errors have serious consequences?	Is task of short duration?	Is area windowless?	Final service illuminance (lx)
Storage areas and plant rooms with no continuous work	150					150
Casual work	200				no → 200 / yes ↑	200
Rough work — Rough machining and assembly	300	no → 300 / yes ↗	no → 300 / yes ↗	yes ↑ / no → 300	no → 300 / yes ↗	300
Routine work — Offices, control rooms, medium machining and assembly	500	no → 500 / yes ↗	no → 500 / yes ↗	yes ↑ / no → 500	→ 500 / ↗ 500	500
Demanding work — Deep-plan, drawing or business machine offices; inspection of medium machining	750	no → 750 / yes ↗	no → 750 / yes ↗	yes ↑ / no → 750	750 → 750	750
Fine work — Colour discrimination, textile processing, fine machining and assembly	1000	no → 1000 / yes ↗	no → 1000 / yes ↗	yes ↑ / no → 1000	1000 → 1000	1000
Very fine work — Hand engraving, inspection of fine machining or assembly	1500	no → 1500 / yes ↗	no → 1500 / yes ↗	yes ↑ / no → 1500	1500 → 1500	1500
Minute work — Inspection of very fine assembly	3000	no → 3000 / yes ↗	no → 3000 / yes ↗	yes ↑ / no → 3000	3000 → 3000	3000

the two luminances are the same, it might be assumed that they would look the same. Unfortunately, they will not; the grey will still look greyer than the white *unless* they are not viewed together (say each is viewed through a tube in such a way that each surface covers the whole of the observer's field of view). Only under these very specific circumstances will the two appear to have similar luminances. Because an object exists within a frame of reference which contains other objects and surfaces, well-defined textures, contours, contrasts and colours, the optic cortex interprets the stimuli in terms of past experiences and expectations to ensure that the visual 'world' remains 'constant'.

Because of this phenomenon, Hopkinson and Collins suggest that contrast should be expressed not in terms of the actual luminance levels but of the difference between the 'apparent brightnesses' of the object and the surround. This rests on the assumption that everything that we see is evaluated, as far as brightness is concerned, in terms of some reference level which Hopkinson and Collins suggest is associated with the state of adaptation of the eye at the time. Light entering a large window, therefore, is likely to alter the eye's adaptive state and so affect vision by altering the apparent brightness of, say, characters on the visual display screen. Hopkinson, Waldram and Stevens (1941) have produced a set of curves from which one can read the apparent brightness of the object or surround given their respective brightnesses.

Although a high contrast is clearly important in ensuring that the object is perceived accurately, it is also important that the *direction* of the contrast effect is considered, for two reasons.

First, as was discussed in Chapter 5 some evidence exists to suggest that dark characters on a brighter background (negative contrast) lead to slightly higher performance and 'preference' ratings than the reverse (Bauer and Cavonius, 1980; Radl, 1980). This is possibly because the printed page is normally also in negative contrast so that adaptation is maintained when the gaze has to move from the screen to paper and back again.

The second reason for being concerned about the contrast direction arises if the surround is *considerably* brighter than the object, perhaps because of reflected light falling on the screen. If this occurs then both the visibility of the object and the visual comfort of the observer are likely to be reduced owing to glare. This will be discussed in more detail below.

As an example of the importance of contrast to efficient visual performance, in their illumination study Gilbert and Hopkinson (1949) asked their subjects to read the letters on a Snellen chart under different levels of illumination, using different contrast ratios between the letters and the background. Their results indicated strongly that as the contrast was increased the subjects' ability to read the letters accurately also increased. This effect was particularly marked at the lower levels of overall illumination, whereas the performance increase was not so marked when the overall illumination level was reasonably high.

When the eye has to move from one visual area to another the importance of considering the contrast ratios between the two areas becomes greater owing to the eye's adaptation level. Looking out of the window, for example, is likely to ensure that the retina is adapted to fairly high light levels; if the observer then attempts to read text on a desk inside the room, it is likely that the retina will take time to adapt to the new luminance levels. For this reason, for visual display units it is generally agreed that contrast ratios of screen background to the external work environment should be 1:3 (i.e. the external conditions should be no more than three times as bright as the screen) for areas immediately surrounding the workplace (near field) and 1:10 for other areas (far field) (Dainoff, 1982). Less agreement is found for character-to-screen background luminance ratios. Recommendations range from 3:1 (as a minimum) to 30:1, but the region of 7:1 to 10:1 seems to be regarded as optimal. However, consistent measurement procedures for appropriate symbol luminance values to be used in computing these ratios are needed (Stammerjohn, Smith and Cohen, 1981). Furthermore, when considering contrast effects, the possible presence of screen reflections needs also to be taken into account, as discussed below. A few data have been published which provide details of luminance contrast ratios measured in different workplaces (for example, Hultgren and Knave, 1974; Läubli, Hünting and Grandjean, 1981).

Glare

Glare results whenever one part of the visual field is brighter than the level to which the eye has become accustomed and such excessive luminance levels can arise in one or both of two ways. First, direct glare occurs when the light appears directly from the source itself, such as the headlight of a car at night, from the sun during the day, or perhaps from a badly positioned light. Second, and perhaps more insidious, reflected or specular glare is caused by reflections of high brightness from polished or glossy surfaces. As will be seen later, the VDU screen itself often acts as a very good reflector of specular light, as does glossy paper and even the keys on a keyboard. White walls and ceilings can also be a source of specular glare. The effects of these glare sources can often be unpredictable since they may occur under various circumstances—for example, the glare may only occur when the object is placed at a certain angle to the light, when two or more lights are brought together, or at certain times of the day when the sun is being reflected off other surfaces.

Glare is commonly described as being of two types. If there is direct interference with visual performance, the condition is referred to as disability glare. However, if performance is not directly affected, but the bright stimulus still causes discomfort, annoyance, irritation or distraction, the condition is called discomfort glare. As Boyce (1981) points out, the distinction between these two terms is often blurred—the same lighting conditions can produce disability and discomfort simultaneously and, to confuse matters further, different lighting conditions can cause disability and create discomfort independently. However, disability glare, in essence, refers to the effects of a non-uniform luminance distribution on the visibility of objects; discomfort glare refers to the sense of discomfort the non-uniform luminance distribution produces.

The effects of both types of glare may eventually be to cause reduced performance, through distraction, through increased arousal or, because having to avoid the glare can constitute another task that the operator has to perform, through reduction in the available spare mental capacity. Furthermore, because the eye always tends to move to the brightest part of the visual field (the so-called phototropic effect), a consequence of glare can often be to draw the eyes away from the task in hand. For example, Hopkinson and Longmore (1959) have demonstrated that the eye makes more frequent, jerky darts towards the brighter area of the visual field.

Disability glare

The reduced ability to see accurately owing to interference from a bright light source has probably been experienced by all at some time or another, so the potential disabling effects of glare are well-known.

At a descriptive level, two of the earliest workers in the field, Luckiesh and Holladay (1925) considered disability glare to be of three types. Veiling glare, they felt, was due to light from the glare source being scattered in the fluids of the eye, so reducing contrast and hence visibility. An effect is caused, therefore, which is similar to illuminated fog or mist. This was illustrated by Stiles and his colleagues (Stiles, 1929; Crawford and Stiles, 1937) who performed an experiment in which the glaring light source was presented on the blind spot of the retina. Although the light source itself was invisible, its veiling effect was still present.

The second type of disability glare, which Luckiesh and Holladay describe as 'dazzle glare', occurs as a short-term effect for the duration of the glare source. Finally 'blinding glare' lasts beyond the period of the glare stimulus owing to the formation of 'blinding after-images'.

In a comprehensive series of experiments Holladay (1926) investigated many aspects of disability glare and he is perhaps best remembered for producing a glare formula which is still used today. His experiments indicated that the amount of glare (defined in terms of contrast reduction), is determined by both the position of the glaring source with respect to the observer and the amount of light entering the observer's eye. Thus:

$$\text{Contrast reduction} = \frac{k \times \text{illumination produced by glaring source at eye}}{(\text{Angle at eye between source and object being viewed})^{2.4}}$$

The value of k in this formula appears to depend on the age of the observer since age causes changes in the consistency of fluids in the eyeball (Christie and Fisher, 1966).

There are two important implications of Holladay's formula. First is its suggestion that the extent of the glare will decrease as the angle of the glare source to the observer increases. As Hopkinson and Collins (1970) point out, the effect will be the same whether the glaring source is a small source of high illuminance or a large source of low illuminance—provided the illumination at the eye is the same. This means that a dark sky, for example, seen through a large window can cause as much disability glare as a small, more intense bulb—even though its brightness may not be sufficiently high to cause any discomfort.

Discomfort glare

Paradoxically, discomfort glare appears to have been studied more extensively than disability glare, and a number of formulae have been derived which relate various physical parameters of the glare source to levels of 'discomfort' (see, for example, Murrell, 1971 or Boyce, 1981 for a list and description of many of these formulae.)

The discomfort produced by a glare source appears to have a different physiological origin than does disability glare. Thus Hopkinson (1956) has demonstrated a link between the level of discomfort and the activity of the eye musculature which controls the iris. This relationship, however, is not perfect and Hopkinson concludes that discomfort sensations were due only in part to the conflict which arises between the requirements for pupil control between the areas of the retina stimulated by the glaring source, and those receiving lower levels of illumination.

The most modern glare formula, which has become generally accepted, has been accepted by the Illuminating Engineering Society based on empirical work developed by the Building Research Station in Great Britain. This work was carried out over a number of years by Hopkinson and his colleagues (see, for example, Hopkinson, 1940, 1972; Petherbridge and Hopkinson, 1950). The results of the various investigations produced the following glare formula:

$$\text{Glare constant } (G) = \frac{B_s^{1.6} \times w^{0.8}}{B_b \times \theta^{1.6}}$$

where:

B_s is the luminance of the source

w is the solid angle subtended by the source at the eye (i.e. this is related to its apparent size)

B_b is the general background luminance

θ is the angle between the direction of viewing and the direction of the glare source.

The glare index, then, is computed by summing the glare constants from each source in the visual field, obtaining the logarithm of this sum, and multiplying this figure by a factor of 10. Thus:

$$\text{Glare index} = 10 \log_{10} (\text{sum } G)$$

Although the values of the exponents in the formula depend to some extent on the experimental conditions, it is possible to see that decreasing the size and luminance of the source would increase glare, as would increasing the background luminance. In practice, however, increasing the source luminance is also likely to increase background luminance. Furthermore, as with disability glare, increasing the angle between the glare source and the observer also decreases glare. As a rough guide Hopkinson and Collins (1970) state that a glare index of less than 10 is rated as 'barely perceptible' glare while a value of over 28 is rated as 'intolerable'. Unfortunately, however, as Boyce (1981) has shown, there is wide individual variability in the extent to which glare (as measured by the glare index) causes discomfort.

Veiling reflections

In addition to these two types of glare, a special case of glaring sources can occur when the high levels of background illumination appear in the visual field and cover the objects of interest. For obvious reasons, these are called veiling reflections and their effect is to increase the overall levels of both the object and the background luminances. To measure the contrast between the object and surround, therefore, the basic formula discussed earlier needs to be modified slightly to include the luminance of the veiling source (B_v). Thus the new task contrast (C) will be:

$$C = \frac{(B_o + B_v) - (B_b + B_v)}{B_b + B_v}$$

In an attempt to discover how veiling reflections affect viewer satisfaction, De Boer (1977) asked subjects to read two journals, one printed on a moderately glossy paper, the other on semi-matt paper, and a piece of text written in pencil on matt paper. Figure 6.9 shows that there is a clear relationship between comfort and veiling reflections, with the 'just disturbing' category having a contrast ratio of about 0.6.

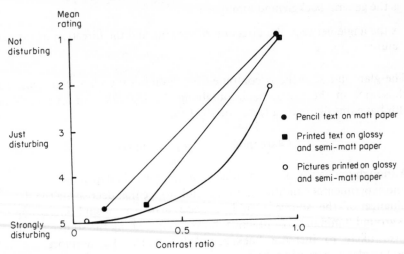

Figure 6.9.   Effect of different contrast ratios, arising from veiling reflections from various surfaces, on perceived disturbance (De Boer, 1977). Reproduced by permission of the Chartered Institution of Building Services.

Typically, at the computer workstation veiling reflections are likely to present themselves mainly as reflections from the VDU screen. However, they can also occur over shiny keys of the keyboard and on glossy source document paper. As far as the screen is concerned, Cakir, Hart and Stewart (1980) point out that the smooth glass surface of a screen face typically reflects about 4% of the light which falls on it, which is quite sufficient to produce clearly visible and sharply defined reflections. When the phosphor is bonded directly on to the inner surface of the screen glass, without any intervening filter, this reflectance can rise to 22–27%.

   Cakir, Hart and Stewart also point out that veiling reflections can affect the eye's accommodation. Reflections on the face of a VDU screen, for example, represent an additional image which is interposed between the operator's eye and the plane on which the character images are displayed. Thus a 'double image' occurs which the optic cortex attempts to resolve (often unsuccessfully) by using the ciliary muscles to alter the lens curvature. This, in the long term, is likely to lead to visual fatigue.

Reducing glare

From the above discussion, it is clear that glare arises mainly from two sources: specular glare reflected off the screen, keyboard, source document, etc., and glare arising from large light sources such as windows or badly positioned lights.

Glare from screens

Perhaps the most obvious way to control reflected glare from VDU screens is to control the glaring source; to pull blinds, to position the screen so that the window does not shine on it, to arrange lights so that they are not reflected, etc. Often, however, this is not possible or convenient. For example, sun shining through a window at such an angle or intensity to be reflected on the screen may only occur for a relatively short time, say a few hours in the morning or late afternoon. Rearranging the workstation to take account of such possibilities may not be a feasible proposition. For these types of situation, screen filters are often used by manufacturers and individual operators to combat the problem of screen reflections.

Unfortunately, little work appears to have been reported which has investigated the efficiency of different types of screen filter. Nevertheless, Cakir, Hart and Stewart (1980) present a useful discussion of the different types of filter presently available and the advantages and disadvantages of each. As they point out, however, screen filters can have only limited value. It is not possible to place a filter between the eye and visual display and thereby improve all of the characteristics that contribute to the 'quality' of the display. Whilst the use of an appropriate filter can be effective in reducing screen reflections, it is invariably accomplished at the expense of reduced character brightness and resolution.

Cakir, Hart and Stewart suggest that there are essentially seven types of screen filters that can be used with varying effect:

1 *Filter panels* can be installed in front of the screen and may be coloured. However, as the authors point out, such panels themselves are often glossy and can produce a highly reflective surface.
2 *Polarization filters* polarize the incident light and later diperse it after reflection back from the screen. Again, however, these often cause as much reflection as they reduce.
3 *Micromesh filters* are generally black in appearance and are placed directly on the screen. The micromesh behaves effectively as a large number of very small tubes that restrict both the light striking the screen and that reflected from it. Depending on the coarseness of the mesh, however, the display can be obscured when viewed at certain oblique angles. Furthermore, it can also absorb much of the light emitted from each character, sometimes up to 70%, so making the characters appear less bright. The authors suggest that micromesh filters can be used to advantage only if the ambient illumination, including that from all surfaces, exceeds about 500 cd m^{-2}.
4 *Etching the screen glass surface* can reduce direct reflections from about 4% to around 2%. Again, however, this is likely to be at the expense of reduced clarity. As with micromesh filters, etching can reduce the character brightness by up to 80%.

5 *Spray-on anti-reflective coatings* scatter the light as it passes through the coating. This, however, reduces the sharpness of the character.

6 *Vapour deposited screen coatings* can overcome some of the disadvantages of spray-on coatings.

7 *Thin-film layers* produce an effect similar to the vapour deposited coatings by placing a very thin film layer, having a thickness equal to one-quarter of the wavelength of light, on the screen. The authors suggest that, despite its high cost and the fact that finger smudges can reduce its sensitivity, this is possibly the most effective type of filter.

Finally, Cakir, Hart and Stewart point out that a tube-shield, although not a type of filter, placed over the screen between the operator and the screen can considerably reduce the level of ambient light falling on the screen. Provided that the tube does not cause the operator to have to adopt an unnatural posture, they suggest that this is likely to be the most effective form of reflection reducer for otherwise untreated VDU screens. This type of screen, however, is likely to be less effective if the operator is not seated in a 'fixed' position at the terminal but moves around the workplace, periodically reading data presented on the screen.

With regard to the effectiveness *and* acceptability of these types of screen filters Cakir, Hart and Stewart make a number of recommendations (although, unfortunately, they present no reference to the studies performed):

> CRT displays with fine-grained anti-reflection coatings ... or with a high quality etched surface are more highly ranked by VDT operators than other types of filter both as regards their effectiveness in reducing reflections and the legibility of the display. From the point of view of reducing reflections alone, micromesh filters have been judged to be equally reflective.

> Displays with glass or polarization filters are usually less favourably judged, especially from the point of view of display legibility which, under typical office conditions, is far less than that of other types of display. For as long as the optical quality of this type of filter cannot be improved, their use cannot be recommended.

> Black micromesh filters are also poorly judged by most VDT operators, again due to their effect in reducing display legibility. Only when the ambient illuminance exceeds 500 lx (500 cd m^{-2}) and the problems of reflections cannot otherwise be resolved can micromesh filters be used to advantage.

Glare from windows

Consideration of the glare formula discussed earlier suggests two features of the illumination environment that can contribute to increased glare from large areas such as windows. Thus glare is increased as the luminance level of the glaring source (B_s) is increased and as its angle to the observer is decreased. This suggests that simply reducing the amount of light entering the room will go some way to reducing glare—but not the whole way. Hopkinson (1972), therefore, suggests that if the simple expedient of window blinds is not appropriate, architectural techniques can be employed such as using tinted glass, limiting the area of sky visible from any position in the room using large, vertical fins on the window or fitting translucent blinds, by building an overhang above the window or, to increase the angle of the glaring source, by having windows higher up the wall. Furthermore, remembering that glare is a contrast effect, he suggests that it might be reduced if this contrast is also reduced, for example, by painting the window surrounds a very light colour (possibly even white). Care needs to be taken in this case, however, to ensure that the white surrounds do not, themselves, become glaring objects.

Windowless rooms

If glare from windows is a serious problem, one obvious design possibility is to remove the windows and install lights, the intensity and angle of which are under the control of the operator. Research data suggests, however, that to do so can often create problems of a different form, possibly of reduced satisfaction with the workplace. Boyce (1981) presents a valuable review of such studies, which have demonstrated mixed reactions to windowless rooms, often depending on the room function and the number of other occupants that it contains. For example, Ruys (1970) surveyed occupants in five different buildings in America, each containing a number of windowless offices. Whereas there appeared to be few complaints about the level of artificial lighting provided, nearly 90% of the occupants expressed dissatisfaction with the lack of windows. Those office workers who often had to work alone complained that a lack of windows meant a lack of daylight, poor ventilation and an inability to know about the weather or to have a view. It also gave an impression of being cooped up and led to feelings of depression and tension.

On the other hand, studies performed in factories, which are often windowless but in which space is usually large and contains a number of other people, suggests few complaints (Pritchard, 1964). Boyce also reports similar findings from studies investigating the effects of windowless classrooms on school children. Indeed, in some cases the children performed better in rooms without windows.

Contradictory data such as these led Boyce to suggest that it is not the lack of windows *per se* which is a cause for discontent but the social setting of the environment and the size of the windowless space. In environments in which there was adequate scope for social interaction (factories and schools), with larger rooms, the complaints were rare. In smaller office-type environments, however, with reduced chances for social interaction, complaints were heard. Furthermore, Boyce argues that equality of circumstances is important in such cases. For example, Sommer (1974) found that the dislike of a windowless environment in the underground offices that he studied was amplified by the fact that the executives had offices above ground with windows overlooking fine views.

NOISE

Noise is quite simply airborne vibration that is received at the ears. It is conveniently and frequently defined as 'unwanted sound', a definition which, in its looseness, enables a sound source to be considered as 'noise' or 'not noise' solely on the basis of the listener's reaction to it. Furthermore, sounds which are labelled as being 'noise' by one individual on one occasion may not be so labelled on other occasions or in a different environment.

Although the sounds that we can perceive all around us, from speech, from machines, from traffic, are very complex in nature, for analysis and measurement purposes they can all be reduced to a group of very simple, sinusoidal, waveforms, each having a single frequency and intensity level. A description of this process, known as Fourier Analysis, is outside of the scope of this book, although it is appropriate to provide a short description of the units of frequency and intensity that are used.

In terms of the frequency, for the human listener sound is defined as acoustical energy between 2 and 20,000 Hz (2 Hz to 20 kHz) (Kryter, 1970), the typical frequency limits of the ear. The ear is still able to separate wave changes of the air below about 16 Hz but the sensations are perceived as 'beats'. Above about 16 Hz, however, the beats begin to fuse to produce a tonelike quality.

The intensity of a pure tone is defined in terms of the pressure changes associated with the compression and refraction in the air cause by the sound source. The description of sound intensity, therefore, is in terms of the sound pressure level (SPL) and is measured in the logarithmic units of decibels (dB).

Because the decibel scale is logarithmic in nature a simple, linear relationship between decibel level and sound intensity does not exist. Indeed each 20 dB increase implies a difference in pressure of 10:1. Thus 80 dB is not twice as intense as 40 dB; its pressure level is 100 (i.e. 10^2) times as intense. The starting point of the logarithmic scale (0 dB) is arbitrarily set to be at the average threshold of hearing for a 1000 Hz tone obtained after audiometric surveys of many thousands of subjects. For this reason it is possible to have a sound intensity which is so quiet that it registers on a sound level meter with a negative dB level.

Just as the ear converts acoustic energy into nerve impulses to be decoded and 'measured' by the auditory cortex, electrical sound level meters also convert the sound received from the microphone into electrical energy which is then analysed by the machine. The ear, however, does not respond equally to all frequencies—it is more sensitive to some than to others. Unless modified, however, the microphone and amplifier would treat all frequencies in the same way and, for this reason, electronic weighting networks are often included in sound level meters—the three internationally recognized scales being the A, B and C scales. Because they affect any readings which are made, the scale should always be quoted in any noise level report.

Like any environmental pollutant, noise can affect operators in any or all of three ways: first it can damage health by causing deafness, second it can affect performance, and third it can cause annoyance. The first of these, of course, is unlikely to occur in environments that also house computer systems—the noise levels created by the computer are unlikely to be high enough. It is possible, however, for the types of noise experienced in offices to cause annoyance and, sometimes, performance reductions—particularly for the perception of acoustic displays such as speech.

Noise sources

The types of noise likely to be received by operators working with or near computer equipment will generally arise from one or both of two sources: from the office environment itself (from the machines and people that it contains), and from the outside (from traffic or from aircraft), particularly if the windows are left open. Each of these sources can affect performance and feelings of well-being.

As far as the internal noises are concerned, computer machinery and speech from other employees are likely to be the main causes of this type of unwanted sound.

In a questionnaire survey of nearly 2000 users of large offices, Keighley (1970) demonstrated that noise was definitely the worst rated feature of the office environment, particularly the noises that originated from inside the rooms. Telephones, various types of business machines and 'thoughtlessly loud conversations' were frequent causes for complaints. Similar findings were obtained by Nemecek and Grandjean (1973) in landscaped offices. As can be seen from Figure 6.10, of those employees who considered that they were disturbed by noise, nearly 50% of the 400 surveyed felt that the noise produced by conversations was most annoying. Interestingly, further questioning revealed that the majority who indicated that conversation noise disturbed them most felt that it was the content of the conversation rather than its loudness which was the most disturbing.

As far other noise sources within buildings are concerned, Croome (1977) lists mechanical engineering services (heating, ventilation, etc.), electrical services (lighting, particularly fluorescent lights), circulation services such as lifts, process machines (typewriters, printers (see Busch-Vishniac and Lyon, 1981), etc.) and people (talking, walking, slamming doors, etc.).

Unfortunately, however, as Croome also points out there is a limited amount of acoustical data available to determine the extent to which any one member

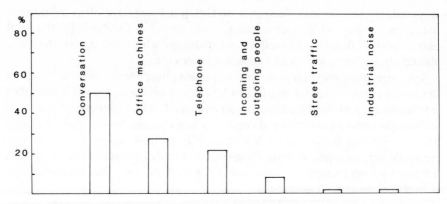

Figure 6.10. Proportion of respondents reporting disturbance from various noise sources in landscaped offices (Nemecek and Grandjean, 1973). Reproduced by permission of Butterworth Scientific Ltd.

of these categories contributes to the total sound source. Nevertheless, large amounts of data are available on ways to attenuate the sounds which do arise from these sources.

Noises arising from *outside* of the office environment are likely to be due primarily to sources such as road or air trafic, although features such as the air-conditioning systems of nearby buildings can also contribute to the general level of acoustic energy. As would be expected, these different types of noises interfere differently with operator behaviour. Thus, Ahrlin and Rylander (1979) have demonstrated that road traffic noise interfered significantly less with speech than did train noise, although both types of noise caused roughly the same interference with rest and sleep. Unfortunately, little detailed work appears to have been performed in this area either to substantiate such conclusions or to equate the effects with some of the physical parameters of these noise types.

Whatever its form, however, this type of external noise is unlikely to be a general problem. For example, some of the data from Nemecek and Grandjean's (1973) study of survey of noise in landscaped offices (shown in Figure 6.10) suggest that only very few of the respondents considered that street traffic and industrial noise was a source of distress. The extent to which this type of noise is intrusive, then, will be specific to particular offices and will depend primarily on the location of the office, both geographically and its position within the building. Furthermore, the problem is likely to be more acute at certain times of the year, for example in the summer when windows are opened for ventilation (using complaints statistics, Beranek, Kryter and Miller, 1959, demonstrated that aircraft noise was more intrusive during the warm summer months.)

Effects of noise

As far as an office environment is concerned, noise effects are likely to lie in the spheres of performance decrements and increases in annoyance levels. Of course these effects can, themselves, lead to other problems: reduced performance can lead to safety reductions and accidents; continued feelings of annoyance can lead to dissatisfaction with work, increased turnover and even mental illness.

Performance effects

Communication

Speech is one aspect in the working environment that can be interrupted by noise. Effective verbal communication depends both on the ability of the speaker (whether the speaker be another person or a machine synthesizer) to produce the correct speech sounds, and on the ability of the listener to receive and decode these sounds. A noisy environment can interfere with this last stage in the speech transmission, owing to an effect which is described as masking.

A great deal of work has been done over the years to determine how masking occurs and the parameters which define it. It is not the purpose of this book to review even a fraction of these studies; such reviews can be found in other texts such as Kryter (1970), or Oborne (1983). However, it is appropriate to consider briefly some of the more important aspects of the masking phenomenon so that the effects might be minimized.

Levels of the masking effect are dependent on almost any aspect of the signal (speech or auditory display) and of the masker (noise) that could be considered: their respective frequencies, intensities, durations, meanings to the listener, phase relationships, etc. However, one general rule is able to be distilled from all of the data obtained when investigating these relationships: higher levels of masking will occur the more similar the signal and the masker become. Thus, greater masking occurs when the signal and masker frequency spectra are the same, when they are heard at the same time, when they have similar meanings for the listener, etc. The only exception to this rule is the case of intensity: more masking occurs as the masker becomes louder. The implications of such findings to the design of the acoustic environment, then, is that the noise types and levels that are present should be as different as possible from the signals that are likely to occur. This is particularly important when considering their frequency relationships.

Kryter (1970) indicates that speech (for males and for females) tends to predominate at around 400–500 Hz, but includes frequencies up to 5000 Hz. Furthermore, speech energy below 200 and above 7000 Hz contributes almost nothing to speech intelligibility. Clearly, therefore, significant environmental noise having frequencies in the range 400 to about 1000 Hz should be avoided.

With regard to noise intensity, however, the problem is rather more complex. This is because, as French and Steinberg (1947) point out, one of the distinguishing characteristics of speech is its dynamic quality. Conversation at the rate of 200 words per minute is not unusual and, during the brief period that a sound lasts, the intensity is not constant. It builds up rapidly, remains relatively constant for a while and then decays rapidly. As was discussed in both Chapters 4 and 5, the various sounds differ from each other in their build-up and decay characteristics, in length, in total intensity and in the distribution of intensity with frequency. For these reasons, a relatively constant level of masker is unlikely to mask completely the speech sounds; it will mask parts of the sounds only, the proportion of the sounds masked being related to the characteristics of the sound. Furthermore since understanding speech depends also on the probability that a particular word in a sentence will occur, the extent to which noise masks speech will be related also to the amount of redundancy and the frequency with which the words occur naturally in the language.

A further reason for the difficulty in defining precisely which noise intensities are likely to mask speech is that the normal behavioural response to increased ambient noise will be for the speaker to raise the voice. However, as Kryter (1970) points out, the increase in effort is often not sufficient to override the noise level completely. Indeed, Korn (1954) showed that speech intensity needs to be increased by about 3.5 dB for every 10 dB increase in room noise. Of course, the increased speaking volume will, itself, add to the ambient noise levels.

If the signal is masked by noise which is interrupted by periods of quiet, then the degree of masking changes in quite a complex manner which is related to the rate of interruption. Miller and Licklider (1950), for example, explain the relationship as follows:

> At interruptions of less than 2/sec, whole words or syllables within a word tend to be masked; at interruption rates of between 2 and 30/sec, noise detection is so brief that the listener is able to hear a portion of each syllable or phoneme of the speech signal, thereby tending to reduce the amount of masking; when the interruption rate is more frequent than 30/sec the spread of masking in time around the moment of occurrence of a burst of noise results in increased masking until by 100 interruptions per second there is, effectively, continuous masking.

In conclusion it should be pointed out that most studies of this nature have been conducted using young (usually male), articulate subjects with normal hearing in situations where no face-to-face contact is permitted (analogous to, for example, telephone conversations). Little attention has been paid to the social and non-verbal cues which also occur between people who are speaking. For example, Waltzman and Levitt (1978) reported that face-to-face encounters using visual cues improves the intelligibility of noisy messages quite considerably. Furthermore, Webster (1973) has shown that the speech intelligibility criteria that are used, which are based on speech without visual cues, overestimate the effect of noise for face-to-face communication by as much as 20 dB. Finally, as Jones, Chapman and Auburn (1981) point out, virtually nothing is known of the skills that we use to perceive speech in noisy conditions. This is despite the fact that there is ample anecdotal evidence to suggest that individuals who are practised at conversing in noisy settings are able to pick out speech more accurately than those who are not practised.

Cognitive performance

There is at present much controversy raging over the question of whether environmental noise affects anything other than auditory-based performance, particularly when the task requires elements of an operator's vigilance. This controversy has revolved around questions of both experimental design and whether or not any effects are due to the masking of 'inner speech'. Since the effects of noise on vigilance performance, if it has any detrimental effects at all, occurs only in environments with very high intensity noise levels (greater than 100 dB(A)) which are unlikely to be experienced by computer operatives, and since the controversy has raged without complete conclusion in the experimental literature for a number of years, a detailed discussion of the effects of noise on vigilance behaviour will not be considered here. The interested reader, however, can turn to a number of sources which will advance one or other of the competing views (for example, Broadbent, 1954, 1971, 1978; Poulton, 1976, 1977, 1978).

Apart from vigilance, however, there are some cognitive functions which do appear to be affected by noise, although again only in intense noise. One of these is time estimation. Jerison (1959), for example, exposed subjects to intense (114 dB) noise for over two hours and, in addition to other tasks, asked them to press a key at what they considered to be 10-minute intervals. His results show that throughout the experimental period his subjects progressively contracted their internal time-scale when in the noisy condition but not in the 'quiet' (77.5 to 83 dB(A)). Whereas in the first 15 minutes of noise the key was pressed after an average period of 8.75 minutes (to signal the end of the 10-minute period), after 2.75 hours '10 minutes' was contracted to about 7 minutes.

Environmental noise can also affect memory, although it is not entirely clear whether this occurs only at the input (memorizing) stage, at the output (retrieval) stage or both (for example, see Thomas, 1978). Furthermore the direction of the effect (an improvement or reduction in memory) is equivocal. Some studies have suggested that noise improves immediate retention (for example, Archer and Margolin, 1970) while others have shown an impairment

(McLean, 1969). Indeed, still others have suggested that noise has no effect on immediate retention (Sloboda and Smith, 1968).

The levels of noise used in experiments of this nature, however, have generally been very high (greater than about 80 dB(A)). When slightly lower noise intensities are used (65 dB(A)) *improved* immediate recall is generally the result (for example, Berlyne *et al.*, 1965; Wesner, 1972). This is probably because of the operation of the inverted-U, arousal–performance relationship discussed in Chapter 1. Thus, moderate increases in noise increase body arousal so that performance incrases. If too much noise is perceived, however, the arousal increases become too great with resultant *reductions* in performance. This suggests, therefore, that noise acts on cognitive behaviour as a general stressor, and that any performance increases or decreases in noise can be explained in these terms. This possibility will be considered later.

Annoyance effects

Annoyance is a common subjective response that we have all exhibited in the past when exposed to something which we do not want. Since, by definition, noise is unwanted sound, in whatever form it presents itself (speech, music or random acoustic energy) it is likely to cause annoyance. The extent to which particular sounds are likely to cause annoyance, therefore, will be determined not simply by their physical characteristics, but by the extent to which they are unwanted by the listener. This means that what is annoying to one person may not be so to another and so it is not possible to define strictly the acoustic conditions likely to cause annoyance (as it is possible, for example, to define the conditions likely to lead to deafness or to reductions in speech intelligibility). Nevertheless, there are some physical aspects of noise which are more likely to be annoying than others.

Physical aspects of noise annoyance

Kryter (1970) suggests that five aspects of a noise stimulus can be identified as affecting its annoyance level: (a) the spectrum content and level, (b) the spectrum complexity; (c) the sound duration; (d) the sound rise time (that is, the length of time that it takes to reach its maximum level); and (e) the maximum level reached (for impulsive sounds such as a door bang).

The relationships between most of these parameters and annoyance are likely to be fairly obvious. For example, annoyance increases the louder the sound, the longer it remains, etc. With regard to the content of the spectrum, however, the relationship is not so straightforward. By asking subjects to adjust tones of different frequencies to make them equally 'noisy', Kryter and Pearsons (1963) were able to produce bands of equal 'noisiness' over a frequency range of 40 to 10,000 Hz (a distinction was made between

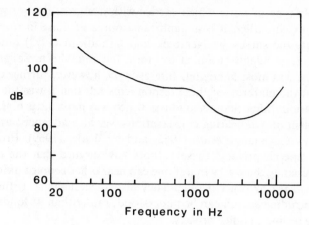

Figure 6.11. An equal noise annoyance contour (Kryter and Pearsons, 1963). Reproduced by permission of the American Institute of Physics.

'noisiness' and 'loudness'). These bands indicated that the higher frequencies (above about 2000 Hz) tend to contribute more to the sound noisiness (and thus are likely to be more annoying) than the lower frequencies—even though they were equally loud. This relationship can be seen in Figure 6.11: as the noise frequency increases above about 1000 Hz it appears to become more 'noisy' (or, interpreting the graph literally, with increasing frequency a lower intensity is needed to maintain the same noisiness level). Although the same relationship is apparent when the sounds are made to be equally 'loud', the increase in sensitivity for higher frequencies is not so marked.

Details of the procedures used to record and measure noise levels at a workplace are provided by Michael and Bienvenue (1983).

Subjective aspects of noise annoyance

In many respects, what is conveyed by the term 'annoyance' is not just 'noisiness'; annoyance implies something more. It commonly signifies one's reaction to sound that is based not only on physical characteristics of the stimulus but also on what it means; the emotional content and the novelty that the sound can have for the listener. As Wilson (1963) suggests,

> The annoyance may be ascribed to the 'information' which sounds may carry from the source to the recipient. The physical energy in the noise of a creaking door, a crying baby, or a distant party may be very small, and if distributed in the form of random noise probably would be quite unnoticed. But it may convey manifold suggestions of alarm, neglect, sadness, loneliness, and so in some people it has an emotional effect out of all proportion to its physical intensity.

Speech is a type of noise which carries with it a great deal of information and, as discussed earlier, it is a significant source of noise in rooms such as offices. Thus, the survey by Nemecek and Grandjean (1973) indicated that 46% of the respondents troubled by noise felt that the noise produced by conversations was most annoying. Interestingly, however, further questioning revealed that the majority of these respondents felt that it was the content of the conversation rather than its loudness which was most disturbing.

The problem of overhearing conversations was also advanced as a cause of annoyance by Cavanaugh et al. (1962) and by Waller (1969). Proposing the concept of 'speech privacy' these authors have argued that the disturbance might be caused by the worry that if one can hear other people talking then one can also be *heard* by other people. They also suggest that it is the degree to which the intruding speech can be understood, rather than its loudness, which destroys the feeling of office privacy.

Some studies have attempted to relate the noise sensitivity of individuals to individual traits. For example, Stephens (1970) examined the relationship between the judgement of loudness and annoyance in conjunction with various personality measures. He found that among tests measuring introversion, need-achievement, test anxiety, social desirability, and general annoyance, only the test anxiety scores correlated significantly with noise sensitivity. He ascribed this result to the tendency for anxious subjects to give extreme responses to very different stimulus levels. Interestingly, noise annoyance did not correlate at all well with noise sensitivity.

On the basis of questionnaire responses obtained before students arrived on a University campus, Weinstein (1976) distinguished two groups of respondents—noise-sensitive and noise-insensitive. As would be expected, throughout the year at college the noise-sensitive students were bothered much more by dormitory noise and became increasingly disturbed during the year. The noise-insensitive students, however, showed no change in disturbance. In an extension to the study, sensitivity scores and scores from a range of personality tests were also examined. The results suggested that noise-sensitive subjects were generally lower in dominance, capacity for status, sociability and social presence. In addition, the results demonstrated that higher noise-sensitivity scores were related to increased intraversion scores. Commenting on these results, however, Jones, Chapman and Auburn (1981) point out that since the sensitivity scales emphasized the importance of noises produced by other people, the question needs to be asked whether the association between sensitivity and sociability simply reflects a lack of social skills on the part of some of the respondents.

Despite valid experimental arguments such as these, however, evidence is available to suggest that continued noise does detrimentally affect social behaviour. For example, in a series of studies Mathews and Cannon (1975) investigated the influence of noise on the willingness to help an experimenter's confederate pick up materials that have been 'accidently' dropped. Those subjects who were exposed to 85 dB(A) noise were less likely to help than those exposed to a maximum of 65 dB(A). Similar results were obtained in more naturalistic settings. In addition, a study by Crook and Langdon (1974) of classroom activity in schools around London Airport demonstrated the distracting effects of noise and the results that this can have on social interaction. In addition to the aircraft noise interfering with lessons, the authors also reported changes in the style of teaching on the noisier days (lessons abandoned and more pauses in the flow of the teacher), increased pupil fidgeting, and a reduction in the teacher's satisfaction with the class as a whole. Thus teachers often felt that the noise caused the whole atmosphere of the proceedings to deteriorate, that they and their pupils became irritable and tired, that they developed headaches and that the pupils became noisier and less inclined to work.

Noise as a stressor

All of the discussion so far has reinforced the concept that, in addition to its direct affect on hearing, noise acts in the way of a general stressor. This might increase the body's arousal level which, if arousal increases above an optimum level, can reduce performance.

However, there is general agreement that stress not only brings about quantitative changes in performance but also qualitative changes. Easterbrook (1959), for example, proposed that in over-aroused subjects attention tends to be concentrated on the dominant and obvious aspects of the situation. This suggests that some aspects of task performance might be relatively unaffected by stress but that performance on other, either more difficult or less important, aspects of the task may be impaired. For example, Boggs and Simon (1968) examined noise effects in relation to task complexity. They found a reliable noise/complexity interaction in which noise produced more errors in complex rather than simple tasks.

Views such as this have been extended recently to emphasize that stress also reduces the stability of attention and interferes with the capacity to discriminate relevant from irrelevant aspects of a task (for example, Kahneman, 1973). Since stress is also likely to narrow the span of attention in the way described above, Jones (1979) suggests that the qualitative result of stress is that it seems to produce strategic changes in behaviour rather than simply depressing performance.

The idea that coping with noise involves some cognitive intervention has also evolved in other areas of inquiry. Over the past decade or so there has been an increasing amount of interest in the notion of 'perceived control' as a means of alleviating the deleterious after-effects of noise. For example Wohlwill *et al.* (1976) suggest that individuals are able to cope with noise through increased concentration and effort. They make the observation that subjects in such experiments sometimes experience considerable 'release of tension' after the experience—even to the extent of breaking down to cry. In a series of studies (Glass and Singer, 1972) subjects exposed to loud intermittent noise over which they had no control did not show detrimental effects in their performance *during* the noise (indeed physiological indices indicated that the subjects had adapted to the noise), but they performed badly when the noise had ceased and they moved to another room. These results contrasted with those from similar groups of subjects who were told that they could terminate the noise although they were encouraged not to do so. These subjects showed no detrimental effects after the noise.

Finally, one extreme response to noise as a stressor that has been documented slightly is that of reduced mental health. In this case, several lines of indirect evidence point to some increase in incidence of minor psychiatric disturbance as a result of exposure to noise. For example, Cohen, Glass and Singer (1978) have suggested that:

> Existing evidence suggests that noise may indeed have some responsibility for the personal disorganization of those living or working in noisy environments. Industrial surveys, for example, report that noise exposure results in increased anxiety and stress responses. Workers habitually exposed to high intensity noise show increased incidence of nervous complaints, nausea, headaches, instability, argumentativeness, sexual impotency, changes in general mood and anxiety. ...Jansen (1961) reports that workers in the noisiest places in a steel factory have a greater frequency of social conflicts both at home and in the plant.

Cohen *et al.* do point out, however, that it is difficult to ascribe these effects solely to noise. There is a variety of other stresses associated with noisy work places and a number of variables which are related to the types of people who are likely to work in them. At the very least, however, the evidence is suggestive of some distinctive social effects.

Industrial music and productivity

Before concluding the discussion of the effects of noise at work, one final aspect needs to be considered and this relates to the use of background music in factories and offices. In many respects, of course, this topic should not be considered in a section which discussed the effects of noise since noise, by definition, is unwanted sound. Music, on the other hand, is often wanted and is enjoyed by many workers. The effects of music on performance will be discussed here, however, since it is an acoustic stimulus which, it has been argued, may possibly affect performance. As with the effects of noise on some aspects of cognitive performance, however, the evidence regarding music and productivity is also controversial.

Fox (1983) distinguishes between two types of music at work—background music and industrial music. Although each might be said to be used in an attempt to increase commercial profitability, they are quite different in their modes of operation. Background music, then, is the type of music often heard in shops and supermarkets; it is an endless stream of light, quiet music designed to put shoppers at ease. Industrial music, however, is generally of varying types and does not occur all of the time but only at selected periods during the day. Indeed, if it were to be played all of the time, it would defeat the basis for having the music.

The theoretical basis for suggesting that music might aid performance lies in the alleviation of boredom and fatigue that often accompanies repetitive work. Again, then, the inverted-U, performance–arousal relationship is invoked (Fox, 1971). Thus the normal stimulation which is received by the operator from the task is used not only to give information about the job, but to provide stimulation for the part of the brain known as the reticular activating system (RAS) which determines how much attention, alertness or vigilance the operator will bring to the job. This, in turn, is related to the irregularity, rate of occurrence and variability of these signals, but not necessarily to the intensity or frequency of the acoustic stimuli. Repetitive work with little stimulation, therefore, can lead to under-arousal and a loss of efficiency. The basis of industrial music, therefore, is that varying, secondary stimulation might provide the stimuli needed to 'reactivate' the RAS.

With music, however, other influencers of performance might also be present. Thus music may influence not only attention and vigilance but feelings of well-being and job satisfaction, and these effects could be reflected by reductions in absenteeism, bad timekeeping and labour turnover which are likely to increase overall productivity.

Studies investigating the effects of industrial music on productivity have been reviewed by Fox (1971, 1983). Although many were poorly controlled he concluded, from both laboratory-based and industrial studies, that under the right conditions music is beneficial. Thus subjects increased their performance in the laboratory, and the industry-based studies showed reductions in errors, poor timekeeping, staff turnover and accidents, and increases in output and production quality.

When considering the music to be used for such purposes, two questions are important: 'When should the music be played?' and 'What type of music should be played?' The answers to these two questions are based in the theoretical rationale for using industrial music—that of increasing arousal.

With regard to the times for music, then, on the basis of the inverted-U arousal–performance hypothesis, the suggestion is made that it should be played at those times during the day when arousal would otherwise be low. Daily variations in human performance and efficiency have long been recognized (Rutenfranz and Colquhoun, 1979) which are generally termed 'circadian rhythms'. For example, Blake (1971) demonstrated increases in performance between 08.00 and 10.30 hours, with a 'post-lunch' dip at about 14.00 hours. Fox (1983), therefore, strongly urges that music is played only at the times when arousal is low. Unfortunately precise times during the day for these peaks and troughs are not available (see Folkard and Monk, 1979) and so the appropriate times need to be determined empirically within each working situation.

Finally, with regard to the content of the music, a series of studies carried out by Fox and Embrey (1972) suggest that the workers themselves should be able to choose their music. In a laboratory experiment they tested six subjects on a detection task using four conditions:

1 no music;
2 music played during the 15th to 20th minute of the test session using a programme of randomly selected music;
3 as in (2) but using a commercially prepared, lively programme;
4 as in (2) but allowing the subjects to select a programme from the tapes used in (3).

Their results demonstrated that average detection efficiency increased significantly from the 'no music' to the 'commercial music' conditions, with detection rate being higher when the subjects were able to choose their music ((4) rather than (3)).

THE THERMAL ENVIRONMENT

The thermal conditions present in the environment can play a large part in the comfort and efficiency of people who live and work in that environment. To take an extreme example, quite small departures (greater than about 5°C, Oborne, 1982) from optimal body temperatures can lead to death. Of course, the temperatures being considered in these cases refer to those that are experienced deep in the body structure, and not the thermal conditions which apply at the skin surface. Nevertheless, as will be illustrated later, fairly small departures from ideal skin temperatures can lead to discomfort and reduced efficiency.

The body's physiological response to the thermal environment depends on a very complex balance between the levels of heat production and heat loss. The heat which results from the normal body metabolism, particularly during work, and from convection and radiation in the environment maintains the body at a temperature well above that of the normal surrounding environment. At the same time heat is constantly being lost from the body by radiation, convection and evaporation so that under normal resting conditions the body's core temperature remains within a narrow range of between 36.1 and 37.2°C (97–99°F).

Thermal variables

Environmental variables

A detailed examination of the thermal balance model described above suggests that a number of thermal variables are important to maintain the balance; to allow the body to maintain its warmth but to lose heat when it has too much. The important variables, then, will be first the level of dry heat in the environment which helps to maintain the body's warmth. This arises from both convection of heat from structures such as heating systems and from radiation from, for example, the sun. It is normally measured with a standard thermometer.

Secondly, the amount of water vapour in the environment (humidity) influences the degree of cooling that can occur through sweating. Thus, if the humidity is too high, less sweat is able to evaporate. At the other end of the scale, however, very low humidities are likely to cause discomfort by drying the normally moist membranes in the eyes, nose and throat—particularly if the air temperature is rather high.

The final major variable is the degree of air movement. When the air moves over the body it has a cooling effect as a result of both helping to evaporate the sweat and by dissipating the heat from the body surface. Naturally, if the body is too hot, this is likely to result in increased comfort. Too large an air velocity, however, is likely to lead to complaints of draughts and, as with low humidity, it can help to dry the normally damp membranes in the eyes, nose and throat. It should be remembered, however, that velocity is a relative term which, in this case, applies to the motions of the air and the observer. If the observer is stationary the relative velocity is equal to the air speed. The velocity of air relative to a moving observer, however, is determined both by the speed and the direction of the observer relative to the air speed and direction.

Individual variables

In addition to the three primary variables described above, the behaviour and constitution of the operator can also affect the extent to which an optimal thermal balance is maintained. In this respect the important aspects can be seen to be the person's activity, clothing, age and sex.

Activity

It should be easy to understand how activity can affect the thermal balance. Thus, as muscular work is done heat is generated in the muscles, and this helps to raise the body's core temperature. Table 6.4 illustrates the metabolic rates measured whilst performing different activities and, as can be seen, nearly

Table 6.4. Metabolic rates for different activities.

Activity	Metabolic rate of heat production per unit surface area (W/m²)
Basal metabolic rate	45
Seated at rest	60
Standing at rest	65
Office work	75
Light work, standing	90
Walking on ground level at 3.2km/h (2 mph)	115
„ „ „ „ „ 4.8 „ 3 „	170
„ „ „ „ „ 6.4 „ 4 „	240
„ „ „ „ „ 8.0 „ 5 „	340
Heavy manual work	250

twice as much heat is generated when performing even fairly sedentary activities such as office work than at the basal rate.

Clothing

The transfer of dry heat between the skin and the outer surface of the clothed body is quite complicated and involves the processes of internal convection and radiation in the intervening air spaces, and conduction through the cloth itself. These variables are accounted for by the now internationally accepted, dimensionless unit of thermal resistance from the skin to the outer surface of the cloth—the 'clo' (1 clo = 0.16 C/W).

Unfortunately, it is difficult to measure the clo value of any clothing system since the process requires a life-sized heated manikin and the relevant electronic sensors. Thus only a few full clothing ensembles have been measured, although Fanger (1970) lists twelve.

In addition to the conductive resistance of the textile itself, the air between textile layers also acts as an important insulator (which is not taken into account by the clo value). The quality of tailoring and fit, therefore, will influence the overall thermal resistance of the clothing by allowing or not allowing air to enter between the clothes and skin and so help to cool the body surface.

Age

Since thermal balance depends to some extent on metabolic rate, and since metabolic rate decreases slightly with age, it would be reasonable to expect the elderly to prefer higher temperatures than younger people. Furthermore the elderly are less likely to lead an active life which would help to maintain a high metabolic rate. The research which has been carried out in this area, however, suggests that, provided their physiological regulatory mechanisms remain effective, the thermal preferences of the elderly are no higher than for younger subjects (Rholes, 1969; Fanger, 1970). Fanger ascribes the failure to show differences in preference to the body's bioregulation system. His measurements indicated that 'insensible' sweating (in other words, the evaporation of imperceptible amounts of sweat from the body which help to maintain thermal balance) in the elderly decreased in proportion to their reduced metabolic rate. Thus, although less heat is produced in the body, less is lost.

Sex

In an experiment which measured the metabolic rate of subjects carrying out different levels of activity, McNall *et al.* (1968) demonstrated that males have higher metabolic rates than females. Again, therefore, the argument could be proposed that females might prefer warmer environments. Unlike with the variable of age, however, some slight evidence does exist to suggest that this is indeed the case. Thus Beshir and Ramsey (1981) exposed subjects to different temperatures and asked them to rate their thermal sensation on a nine-point scale ranging from 'cold' to 'extremely hot'. Female subjects consistently rated lower (i.e. cooler) than the males, although no statistical data are provided to assess the significance of the difference. Similar work (using a five-point scale) by Fanger (1970) resulted in similar conclusions although, in this case, the male–female difference was slight and statistically non-significant for Danish subjects but just significant for American subjects. Even the American difference, however, was very slight: the females preferred, on average, temperatures 0.3°C higher than the males.

Once again, the reason for the lack of any significant difference between the thermal preferences of the two sexes could lie in the respective levels of insensible sweating. Thus Fanger's data suggest that males sweated slightly more than females.

Thermal comfort and performance

In the literature, there is considerable evidence to suggest that fairly large departures from optimal thermal (that is, 'comfortable') conditions result in reduced performance, both motor and cognitive (see, for example, Oborne, 1982; Kobrick and Fine, 1983). There are far less data, however, regarding the effects of only slight variations in temperature on performance.

Reddy and Ramsey (1976) asked subjects to perform four tasks, separately, under three different temperatures (20.0, 25.6 and 28.9°C) with the other environmental conditions (humidity, clothing and air velocity) set to be in the 'comfortable' range. The four tasks were maze drawing, multiplication, reaction time and tracking (following a continuously varying trace), and some of the results obtained are illustrated in Figure 6.12. (The three figures have been arranged so that 'better' performance is indicated by the results occurring higher up the vertical axis.) Although there was no variation in reaction time, Figure 6.12 demonstrates that performance on the other three measures was dependent on temperature, although in different ways. The authors attribute the differences in performance to the effects of the thermal conditions to the subjects' original (basal) arousal levels.

Beshir and Ramsey (1981) also considered the effect of the 'comfort' range of thermal conditions on performance, although their temperature range extended rather higher than that normally considered to be comfortable (i.e. to about 110°C). Their study, however, considered aspects such as the subject's perception of boredom, drowsiness and fatigue at these different temperature levels. Interestingly, their results (illustrated in Figure 6.13) suggest that these deleterious effects occur primarily in the temperature range 90–100°C. Both above and below this range, boredom, fatigue and drowsiness were reduced. Again, an arousal hypothesis could be used to account for such findings.

With respect to the effects of cold environments on motor performance, two factors appear to be important. First, the temperature of the limb which is being used: cold conditions cause a loss of cutaneous sensitivity and muscular strength, and changes in the characteristics of the synovial fluid in the joints. The second important factor is the rate of cooling.

Morton and Provins (1960) demonstrated a significant reduction in dexterity whenever the hand skin temperature fell below 20–25°C (68–97°F), although there was large individual variability. They suggest that the true relationship for any one person may be such that most of the change in performance is spread over only a few degrees. Skin sensitivity remains fairly normal for small drops in skin temperature, but deteriorates considerably after the individual's critical hand skin temperature has been reached.

Data from Clark (1961) tends to support this suggestion of a critical temperature. He showed that as the length of time for which his subjects were exposed to cold increased, their performance decreased as the skin temperature was lowered from 15 to 10.5°C (59–51°F). At a higher overall temperature, however, (13–18°C; 56–65°F) this performance/exposure duration relationship was not apparent.

With regard to the rate of cooling, this was investigated by Clark and Cohen (1960) using a knot-tying task. These experimenters found that slow cooling to a 7.2°C finger temperature (45°F) resulted in more errors than did fast cooling to the same temperature. They suggest that this was because the slow-cooling procedure allowed relatively lower subsurface temperatures to occur.

Because the main factor affecting manual performance in the cold is related

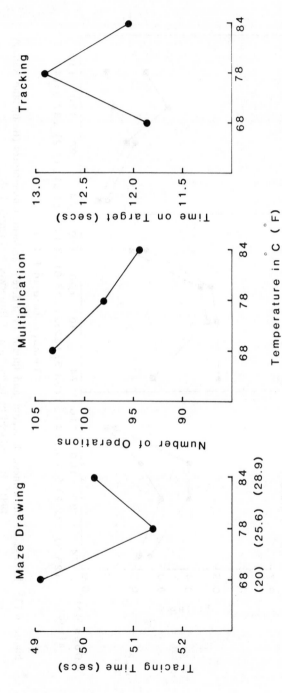

Figure 6.12. Effects of ambient temperature on three different tasks (adapted from Reddy and Ramsey, 1976). Reproduced by permission of the American Society of Heating, Refrigerating and Air Conditioning Engineers.

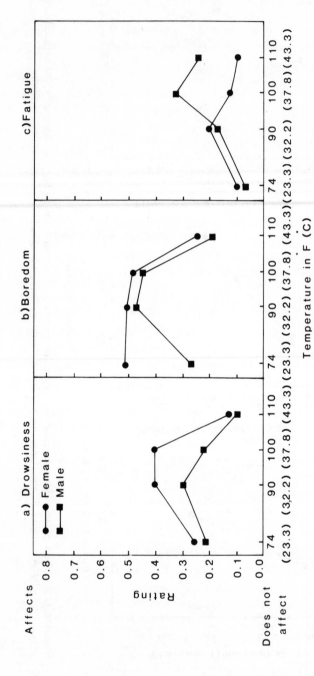

Figure 6.13. Ratings of drowsiness, boredom and fatigue in different ambient temperatures (Beshir and Ramsey, 1981). Reproduced by permission of Butterworth Scientific Ltd.

to the skin temperature of the affected limb, when it is impractical for protective clothing such as gloves to be worn it would appear sensible to attempt some means of warming the skin locally. Lockhart and Keiss (1971), for example, showed that for most tasks the impaired manual performance which was experienced during the cold conditions (when the average skin temperature of the little finger was 12°C (54°F)) was greatly alleviated by applying radiant heat to the hands only (raising the temperature of the little finger to 19.5°C (67°F)). Indeed performance using the radiated heat in very cold conditions (18°C, 0°F) was no worse than working in 15.5°C (60°F) conditions (when the average skin temperature of the little finger was 30°C (80°F)).

Artificially raising the temperature of the affected limb, however, cannot fully overcome the effects of the cold if the rest of the body is not similarly heated. For example, Lockhart (1968) maintained the temperature of his subjects' hands at the 'normal' temperature, whilst cooling the body from 25.5 to 19°C (78–66°F). His results suggest that cooling the whole body affects the operator's ability to carry out some manual tasks even though the hands were kept 'warm'. The tasks affected involved fine dexterity, and Lockhart suggests that part of the reason for the performance reduction could have been due to shivering. Support for this contention has been provided by Peacock (1956) who examined the effects of cold on rifle-aiming steadiness after vigorous exercise. Although steadiness was reduced, Peacock's results showed that if shivering is excluded as a cause of the unsteadiness, rifle steadiness was not seriously affected in the standing position when compared with results taken during normal temperatures.

The effects of cold on manual performance, therefore, appear to be twofold. First, if the cold is applied locally to the operating limb, it can have a direct effect on the muscular control of that limb, reducing such abilities as dexterity and strength. This may be overcome somewhat by locally warming the limb. Cold applied to the whole body, however, can reduce performance by shivering. If the whole body can be stabilized during this shivering, generalized cold would appear not to affect manual performance to any great extent.

SUMMARY

This chapter has considered how the immediate physical and social environments in which computers are operated are likely to affect the transfer of information from the operator to the computer and back again; that is, how the environment can interfere with an otherwise perfect system. Thus, the use of space from the viewpoint of designing the computer workstation, seating and the social effects of personal space and territoriality were first discussed. In each case it became apparent that optimum dimensions exist for maximum performance—dimensions of desk height, position from the operator, seat design, nearness of other operators, etc.

The remainder of the chapter considered less 'visible' features of the environment—the illumination, acoustic and thermal environments. In these cases, again it was shown that optimum levels exist, and slight departures from these optima result in the imposition of stress responses—which can, themselves, lead to reduced performance.

PART III

Software

The essential difference between 'hardware' and 'software' was discussed at the beginning of Part II, the three chapters of which considered ways in which the design and arrangement of the 'hard' components that an operator has to use in a computer system can enhance or reduce overall performance and thus productivity. The chapters in this third part will do the same for the computer's 'soft' aspects, its languages and the concepts that it uses.

Although the impression might have been gained from the introduction to Part II that the hardware is the most important aspect of the system—without it no operator can give instructions to the computer nor can information be returned—the same can also be said for the software. Indeed, it could be argued that the software *is* the computer: it is what gives the computer its unique 'character', its power, its facilities. Without the software there can be no computer: pressing keyboard keys will do nothing; the screen will not display anything useful; the computer will not work!

The problems involved in designing the software so that it can be used by a human operator (so that it is compatible with the operator's behaviour and abilities) are different from those encountered when dealing with the hardware. Thus, most of the hardware problems discussed in the previous three chapters related to interfacing with the operator's peripheral processing capacities: reach, vision, hearing, speech, etc. Although, of course, these processes are associated with the central processing faculties (for example, images are 'seen' by the eye but are decoded by the brain) the problems involved are rather different than those encountered when considering the software. These, then, concern more the operator's central processing capabilities: understanding, language, memory, structured thinking, the cognitive processes involved in reading, etc.

The distinction between the hardware and software problems, of course, can also be made at a different level, at an historical/technological level. Thus,

229

many of the hardware problems of the human–machine interaction have been present for many years. Typewriters were invented over a century ago and questions about the efficiency of both the QWERTY key arrangement and the position of the keyboard were as important to typists of the time as they are to present-day computer operators. Similarly cathode-ray tubes (television screens) have been available for nearly three-quarters of a century. Although some problems relating to aspects such as colour and raster scanning lines, for example, are more recent, there is no doubt that early television viewers were plagued as much with glare, eye strain or sound quality as are the present-day VDU operators or speech production engineers. Taking this type of historical viewpoint further, however, it becomes apparent that the software aspects present very new types of problems. Because computers are such recent technological introductions, the operator's problems of interacting with the languages used and the ideas and concepts that they employ are far more recent and, to some extent, less understood. It will be the purpose of the following two chapters to throw some light on the more recent findings in this area.

The essential distinction between Chapters 7 and 8 will be to consider the software aspects from the point of view of first the computer programmer (Chapter 7) and then the computer user (Chapter 8). Thus, Chapter 7 will consider aspects such as the design and use of computer languages, and some of the behavioural attributes needed for computer programming. Chapter 8, however, will discuss the importance of software design not from the point of view of the computer scientist but from that of the naive user. Thus, features such as screen information layout, the use of colour and other cues, etc. will be discussed.

Of course, in some respects the distinction between the two chapters is one without a difference. Computer programmers are also users; the naive user often has to take the role of the programmer to make the machine operate in the appropriate way. This being said, however, it is possible to make the distinction by suggesting that Chapter 7 will consider the factors that contribute to the ease of use by people who would otherwise fall under the remit of Chapter 8.

CHAPTER 7

Software Psychology

The theme of this chapter will be to consider the important behavioural factors that are associated with the software production, from the point of view of the programmer and the experienced computer user. To all intents and purposes, this concerns the computer languages and the ways in which they are used to program the computer. Within such a categorization, however, it should be realized that the software can take a number of different forms, each having accompanying problems that they present to the user. As an illustration of these different forms, Stewart (1976) suggests that there is a software continuum, which extends from 'hard' to 'soft' software.

At the 'hard' end of the continuum lies the system software: that is, the instructions that actually make the computer operate—its languages, operating procedures, etc. These affect such factors as the computer's response time, its error diagnostics and the facilities that it offers for editing and changing programs. As Stewart points out, these features are outside of the control of many users—particularly those who use computers relatively infrequently. It is because this type is either impossible or extremely difficult for most users to change that Stewart calls it 'hard software'.

At the other end of the continuum is the 'application software'. This forms the programs, packages of programs and applications available to all users—both programmers and naive operators alike. Since the user can often alter these packages to suit his or her own requirements, Stewart describes this end of the continuum the 'soft software' end.

Of course, this continuum is not fixed: as the user becomes increasingly sophisticated and experienced at using computers the hard software becomes more and more 'soft'.

A further distinction which should be made, particularly with respect to the hard-software end of the continuum, is one between computer languages and dialogues. This distinction is both subtle and important from the point of view of understanding psychology's role in software design, and it reflects the discussion of the concept of communication presented in Chapter 1. Thus it was emphasized that efficient communication occurs only when the ideas are transmitted accurately—that the correct *sense* of the message is transmitted from the transmitter to the receiver rather than the precise words having to be received accurately.

The distinction between language and dialogue, then, is similar to that between the 'words' and the 'sense' of the message. The computer language is that which the computer 'understands' and 'reacts' to. It is designed to be of a form which the computer accepts—that is in 1's and 0's. Because it is often difficult for the human programmer to understand or to remember these binary digits, however, more complex and sophisticated languages have been designed which translate some of the words that the programmer uses in his or her everyday speech into the characters that the computer understands. It is at this interface that the language becomes a dialogue. Thus the 'translator' acts to convert the computer programmer's ideas expressed in his or her own language into the instructions that are understood by the computer in its own language. When this translation occurs correctly, when the ideas from the human brain are transmitted efficiently to the computer's central processing unit, then a dialogue can be said to have been set up between the operator and the computer. The more sophisticated the computer language translator that is used, therefore, the more likely it is that the dialogue becomes successful. Thus, it can be seen that the problems of designing software from the behavioural viewpoint lie in the efficient design of human–computer dialogues.

The results of poor dialogue design can be very important and can cause reactions ranging from simple frustration (with its concomitant performance losses) at one end of the scale to large organizational financial losses at the other. Kling and Scacchi (1980) suggest that computing-use failures can fall into four categories: *miscalculations* (for example, deleting the wrong file); *hold-ups* (due, for example, to new operators not understanding the correct procedure); *circumstantial errors* (such as wrong operating system commands); and '*natural*' *accidents* such as hardware failure. Clearly, the first three of these failures can be laid at the door of poor dialogue design since they all involve the operator carrying out a task in the wrong manner. The results of such failures are often time consuming and costly. Thus, Hebditch (1979) reports the cases of three projects which had to be abandoned (with losses ranging from £90,000 to £300,000) because the dialogue that had been designed was quite inappropriate to the user environment. One was too complicated for the users to understand, one was too long-winded for easy comprehension, whilst the third was 'inefficient'.

LANGUAGE AND DIALOGUE TYPES

A great deal has been made so far of the subtle distinction between a language and a dialogue. The message that should clearly have emerged is that it is most important to ensure that the *dialogue*, the dynamic interface between the computer and the operator, is designed appropriately. However, before being able to discuss the behavioural factors important in efficient dialogue design, it is first necessary to consider the types of languages that are available to the computer upon which it operates.

Language types

It has been emphasized many times that computers actually only use one type of language—binary digits composed only of 1's and 0's or 'ons' and 'offs' (that is, the presence or absence of a voltage). Because these make it difficult for a programmer to operate at a conceptual level, some form of software 'translation' device is used, the basic type of which is known as assembly language (or, sometimes, 'machine code'). This operates using at least the letters of a natural language such as English so that programming concepts devised using some semblance of a natural language are 'transformed', or assembled, into the machine's binary digits. For example, to store information in a particular memory location in the computer the programmer might instruct the computer to STA (that is, to store the information at location 'A' in the computer's memory).

Because it represents only a basic 'translator', however, assembly language is still very complex to use and, although very powerful programs can be written, it offers the programmer very little flexibility outside of the confines of the few 'statements' available. For this reason, most computers operate with higher level languages which, because they offer more flexibility in the use of natural languages, have to perform more 'translations' and are thus generally slower. Formally, they are of two types—interpretive and compiled.

With an interpretive language, such as BASIC (an acronym for Beginner's All Symbolic Instruction Code), the instructions are programmed into the computer using what can be recognized as words from a natural language (such as IF, THEN, GO, etc). The computer then transforms (interprets) these words into its own binary digit form *each time that it encounters a representation of the word or phrase in its own memory*. A compiled language like FORTRAN (FORmula TRANslation), on the other hand, operates more efficiently. This interpretive process is done only once, and then the computer operates much quicker on the translated (compiled) code on each subsequent occasion. The most obvious difference between the interpretive and compiled languages, then, is one of computer operation speed although, of course, there are other operational differences between the two types.

Whatever type of language is used, a more useful distinction between them has been proposed by Fitter (1979) which is based more on the facilities that are made available to the operator. His is more a 'dialogue-type' distinction, therefore and, indeed, he later relates his language categories to different types of dialogue style. In his review he distinguishes between 'navigational' and 'non-navigational' languages.

As its name suggest, a navigational computer language is one in which the user needs to 'steer through' the language's grammatical rules. As Shackel (1980) describes it:

> 'The user must not only describe the actions/data required but also encase his described requirement within a set of artificial syntactic, constructional (or navigational) elements.'

In practice, then, all of the initiative and ingenuity arises from the user who has to instruct the system how to find its way to answer the problem. This can place quite heavy burdens on the user's cognitive capacities—particularly on remembering the appropriate instructions.

The navigational languages can be further sub-divided into linear structures in which each instruction follows each other (as with many of the more well-known formal languages) and those which are two-dimensional or diagrammatic. Comparing linear and diagrammatic languages, Fitter (1979) suggests that if the graphic notation can reveal the structure inherent in the underlying data or the process by which entities are manipulated, then a diagrammatic language will be superior to a linear symbolic language.

Despite their apparent rigidity in form Fitter (1979) does commend navigational languages. He argues that, for all but the most naive of users, the necessary investment of time and effort required to tutor the individual and to provide suitable navigational aids will result in the user having confidence in, and control of, the language. He implies, therefore, that the navigational will eventually prove superior to the more 'natural' non-navigational languages such as a totally natural or a menu-driven language. These, he argues, will

> 'protect the user from the innards and structure of the system, but never allow him properly to comprehend either the total potential of the system, or more importantly, when the system is being used in a way that was not intended by its designer'.

The message, therefore, is clear: the language flexibility of non-navigational languages can be limiting for more advanced users. Nevertheless, as Shackel (1980) points out, the relatively simple types of action required of the user give less opportunity for error and forgetting, and allow more time to concentrate on the essentials of the particular problem without having to be concerned with syntax or special instructions.

Fitter describes the menu-type of non-navigational language as a 'constrained language'. These systems simplify the task for the user by enabling him or her to give instructions via menus, multiple menus (for example, the PRESTEL viewdata system), prompting or form filling. Again, such languages appear to be useful to naive users in well understood but limited applications. As Shackel (1980) points out, however, their drawback is that, unlike the retrieval power of formal languages, the nature of the questions which can be answered is limited by the designer's foresight, planning or model of the user's behaviour and abilities.

Natural languages

If the necessity for a truly interactive dialogue is taken to its extreme, the language which emerges will not be constrained by the computer's syntactic requirements but only by the limits of the user's language. A natural language then, one in which the user would converse with the computer as he or she would another person, is likely to be the goal of dialogue designers. Indeed, it is one which, it has been argued, might possibly be attained. Thus Addis (1977), for example, surveyed attempts up to 1975 to develop natural language systems and concluded that, in due course, a universal 'natural language' processing system could be developed.

Despite Addis' optimism, however, it must remain doubtful whether a truly natural language can ever be designed. Thus, as was emphasized in Chapters 4 and 5 when considering speech input and output, full communication contains much more than simply the words used or spoken in a language. Gestures, intonations, stresses, etc., are all used by the transmitter to convey the message to the receiver and it is unlikely that the present generation of computers will ever be powerful enough to be able to incorporate these 'active' components of a true language. The most that could be achieved are specific subsets of a natural language for particular applications. For example, Shackel (1979) describes the language ROBOT (Harris, 1977) which has proved useful in a number of different, although specific, situations.

Natural languages then, (at least those which have been designed so far) have both advantages and disadvantages, and these have been summarized by Cuff (1979) as follows:

The principal advantages of a natural language (NL) interface for casual users are:

(i) It provides an already familiar way of forming questions.
(ii) It is self-evident that the formulation of any query need be no more complex than its 'natural' statement. Most complicated queries may be posed relatively easily compared with formal languages or menu methods.
(iii) There are often many ways to extract the same data; the user can choose his own wording.

(iv) The user does not have to learn a formal syntax (as such), and his departures from accepted grammar may be tolerated without comment.

Against these, the following points may be noted:

(i) The use of NL encourages an unrealistic expectation of the system's power—it might lead the untrained user into talking to the computer as though it were intelligent.
(ii) The linguistic limitations of such a system are not as well defined as they are with a formal language. They can appear, sporadically and unexpectedly, when the system rejects an unknown word or a grammatical construction, or when it lacks background knowledge.
(iii) NL's richness frequently makes sentences ambiguous.
(iv) Because the vocabulary and knowledge which people want to use when querying a particular database may be specific to the latter, an NL system has to be partially recast for each new domain of discourse.

Some of these disadvantages of using natural language, of course, may be alleviated with proper design. Thus, Biermann, Ballard and Sigmon (1983) describe an empirical investigation of one natural language system which produced, overall, successful processing rates of nearly 74% of the problems set. They did not encounter any of the standard concerns about NL expressed above, such as vagueness, ambiguity or verbosity. Nevertheless, the problems set by the authors were specific to the language system used, again suggesting that the solution of the pros and cons of using natural language will have to be related to the particular situation in which a natural language is envisaged.

Finally, it should be pointed out that, from a behavioural viewpoint, some restrictions on the use of words and syntax within a language does not necessarily produce reduced performance. Thus it will be remembered that, whilst discussing the values of speech input devices in Chapter 4, work of Kelly and Chapanis (1977) was discussed which showed that problem solving performance was not reduced even though the vocabulary available was restricted to 300 words. Similar conclusions were reached by Miller (1981) who describes a study in which subjects used unconstrained natural language to specify procedures for manipulating files in a simulated information and retrieval task. Again, although only relatively few (610) unique words were used to define the fairly complex task, the results suggested that people can communicate within the confines of a limited vocabulary language. Thus, as Shackel (1980) points out:

'Instead of attempting to program computers to interpret all the complexities of human natural language, perhaps a restricted vocabulary and syntax can be derived which is easier for the computer and not significantly limiting to human acceptability and performance.'

Ehrenreich (1981), however, injects a note of caution to such optimism. He argues that, although subjects were able to communicate with a restricted language vocabulary, because the same words often have different meanings in different contexts, the subjects often had many more than 300 different *semantic* entities available to them. Programming a computer using a much restricted language, then, may not be as easy as communicating with another person with the same restriction.

Nevertheless arguments that it is possible to use a restricted language have led, in recent years, to the growing acceptance that it is the meaning rather than the information that needs to be transmitted for efficient communication. In this respect, then, the partial 'fuzziness' of natural language may be an essential characteristic and an advantage under certain conditions. This has evolved to produce languages which are 'fuzzy' in their character, such as PRUF (Possibilistic Relational Universal Fuzzy) described by Zadeh (1978). Unfortunately, the concept of fuzzy languages is rather too complex to be described in detail here.

Diagrammatic languages

The essential feature of a diagrammatic language is that, as its name suggests, it requires the programmer to instruct the computer not by using words so much as perceptual structures that describe the appropriate process. Of these languages, the flowchart is probably the best known example.

Fitter and Green (1981) suggest that diagrams can be very useful as a medium for computer languages. Many of the conventions can be learnt very swiftly and indeed many are already known to the 'man-in-the street', so that they make an excellent communication medium for the naive user. Furthermore, when presented as flowcharts, diagrams appear to aid the user when having to make the type of complex decisions that often are involved in computer programming. Thus, Wright and Reid (1973) presented their subjects with 'difficult' and 'easy' problems and showed that with the difficult material the flowcharts produced fewer subsequent errors than when the material was presented as prose, short sentences or tables. When the material was easy to comprehend, there was no advantage.

Kamman (1975) compared the efficiency of two types of flowchart design which differed both in complexity (the number of choices to be made) and the number of words on the chart. He showed that the more streamlined chart (less complex, fewer words) produced significantly fewer errors (looking up telephone numbers in a directory) than the first. Furthermore, both forms of flowchart produced fewer errors than the normal, linear structured telephone directory.

Kamman's study demonstrated that reducing the number of choice points and making the whole chart simpler made the task easier for the subjects. However, in some cases it may not either be possible or practical to reduce the number of choices—particularly with a complex process such as computer programming. In such cases, however, it may be possible to form small sub-charts, each of which deals with separate sequences in the operation. A more radical solution has been advanced by Jones (1978) who suggests that the material might be rewritten, vertically, in a 'branching list' structure, so that the reader is required to jump from section to section. For example, in a decision making task question 1 might read 'Is the motor turning? If YES continue with question 2. If NO go to question 15'. Wright (1977), however, argues that such a format may be useful in providing specific answers to specific questions but it loses some of the important advantages of flowcharts—primarily the visual appearance of the decision making structure.

Dialogue types

Through the discussion of different types of computer languages, it should increasingly have become apparent that the 'ideal' language is one which relates its requirements to the operator's cognitive and perceptual abilities. For casual or naive users, this implies some sort of non-navigational language; for the experienced user, however, who might wish to extend the capabilities of the system and can understand the system's construction, this implies some sort of navigational language. In both cases the important feature is that an appropriate dialogue is set up between the computer and the user. To do this, there exist a number of different dialogue styles.

In his article dealing with types of language, Hebditch (1979) also discusses dialogue styles in which he emphasizes the practical issues and details of dialogue design. He proposes eight main groups of dialogue styles:

1 *Natural-language based.* These have already been discussed.

2 *Programming-type dialogues.* This form of dialogue presents information to the operator in the form of a computer program. Thus, users have to operate at a more complex level than when using other dialogue types.

3 *Instructions and response.* In this type of dialogue, which Hebditch argues is very suitable for less-frequent users, information is transmitted in the form of questions to which very simple responses have to be made.

4 *Menu selection.* Selecting the appropriate response from a list presented on the screen is a useful dialogue type for very complex data. Unfortunately, as Hebditch points out, with inappropriate choices of alternatives, dialogues of this nature can easily suggest to the user that he or she is stupid.

5 *Displayed formats.* In this type of dialogue, the necessary information is presented to the user as a graphic display. Ramsey and Atwood (1979) suggest that this is not truly a dialogue type, and more will be said about the display of information in the next chapter.

6 *Form filling.* This is a dialogue which has become very popular with the advent of the VDU, rather than having to present information using a teleprinter.In this dialogue users input information in response to questions

asked in the format of a standardized form. Ramsey and Atwood (1979) point out that this is generally faster than standard 'question-and-answer' dialogues because the user often provides several responses in a single transaction. Again, however, the efficiency of this type of dialogue depends largely on the quality of the presented information, and these problems will be discussed in Chapter 8.

7 *Panel modification.* Hebditch recommends that this type of dialogue is only used by experienced operators. Data are displayed on the screen in response to a single input key, and this can also be combined as a form-filling dialogue.

8 *Query-by-example.* This technique is used generally to retrieve information from large data bases; the user starts by indicating the data set to be investigated and the system responds by indicating the data elements in the record concerned. Then the user indicates the limits of the data to be searched, etc. Ehrenreich (1981) and Reisner (1981) have both produced extensive reviews of the benefits and disadvantages of this type of dialogue.

PROGRAMMING BEHAVIOUR

Before considering the factors important in the design of efficient languages, it is useful to discuss the aspects of a programmer's own behaviour which are likely to act either for or against the efficient use of the language to program the computer. These aspects clearly relate to a programmer's cognitive abilities, in particular to the ability to learn and to remember the language syntax and use, to understand the language, and to adopt appropriate cognitive styles in order that performance is maximized and errors are reduced. Some of the cognitive aspects of such performance measures were discussed in Chapter 1. The purpose of this section will be to consider how these abilities might affect the performance using software. With such information, it should then be possible to consider the design of more useful software in a later section.

Learning

In a series of experiments Mayer (1975, 1979, 1981) investigated the factors that a novice has to learn when learning how to program a computer (in BASIC). He suggests (1981) that to learn effectively, students need to be able to liken their actions to some physical or mechanical models, from which they can abstract the programming syntax. Thus, to learn the complexities, students need to be provided with some sort of concrete model of the relevant processes in which the machine's operation and the effects of syntax are demonstrated explicitly either on paper or using physical models.

In a series of investigations, Mayer (1975, 1976) investigated the efficiency of such concrete models for learning BASIC. Initially, subjects were either given a concrete model of the computer or were not, and were then asked to read the manual of a BASIC-like language before being tested on the concepts learnt. The results demonstrated that members of the control (non-model) group learnt the material better and were able to transfer their knowledge to the test material only when the test material was similar to that in the instructional manual. When the test material required the subjects to 'go beyond' that in the manual, those subjects provided with a concrete model performed better—that is, they had learned the syntax better. (In a subsequent experiment Mayer (1980) used the same proceedure to investigate a different language—file management—and reached similar conclusions.)

Mayer (1976) also considered when in the learning process the model should be presented. Thus, in a similar experiment to that above, subjects were given the model either before or after reading the manual. Interestingly the results demonstrated qualitative differences in performance between the two groups. The 'after' group excelled on problems which required some degree of retention of the material, whereas the 'before' group performed better on problems which required creative transfer to new situations.

In addition to investigating ways of increasing understanding and thus the ability to learn, Mayer (1979, 1981) has also considered what *needs* to be learned. He has proposed a detailed decomposition of the knowledge required for BASIC programming into a number of different levels, claiming that the translation between these levels is a critical component of the programmer's skill. Thus, he considers that the features of programming that a novice needs to learn are:

1 *Machine level*, i.e. an understanding of the electronic concepts that are used to operate a computer—logic circuits, electro-magnetic fields, octal numbers, etc. This level of knowledge, whilst being important to the professional, may be too detailed for the novice programmer.

2 *Transactions*. This level acts at the operational level of the computer; the transactions are related to the general functions of the computer and are the building blocks from which the statements are made. Despite their importance in initial understanding, Mayer suggests that the transactional level has not been exploited fully in instructional manuals.

3 *Prestatements*. These are subcategories of statements and are more specific subgroups of statements that contain the same name. For example the action taken by the computer when confronted with the statement A = B, can vary depending on whether B is a memory location or a specific variable. Each of these actions represents a different 'prestatement'.

4 *Statements*. These are, traditionally, the basic level of program understanding. In essence, each statement forms a collection of prestatements which share the same name such as LET, PRINT, etc. Mayer

argues that, although they are the basic levels for computer instruction, a full comprehension and ability to learn BASIC may also involve understanding the implications of the lower levels. Unfortunately, as discussed above, this is not often done in instructional manuals.

5 *Mandatory chunks*. This is a series of two or more statements that must always occur in a particular sequence, such as IF and THEN, READ and DATA or FOR and NEXT. The novice programmer needs to learn these combinations and, essentially, to treat them as one.

6 *Non-mandatory chunks*. Like mandatory chunks, these also are statements that often appear together, although they do not have to do so. They are composed of two types: basic and higher non-mandatory chunks.

Basic non-mandatory chunks are a series of statements that often go together to accomplish some action, such as obtaining a count of the number of subjects processed by the program, or continually reading data from within the program. They could be termed basic 'procedures'. *Higher* non-mandatory chunks, on the other hand, are groups of statements and transactions that not only often go together, but have a specific sequence of operation. Mayer argues that, as the learner gains more experience, the size and number of chunks (or 'superstatements') he or she knows will grow.

7 *Programs*. These are the highest levels of knowledge for a programmer to learn. They represent the total set of chunks, statements and prestatements needed to operate the computer in the manner in which the operator wishes. At this level of knowledge, Mayer argues, many other programming skills are required, some of which will be discussed later.

Memory

An ability to learn the formats of statements, chunks, etc., necessary for succesful programming is clearly an important feature of efficient programming. As such, it has implications for the design of computer dialogues as will be discussed in the next section. Learning, however, is only one aspect of the programmer's cognitive abilities that need to be used to remain efficient; another is clearly the ability to retain the information learned—that is, memory.

The presence and use of a complex human memory system forms the basis for most models of computer programming behaviour that have been advanced (for example, Brooks, 1977, or Shneiderman and Mayer, 1979). Most divide human memory into two subsystems (short-term and long-term memory), although Brooks (1977) adds a third—'external memory'—which, he suggests, represents the 'hard-copy' memory aids available to programmers such as writing program segments on pieces of paper. Although this is not a model of the cognitive components of memory (as is the hypothesis of two 'working areas' in the brain), the presence of such capacities and their relevance to overall theories of programmer ability and behaviour will be discussed later.

The little empirical work that has been performed to investigate the role of memory in programming behaviour has considered the problem primarily from the viewpoint of attempting to increase the memorability of program structures through the use of both appropriate file and variable names and of concrete models. The practical application of this work, then, has been to aid the programmer when the program has been written—that is, to help in the elimination of errors from the program. This process is called 'debugging' and will be discussed in detail later.

In a simple experiment Shneiderman (1976) asked subjects to memorize two identical FORTRAN computer programs, both printed on a line-printer. Although the first was printed as a complete and working program, the second was a jumbled version of the first. The two listings were given to a wide variety of subjects, from non-programmers to expert programmers, who were asked to recall the two programs (Shneiderman describes this as 'reconstruction'). His results suggested that experience had no effect on the ability to recall accurately the 'shuffled' version of the program. With regard to the complete and working program listing, however, although non-programmers did no better than they did with the shuffled version, the amount recalled and the degree of reconstruction performed did increase with programming ability. Shneiderman attributes these results to a person's increased ability to recognize program sub-structures with experience:

'When asked to reconstruct a program, the subjects applied their knowledge of the programming language syntax and reconstructed their statements as best they could. Often the experienced subjects would write functionally equivalent but syntactically varying forms.'

In other words, since memorization of complex material such as computer programs cannot be accomplished by rote it would appear that competent programmers are able to memorize more material owing to their increased skill at imposing structure on the information.

In a later article Shneiderman (1980) took the argument further to suggest that research performed on the memorization of English sentences (for example, Bransford and Franks, 1971; Barclay, 1973) can be used to imply that programmers store the semantics rather than the syntax (that is, the meaning rather than the rules) of computer statements. They then extract the semantic information and recode groups of statements into higher level semantic structures which can represent the operation of a group of statements. This argument is similar to one proposed by Atwood and Ramsey (1978), who suggest that the information contained in a program is represented in a programmer's memory as a 'connected, partially ordered list (hierarchy) of "prepositions"'. Using arguments of this nature, Shneiderman suggests ways in which programmers can be trained to increase their memory for program structures, and these will be considered later.

A similar technique to using concrete models to improve the memorability of program structures has been proposed in a different context by Ausubel (1968) who has argued that learning new technical prose may be enhanced by providing an *advance organizer*. This normally takes the form of a short expository introduction, presented prior to the text. It contains no specific pieces from the text but provides the general concepts and ideas that will be used in the text. West and Fensham (1976) and Mayer (1979) have investigated the use of such advance organizers for computer programmers and demonstrated that they have their major effects in situations where the material is new or difficult for the learner (for example, for 'low-ability' or inexperienced students, or where information has to be transferred from one situation to another).

A slightly different approach to investigating the memorability of programs was taken by Love (1977). He studied the effects of complexity of the program and the extent to which it appeared as paragraphs (that is, its structure) on the same type of memorization/reconstruction ability as used by Shneiderman. He showed that paragraphing did not facilitate reconstruction at all. Experienced programmers, however, did benefit from having the simpler programs to deal with (non-programmers did not improve their performance with the simpler programs). Similar results have been obtained for 'indented' versus 'non-indented' program listings (an indented listing is one in which program sub-sets, such as FOR...NEXT, are indented from the left margin). Such data, therefore, suggest strongly that memorization is not related to listing readability but to program complexity. Further evidence of this assertion can be seen in a study by Sime, Green and Guest (1973) who found that nested conditional statements (IF...THEN...ELSE) reduced the error rate and solution time compared with GO TO statements. They explain this result on the basis of lower short-term memory requirements for the nested statements although, again, an argument could also be proposed that the IF...THEN...ELSE types of statements help to provide more structure to the program than does a sequence of simple GO TO's.

In his investigations of the effects of concrete models on programming behaviour Mayer also considered their relevance to remembering program structures. It will be remembered that his technique was to provide some subjects with a BASIC manual and a model of how the language operated, whereas others were provided simply with the manual. In one experiment (Mayer and Bromage, 1980), students were provided with the model either before or after reading the manual, and were subsequently asked to recall all they could about portions of the manual. The results showed qualitative differences in the type of information recalled. The 'model-before-manual' group recalled more conceptual information (i.e. relating to the internal operation of the computer), whereas the 'model-after-manual' group recalled more technical and format information relating to the programming language and ways in which a computer is programmed. The model, therefore, had a strong effect on the way that the information was encoded by the subjects.

The available evidence, therefore, suggests that programmers are able to remember the structure of their programs by rearranging the program into meaningful, semantic, chunks. The value of a concrete model in Mayer's studies suggests that the chunks may be arranged along the lines of such models. These observations lead to a number of possible ways for training programmer memory and effectiveness.

First, as Mayer (1981) points out, the use of concrete models in training can lead to better recall. Thus, making little distinction between the process by which information is absorbed (learning) and retained (memory), he argues:

> 'If your goal is to produce learners who will not need to use the language creatively, then no model is needed. If your goal is to produce learners who will be able to come up with creative solutions to novel (for them) problems, then a concrete model early in learning is quite useful.'

Second, given the results of Shneiderman regarding the memory performance of experienced programmers and their imposition of semantic structure on the programs, he suggests that 'if the program is well organized and the problem domain familiar, we see no limit to the size of the program that can be commited to memory'. Furthermore he suggests (1978) that programmers might be trained to look for familiar patterns of templates such as an IF statement in a DO loop. Similarly, program composition should be taught by the development of templates which are organized into modules.

The memorability of programs, of course, should also be able to be increased using many of the memory techniques known to behavioural scientists—particularly for helping the programmer to remember the names given to different variables.

Carroll (1981) discussed the implications for meaning and memorability of the names that are often given to abstract structures and he also surveyed (1982a) the range of names that users gave to their computer files. He found that users often imposed a common structure on the names of their files and adopted common strategies for such creative naming. Such findings are consistent with those from cognitive psychologists such as Garner and Whitman (1965) who have found that lists of nonsense words are more easily learned and remembered when they display internal consistency. For example, the list BROZ, BRAZ, BROJ, BRAJ, PLOZ, PLAZ, PLOJ, PLAJ is more efficiently remembered than, say, BROZ, BRAJ, PLOZ, PLAJ, BLOJ, BLAZ, PROJ, PRAZ. Thus, in the first list, the first two letters of each word

(BR and PL) become redundant due to their continuation in the sequence, and the sequence itself has consistency (--OZ, --AZ, --OJ, --AJ).

In his survey of file names, Carroll found that consistency was structured into the majority of names in terms simply of either truncating the file content (for example, SURvey) or of blending together multiple words (for example, SURVDATA). Unfortunately, he did not investigate any relationship between the use of such strategies and the memorability of the names produced. Had he done so, however, it is unlikely that any definite relationship would have emerged, particularly given the results that have been obtained relating to the memorability of variable names that are given mnemonic structures. For example, Shneiderman (1980) reports two experiments, a comprehension experiment which showed mnemonic names to be more effective, and a debugging experiment that found no such effects. Furthermore, Sheppard *et al.* (1979) found no evidence that mnemonic names helped professional programmers to remember about 50-line FORTRAN programs. Sheil (1981) suggests that such inconclusive results might have been due to individual programmer/program variability in needing such mnemonic techniques; the names might have been more useful for programs with which the programmer is less familiar. Furthermore, it could be suggested that mnemonics proposed by the programmers themselves rather than by the experimenters might be more successful.

Another way of increasing the memorability of a program structure, particularly when it may later have to be debugged, is to include comment statements at appropriate points in the program. These non-executable statements are always printed out with a program listing to aid the programmer to remember the meaning of different variables, the actions that a particular subroutine will take, etc. Indeed, the judicious use of comments is almost universally considered to be good programming practice. Unfortunately, however, the evidence available is not entirely conclusive. For example, Weissman (1974) found that appropriate comments caused hand simulation of programs to proceed significantly faster, but with significantly more errors. On the other hand, Shneiderman (1977) contrasted students' modification and recall of FORTRAN programs with either high level or low level comments (that is, comments relating either to the program structure or to descriptions of individual statements). The programs with the higher level comments were found to be significantly easier to modify although, unfortunately, Sheppard *et al.* (1979) were unable to repeat these conclusions. They found that neither high nor low level comments had any reliable effect on either the accuracy or the time taken to modify small FORTRAN programs. Sheil (1981) argues that such equivocation might be the result of differences in the value of the comments to the individual subjects. Thus a comment is only useful if it tells the readers something that they either do not know or cannot infer from the program itself.

Cognitive style

The evidence that is arising suggests that successful programmers develop strategies for coping with the very complex material that they have to deal with. These strategies include breaking down the problem into meaningful and manageable chunks. The question needs to be posed, therefore, whether a particular style of thinking exists which allows a programmer to perform successfully.

Witkin and his associates (Witkin *et al.*, 1954; Witkin *et al.*, 1962) have described cognitive style variously as a person's preferred strategy for encoding, as structures for filtering incoming stimuli, as control structures for directing mental coding, or as mental programs for input. They have also referred to it as 'field articulation','psychological differentiation', or 'field dependence'. In short, therefore, 'cognitive style' refers to the ways in which we treat information within our world. Such individual styles, Witkin and his colleagues have shown, are stable over the lifetime of an individual despite external influences. Tyler (1974) defines cognitive style slightly differently, and relates it to the ability to differentiate parts or aspects of a confusing situation or the ability to deal with confusion. Often the stimuli used to measure subjects' field-dependence are ambiguous figures, and individuals who have high scores are those who are able to extract relevant information more efficiently.

Doktor (1976) has proposed that cognitive style reflects two alternative modes of processing information: *analytic*, which is sequential, linear, verbal-symbolic processing and is dominated by the left hemisphere in the brain, and *heuristic*, which is intuitive, global, pictorial processing and is right-hemisphere dominated. As Egly (1982) points out, the common thread in these views is that cognitive style corresponds to a difference in the ability to detect and to analyze details.

To investigate the effect of cognitive style on programmer performance, Egly (1982) asked subjects, who previously had had their cognitive style determined, to use a computer program and set of data to answer a series of questions. She found that cognitive style was significantly related to the number of questions answered successfully, with field-independent individuals performing particularly well. These results are similar to those of Coombs, Gibson and Alty (1982) in their investigation of the success rate of novice computer programmers:

> Successful learners worked from 'inside' the language, paying close attention to the procedural representation of logical relations between individual language structures. Less successful learners sought to determine important structural detail with reference to factors external to the program language itself, e.g. features of the local machine, and to represent this knowledge in descriptive rather than procedural terms.

Less successful learners, then, were more field-dependent.

DIALOGUE DESIGN CONSIDERATIONS

One of the important messages to have emerged from the data presented in the previous section is that programming and interacting with computers involves a compound set of cognitive behaviours. Efficient computer interaction is a learned skill which involves, essentially, being able to analyse the programming problem into meaningful chunks and to translate these chunks into usable computer program code. Only by performing such semantic and syntactic analyses will the complex nature of the task, which involves a great deal to be remembered and learned, be able to be performed efficiently.

These aspects then represent both the abilities and the requirements of the programmer. The next question to be asked in the search for efficient dialogue design is how the program or the language can themselves by designed to interact with the programmer; to fit the programmer's abilities and requirements. Questions of this nature are usually answered by suggesting that the language, the program, and even the displayed information needs to be 'user-friendly'. As will become apparent in this section, however, this jargonized phrase itself begs the question 'What is user-friendliness', and how is it attained?'

User-friendliness

The concept of user-friendliness can best be explained by remembering that, for efficient operation, a dialogue needs to be set up between the computer and the operator. The essential feature of this dialogue is the dynamic transmission of information between the two components; both need to understand the message produced and to operate in an environment (social and physical) that facilitates this understanding. As with any communication acts between two or more humans, however, irrespective of the physical conditions (such as intense noise), the message can often be lost or distorted if the social and cognitive abilities of the transmitter and receiver are at variance; for example, if one person dislikes or mistrusts the other, or one person operates with higher thought processes, using more complex words and sentence constructions, than the other. Since the same is also true for the interaction between humans and computers, the concept of user-friendliness is one which suggests that human–computer communication should operate at the same 'level' as friendly human–human communication.

Morton *et al.* (1979) suggest that one reason why a dialogue may *not* be user-friendly is because languages are often 'computer-centric'. The software designers have, for one reason or another, assumed either that the users share their specialist knowledge and experience, or that they will learn to adapt to it. Just as a person can be 'ego-centric', therefore, a computer-centric dialogue would insist that the computer is at the 'centre of events' and that all commands, operations, etc. are performed in one 'direction' only: for and towards the computer. As will be discussed later, this can lead to mistakes in interpreting the meaning of command words, particularly if the user does not either understand or 'naturally' adhere to such computer-centricity. In these cases the computer commands are not compatible with the user's expectations.

To the newcomer to computers, one way in which computer-centricity often appears is through the use of jargon—words, phrases or commands that are meaningful only to members of the particular population that they are used by—in this case computer experts. Jargon can occur both within the computer program or system itself and in the documentation that is often supplied with the system. Overuse of jargon can lead to misunderstandings by the user and to negative attitudes towards both the programmer and the system.

Jones (1978) describes a number of examples of the ways in which jargon can interfere with efficient dialogue, ranging from using completely idiosyncratic terms known only to 'experts', to demanding that the user input information to the computer in particularly idiosyncratic ways—ways which might be logically correct and understandable by an expert but which are not immediately obvious to a naive user. Figure 7.1 provides an example of these two forms of jargon (in the second, the user was supposed to type either 'Q' to quit from the computer or 'C' to continue computing).

Other examples of the computer-centricity with regard to the inputting of information are supplied by Wasserman (1973). He quotes the example of a program which will not accept any response other than the three characters which make the word 'YES'. Thus '(space)YES', 'YES(space)' or even 'yes' would not be acceptable despite the fact that the user is, in all three cases, trying to signal agreement. He suggests further that synonyms, such as

---

a) *Information which is understandable only by those who understand the particular computer system*

ERROR BB NO ENVIRONMENT PRESENT FOR RETURN

b) *Incomplete information and unhelpful instruction* (the appropriate response is 'Q' or 'C')

(Computer display)	(User response)
QUIT?	NO
QUIT?	YES
QUIT?	YES
QUIT?	NO
QUIT?	NO
QUIT?	N
QUIT?	Y

(At this point the user gave up in desperation)

Figure 7.1. Two examples of jargonized dialogue provided by Jones (1978).

'SURE' and 'CERTAINLY' should be allowable. Cheriton (1976) takes the argument further to suggest that command words should also be allowable in abbreviated form. Each of these suggestions, of course, is likely to lead to the user having to maintain fewer key words in memory, and may thus lead to fewer errors.

The concept of user-friendliness also applies to the way in which the computer dialogue responds in the event of an error. In human–human communication, one would attribute rather unfriendly attributes to a person who, disagreeing with some information during a conversation, simply replied 'Error' or even 'Error number 43'. In addition to being uninformative and unhelpful for future communication and learning (Hansen, 1971, notes that computer program learners have a great deal of curiosity to find out what happens when they do something wrong), such a response would be likely to lead to reduced motivation to continue the conversation or to listen further to the arguments being put. The same is clearly true also for human–computer communication.

Since users clearly do make errors and since, with the present generation of computers at least, information needs to be input to the program in fairly well-defined ways, error messages are important aspects of a program. Shneiderman (1979) argues that a well-designed error message should be understandable, non-threatening and low-key. The important point, then, is that they should not simply tell the user that he or she has made a mistake, but also how the user can rectify the mistake.

With regard to the timing of the error message, Shneiderman (1979) refers to a study by Segal (1975) which

'.. suggests that human performance improves if errors are issued immediately and the disruption of user thought processes by immediate interruption is not a serious impediment'.

However, Martin (1973) also cautions that the message should not be too abrupt ('a split-second error response in midthought is jarring and rude').

The discussion of error messages leads, clearly, to consider the levels of help that a user-friendly dialogue should provide. For example, inexperienced users require different types and levels of information about the system or the program than do experienced users. Furthermore, as well as providing assistance for inexperienced users, all users tend to forget aspects of the system over time and so some form of help facility can be a convenient aid. Kennedy (1974) also points out that help facilities can give confidence to the casual user:

'If the user can ask the computer what to do at any stage or explain how a particular function works, the procedure of familiarization proceeds fairly rapidly.'

Gaines and Facey (1975) describe a particular technique for providing tutorial help which they call 'query-in-depth'. At any point where the user is requested to make an input to the program, a question mark can be typed to indicate a lack of understanding. This produces information about what is required from the user or a list of sample inputs.

Human–human communication, of course, includes many more variations than simply verbal communication. As Jones (1978) stresses when discussing computer dialogues, the importance of non-verbal signals such as voice intonation or body movements in everyday communication should not be overlooked. He argues, therefore, that computer dialogues should include non-verbal signals to enrich the 'conversation'. Such signals might include bells, bleeps, 'reverse video' (that is, dark characters on a light background), colour or flashing characters. Shneiderman, however, does caution against the overuse of such extra facilities, for example a bell might 'embarrass' the user. Stewart (1976) also points out that, whereas flashing characters can be used to distinguish important information, they may also disrupt the user's thought processes. Of course, if too many different non-verbal signals are presented to the user at a time, the classic symptoms of cognitive overload that ergonomics principles seek to avoid may occur.

Finally, before considering other aspects of computer programming or system design that can lead to user-friendliness or unfriendliness, it is important to realize that overemployment of the concept of user-friendliness has recently been criticized. For example, Stevens (1983) points out that too much friendliness on the part of the dialogue can lead to a restrictive or misleading view of computer capabilities. The user might come to believe that the computer can do more than it can, in fact, do. A similar argument has been advanced by Thimbleby (1980) who suggests:

> 'If computers are to be symbiotic in a positive sense then ... they can do this best by being better computers rather than approximating humanoids.'

Secondly, Stevens argues that too much user-friendliness can lead to a wrong expectation of the extent to which computers can replace human operators. Also, overuse of 'help' facilities can lead to user exasperation, particularly from experienced users.

This last caution against too much friendliness is particularly important since providing too much help can actually lead to reduced performance. Thus Klensin (1982) argues that although help facilities may increase inexperienced users' performance, if they are unable to be halted they can slow down experienced users who do not need them; if the system is too 'friendly' it is likely to constrain the experienced user in its use. For example, for reasons of ease or friendliness it might be that information is able to be input only in certain ways or formats, or that only certain types of analyses can be performed. Such formats, however, may be restrictive to the aims of more experienced users. Stevens also points out that over-friendly help facilities can lead to a rather purile form of 'conversation' occurring which, if it were to have occurred in a human–human conversation would, very quickly, appear to be 'false'.

Wasserman (1973) suggests that the problem might be overcome by providing two distinct dialogues within a program or system: 'NORMAL' for relatively inexperienced or casual users and 'QUICK' for experienced users. However, Maguire (1982) argues that this division of users into 'new' and 'experienced' is too simplistic, supporting Stewart's (1976) suggestion that there is really a continuum of users ranging from 'new' to 'experienced', with people at many different levels of knowledge and experience of the system. For this reason, he argues for Gaines and Facey's 'query-in-depth' approach described earlier. Users can then use the help facilities when they wish to do so.

Comprehensibility

One of the major determinants of whether or not a program or a system is user-friendly will clearly relate to the extent to which it is comprehensible to the user. One which is not comprehensible, which involves unnecessarily complex structures or uses jargon understandable only to the person who developed it, is likely to lead to poorer user behaviour than the same program written in a comprehensible manner.

The concept of comprehensibility has already been introduced earlier when discussing Shneiderman's work (1977, 1978) dealing with the extent to which programs can be reconstructed after having been rearranged. Thus it was shown that the less complex programs were easier for the subjects to remember and to reconstruct. On the basis of such evidence he argues (1978a) that such a procedure provides a good test of the comprehensibility of the program and suggests that every 'module' should meet a '90–10' rule: that a competent programmer should be able to reconstruct functionally 90% of the program after 10 minutes study. Although such a procedure does have some face validity ('a competent programmer should be able to grasp the module's meaning and operation in approximately 10 minutes') he does accept (1980) that the proposal needs further testing and evaluation if it is to be used to select programs or programmers.

Although Shneiderman proposes a technique to *test* the comprehensibility of program structures, it is still important to consider how to *produce* a comprehensible structure. A partial answer to questions of this nature has been provided by studies in applied psychology, as Green (1980) describes. Most of this work has revolved around the use of conditional statements within the program: IF ... THEN ... ELSE (for example, IF A = B THEN PRINT 'YES' ELSE (otherwise) PRINT 'NO'). Since it is this type of statement that essentially gives the computer its decision making powers and makes it something other than a fast abacus, it is appropriate that the little work which has been performed in this area has been to consider the use of such statements.

One of the earliest studies to consider this question was performed by Sime, Green and Guest (1977) (see, Sime, Arblaster and Green, 1977). They compared the IF... THEN... ELSE structure (for example, IF p THEN do A ELSE do B) with its logical equivalent: If p THEN do A; Not p THEN do B. Their results suggested that both novices and professionals found the second form easier to use and that novices corrected their mistakes ten times faster using the second form. These findings have been supported by Green and Manton (1978). One possible reason for this finding is that the IF... THEN ... ELSE structure involves both a positive and a negative form to be evaluated within the same structure—IF positive THEN... ELSE IF negative THEN .... The form suggested by Sime, Green and Guest makes this implied structure more explicit.

Examples of the use of complex language structures in programs, and their effects on program comprehensibility, can further be seen when using these conditional statements in a 'nested' form: IF ... THEN ... IF ... THEN ... ELSE ... IF ... THEN ... ELSE, etc. In this case, a series of conditional statements are linked together and the programmer is required to remember

Problem:		
	CHOP AND FRY:	All things which are tall and not hard.
	PEEL AND ROAST:	All things which are green and not hard.
	BOIL:	All things which are juicy, not hard and not tall.
	PEEL AND GRILL:	All things which are hard and not green.
	ROAST:	All things which are not tall, not hard and not juicy.

GOTO	Nested
IF hard GOTO L1	IF hard peel
IF tall GOTO L2	IF green roast
IF juicy GOTO L3	NOT green grill
roast: stop	END green
L1 IF green GOTO L4	NOT hard
peel: grill: stop	IF tall chop: fry
L2 chop: fry: stop	NOT tall
L3 boil: stop	IF juicy boil
L4 peel: roast: stop	NOT juicy roast
	END juicy
	END hard

Average Errors:	
Semantic: 0.40	0.04
Syntactic: 0.20	0.13

Figure 7.2. Two forms of the IF-statements used for cookery instructions by Sime, Green and Guest (1977); reproduced with permission. Copyright: Academic Press Inc. (London) Ltd.

each of the conditional pathways. Despite the fact that such 'steep' nesting (Green, 1980) forms the basis for some languages—for example, the artificial intelligence language LISP—it is not recommended by a number of authors. For example, Weinberg, Geller and Plum (1975) suggest that no construction should ever be nested inside itself, and Kernighan and Plauger (1974) recommend the programmer to avoid nesting 'IF' statements inside each other. After reviewing the few studies to have considered this problem, however, Green (1980) argues that nesting does not produce too many difficulties provided the structures are not too complex and the boundaries of the nests are well-defined with suitable lexical markers to tell people where the nested structure ends.

The main purpose of the study by Sime, Green and Guest, described above, was to determine the extent to which IF-statements should be nested or should use the 'GO TO' statement. In accord with Green's argument mentioned above, their study demonstrated that fewer errors were produced by subjects when using a nested structure as opposed to one which used GOTO's. Examples of the two forms, for cooking various foods, are illustrated in Figure 7.2. The essential features of their conclusions have been supported by Smith and Dunsmore (1982). Sheil (1981) provides a useful summary of the 'IF-THEN ELSE'/'GOTO' controversy.

Cognitive compatibility

One of the central themes which this book advocates, and which the reader should have comprehended by this point, is that the efficient interaction between a person and the environment in which that person operates will occur only if the two are matched in requirements and abilities; for example, if the user can perceive the information from the environment in the time and format that the machine provides, or if the machine can allow sufficient flexibility for the operator to be able to exercise appropriate controlling movements. If the two components are not compatible—if the user's visual system cannot perceive and recognize the stimuli in time or the physical environment is too harsh to allow appropriate control to be exercised—then, for many of the reasons outlined in Chapter 1, performance is likely to be reduced with a concomitant increase in error rate and reduction in satisfaction.

Just as it is necessary to ensure physical compatibility between the user and the computer system, so it is important that they are compatible at a cognitive level. This means that the computer's conception of what the user is able to do (that is, its conception through the programmer) needs to be compatible with what the user actually can do. Similarly, the user's conception of what the computer can do needs to be matched to that which the computer is able to do. In other words, the machine's model of the user's behaviour needs to be compatible with the user's model of the machine's.

The importance of such cognitive compatibility in computer programs and system commands has been highlighted by workers at the Applied Psychology Unit in Cambridge (Morton *et al.*, 1979; Barnard *et al.*, 1981; Hammond *et al.*, 1981; Barnard *et al.*, 1982). Their concern was the concept of computer-centricity discussed earlier; that is, that the programmer's model of the computer being at the centre of events might not be compatible with the expectations of the user. In essence, they extract three forms of cognitive incompatibility which can occur: linguistic, memory and perceptual.

Linguistic incompatibility can occur at both a syntactic and at a semantic level. As an example of the syntactic level, consider interactive commands that are often used by computer systems such as DELETE (to delete an entry or a file), MOVE (usually to move one piece of file to another area), INSERT (to insert information into a file), etc. Accompanying each of these commands, following the control word—DELETE, MOVE, INSERT—there are usually two further pieces of information: the information to be deleted, moved or inserted and the file or memory area from which or to which the information is deleted, moved or inserted.

The incompatibility often arises because the information following the commands DELETE, MOVE, INSERT, etc., often have to be used in abreviated forms, such as DELETE X,Y; MOVE X,Y; INSERT X,Y. In 'natural' language, that is the language used by the operator, the above abbreviated commands might well be interpreted as DELETE (information X) from (File Y), or MOVE (information X) to (File Y), or INSERT (information X) into (Area Y). If this is how the computer programmer or system designer intended the actions to take place, then there is no syntactic incompatibility. Often, however, commands of the form such as DELETE X,Y imply the reverse of what is expected in natural language, that is DELETE Y from file X.

Semantic linguistic incompatibility can occur in a similar way—that is the system designer's view of the user's behaviour is at variance with the user's expectations. In this case, however, the problem arises over meanings of commands—particularly when the commands are computer-centric. Examples might include the use of the terms PUT and GET or LOAD and DUMP. Both pairs of commands are often used to transfer information from the computer to some storage medium, and vice versa. However, the *direction* of the transfer is only immediately obvious if the user has already accepted that the computer is at the centre of the operation. Then PUT, for example, implies putting information onto the storage medium and GET suggests retrieving it. However, if the operator shifts attention from the computer towards the storage medium itself, so that this is seen temporarily as the centre of the operations, then the actions of PUT and GET become cognitively incompatible. Similar problems also exist with the commands LOAD and DUMP. Although a computer-centric user would possibly understand that information is DUMped to a file, the word LOAD does not immediately imply that the information is LOADed from the file to the computer. Carroll (1982b) also discusses some of these semantic incompatibility problems.

The second form of cognitive incompatibility which has been suggested is a *memory incompatibility*. In this case, the machine's requirements of the user's memory capabilities can be incompatible with the user's actual abilities. Again, linguistically incompatible terms can increase the memory load required because they require the user to remember, for each command, the relationship between the variables X and Y.

Finally, there is proposed *perceptual incompatibility*. This relates primarily to the presentation of information as displayed on the computer screen and its relationship to the operations required of the user. As such, it will be dealt with in more detail in the next chapter.

Modularity and structured programming

It has already been seen that a programming approach which emphasizes the structure of the program, perhaps through such constructions as IF ... THEN statements, may help the user to understand what the program is meant to do and to use it more efficiently. This concept, however, can be extended to suggest that a program which is built up from modules—smaller sub-programs—might further aid the user in understanding.

That this might be the case was suggested by studies described by Shneiderman and Mayer (1979). They asked subjects to attempt to understand the structure of a program which was either (a) divided into modules (each module having an explicit function, with a 10-line main program and three small sub-routines), (b) non-modular (which was simply a sequentially arranged program), or (c) random modular (the program was divided into sub-routines, but without each having a clear function). The comprehension scores obtained suggested highest program comprehension occurred using the modular approach and lowest using the random modular approach. It would be wrong, however, to take the conclusions too strongly since the significance of the difference between the groups was not high. Nevertheless, the results are suggestive of the direction of the difference and, as Shneiderman and Mayer point out, individual differences in programmer ability can play a very large part in affecting the value of such an approach: 'Excellent programmers can perform surprisingly well even in adverse conditions.' They also argue that the implications of the results are that modularity is likely to be helpful to experienced programmers, who have developed the semantic and syntactic skills needed for efficient programming, since modularity is likely to help the programmer to develop further an understanding of the internal program structure.

A suggestion of how the modularity of programs could be measured has been made by Stevens, Myers and Constantine (1974) who invoke the concept of structural complexity. They suggest that a modular program's complexity arises as a result of the number of communication links between the modules. In this context they suggest two measures of structural complexity: *absolute complexity* which is simply the number of modules present, and *relative* complexity which is the ratio of the number of module linkages to the number of modules. Although they provide no experimental data, they do argue that the goal of a modular program should be to minimize the number of connections between modules, so eliminating paths over which changes and errors could propagate and making it easier to understand each module without reference to others.

To define the strength of association between two modules, that is the extent to which they are independent or interdependent, the authors discuss the concept of *coupling*. Strong coupling complicates a system since a module is harder to understand, change, or correct by itself if it is highly interrelated with other modules. Unfortunately, however, the amount of coupling is highly dependent on a number of factors (for example, how complicated the coupling is, where the coupling link actually occurs—at the beginning or inside the module—and the material being sent or received). For this reason, the authors suggest, there will be no single simple measure of coupling complexity. However, coupling complexity is likely to be reduced if the relationships between the elements within a module are maximized. This factor the authors call *cohesiveness* and use the degree of *binding* as its measure. They argue, therefore, that the goal should be high levels of binding, and suggest a number of techniques for increasing the amount of binding within a module. Unfortunately, however, as was mentioned above, none of these suggestions has been put to the empirical test.

Response time

A further indication of the friendliness of the partcipants within a communication system is the time that one takes to respond to the overtures of the other. When one member takes an inordinate length of time to reply to a question posed by the other this is sometimes taken to indicate rudeness or a lack of friendly communication, often with concomitant implications for the quality of the communication act. Furthermore, if the response that is required is one which should take the form of performance feedback, then a long response time can also affect the quality of learned performance. The same can well be true, too, when one of the participants in the communication net is a computer.

In addition to adverse attitudes being formed, the disruptive effect of response times which are too long can occur as a result of interference with the user's 'continuity of thought' and limited memory capacity. Thus Miller (1968) has argued that if the system response time is delayed by more than a few seconds beyond the time that the operator is ready to begin the next transaction, operator performance will decrease and errors increase. Certainly, in terms of increased performance time (over and above the extra time taken by the system), such predictions have been borne out (for example, Morfield *et al.*, 1969; Goodman and Spence, 1978; Barber, 1979). However Barber (1979) did not find that errors also increased.

In some situations, response time *variation* may be a more important consideration than simply the delay *per se*. For example, Miller (1977) demonstrated that increasing the variability in response time generates poorer performance and lower user satisfaction. As Shneiderman (1980) points out:

> 'Users may prefer a system which always responds in 4 seconds to one which varies from 1 to 6 seconds. Apparently users can devote 3.9 seconds to planning if they are sure that the time is available.'

The problem cannot be solved, however, simply by reducing the response time of the system effectively to zero. Firstly, reducing the response time, particularly when the time has been increased because the system has to cope with a number of simultaneous users, carries with it quite a considerable increase in hardware costs. Secondly, too fast a response might well begin to overload the user's cognitive capacities. As Kennedy (1974) suggests:

> 'At high data rates, fatigue due to heavy concentration causes comprehension to be achieved only for short periods.'

Suggestions for an appropriate response time for a particular system, therefore, are difficult to provide since they depend on a number of factors. Two approaches, however, can be discerned in the literature.

The first, advocated by Miller (1968), is to provide varying response times for different types of commands. Thus, users might have to wait several seconds for a file to be loaded or for a program to be executed. However, they might expect to be provided with almost immediate responses to editing commands or to emergency requests. Table 7.1 provides some of Miller's suggested response times for seventeen command types.

The second type of approach, suggested by Spence (1976), has been to consider the user's perception of the task to be completed. He invokes the concept of 'psychological closure' to suggest that an operator considers a task to be 'closed' when it has been completed fully. Thus, an operation such as dialing a 6-digit telephone number is closed when the number has been completely dialled. Each of the task components—dialling each of the six digits—carries its own level of closure which is less than the closure for the total task. Spence's suggestion, therefore, is that the stronger the task's closure, because the task is completed the more will the user be tolerant to

Table 7.1. System response times for different types of activity suggested by Miller, 1968

User activity	'Maximum' response time (sec)
Control activation (for example, keyboard entry)	0.1
System activation (system initialization)	3.0
Request for given service:	
simple	2
complex	5
loading and restart	15–60
Error feedback (following completion of input)	2–4
Response to ID	2
Information on next procedure	<5
Response to simple inquiry from list	2
Response to simple *status* inquiry	2
Response to complex inquiry in table form	2–4
Request for next page	0.5–1
Response to 'execute problem'	<15
Lightpen entries	1.0
Drawing with lightpens	0.1
Response to complex inquire in *graphic* form	2–10
Response to dynamic modelling	—
Response to graphic manipulation	2
Response to user intervention in automatic process	4

some delay. Conversely, the weaker the closure, the shorter should be the corresponding response delay.

Finally, in addition to the time that the system takes to respond due to its own slowness, in recent years another means of slowing down the user's response rate has been developed which is known as 'artificial lockout'. This involves the program itself restricting the user's speed by holding up the next part of the interactive sequence, even though the system could respond. Atwood and Ramsey (1979) suggest that there appears to be some evidence that, in a complex problem-solving situation, this may cause the user to concentrate more on the problem to be solved and less on the tactics used to solve it. This, then, is likely to result in improved performance, although at some cost in 'user satisfaction'.

Uniformity and consistency

A final consideration when discussing important factors in programming languages is the extent to which the language or program semantics and syntax are consistent. As Gaines (1981) points out, users become familiar with a particular dialogue and, if they occasionally find that what they have leant does not always apply, this can have two unfortunate consequences. Firstly, it puts an additional memory load on users—not only do they have to learn extra commands but they also have to learn the cases when one command syntax is used and those identical cases but in a different situation when another might be used. Similarly with programs: using different abbreviated variable names for the same type of variable, or different syntax, can help to overload the memory capacities of the operator. This problem, of course, also relates to the question of semantic and memory compatibility discussed earlier. The second unfortunate consequence of inconsistency to which Gaines alludes concerns a naive user who

'has at last gained confidence in his familiarity with the system and then suddenly finds that his trust in himself (and system and its designer) is misplaced'.

Such experiences, Gaines suggests, can be 'devastating psychologically'.

PROGRAM DEBUGGING

From the previous discussions about computer programming practice, it will have become apparent that a number of quite complex cognitive skills are involved, including memory, comprehension, decision making, etc. However, the programming process is not completed simply at the stage of having produced an appropriate 'first-draft' program; even expert programmers write programs that initially contain errors and these mistakes and inaccuracies often become apparent only when the program is entered into the computer and is run. These mistakes are, in the jargon of computer programmers, called 'bugs', and the successful 'debugging' of a program is often required before the full programming process can be said to be completed.

Unfortunately, the debugging process often constitutes a large portion of the total programming time. Indeed, Delaney (1966) has estimated that the successful correction of errors takes about 25% of the time required to complete a large software system (including the time taken to formulate the problem, generate a plan, etc.); it takes an even greater proportion of the individual programmer's time (Grant and Sackman, 1967). Furthermore debugging has been reported to take three times longer than the original coding process (Rubey, 1968), although the range of individual differences in debugging is quite large (Grant and Sackman, 1967; Gould, 1975).

Gould (1975) distinguishes between two types of program bugs. Firstly are *syntactic* bugs that arise as a result of the programmer using an inaccurate command or language syntax—for example, forgetting to put commas or other statement delimiters at appropriate points in the program, or using the wrong number of arguments in a data array. Since these prevent the program from actually being run, they would normally be detected and indicated by the computer's operating system. Secondly are *non-syntactic* (but not necessarily semantic) bugs. These are not likely to interfere with the running of the program, but usually appear when the program results are inspected. It may be, for example, that the wrong variables are used in a computation or that the output is formatted incorrectly. Of course, sometimes these non-syntactic bugs may also interfere with the program's execution. For example, on occasions a simple division computation using variables rather than actual numbers may 'crash' (that is, fail to run) because the value of the denominator is zero.

Perhaps one of the earliest studies of programming errors was reported by Youngs (1974) who analysed the error performance of experienced and novice programmers using several different languages. The main thrust of his study was to investigate the *types* of errors commonly made, although he does provide some data on the extent to which his subjects corrected their errors as they progressed through the program development sequence, attempting to validate different forms of the program. Thus, although both groups of subjects recognized similar proportions of errors on their first program draft (beginners: 46%; experienced: 52%), the experts removed their errors more quickly on subsequent runs. On average, beginners corrected or avoided approximately 30% of the remaining errors on each run, whereas the advanced programmers eliminated 40% of the remainder. Youngs suggests that this was due, not so much to the experts' generally superior diagnostic skills, but to their ability to correct the more superficial semantic and syntactic inconsistencies quickly. This provided more chance for them to concentrate on the logical errors.

Gould (1975) also considered the effect of experience on debugging performance. In his study, he introduced different types of bugs into programs and asked subjects to find them. Although he was unable to find systematic performance improvements from practice with the different programs, he did show practice effects specific to programs and types of bugs. Thus, the average debug time decreased from about 14 minutes to about 5 minutes after the subjects had seen a particular program once. Similarly, on being confronted with the same type of bug in subsequent programs, detection time fell from about 15 minutes on the first occurrence to about 7 minutes on the second and subsequent occurrences. Experience with the particular problem, then, is likely to increase performance.

In an earlier experiment Gould (Gould and Drongowski, 1974) considered the effect of the type of bug on detection time. They found that bugs such as endless loops (in which the computer endlessly follows the same computational path) and array errors were detected more quickly than bugs such as assigning values to variables which required a comprehension of the way that the program was meant to operate. Sheil (1981), however, does caution against taking the results of Gould and Drongowski too literally. He suggests that it is the implication of the bug for the program, rather than the type of bug, which is important. Thus the 'same' bug in one program may be easier to detect than in another because in the first it represents a syntactic error whereas in the second it might occur as a semantic or a logical fault.

In their study, Gould and Drongowski (1974) also considered the effect of various debugging aids on performance. One group of subjects was given a listing of the program to be debugged (the listing included a description of what the program should achieve); a second group was given the listing plus an example set of input values and the resulting output; a third group was given the same materials as the second, plus the output that the correct program would have produced; finally, the fourth group was given the listing and told the type of bug that the program contained.

Unfortunately, the results of the experiment indicated that none of the debugging aids helped performance, either in terms of the number of bugs found or the time to find them. The authors explain their results in terms of the subjects' abilities to adapt to the particular debugging aid provided, and emphasize their arguments with reference to apparently different strategies adopted by the different groups. For example, group 2 (that given the input-output relationship) seemed more selective in the statements that they attended to than the group which was given the listing only (group 1). Despite the surprising nature of these results, other experimenters (for example, Shneiderman and McKay, 1976) have also found that aids are not as useful as might be thought (they used flowcharts to indicate to subjects how the program should progress).

The lack of any empirical support for the value of debugging aids also appears to extend to the format of the program print-out which the programmer uses to trace the flow of the program. In particular, studies have been performed to consider the value of indenting sections of the program listing, particularly when structures such as nests or sub-routines are used (in much the same way as shown earlier in Figure 7.2). Although it might be suggested that such an aid could help the programmer to understand the structure of the program, Weissman (1974) (reported in Sheil, 1981) found no performance improvements for modifying, hand simulating, or answering questions about programs which were listed using either the indenting or non-indenting techniques. Similar results were obtained by Shneiderman and McKay (1975) and by Love (1977). Despite such evidence, however, Sheil (1981) argues that, intuitively at least, such formatting procedures should aid the programmer to understand the program structure and should thus increase performance. He further suggests that the clear individual differences in preference for these techniques that the studies have found might have masked the true value of such 'pretty printing' techniques for some people.

Since debugging takes such a large portion of the total programming time, results such as these are slightly disappointing. It would have been helpful if suggestions for sensible debugging aids could have been made, so that programmer productivity could be increased. However, two points should be made before dismissing entirely the value of such aids. Firstly, the few studies performed in this area have been carried out using a very restricted range of program and bug types. As Shneiderman and McKay recognize, therefore, more experimental data are required using a wide range of programs before the value of flowcharts can be assessed. In this respect, Brooke and Duncan (1980) report that flowcharts do increase the speed with which faults can be identified in very complex tasks. Secondly, the studies have also provided some qualitative descriptions regarding the ways in which subjects attempted the debugging task. Such descriptions may help to produce more useful aids.

Gould and Drongowski (1974) suggest that subjects adopt a hierarchical process of debugging in which subjects first consider violations of the language system grammar and then errors in the substance of the program. If this is so then, as Youngs' study of the error performance of experienced and novice programmers indicated, aids which help the operator to detect the simple semantic and syntactic errors, and thus allow more time to consider the more complex logical errors, should prove beneficial.

SUMMARY OF DIALOGUE DESIGN RECOMMENDATIONS

The overriding theme which has run through this chapter has been to argue that a 'good' dialogue can be defined in two ways: firstly, it is user-friendly (although not over-friendly)—it attempts to work with the user to enable his or her abilities to be used to their maximum; secondly, and subsumed under the first point, it should not overload the users' capacities for memory and comprehension. The various aspects discussed in this chapter all relate to these two points.

Maguire (1982) has produced a useful summary of the various aspects important in dialogue design, which is reproduced in Table 7.2. An interesting feature of this table is that it also includes suggestions for the design of relevant hardware, and so emphasizes the 'system' aspects of dialogues. The recommendations themselves are summarized in columns one and two of the table; column three contains caveats which could be applied to certain recommendations. It also indicates, by means of arrows, groups of conflicting viewpoints, together with comments suggesting possible methods of resolving them.

Table 7.2. A summary of important features in the design of dialogues (From Maguire, 1982). Reproduced by permission of Academic Press.

Area of consideration	Recommendations	Modifications to recommendations and suggestions for resolving conflicts (indicated by arrows)
(1) Knowledge of and communication with the intended user	The designer should familiarize himself with the attributes and tasks of the intended user. Of particular importance are task complexity, frequency of system use and user adaptability A prior demonstration of interactive dialogue will place users in a better position to discuss their requirements	
(2) Use of a specialist intermediary or documents	Do not assume that the user needs to interact directly with the machine. Appointing an intermediary or distributing computer listings may be preferable approaches	
(3) Natural language dialogue	Provides a means of computer access without necessitating the learning of a formal computer language. Most successful when the domain of discourse is limited	Can give a misleading impression of the computer's power The ambiguities and implicit assumptions underlying natural conversation make the development of multi-topic dialogues a very difficult task
(4) Reliance upon programming skills	In future, programming skills will become widespread thus enabling designers to apply ← flexible, programming type interfaces to a wider range of systems It will be difficult for the whole population to become sufficiently adept at programming for interfaces ← requiring this skill to be generally appropriate	Unskilled people may take advantage of the flexibility of a system via natural language interfaces, intermediaries or query-by-example techniques

Area of consideration	Recommendations	Modifications to recommendations and suggestions for resolving conflicts (indicated by arrows)
(5) Alternatives to printed text— graphics and speech	Pictorial displays may be preferable to printed text, particularly when the information contains some form of structure	
	Graphical input devices such as lightpens, tablets and joysticks similarly can enrich a dialogue	There appears to be little agreement on the relative merits of differing devices for positioning a cursor
	Man–computer speech communication frees the man from direct contact with a computer terminal	
(6) Handling different levels of user experience	Novice users will need explanatory dialogues while more experienced users will require a briefer form of interaction. Systems should thus contain two levels of dialogue	There will be many more than two levels of user experience and so a more comprehensive range of dialogues should be available
(7) Hardware considerations	Whereas VDU terminals facilitate high speed data transmission, teletypewriters provide an inexpensive way of obtaining hard copy output	Slow rates of information display may sometimes be preferred
	Custom built hardware may be suitable in some areas despite its high cost and inflexibility	
	Special function keys can be simulated in a more flexible manner using the display screen and lightpen	
	The layout, positioning and appearance of a terminal should be carefully considered in the interests of operator comfort	

Table 7.2—*contd.*

Area of consideration	Recommendations	Modifications to recommendations and suggestions for resolving conflicts (indicated by arrows)
(8) Input precision	Make use of input data expressed in vague terms	
(9) Command synonyms and abbreviations	Unsophisticated users will expect synonyms of commands to be acceptable A wide choice of inputs will be confusing for the novice	Guide users to the correct form of a command via a help facility which can detect the use of command synonyms
	To reduce the typing required, command inputs should be accepted up to their minimal unambiguous form	Serious misunderstandings can arise when simple errors are made
(10) Literal responses	The system should be deterministic, initiating a minimal number of unsolicited actions	In order to give natural replies to users' queries it may be desirable to include additional information not explicitly requested If an intelligent system can detect that the user is not following the optimum path through a database he should be informed of this
(11) System response times	Minimize all response times Reduce response variability Link the response time to the computer operations triggered by each input Relate response times to the strength of 'closure' corresponding to each input Provide interim responses during long delays	Minimize response times within a limit of response variability particularly for intermediate user inputs prior to task completion (weak closure). Linking delays to input complexity is appropriate to experienced users only
(12) Prevention and cure of operator errors	Reduce the possibility of errors by making inputs seem natural and consistent	

Table 7.2—*contd.*

Area of consideration	Recommendations	Modifications to recommendations and suggestions for resolving conflicts (indicated by arrows)
	Provide the user with enough information to help him identify his own errors	
	Error messages should be understandable, non-threatening and low-key	
	The immediate transmission of error messages will speed up the interactive process ←⌐ Point out mistakes *after* the completion of inputs to avoid ←⌋ disrupting the user	The need for inputs to be formed correctly at first attempt and user sensitivity to interruption may point to one of the two approaches
	Query inputs which lie outside their expected range ←⌐ As valid data frequently lies outside preselected 'norms', ←⌋ system checking can cause frustration	Provide a flexible data validation mechanism which can be modified or suppressed by the user
	Encourage operation by experiment	

SUMMARY

This chapter has emphasized the importance of considering the communication act when designing and using computer software. Thus, stress was laid on the value of ensuring that the information that is passed from the communicator to the receiver (in this case via a common language) is transmitted efficiently.

In the case of computer operations, the language that the operator and the computer normally use are completely at variance with one another. To enable this communication (usually instructions) to be performed in a language which is understandable both by the human operator and the computer, some form of translation device is required—and this is the computer's operating 'language'. This chapter considered features of different languages which could enhance the translation facilities offered.

CHAPTER 8

Displaying the Information

This chapter will discuss what is probably the final link to be put into making an efficient interface between the computer and the operator. Previous chapters have discussed how operators should be able to communicate physically with the machine (to enter and to receive information) and how the machine's operating system can be designed to be compatible with the operator's cognitive capacities. The final link, then, will deal with the ways in which the computer software enables the information to be displayed to the operator; how understandable it is; and how it can be used effectively by the operator.

The forms of output hardware that are available to the programmer and their advantages and disadvantages were discussed in Chapter 4. For most applications the output is likely to be displayed via two of the operator's senses—visual (using VDUs or printers) and auditory (using speech). The behavioural problems involved in speech output (and input) were discussed at length in Chapters 4 and 5 and so will not be considered in detail in the present chapter. This chapter will concentrate primarily on the problems of displaying information visually, usually text or graphics on the computer screen, although the ways in which written information should be presented (usually in the form of computer manuals) will also be considered.

The reason for displaying text or numbers, pictures on a computer screen, for example, is generally very simple: through the computer the programmer wishes to inform the operator that some action has been performed by the computer, that results have been produced and, perhaps, that some further response is required. For the desired effect to occur, however, some very complex behavioural processes need to take place, which involve the operator perceiving and recognizing the characters of the text (reading the words, for example) and comprehending the message. As this chapter will demonstrate, the use of different display formats can help to enhance or disrupt these

267

processes. The first aspect to consider, then, is how textual information is perceived and recognized.

THE READING PROCESS

Eye movements

Whereas is is possible to hear speech and sounds quite passively, reading is a very active process. Because the most acute part of the retina is towards the centre, near the fovea, the eyes constantly have to be moved to bring into view the appropriate parts of the displayed material. However, if the eyes were moved at a constant rate over the material (like a pen moves over paper during writing), then the resultant image would be both confused and blurred. Since a stable image is only formed when both the eyes and the object are stationary, the movement of the eyes over the material during reading is characterized by a succession of fast movements and stationary periods. The fast jerks are called *saccades* and the stationary points are termed *fixations*. (Rayner, 1978, points out that this term 'fixation' is something of a misnomer since the eye makes relatively small tremors even during each fixation.)

The existence of saccadic eye movements during reading has been known since the turn of the century, and so there is a large amount of experimental literature available which deals with the subject (see Matin, 1974, for an historic review). It is only in more recent times, however, with the development of sophisticated monitoring equipment, that the investigation of these movements and their implications for understanding the cognitive processes involved in reading and comprehension, have been able to be performed with any accuracy (see Young and Sheena, 1975, for a survey of the techniques used).

The two important parameters of saccadic movements that relate to reading efficiency are the duration of each fixation and the number of fixations required. In this respect, the average length of a saccade appears to be about 2° of visual angle (about 6 ten-pitch or 8 twelve-pitch character spaces) and, for skilled readers, the average fixation durations lie between 200 and 250 msec (Rayner, 1977). However, there is a great deal of individual variability in this matter. For example, Rayner (1978) reports that, even for a single person reading a particular passage, saccade lengths often range from 2 to 18 character positions or more, and fixation durations range from 100 to over 500 msec. It is this variability in reading skill which relates to an individual's reading efficiency.

A simple exercise in introspection, of course, would indicate that saccadic eye movements do not take the form simply of continuous movement from, for European texts, left to right over the page. The eye's movements also include the third characteristic of saccadic movements—that of *regressions*. A regression is a movement in the opposite direction to the normal saccadic scan (that is, for English, in the right–left direction) and occur approximately 10–20% of the time in skilled readers (Rayner, 1978). They are assumed to occur when the reader has difficulty understanding the text, misinterprets it and/or when the reader overshoots the next fixation target. They also occur, of course, when the reader reaches the end of one line and needs to start processing the text on the next (although Rayner, 1978, suggests that these movements should be distinguished from a regression, both because they are necessary to continue the reading process and because there is some suggestion that they involve different cognitive control processes).

An example of the saccadic process can be seen in Figure 8.1 (from Bouma, 1980) which illustrates the three types of movement for readers of Dutch text. As can be seen, Bouma distinguishes between the two types of regression saccades, describing them as either 'correction saccades' or 'line saccades' (the latter being the movement from one end of a line to the beginning of the next). Interestingly, the termination of a line saccade generally appears to occur not at the beginning of the next line, but at least one fixation into the line, possibly because the eye undershoots the necessary movement. This, then, requires a further correction (regression) saccade to the line beginning, which again is likely to reduce reading speed. However, Shebilske (1975) has demonstrated that the duration of the fixation following a return sweep is often very short, and suggests that its purpose is to program a corrective saccade and not to abstract textual information.

Discussing the relationship of line saccades to the reading process, Bouma points to the importance of typographical design:

> The horizontal extent of line saccades is controlled by visual information in the left visual field, concerning the far left-hand margin, which should therefore be in a straight vertical line ... with a sufficiently wide margin... .
> The vertical extent of line saccades is controlled by perceived inter-line distance. If this vertical component is inaccurate, the eye may mistakenly jump over two or perhaps even three lines.

The use of such information to the appropriate design and layout of text will be considered later.

Two major positions have traditionally been taken with regard to the reason for the fixation periods during reading. Rayner (1977) describes these as the *cognitive lag hypothesis* and the *processing monitoring hypothesis*. The cognitive lag hypothesis suggests that the eye movements are so rapid and the durations of the fixations so short that the semantic processing of the text must necessarily lag behind the perception of the stimulus. The process monitoring hypothesis, on the other hand, suggests that semantic processing is more rapid and immediate, since it argues that the eye movements are affected by the cognitive processes occurring at the time of the fixation. More difficult words and passages, therefore, should lead to longer fixation periods. On the basis of

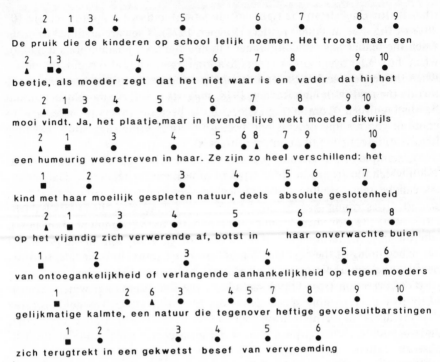

Figure 8.1. Eye fixations during the silent reading of a piece of Dutch text (Bouma, 1980). Three types of eye saccade are indicated: reading (circles), correction (triangles) and line (squares). The numbers indicate the order of the fixations within each line. Reproduced by permission of Taylor & Francis Ltd.

an experiment which showed that fixation durations were affected by the types of words in the sentence and that the frequency of fixations was related to word position within the sentence, Rayner (1977) has argued that the processing monitoring hypothesis operates during reading. That is, that the eye movements are mediated by cognitive processes rather than being simply an inability of the reader to 'keep up with' the eye movements.

Although information regarding the eye's saccadic movements provides details of the control movements and possible times that a reader takes to process a piece of text, it is not the full story. Information is also required regarding the amount of information that the reader can process at any one fixation. This is known as the 'span of perception' and is another aspect which determines reading speed and accuracy.

During reading, a piece of text can fall on one of three areas of the reader's retina. Firstly, the foveal region (which incorporates an area subtended by a visual angle of 1° to 2° around the central fixation point) is, as discussed earlier, the area of clear visual acuity in which a great deal of detail is visible. It is to enable the main part of the text to fall on this area that saccadic eye movements occur. Secondly, beyond the foveal region at visual angles between about 2° and 10°, is the parafoveal region in which visual acuity falls off markedly. A subject's ability to identify characters correctly becomes progressively worse with increasing movement into the parafoveal region. Finally, beyond the parafovea is the peripheral region in which correct identification of information is very poor although, because the area is well-served with retinal cells called 'rods', the detection of general contour differences—between an area of text and an area of 'white paper', for example—is very good.

Studies of the size of the area from which a person picks up information have been conducted for a number of years, and take many different forms. Some of these studies and designs have been reviewed and criticized by Rayner (1975) who suggests (1978) that, because of experimental and conceptual deficiencies, none appears to provide very definitive answers to the problem. One technique suggested by McConkie and Rayner (1975), however, does appear to help produce some more definite conclusions.

McConkie and Rayner used a computer controlled system to present text to subjects on a VDU. The system was designed in such a way that only the area of the display to which the subjects directed their gaze (i.e. fixated) was understandable. Text outside of the variable width 'window' was, in different ways, mutilated. Thus, the subject's display was continually changing as the eyes moved over the text although, where the reader looked, there was normal text to be read.

For each window size (which varied between 13 and 100 characters—between 6 and 50 characters on each side of the fixated character), three forms of word mutilation were introduced: firstly (X) all characters outside of the window were replaced by an 'x'; secondly (C) all characters were replaced by another character which was visually confusible with the original; and thirdly (NC) replacing characters with non-confusible letters. In addition, each of the three types of mutilation took two formats: either the spaces between words remained (S) and took one 'character' position or they were removed (F). Examples of these six forms are shown in Figure 8.2.

```
       Graphology means personality diagnosis from handwriting.  This is a

X5     xxxxxxxxxx xxxxx xxxxonality diagnosis xxxx xxxxxxxxxxx.  Xxxx xx x

XF     xxxxxxxxxxxxxxxxxxxxxxxxonality diagnosis xxxxxxxxxxxxxxxxxxxxxxxxxxxxxx

C5     Onojkaiazp wsorc jsnconality diagnosis tnaw kori mnlflrz.  Ykle le o

Cf     Onojkaiaqpewsorcejsnconality diagnosisetnawekoriemnlflrqeeeYkleeleco

NCS    Hbfxwysyvo tifgl xiblonality diagnosis abyt wfdn hbemedv.  Awcl el f

NCF    Hbfxwysyvoctifdlexiblonality diagnosiseabytewfdnehbemedveeeAwclcclef
```

Figure 8.2. Example of the ways in which McConkie and Rayner (1975) mutilated text to investigate the amount of peripheral vision required for accurate reading. On each line a window size of 17 is shown, assuming the letter *d* in *diagnosis*.

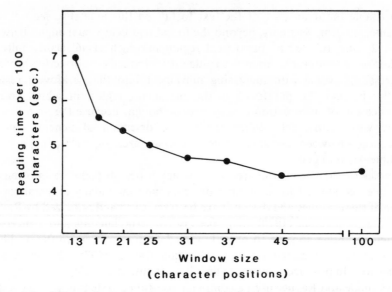

Figure 8.3. Effect of window size on the time taken to read 100 characters of text (McConkie and Rayner, 1975). Reproduced by permission of the Psychonomic Society.

Two interesting results were obtained by the authors regarding the effect of window size on the span of perception. Firstly, as shown in Figure 8.3, the smaller the window, the longer it took for subjects to read the text. Thus reducing the size from 100 to 13 characters caused the time to read each successive piece of 100 characters to increase from 4.3 to 7 seconds, approximately a 60% increase in reading time. Most of this increase (76%) was due to increases in the reader's fixation time. As Figure 8.3 illustrates minimum reading time was only reached with the larger window sizes, with windows approximately 18–22 characters on each side of the fixation point. The data also indicated that these window sizes produced the maximum saccadic length.

The second interesting result relates to the effect of window size on the number of regressive saccades made by the subjects in terms of the type of character mutilation outside of the windows. Their results demonstrated that the minimum number of regressive movements occurred when the letters outside of the window carried no information whatsoever (that is, when they were simply x's). The maximum number of regressions occured when they had some information content (i.e. the compatible condition). At the optimum (larger) window sizes, however, the difference between the three types of mutilation was reduced considerably. These results suggest, therefore, that readers do register information that falls outside of the normal perceptual area. To what extent it is used in the comprehension, rather than the eye control, process, however, is debatable since McConkie and Rayner did not test subjects' subsequent recall of the information read under the different conditions. However, McConkie later (1976) suggested that readers obtain different types of information from different regions within the perceptual span during a fixation in reading. Information falling on the fovea is processed for its semantic content and information from the parafoveal area is limited to rather gross featural information such as word shape and word length.

In a subsequent experiment McConkie and Rayner (1976) investigated the symmetry of the perceptual span and demonstrated that it appears to be shifted to the right of the fixation point. Using a 25-character window with either 4-left and 20-right characters unmutilated or 20-left and 4-right, and comparing the results with an unshifted 40 character window, the authors demonstrated that the right-shifted pattern (with only 4 characters on the left) produced no reductions in reading performance. There were significant reductions, however, when the left-shifted pattern was used. They suggest, therefore, that readers acquire more information from the right of a fixation than from the left.

Recognizing words

Visual recognition

One of the fundamental problems confronting anyone who studies the reading process is to identify the basic unit of perception. What is it about the characters which make up a word that we recognize? This clearly has important implications for the design of text on, say, the computer screen. Various levels have been proposed in the past, ranging from an analysis of particular features of each letter to the perception of whole words (Adams, 1979).

Letter-based hypotheses

One of the original hypotheses to be proposed relates to the identification of words through an analysis of their individual component letters. The attractive feature of such a model lies in its simplification of the reading task—once the twenty-six letters of the alphabet (in both their upper and lower case forms) have been learned, innumerable combinations of these symbols can be analysed. Smith (1971) suggests that such identification can occur as a result of two methods: matching the symbol with an internal representation or 'template'; or by analysing characteristic features of the letter which distinguish it from other letters.

Although a *template model*, in which the reader matches the symbol on the page to an idealized 'internal' model of the symbol, may at first appear to make sense, a number of damaging criticisms may be directed towards it. For example, Reed (1982) points out that the comparison requires the template to be in the same position and orientation, having the same size, as the pattern to be identified. This means that the size of templates would have to be continuously adjusted to correspond to the position, size, orientation, etc. of the symbol—a process which would considerably slow the reader. Secondly, the template would have to be able to accommodate the wide variety of patterns produced by different people writing the same character. It would be difficult to construct a template for each letter that would produce a good match with all varieties of that letter. Thirdly, the model does not allow for the fact that we perceive characters in relation also to the context in which they appear. For example, take the shape ' ℯᴜ ': It is perceived as a 'w' in the sentence 'Let us take a ℯᴜalk', but as a combined 'e' and 'v' in the sentence 'It was a momentous ℯᴜ ent'.

The *feature analysis model* of individual letters makes no attempt to match the stimulus with an internalized template. Instead, it suggests that we make a series of tests on different features of the letters until all possible alternative responses are eliminated. Gibson (1969) has produced a set of features for upper case letters as shown in Figure 8.4 which might be able to be used to predict the confusability between letters. For example, the only difference between P and R is the diagonal attached to the R and this is likely to lead to confusion between the two, and to longer recognition times.

Although a feature analysis model might predict behaviour better than a template model, any model based solely on an argument that we recognize text as a result of analysing individual letters still cannot provide the full explanation of reading behaviour. For example, Smith (1971) points out that a letter recognition model does not take account of the extent to which expectation influences word identification. For example, the fourth letter of the sequence 'SEQI' may be interpreted as a 'U' when reading the letters quickly—not because of any physical similarity between the two letters but because it is expected that 'u' should follow 'q'.

A further problem with the letter-by-letter hypothesis has been exposed by Cosky (reported in Gough and Cosky, 1977). He reasoned that if words are recognized by means of their component letters, then the difficulty of recognizing words should be related to the difficulty of recognizing their letters. In his experiments, the times taken to recognize words did increase with word length but was unaffected by letter difficulty. It would appear, therefore, that reading does not proceed by serial, letter-by-letter processing.

Whole-word hypotheses

The suggestion that the shapes of individual letters (both upper and lower case) cause different space envelopes around words, and that these relate to the ease

Figure 8.4. A set of features for capital letters (Gibson, 1969). Reproduced by permission of Prentice-Hall Inc.

Features	A	E	F	H	I	L	T	K	M	N	V	W	X	Y	Z	B	C	D	G	J	O	P	R	Q	S	U
Straight																										
horizontal	●	●	●	●	●	●	●								●											
vertical		●	●	●	●	●	●	●	●	●				●		●		●				●	●			●
diagonal /								●	●	●	●	●	●	●	●								●	●		
diagonal \								●	●	●	●	●	●	●	●								●	●		
Curve																										
closed																●		●			●	●	●	●		
open V																				●						●
open H																	●		●						●	
Intersection	●	●	●	●			●	●					●			●							●	●		
Redundancy																										
cyclic change		●							●			●				●									●	
symmetry	●	●		●	●		●	●	●		●	●	●	●		●	●	●			●					●
Discontinuity																										
vertical		●	●	●	●	●	●	●	●	●				●		●		●				●	●			
horizontal		●	●			●	●								●											

of reading the word, has been made already when discussing the relative advantage of upper and lower case letters. The whole-word model, therefore, takes a similar form to the letter analysing models by suggesting that individual words are matched to some internalized word template. Indeed much of the reading research conducted around the turn of the century was directed towards discovering the aspects of words' shapes that cue their identities (see Woodworth, 1938, for a critical review).

Unfortunately, however, the evidence appears to be as much against the suggestion that we read by distinguishing whole words as it was against a letter-by-letter model. For example, Adams (1979) argues that analysing by word would be a very time- and memory-consuming process:

> 'We can recognize words in an innumerable variety of typestyles and scripts: does this mean that a given word has as many internal representations? Depending on the goodness-of-fit required for word recognition, the necessary number of internal models would approach infinity.'

A word recognition hypothesis also suggests that if the word is disrupted in any way, recognition should be affected. To test this, Smith, Lott and Cronnell (1969) presented words for identification that were printed in a mixture of upper and lower case type, for example 'qUiTe', 'eveN'. Subjects were required to find the target words embedded in text. As many mixed-case target words were identified within a set time period as single-case words.

Perhaps the strongest objection to the hypothesis is that it implies that we process familiar and unfamiliar words differently and also, therefore, words and non-words. However, it has been repeatedly demonstrated (see Adams, 1979) that, provided they conform to the orthographic rules of English suggested earlier, non-words are recognized as easily as familiar words. However, orthographically correct non-words are recognized quicker than strings of unrelated letters. As Adams suggests, these two sets of results suggest that the unit of perception is smaller than a word but greater than a single letter.

Letter cluster hypotheses

The advantage of this intermediate position—that most words are identified through the recognition of groups of letters—lies in its ability to account for the ease with which subjects identify pseudo-words (that is, nonsense words which conform to orthographic rules of English). Simple introspection and observation suggests that a reader who is presented with an unfamiliar word tends to break it down, not into its component letters, but rather into groups of letters or syllables. For example, Gibson *et al.* (1962) have suggested that reading depends on the decoding of spelling patterns where a spelling pattern is defined as any 'letter group which has an invariant relationship with a phonemic pattern'. (A phonemic view of reading behaviour will be discussed later.)

Unfortunately, however, the letter-cluster hypothesis has received a great deal of criticism on pragmatic grounds. Thus, Smith and Spoehr (1974) have suggested that the model needs first to establish on what bases readers break up (parse) the words. If the units of perception were either single letters or whole words, then the initial parsing could be made on the basis either of either physical characteristics of the letters or the presence of spaces between words. No such simple solution is apparent for spelling pattern units. The meaning of a word depends not only on the position of the cluster within the string of characters, but also on its own position in the phrase or sentence.

In summary, then, it would appear that the models of reading that are based on the view that we perceive words in terms of the shapes of their components (the components ranging from single letters, through clusters of letters to the word itself) have their defficiencies. While there are arguments that can be proposed to support each of the models, none of them in isolation is adequate to explain the full range of phenomena associated with word recognition, and it can only be concluded that a combination of each is involved.

Phonetic recognition

The previous section dealt mainly with the ways in which we perceive words visually—that is, extract the features from their shapes or from the shapes of their components in order to decide which word is printed. This section will consider how we transform visual stimuli into cognitive responses. This is normally considered to be the process of 'lexical access' and occurs in terms of speech sounds themselves. The process can be explained in terms of two extremes of view: on the one hand is the view that silent reading takes the form of covert speech (subvocalization) and is accompanied by implicit speech muscle activity. On the other hand, the view is taken that reading is not simply silent speech but a process by which the speech sounds are encoded and are represented cognitively.

Subvocalization

The idea that we read text in the same way that we would speak it, except that no sound is made, has received a great deal of attention since about the turn of the century. Evidence that some subvocalization does occur, particularly with difficult text, was provided by Sokolov (1966) (reported by Baddeley, Eldridge and Lewis, 1981) who examined its role in a problem solving task. He recorded the speech muscle activity using a laryngeal electromyogram and found that, as the problem became more difficult, the amplitude of articulation increased. He went on to suggest, however, that subvocalization was not a necessary step in thinking, but rather represented just one possible source for the processing of coded information, and was relied upon to a greater extent with complex or difficult material.

Further evidence that subvocalization occurs is provided by experiments which demonstrate confusion occurring when reading acoustically similar words. Thus Conrad (1964), for example, demonstrated that the most likely confusions for visually presented material are between items which sound alike. Thus, when subjects were required to recall letters of the alphabet, memory errors tended to consist of substitutions of letters acoustically similar to the test letter, for example 't' and 'd'.

Hintzman (1967) has proposed two hypotheses about the nature of the system used to store the acoustic information that such a subvocalization process would produce. The *auditory* hypothesis postulates that visual stimuli elicit an associated image of the corresponding auditory stimuli, so that confusion could occur between acoustically similar terms. The *active rehearsal* hypothesis, on the other hand, assumes that the reader subvocally pronounces the visual stimuli and produces small movements in the vocal apparatus. This activity, in turn, produces kinaesthetic feedback which is monitored for retrieval purposes. The hypothesis predicts, therefore, that confused items will be those which have similar patterns of articulation (rather than simply *sounding* the same). An experiment of his own suggested that the errors were, indeed, related to articulatory confusions, suggesting that active rehearsal does contribute to the storage of visually presented verbal material. Such an argument, then, gives credence to the suggestion that efficient reading is as much a motor as a cognitive skill.

Finally, a practical implication of such a reading process has been suggested by Poulton (1977). He argues that intense environmental noise can interfere with cognitive behaviour by masking any inner speech that is occurring. Such masking, he suggests, takes place in the same fashion as the masking of normal speech by intense noise.

Phonological encoding

From the discussion above, it would appear that reading complex material involves the reader in articulating the speech sounds. For less complex material, however, evidence for subvocalization is not so pronounced. Indeed, evidence provided by Gough (1972) suggests that inner speech is demonstrably slower than even the longest estimates of reading comprehension time probably because of the articulatory mechanisms required for the recoding loop. Furthermore, as Hung and Tzeng (1981) point out, subjects can gain access to the word in the mental lexicon in less than 200 msec, whereas naming a 3-lettered word requires approximately 525 msec. For normal text, therefore, it does not make sense to suggest that readers have to wait to receive subvocal information before they can recognize a word.

For the reading of 'normal' text, therefore, some other form of visual cognitive processing is likely to occur, and this will probably be on the basis of the speech sounds themselves. Again, two models have been suggested. On the one hand is the view held primarily by Hansen and Rogers (1973) that the letter string is first broken (parsed) into its component syllables, for which a representation of the appropriate sounds is then produced. On the other hand is a proposal that the letter string is analysed into its constituent graphemes (composite speech sounds) to which a phoneme is assigned (see McCusker, Hillinger and Bias, 1981).

i. Parsing by syllables

Some evidence certainly exists to suggest that words are encoded by parsing according to syllables. For example, Eriksen, Pollack and Montague (1970) demonstrated that the time needed to start naming either a word or a two-digit number increases with the number of syllables in the vocalization of the response. For example, the subject's reaction time was longer when 'seventeen' was the stimulus to be vocalized than when it was 'fourteen'. Klapp (1971) also found that reaction time increased with the number of syllables in the stimulus when subjects were required to indicate whether two stimuli were the same or different. Both authors attribute their findings to the need for subjects implicitly to speak a word before vocalization.

The notion of 'internal syllabary', as proposed by Hansen and Rodgers (1973), supposes three reading stages: firstly, segmenting the letter string into its component syllables or 'vocalic centre groups' (VCG's); secondly, decoding the VCG's to produce a phonological representation; thirdly, locating the word in the reader's internal lexicon.

The suggested rules for segmentation, or parsing, imply that if a letter string contains more than one non-consecutive vowel, then there must be more than one VCG. If there is only one vowel, or if all vowels are consecutive, then only one VCG exists. However, there are exceptions to these simple rules. For example, some words may contain more than one consecutive vowel but still be parsed into two VCG's if more than one phoneme is also produced, for example, 'LI/ON', 'DU/AL'. Similarly, words ending with a consonant followed by an 'e', such as'GATE', would be parsed into two VCG's rather than one.

Additional rules have been constructed to determine where in the letter string the division should occur. Thus, if the letter string includes the sequence vowel, consonant, vowel (VCV), then the division should fall between the first vowel and the following consonant. If a word includes a sequence VCCV, the division should fall between the two consonants. To account for possible exceptions to these rules, Hansen and Rodgers added the provision that if the initial parsing fails to produce a recognizable phonological representation, then a second set of rules may be used. These allow the sequence VCV to be parsed into VC/V, whilst the sequence VCCV can be parsed into V/CCV.

Despite its simple approach to the question of how we recode visual text into a cognitive schemata, experiments to test the internal syllabary model have not provided conclusive evidence to accept or to refute it. For example, a study by Spoehr and Smith (1973) supports the model's contention that the correct higher order unit is not the syllable but a vocalic centre group. However, both Vygotsky (1975) and Coltheart (1978) suggest that problems exist with the experimental arrangements used which could have confounded the results and Spoehr and Smith's conclusions.

ii. Parsing by graphemes

The alternative suggestion of how we represent the printed word involves the translation of graphemes (rather than syllables or VCG's) into their corresponding phonemes. Such an approach has been taken by authors such as Venezky (1970) and Wijk (1966), and Navon and Shimron (1981) have argued that it applies also to other languages such as Hebrew.

By taking such an approach, however, a major problem becomes immediately apparent and again calls into doubt the speed with which such a procedure can take place: a language such as English, with its deep orthographical structure, does not allow either a one-to-one or an invariant relationship between letters and phonemes. Often, a single phoneme can be represented by two or more letters—for example, in the word 'BROUGHT' (BR/OUGHT); also, a letter can also comprise two phonemes, for example 'X' (EK/S). Before phonemes can be assigned to graphemes, then, the letter strings must first be parsed into single letters or letter sequences which, themselves, correspond to single phonemes. To describe the letter or letter group that corresponds to each phoneme, Venezky (1970) introduced the term 'functional spelling unit'.

Another problem with this approach is that the irregularity of the English language makes it impossible for any parsing procedure to analyse every word correctly into its functional spelling units without the reader being able to call on some prior lexical knowledge. For example, pairs of vowels such as 'ai', 'ea', etc., usually correspond to a single phoneme and so would constitute a functional spelling unit. However, exceptions do exist, for example, DIAS (DI/AS), REAL (RE/AL). The reader needs to know of these exceptions before being able to make phonetic sense of the word. Some attempts have been made to construct sets of rules to enable the correct parsing procedure for every word, but they are very complex.

Finally, further problems exist in the assignment of phonemes to the correctly parsed graphemes since, as has already been pointed out, the relationship between phonemes and spelling units is not invariant. For example, according to Venezky (1970), the spelling unit '0' has seventeen possible phonemic characters, whilst 'A' has ten. Despite this, Wijk (1966) and Venezky (1970) claim that parsing procedures and phonetic assignments yield a correct phonological representation of the majority of English words. Those for which a correct representation is not produced are described as 'irregular' or 'exception' words.

In conclusion, it would appear that the way in which a visually presented letter string becomes represented phonologically is, as yet, far from resolved. The available models suffer from serious limitations. Nevertheless, as McClusker, Hillinger and Bias (1981) conclude, some form of phonological encoding certainly does appear to occur when reading: the problem facing cognitive psychologists is to determine how it occurs.

Individual differences in reading ability

Discussing various hypotheses of the ways in which we read text has two advantages: firstly it helps to ensure that text is presented via the computer in the most readable fashion; secondly, understanding how we read normally should help when considering how and why people read at different rates and with different degrees of proficiency. This would be of value when designing text for either slow or handicapped readers.

Two lines of evidence have been proposed which attempt to account, at least partially, for the observed differences in reading or word recognition in skilled and unskilled (or fast and slow) readers. The traditional view is that individual differences arise owing to the differential use of visual (character/word recognition) and phonological forms of access by skilled and unskilled readers. More recently, however, evidence has been provided which suggests that the reader's skill is reflected in an ability to perform the coding strategies.

The main theme embodied in the traditional approach is that, since phonological encoding involves an extra level of processing, it must necessarily take longer than the more direct visual form of access. This argument was supported by Barron (1973), who suggested that a reader who is free to choose an analysis strategy will normally use the faster, that is visual, strategy. He asked subjects to classify phrases as either making sense or being nonsensical. Two kinds of nonsensical phrases were used: semantically nonsense phrases such as 'I am kill' and orthographically nonsensical but phonemically sensible phrases such as 'It's knot so'. His results suggested that subjects took no longer to classify the latter to be nonsense as the former. This suggests, therefore, that the subjects were analysing the phrases on the basis of their visual appearance rather than their sounds.

If this inference is correct then it seems reasonable to assume that differences in reading abilities reflect differences in reliance on visual and phonological strategies by slow and fast readers. This, indeed, was found by

Barron and McKillop (1975) who examined individual differences in phonemic analysis, visual analysis and in a basic reading task in which subjects were free to use either strategy. Thus, they found that slower readers were better at the phonemic than the visual strategy.

A second approach to the study of individual differences in reading ability focusses on the common assumption that less skilled readers require more time to convert visual representations of words and pseudo-words into the appropriate phonological representations than do their more skilled counterparts. Empirical evidence supporting this assumption has been provided by Mason (1978), who found that in a naming task less skilled readers made more errors and were slower at naming both regular and irregular words than were skilled readers.

Finally, skilled and less skilled readers can be differentiated on the basis of their use of non-lexical information in reading. Whilst this is not so important for the recognition of single words, it is important for processing whole phrases and sentences.

There are several sources of evidence which suggest that skilled readers appear to minimize their workload by efficiently using their knowledge of linguistic and semantic constraints associated with words and phrases (Goodman, 1972). Indeed, Cohen and Freeman (1976) claim that the more proficient readers rely to a greater extent on contextual information and less on vision than do poor readers.

In summary, then, the temporal advantage shown by skilled readers over slower readers may be due to one or all of three factors: firstly, a greater reliance on the faster strategy of visual analysis wherever possible; secondly, when direct visual analysis is inadequate, a superior ability to obtain a phonological representation of a word; thirdly, maximal use of non-lexical information such as context in the processing of phrases and sentences.

Comprehension

Discussing individual differences in reading ability leads on, naturally, to consider how we make sense of the material presented visually to us, that is how we *comprehend* the text. Anderson (1980) argues that comprehension can be analysed into three stages. The first comprises the *perceptual process* by which the message is originally encoded. It is this stage that has been considered until this point. Secondly is the *parsing* stage in which the words in the message are transformed into a mental representation of the combined meaning of the word. Finally is the *utilization* stage, in which the reader actually uses the mental representation of the sentence's meaning to answer a question, to store information, to obey an instruction, etc. The relationship between language and behaviour was discussed in Chapter 1. As Anderson points out, these three stages can occur sequentially or they can overlap. For example, as has already been shown in terms of word context, readers can be making inferences from the first part of a sentence while perceiving a later part.

Parsing sentences

The concept of parsing has already been introduced when considering the syntactic rules of grammar in Chapter 5 and the ways in which the complexity of the rules make it very difficult to produce efficient computer speech synthesis and production systems. Essentially, English sentences are able to be continually broken into constituent parts until the individual words are arrived at, and their relationship to each other can be determined by the shape of the resultant 'tree structure'. The rules which govern such sentence parsing are known as 'rewrite rules' and take the form, for example, of:

'Sentence = noun-phrase + verb-phrase'
'noun-phrase = *either* article + adjective + noun *or* pronoun'
'Verb-phrase = *either* verb + noun-phrase *or* verb + prepositional-phrase'

Such analysis is often referred to as *surface structure analysis* since it considers only the actual words used in the sentence and not their meaning within the total communication act (see Kimball, 1973). Chomsky (1957), therefore, suggests that natural language also consists of *deep structure grammar* which relates to the phrases in the underlying word string. These deep structures would not be syntactically correct if they were directly uttered as subjects of an English sentence. However, Chomsky argues that they are able to be related to the uttered surface structures by means of *transformations* which, themselves, have their own set of rules. It is not necessary to consider the rules here, although it should be remembered that by using the complete set of such rules it should be possible to parse the available text. Then, by examining the extent to which the 'tree structure' is 'right', 'left' branching or is 'self-embedded', it should be possible to determine the text complexity.

When considering sentence parsing and its relationship to comprehension, Anderson (1980) also invokes the concept of 'patterns'; that is, a reader may parse sentences not simply according to grammatical rules but by groups of word types that he calls patterns. For example, the sequence 'noun-verb-noun' (such as 'man bites dog') suggests that the action (verb) was performed by the first noun on the second. In contrast, the pattern 'noun *was* verbed by noun' (such as 'man was bitten by dog') relates the action of the second noun to the first. Such patterning rules, Anderson calls *parsing productions*. Clearly, these patterns relate more to deep structure analysis than to the formal grammatical rules discussed earlier. Thus they help to guide our comprehension of the sentence and our behaviour towards the message.

Although parsing sentences in this way seems, intuitively, to provide a useful starting point to consider how readers comprehend text, Anderson does point out that even at a very simple level of analysis, a piece of text of the length of an average paragraph in this book would produce many millions of different combinations of possible word patterns. For this reason it is highly unlikely that we learn the complete set of possible word patterns through the course of our language development; it is more likely that we learn to process sub-patterns, or phrases, and to concatenate them to form understandable sentences. Thus, Anderson suggests that the important features of parsing consist of:

1 The use of language-processing productions in which the reader looks for typically occuring sentence patterns or constituents, such as *noun* or *person-verb-object*.
2 These productions build in memory the semantic interpretation of these patterns.
3 A total sentence is then processed through the concatenation of a number of pattern recognizing productions.

Finally, Anderson argues that the productions rely for their success on the fact that the sentences contain various clues (word order, key words such as *who*, inflections, etc.) that allow the constituents to be identified (see also, Irwin, Bock and Stanovich, 1982).

One practical application of this type of analysis, from the point of view of designing the most useful ways of presenting text to readers, has been demonstrated by Graf and Torrey (1966) (described by Anderson, 1980). They argued that a sentence would be more easily understood as its constituent structure becomes more identifiable. Thus, they presented subjects with two forms of a sentence that had been split over a number of separate lines. In the first the break at the end of each line corresponded with a major constituent boundary; in the second it did not. For example:

Form A (Split according to constituent boundaries)

During World War II,
even fantastic schemes
received consideration
if they gave promise
of shortening the conflict.

Form B (Split haphazardly)

During World War
II, even fantastic
schemes received
consideration if they gave
promise of shortening the
conflict.

As they expected, their subjects showed better comprehension in Form A than in B. Such conclusions are also substantiated by Anglin and Miller (1968) who found that recall was higher when phrases in a prose passage were intact than if the phrases were broken, and Cromer (1970) who reported similar findings for comprehension.

Sentence construction and comprehension

From the above discussion, it is clear that the ways that we break up text can affect our understanding of the message being transmitted. However, a number of factors can influence this parsing procedure—each related to the way in which the text is constructed. These factors include the presence of ambiguity, the imagery contained in the sentence, the degree of activity or passivity implied by the sentence, and whether or not it is couched positively or as a negative.

Ambiguity

What has been discussed so far is the process of dividing up sentences according to the syntactic characteristics of their constituent words. It must be remembered, of course, that the words themselves convey meaning and that parsing syntactically may not produce the understanding of a message that was intended by its transmitter. This can apply particularly when the sentence is ambiguous, that is when the semantic patterns do not necessarily relate to the syntactic patterns. Because different interpretations are able to be placed on the same piece of text, ambiguity can cause major problems for the reader's comprehension and subsequent behaviour.

In essence, linguists distinguish between two main forms of ambiguity: structural and lexical ambiguity. *Structural* ambiguity arises when an entire phrase or sentence can have two or more meanings; *lexical* ambiguity, on the other hand, arises when only a word in the sentence can have two or more meanings—for example 'light ('set fire to' or 'illuminate') the paper'. In addition, however, it is also useful to distinguish between *permanent* and *transient* ambiguity. Thus, the ambiguity in a sentence which is permanently ambiguous remains even after the sentence has been completed. During transient ambiguity, however, the ambiguity is resolved by the words contained in the remainder of the sentence—before the sentence is completed; for example, 'the briefs were read by the lawyer'. Clearly, permanent ambiguity can lead to misunderstandings whilst transient ambiguity, depending on the extent of the ambiguity, can lead to increased comprehension time. Such results were obtained by Bever, Garrett and Hartig (1973) who asked subjects to complete partial sentences having differing degrees of ambiguity. Interestingly, however, they also showed that once a reader has resolved the ambiguity of a constituent in a sentence, and has settled on a particular interpretation, the ambiguity has no further effect on processing the remainder of the sentence or text—provided that no further change in interpretation is made.

Both forms of ambiguity can arise in a number of ways. For example, if apparently redundant words are removed from the text, meaning can be affected owing to the various possibilities that result from alternative parsing. Ambiguity can also arise if the information presented to the operator is incomplete, misleading or if it is too verbose. Chapanis (1965b) presents a number of examples to illustrate these points.

Imagery

The effect of imagery on a number of cognitive processes has been studied extensively for many years. For example, high imagery words are recalled faster than those which do not easily conjure up an image (Paivio, 1971; Postman, 1975). Similar results have been obtained concerning the memorability of high-imagery sentences (Marschark and Paivio, 1977). Furthermore Ernest (1979) has shown that subjects with high imagery ability are able to recognize unfamiliar pictures more quickly and at lower threshold levels than subjects with low image ability.

If imagery is so important in these cognitive processes, it is not unreasonable to suggest that it also mediates sentence comprehension. Indeed, this was shown to be the case in a study performed by Eddy and Glass (1981), and Holmes and Langford (1976) have also related comprehension to the concreteness or abstractness of sentences. As an explanation of these types of results, Begg and Paivio (1969) had suggested that we code abstract and concrete sentences differently in memory. Thus they proposed a dual coding hypothesis which suggested that concrete sentences can be coded in the form of non-verbal spatial imagery as well as in a verbal association form. Abstract sentences, however, can be coded imaginally only with difficulty.

The implications of such results, that picturable material is easier to understand than non-picturable material, are summarized thus by Paivio and Begg (1981):

'The thoughtful student can readily see some of the implications of this for such matters as the appreciation of literature. One reason why Shakespeare is so appealing, for example, may be the fact that his plays are unusually high in literary imagery.'

As an aid to choosing the most image provoking words, Paivio, Yuille and Madigan (1968) produce data relating to the 'concreteness', 'imagery' and 'meaningfulness' of nearly 1000 nouns.

Sentence activity

It is often possible to convey the same message in different forms, one distinction being along an activity dimension. Thus, a sentence can often take the form simply of a passive statement or can be made in an active or an imperative fashion. For example, a passive instruction could be 'The return key is pressed', whilst its active counterpart would take the form: 'Press the return key'.

The available evidence suggests that comprehension time is reduced for the active form of the text. For example, Gough (1965) demonstrated that active sentences are verified as being 'true' quicker than are passive sentences. Similar results were obtained by Greene (1970). Olsen and Filby (1972), however, demonstrated that the relationship is a strong function of the *focus* of the sentence. Thus, the active sentence advantage is maintained only when the receiver of the sentences can identify with the active part of the sentence. When the event described by the sentence was coded in terms of the receiver of the action, passive sentences were more easily verified. The same results were found for answering (rather than simply identifying) active and passive sentences.

Finally, there is also evidence to suggest that the active advantage holds only for text in which a sensible active–passive transformation can be made. For example, Slobin (1966) measured the verification time for reversible sentences such as 'The boy is being hit by the girl' (in which the subject and object can be interchanged to the active form 'The girl hits the boy'), and non-reversible ones such as 'The boy is raking the leaves'. He found that active reversible sentences were verified more quickly than passives, but that the verification time did not differ for active and passive non-reversible sentences. Paivio and Begg (1981) suggest that such results arise because in non-reversible sentences it is easy to determine which noun is the logical subject so that passives do not cause any problem. With reversible sentences, however, it is more difficult to determine the subject, so that passives are more difficult.

Positives and negatives

Just as a sentence can be couched in terms of different degrees of activity so, too, can it be arranged along a dimension of positive to negative. For example, the positive instruction 'Press button A' could also be put into its negative form 'Do not press button B'. Words such as *not, except, unless* each have negative elements, as in some circumstances do words such as *reduce* (Wright and Barnard, 1975)

Again, the evidence appears to suggest an advantage of one form over the other—in this case the positive form of a sentence is generally comprehended faster than its negative counterpart (for example, Gough, 1965; Greene, 1970).

Despite this general conclusion, however, it would appear that contextual aspects can, again, affect the positive form's advantage. Thus Wason (1965) has argued that if the negative form carries with it more information than its positive counterpart—if it is both plausible and performs its natural function of contrasting and distinguishing the exception from the norm—then the positive form is not easier to comprehend. This he calls the *plausible denial* hypothesis. For example, since most people go to work in the morning saying 'I went to work yesterday' carries very little information. The statement 'I didn't go to work yesterday', however, tells us something new. In such cases Wason found that the reaction times to plausible negatives were significantly shorter than to both positive and negative implausible forms of the sentence. Nevertheless, it was still the case that the plausible, positive sentences were reacted to fastest. These results have been confirmed by Arroyo (1982).

Readability

Having considered some of the factors which can affect how well textual material is likely to be comprehended, it is appropriate to consider how to measure the readability of the material. In many respects readability is largely subjective, with individual styles of writing being able to be discerned in different pieces of work. As Klare (1963) points out, however, although there are rules for efficient writing such as those discussed earlier, careful adherence to them does not guarantee good writing. Writing is an art, not a science; a writer can use the same words as Shakespeare but produce a pedestrian piece of text because of the ways in which the sentences are constructed or the ideas are formed, etc.

Klare does point to three general principles which the writer must bear in mind, however. First the writer must know something of the reader for whom the text is being written—educational level, motivation and reading experience. Second should be considered the writer's own reason for writing the piece—to teach, to entertain, etc. Third, as emphasized earlier, words need to be selected carefully—to ensure that they are not ambiguous, that they are active and affirmative, etc. It is the words used and their construction into sentences which make the prose readable.

To produce some standard in the readability of material, various readability formulae have been proposed, which operate by analysing the words used in selected passages in the prose. Klare (1963) describes many such formulae, but perhaps the most popular was produced by Flesch in 1948.

To compute Flesch's 'reading ease' score, a 100-word sample passage of the prose to be analysed is first chosen. Then the number of syllables (*wl*) in those 100 words are counted in the way in which they are read aloud. For example, 1985 will have five syllables (*nine - teen - eigh - ty - five*). Second, the formula requires the average number of words per sentence (*sl*) to be computed. With this data reading ease can be calculated using the formula:

$$\text{reading ease} = 206.835 - 0.84wl - 1.015sl$$

Thus, the higher the number of syllables in the text, and the higher the number of words per sentence (all of which make the text more difficult to read), the lower will be the score. The formula puts the piece of writing on a scale between 0 (practically unreadable) and 100 (easy for any literate person). As a more detailed guideline, however, Flesch produces a table of typical scores for different types of prose (see Oborne, 1982).

PERCEPTUAL ORGANIZATION AND VISUAL SEARCHING

The previous section considered in detail how, after having recognized that particular marks or shapes on a piece of paper constitute text, the material is organized and scanned in such a way that its meaning is obtained. The purpose of this section is, in some respects, to consider one stage before the reading process—the perceptual stage that is involved in the decision that the information presented is, indeed, text; that the eyes need to be moved to scan the material rather than its background; that particular portions of the text are more 'important' than others. In short, how we organize our perceptual processes in the most efficient fashion to scan material presented to us. Of course, it is also important to have considered the processes involved in textual comprehension since, as was demonstrated in the previous section, the efficiency with which we are able to parse text for optimum comprehension is determined by the way that we organize the sentences. Again, then, the perceptual organization process is likely to affect not only what we see but how we see it and what we understand.

Perceptual organization

A number of models exist to explain the process of perceptual organization (see, for example, Vickers, 1979) but one of the most enduring theories to have emerged over the years arose in the 1920s from the German *Gestalt* school of psychology. The Gestaltist's predictions regarding perceptual organization provide some very simple suggestions as to how textual (and other) information should be arranged for easy perception.

The essential feature of the school of thought is that individual stimuli are grouped together during perception into wholes or *Gestalts*. Such Gestalts possess features of their own that are not obvious from an examination of their individual parts. Take, for example, the object that you are now observing, what you see is A BOOK. This book is an entity in itself; it has meaning to you as a book. Although the book is composed of separate pages, each page containing printed words, each word being composed of individual letters, each letter having different features, you do not see the object in this way. You see it as a 'whole', and one of the principal aims of the Gestalt psychologists was to specify the principles by which individual items are combined into larger, organized wholes. They also sought to find the principles by which these wholes are perceptually segregated and separated from other wholes. In other words, how the figure stands out from its background. Many of these principles are described by Wertheimer (1958) and are based on subjects' reactions to simple patterns of dots and line drawings. Examples of these principles are shown in Figure 8.5.

Perhaps one of the most important of the principles is that of *proximity* which states that organization of individual elements into groups occurs on the basis of distance: the smaller the distance between elements, the more likely will it be for them to be treated as a whole—as a figure that stands out from the ground. As an example, simply flick through the pages in this book: small sections of text with headings, stand out as being separate from the remainder of the text because of their distance from the last line of the previous section.

Along with proximity is the principle of *similarity*. Similar features are likely to be grouped together so that, for example, the pictures in this book are seen to be different from the text. The use of special highlighting features such as colour or underlining can help to create an appearance of similarity. If a particular pattern consists of elements which conform to the principles both of proximity and similarity, Hochberg and Silverstein (1956) demonstrated that the principle of similarity is stronger than that of proximity.

Two elements will also be organized together if they share the same *common fate*. Thus if two portions of the text are flashing, or two areas of graphic symbols move in the same way, they will be treated as a whole, possibly as endpoints of an imaginary moving line.

This suggestion of an imagined continuation line between two common features is extended in the fourth Gestalt principle, that of *good continuation*. This states that the elements that are organized into wholes are those that produce few interruptions or changes in continuous lines. Of course, where interruptions do occur, the principle of closure (described below) might be invoked to produce a set of smaller, individual 'wholes' (see Figure 8.5d (i)). This principle also explains why it is sometimes difficult to perceive a particular shape embedded in another. For example, the continuation lines on the number 5 in Figure 8.5d (ii) make the whole shape into the 'figure' and the white paper surrounding it into the 'ground', rather than the '5' standing out as the figure and the remainder of the image as the ground.

Related to the principle of good continuation is the principle of *closure*. This states that our organization of elements tends to form them into simple, closed figures, independent of other continuation, similarity or proximity properties. Such closed figures are often referred to as 'good figures'.

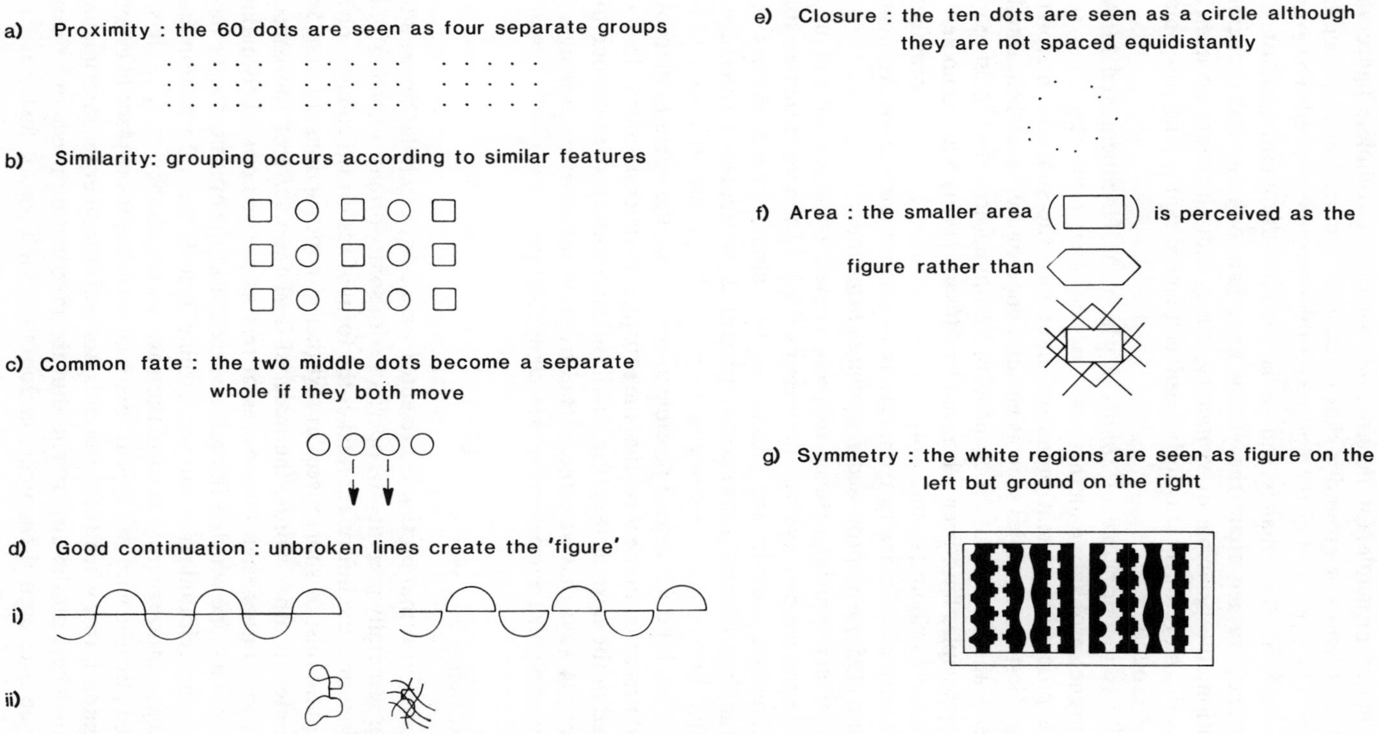

a) Proximity : the 60 dots are seen as four separate groups

b) Similarity: grouping occurs according to similar features

c) Common fate : the two middle dots become a separate whole if they both move

d) Good continuation : unbroken lines create the 'figure'

i)

ii)

e) Closure : the ten dots are seen as a circle although they are not spaced equidistantly

f) Area : the smaller area ( ) is perceived as the figure rather than

g) Symmetry : the white regions are seen as figure on the left but ground on the right

Figure 8.5. Examples of Gestalt principles for perceptual organization.

One major principle for determining whether a complete figure will be perceived as figure or ground is that of *area*: the smaller of two overlapping figures will be perceived as the figure and the other the ground. For example, in Figure 8.5f, the smaller square is seen as the figure against a grid background, rather than the hexagonal shape. A second principle of segregation, the principle of *symmetry*, states that the more symmetrical a figure is the more likely it is to be seen as a closed figure, and this isolates it from the ground.

Finally is the principle of *simplicty* which, as Hochberg and McAlister (1953) argue, probably underlies many of the other principles. They suggest that the processing system organizes input into the simplest interpretation possible. Gestalt principles such as closure, good figure, etc., then, simply are statements about which of the elements of a stimulus are the simplest to group. Similar principles have been advanced by Musatti (1931) who combined all of the Gestalt principles into one comprehensive law of *homogeneity*: homogeneity as to place (proximity), as to quality (similarity), etc., and by Hochberg (1957) who proposed a *minimum principle*.

In summary, the importance of these Gestalt principles should be quite evident. Since we perceive stimuli in terms solely of the ways that we arrange our perceptual world, and since, as has already been discussed, our understanding of the information presented is guided largely by such perceptual organization, employing many of the principles suggested by the Gestalt school should make it possible to ensure that the operator perceives the material presented in the ways that the software designer intended. This will be discussed in the next section, but first it is important to consider one further aspect of the ways that we extract detail from the information presented—that is how we organize our perceptual searching facilities.

Visual scanning and search

The type of information that is presented via a computer, whether on a screen or paper, generally presents the operator with some form of search task. More often than not, the information takes the form of results (in columns or rows) of computations; of short pieces of text that give instructions; of diagrams or graphs; etc. In other words, the material is of the nature of short pieces of information, rather than long pieces of text as in this book. This makes the operator's task one which is initially a search task: the eyes need to be directed towards the relevant part of the display before the information can be processed. Although this is also the case with ordinary text, as has been discussed already, with this type of material scanning takes place in essentially a sequential form; when the material is not text, the relevant information can occur anywhere on the display and thus the information needs to be searched for. Of course, even if the material does take the form of text, parts of the task often involve the operator searching for a particular display characteristic—for example, searching for the cursor among the text during word processing.

The available data relating to the visual search process can be divided, essentially, into studies which have considered the effects of different display arrangements on the task and those dealing with the subjects and their tasks.

Display features

Perhaps one of the first important aspects to be considered when discussing display characteristics and their effects on scanning and search behaviour is the effect of the position of the information on either the screen or on paper. Clearly, this can determine the part of the retina on which the stimuli fall and, because the retina is differentially sensitive, the stimulus position is likely to affect search performance.

A number of experimenters have shown this prediction to be true, both in terms of the probability of correctly identifying characters (for example, Bouma, 1973; Wolford and Hollingsworth, 1974a) and for variations in the time taken to identify characters (for example, Schiepers, 1980) at different screen positions. In all cases, the evidence suggests that the further the character is displaced from the gaze fixation position, the less likely it will be identified correctly and the longer it takes to identify. For example, Smith (1961) demonstrated an inverse square law to exist between search time and the visual angle of the target (θ) to the observer's eye (i.e. time is proportional to $1/\theta^2$). The same type of inverse relationship (although not an inverse square relationship) was demonstrated by Bouma (1973) in terms of the legibility and correct detection of words placed at different distances from a fixation point at the centre of the screen (see Figure 8.6).

Of course, it should be remembered that the 'central point', in these studies implies the point at which the eye is fixated initially—not necessarily the centre of the VDU screen. Brighter parts of the display, for example, can cause the eyes to be directed towards these areas so that these areas become the fixation point. This might then mean that information at the central part of the screen falls on the periphery of the retina.

With regard to the serial position of characters in a display, some evidence exists to suggest that identification is enhanced when gaps appear in the character string. Both Estes and Wolford (1971) and Wolford and Hollingsworth (1974b) have shown that the presence of a gap improves reporting accuracy for the letters appearing on either side of it. For example, take the following two arrangements of a character string:

AVFTYUIOPLE

AVF   IOPLE

Computers at Work

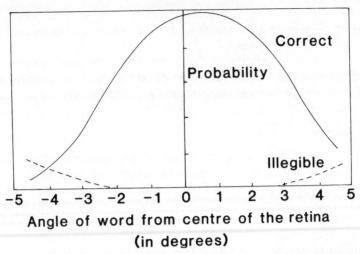

Figure 8.6.   Probability of recognizing words as a function of the angle of the word to the centre of the retina (adapted from Bouma, 1980). One degree of visual angle represents about four letter positions. Reproduced by permission of Taylor & Francis Ltd.

Accuracy for reporting the 'F' and the 'I' in the second string would be about 20% better than in the first string. This is possibly because the gap creates the appearance of two substrings and allows attention to be directed to the letters on either side of it. As Gould (1976) suggests, 'people fixate on contours much more frequently than they fixate on homogenous areas'. Furthermore, the evidence suggests that the letter preceding the gap (F) benefits more from the gap than that following it (I). Adequate spacing of displayed material, therefore, is likely to lead to increased detectability of individual items. Spacing is one of the aspects of user-friendly dialogues suggested by Stewart (1980).

The efficiency of detection is also related to the material that is displayed—particularly in terms of the display complexity, the probability of the item being present, and the ability to distinguish the displayed items.

In terms of complexity, Harris (1966) demonstrated an almost linear reduction in detection performance with both the number of items to be searched and with the complexity of the items themselves. Although Harris's study was performed using an industrial inspection task, this finding of an increase in detection time with increased display density is consistent with a number of other studies that have employed laboratory paradigms of visual search. Teichener and Krebs (1974), for example, have reviewed many of these studies and have shown that the detection time for stimuli in simple arrays increases only slightly with array density up to about 200 stimuli. Above this,

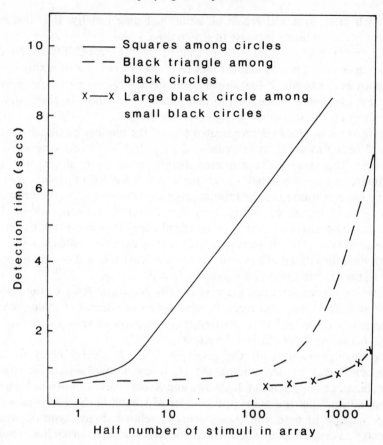

Figure 8.7. Relationship between detection time and the number of items to be searched, for different types of display arrays (adapted from Teichener and Krebs, 1974). Reproduced by permission of the American Psychological Association.

however, the detection time for each stimulus increases dramatically (see Figure 8.7).

The shape of the curves shown in Figure 8.7 suggest that we process information for searching on both a parallel and a serial basis, depending on the number of items to be searched. For 'few' items, therefore, in which the increase in search time with the number of items in the array remains relatively static, it would appear that we process the information in a parallel form—the complete array is processed at once (almost as a Gestalt) so that additional stimuli do not increase the processing time significantly. After a point, however, our ability to process on a parallel basis breaks down and we have to resort to serial processing. Thus, additional items are searched sequentially so that each extra item will create an additional time penalty. It is this which causes the almost linear increase in search time.

Since most human behaviour is shaped by the probability of an event occurring or not, it is reasonable that this is also the case for detecting items in a display. For example, it has already been discussed how past experience can 'set' the observer's perceptual organization. The same is true, too, for detection tasks that include a vigilance component. In a vigilance test, for example, Jenkins (1958) demonstrated that as the number of signals that had to be detected in an array increased, the number of correct detections also increased. This view was later altered slightly, however, to suggest that it was not the frequency of 'wanted' signals *per se* which was the important criterion, but the ratio of wanted to the total number of signals—that is, the probability of a wanted signal occurring (see, for example, Jerison, 1966). These assertions have also been tested using an industrial inspection task by Fox and Haslegrave (1969). Their results indicated that detection efficiency increased almost linearly with an increase in the probability that a fault would be present (that is, the probability that a signal would occur).

However, a corresponding increase in false detections (that is, the rejection of good items) also occurred. It would appear, therefore, that Fox and Haslegrave's inspectors were altering their criterion of rejection rather than simply becoming more efficient detectors.

The distinguishability of the displayed items is clearly likely to be an important factor in determining the efficiency of any search activity. For example, a cursory glance at Teichener and Krebs' curves shown in Figure 8.7 would indicate that the point (the number of stimuli in the array) at which a sharp increase in detection time occurs is related to the type of stimulus presented. For example, when asked to detect squares in circles, subjects' performance deteriorated when only about 10 stimuli at a time were presented. The deterioration point for black triangles among black circles, however, was not until about 200 stimuli were presented. With even greater distinguishability between the array elements, that is detecting a large black circle among small black circles, very little deterioration in performance occurred even with about 2000 display elements. A similar type of relationship, although indicating different optimum array sizes, has been demonstrated by Christ (1975) for more complex stimuli such as aircraft shapes.

As an index of the effect of discriminability on search time, Howarth and Bloomfield (1979) suggest that the two factors are related according to an inverse square law. Thus, search time is proportional to $1/D^2$. In many cases, of course, it is difficult to determine the value that D (the difference in discriminability between the stimulus and the other items in the array) should take. For simple shapes such as circles and squares it is easy (diameter, length, etc.) but for more complex shapes it is more difficult either to measure the differences between the criteria decided upon or, indeed, to select appropriate criteria. However, Bloomfield (1983) suggests that, in such cases, a separate panel of judges can reliably rate stimulus differences to provide some quantitative measure. When he obtained difference measures in this way, Bloomfield was able to substantiate the inverse square relationship for complex coloured stimuli but not when the stimuli were monochromatic. It is possible, therefore, that the extra colour dimension made the searcher's task easier so that the relationship holds for simple stimuli but not for more complex ones.

Teichener and Mocharnuk (1979) argue that the important feature between the stimuli and the arrays is not so much the quantitative value of a difference between the two (*D*) but the amount of information or uncertainty contained in the stimulus and the array. This variable is related to the number of different features of the target and array that have to be considered. For example, in an array of triangles all but one of which had the same size, there would be little uncertainty in searching for a target that was defined simply as a triangle of different size. However, the more different sized triangles that appear in the array, the greater the uncertainty associated with the target stimulus. In an array of triangles varying simultaneously in size and colour, there is even greater uncertainty associated with distinguishing the target from the array. In other words, information varies not only with the number of features within a dimension, but with the number of dimensions. As Teichener and Mocharnuk (1979) explain the point:

> 'A two-dimensional target in an array of 10 two-dimensional stimili has more information than a one-dimensional target in an array of 10 one-dimensional stimuli.'

In their own study, they demonstrated the reliance of search time on display information load. Thus search time decreased and stimulus processing rate increased as the number of target dimensions increased.

The reason for the increase in search time in such circumstances, of course, lies in the increased cognitive load placed on the searcher as the display information load increases. This effect was also shown by Gould and Schaffer (1965), in terms of eye fixation times during reading. In their experiment subjects were shown a display such as in Figure 8.8 in which their task was to fixate on the centre three digits, add them up, and then determine how many of the corner digits summed to the same value. Eye fixation durations for each set of digits were about three times as long as those obtained for more simple tasks. Indeed, the fixation durations were determined largely by the magnitude of the sum of the centre three digits and, in the light of the discussion above, by the similarity of the sum of the centre digits to those in the corners.

Finally, an important aspect of the display layout that can affect the observer's searching abilities relates to the extent to which special aspects of the display stand out from the background in terms of their colour. As an

486   532

356

725   866

Figure 8.8.   Typical display used by Gould and Schaffer (1965) to demonstrate the effect of cognitive load on search times. The distance between the left and right numbers produced a visual angle of 16 degrees.

important variable in modern displays, particularly for coding specific items, colour will be dealt with in more detail in a following section (p. 303). The purpose of the present discussion will be to consider its effects on search time.

In the light of the previous discussion it is not unreasonable to expect that if colour is used as one of a number of dimensions present in the display, then visual search time will be increased. Such an argument is substantiated in results of a study by Green and Anderson (1956), who concluded that search time was slightly longer for multicoloured than for single-colour displays when subjects were not informed of the target's colour. Similarly Cahill and Carter (1976), who asked subjects to search for numbers in displays of 10 to 50 items coded in 1 to 10 colours, found that search time increased as the number of colours used increased—even when the number of items in each colour category remained constant.

The studies imply, therefore, that a search time penalty is incurred if too many different colours are used in the same display. However, there is no doubt that, on unidimensional displays, the use of colour to highlight the target item does reduce search time. Thus, Christ (1975) reviewed a number of studies that had used colour as a display coding attribute. In all of the studies considered, the time needed to locate colours was short compared with the time needed to locate other non-colour attributes of the target such as shape or size (see also Smith and Thomas, 1964). Again, then, the argument appears to be one that presenting too much information to the operator is likely to overload cognitive capacities and degrade performance.

Observer's features

In addition to the actual characteristics of the display, the other important factor in determining whether or not an item will be noticed, and the speed with which it is noticed, relates to some of the individual's own characteristics—perhaps the most important being the information that the person wishes to extract from the display. For example, Buswell (1935) showed that people's faces and hands are the most fixated areas of pictures that contain, among other things, people. (Kolers, 1976, describes in detail some of Buswell's findings regarding perceptual span in reading and looking at pictures.) Mackworth and Morandi (1967) showed that parts of pictures that were rated as being most informative by one group of subjects were fixated most by another group of subjects.

Related to the importance of aspects of the display to individuals, however, is the individual's motivation for viewing the display—thus, people often search displays for meaning rather than to perceive specific targets. In these cases, many of the visual search experiments and results described earlier are not so useful in determining how an operator will use a display. Of more value is to consider how people fixate on aspects of the display. In this respect Boynton (1960) has pointed out that good searchers make many brief eye fixations, whereas poorer searchers make fewer, but longer, fixations. Furthermore Loftus (1972) has found that the more fixations a person makes on a picture during a fixed viewing time, the higher the probability that the picture will be recognized later. Interestingly, neither the duration nor the sequence of fixations affected how well the picture was remembered.

That observers are able to vary their search or scan patterns with their intentions was demonstrated well by Yarbus (1967). He showed subjects pictures of different scenes, such as a group of individuals in a room, and asked them to infer different things from the picture. For example, when asked to estimate the ages of the individuals, most eye fixations occurred around the facial regions; when asked to consider their social standing, most fixations related to the clothes and furniture, etc. Clearly, then, the search and fixation pattern was related to the search intent.

DISPLAYING THE INFORMATION

A considerable amount of information has been presented in this chapter to suggest that the way in which the software is displayed to the operator can significantly affect whether or not the message will be received and understood. Considerations of how we read, search, organize and understand the material presented - whether in the form of text or pictorially - are needed in order that the displayed information is able to be made to be compatible with the user's expectations, requirements and abilities. The purpose of this section, then, will be to consider what ought to be presented, how and where.

Typographical aspects

As many newspaper editors and compositors already know, the layout of a piece of text or other information is possibly as important as its contents. Layout can help to catch the reader's eye during the scanning process, organize perceptual input during the reading process and aid the reader to understand the message during the comprehension process. As Stewart (1980) argues:

'Good formats need to be designed and tested, not left to chance or to the most junior programmer on the team.'

Poulton, Warren and Bond (1970) provide an interesting summary of some of the more important typographical points to be considered when deciding on an appropriate layout, some of which are expanded below.

Sectioning prose

Dividing the text into meaningful sections has three advantages for the reader. First it provides structure to the prose, informing the reader where one set of ideas ends and a new set begins. Secondly, through the Gestalt features discussed earlier, it allows the structure of the material to be organized perceptually. Thirdly, it provides a chance for the reader to 'collect the thoughts' and to prepare for the next section. Regarding the design aspects, Hartley and Burnhill (1976) have suggested that leaving an empty line between paragraphs is a more effective cue for the reader than simply indenting the first line of a new paragraph. Furthermore, vertical spacing can be used to separate out and to group related sections within the text. Another possibility, suggested by Wright (1977), is to colour either the print or the background.

Problems with the use of colour in the text, from the point of view of presenting too much information to the reader, have already been introduced and will be discussed in more detail later. However Wright's suggestions regarding the use of coloured backgrounds would be less burdensome to the reader's information capacity. She argues, that a coloured background can provide supplementary indexing information, for example, as with an appendix in a book. It enables the reader to turn quickly from the text to the beginning of the appendix without having to look for page numbers. On a VDU, background colouring could provide information regarding the type of material being processed—for example, with a financial analysis program a red background could indicate the debit columns and a black background the credit areas. Again, however, the error of presenting too much additional information needs to be guarded against.

One of the common ways of sectioning prose is to use appropriate *headings*, and these serve a number of different purposes. Most obviously they assist readers who are searching through a display or printed material for particular sections. Perhaps less obviously they are also extremely valuable to those who have to read the entire material since they provide a structure which assists the reader to integrate the information as it is being read. Each of these may help to increase the reader's comprehension and memory of what is read, as

Dooling and Lachman (1971) have demonstrated. Unfortunately, as Wright (1978) has pointed out, no specific research evidence is available to suggest either the type of text that would benefit most from headings or the form that headings should take.

One aspect of headings that has received consideration concerns the ways of numbering them. Numbering can serve two purposes: it may help to make clear to the reader the way in which the sections are nested together (thus replacing, perhaps, the need for subheadings), and it enables the reader to refer to specific sections that are smaller than a page.

Perry (1952) has suggested that Arabic numbers are preferable to Roman numbers, although this is possibly so only for the smaller values (compare, for example, the ease of interpreting the sets of symbols iv and 4, and xxviii and 28). In addition, Wright (1977) suggests that numbers are probably better for indexing than letters of the alphabet, and the larger the sequence the greater is the advantage for numbers. For example, people are more certain that 8 precedes 10 than that H precedes J.

The size of display areas

Whereas dividing text into distinct section areas facilitates the reader's scanning and search behaviour, the question of the size of the text area relates to the normal reading and comprehension processes. These involve saccadic eye movements and the division of words, phrases and sentences so that they are not frequently split in places that make comprehension difficult.

With regard to saccadic eye movements, it will be remembered that each saccade encompasses about 6–8 character spaces. It will also be remembered that the available evidence suggests that we do not sweep our eyes over the text in a rigid left–right direction, but often make recursive movements, perhaps to correct mistakes or to aid comprehension. Thus, although unfortunately no evidence is available to guide the designer in deciding the optimum width of the text area, it should be clear that it ought not to be either too small or too large. If the width is too small, only a few saccades may be possible on any one line, thus necessitating recursions to previous lines with the attendant problems of directing the eyes to the beginning of another line. If it is too large, too many saccades may be needed to scan the line. More importantly, perhaps, it is necessary to ensure that when the eye is at the extreme the right-hand end of one line it does not have too far to travel back to begin the next line (again, the optic control mechanism can lead the eye to the beginning of the wrong line). In this context, Bouma (1980) relates the length of a line of text (i.e. the distance between the left and right hand margins) to the angle over which the eye travels to reach the next line. This, he suggests, should be approximately 2°. For long lines of text, therefore, the interline spacing should be reduced.

Within the width of the left- and right-hand margins, the number of characters needs to be related to the distance of the observer from the text, which determines the visual angle that each character presents to the eye.

Subsumed under the topic of display width lies the question of whether or not text is better presented as a single block or in a column format as appears, for example, in newspapers and magazines. Again, this question relates to the control of eye movements between lines. With very long text lines (as would occur in a newspaper that did not use a column format) the interline spacing would have to be extremely small to retain the optimal 2° recursive movement to the beginning of the next line. Columns, then, help to keep the line length small.

The experimental evidence that has been produced to support such a contention does suggest that column formats are advantageous, but only under certain circumstances. Thus, Tinker (1963) demonstrated that both speed and comprehension are superior when text is arranged in a two-column layout compared with an arrangement in which it is spread across the page. However, Kak and Knight (1980) report that this column format was beneficial only for normal reading speeds. Subjects who had been taught to 'speed-read' showed no advantage when using such a format, and even some disadvantage. It may be, of course, that the training that these subjects underwent during the speed reading course (for example, to control recursive eye movements, to scan efficiently) may have directly interfered with the eye movement patterns needed for column formats.

Text justification

Whenever characters at the left- or right-hand margin are vertically aligned with one another (as, for example, in this book) the respective margins are said to be *justified*. Whereas left-justification clearly has advantages for the control of line recursive eye movements—consistent feedback from the optic muscles allows the observer to make some degree of prediction about the appropriate point to stop the recursive movement at the beginning of a line—the advantages of right-justified text are less tangible. Unless words are to be broken at sometimes inappropriate places (thus causing difficulties for word recognition), a constant line length can only be maintained if the amount of spacing between the words is varied. In lines which contain a number of words, of course, this will not be too noticeable, but for shorter lines the unpredictable interword spacing may cause problems for the reader. For this reason Burt (1959) recommended the use of the unjustified style in books for small children.

Gregory and Poulton (1970) performed a number of experiments designed to investigate this question, using both good and poorer readers. As stimuli they used three justification formats: right-justified, not right-justified and not right-justified but with words broken by hyphens in appropriate places. Their comprehension results demonstrated that the better readers neither benefited from nor were disadvantaged by the different format styles. However the poorer readers obtained lower comprehension scores for the justified than for the two non-justified formats. A second experiment, using the poorer readers, demonstrated that the non-justified format advantage no longer held when the line length was increased from about 7 to 12 words. In this case, then, the disadvantage caused by the variable interword spacing was reduced.

Coding and cueing

One clear result that emerged from the discussion of visual search processes was that the more conspicuous is the target area, the better is the search performance. Clearly, then, highlighting important areas of the display, by increased display luminance, by typographical techniques such as underlining, italicizing, bolding, capitals, etc. or by colouring different sections can help the reader to pick out the salient points of the display. With regard to written text, for example, Fowler and Barker (1974) found that library textbook readers had inserted some form of cueing such as underlining or asterisks in over 90% of the books.

In addition to aiding the observer in his or her search task, of course, many of these typographic techniques can also be used to code certain display areas or types of information. Colour coding, for example, is a well-known technique in many areas. For example, a flashing red display is often used to indicate danger; green usually signifies safety, etc.

The available research regarding the effectiveness of different typographical cueing techniques is inconclusive—primarily owing to scarcity. For example, the little evidence which is available suggests that the occasional use of italics for emphasizing significant points may be no better than plain text for ease of comprehension, and a complex cueing system may actually impair study.

The research on underlining as a means of cueing is similarly inconclusive. For example, Cashen and Leicht (1970) showed that students who had received offprints with relevant passages underlined in red were better at answering questions both on the underlined statements and also (possibly because the underlining helped comprehension) on the adjacent, uncued passages. It would appear, however, that this advantage is only apparent if the reader is not under some time stress to complete the passage. For example, in a study in which all subjects were allowed the same time to read a passage, Crouse and Idstein (1972) found that cueing led to higher scores when the readers were given some time to study a 6000-word text, but not when they were given a shorter time. Furthermore, it may well be that underlining may actually make the text harder to read owing to the reduction in space that it causes between the lines.

Foster and Coles (1977) considered the relative merits of using capital letters and bold type as cues. Their results indicated that the bold type was a better all-round technique of cueing. Although the capital letters led to higher scores on the cued material, when the subjects were tested on the uncued material they performed worse than those who had had no cueing at all. The authors suggest that when readers used the capital letter cueing technique it hindered their reading performance, perhaps by affecting their reading behaviour so that they had less time available for perceiving the uncued portions of the text.

Finally, the use of colour needs to be considered. Certainly for coding visual information, colour appears to be the most useful technique. For example, Hitt (1961) compared five types of code: numbers, shapes, letters, stimulus position and colour and demonstrated that numerical and colour coding were equally the most efficient. Similar results were obtained by Smith and Thomas (1964) who demonstrated that a colour code consisting of five different colours was more effective than any geometric shape code that they used. In addition, Christ (1975) has reviewed a number of similarly conducted experiments and has shown that colour is superior to size, brightness and shape coding for accuracy of identification. However, in some instances the use of letters and digits were shown to be more efficient, but this is not altogether surprising since the tasks were in the nature of identifying objects. When tasks which involved searching displays were reviewed, colour was superior in all cases. As far as coding is concerned, therefore, colour would appear to be the most useful 'all-round' method. However, it should be remembered that it does have its own limitations—particularly in environments containing coloured ambient illumination, and if the observers are 'colour blind'.

With regard to the effect of colour as a highlighting cue for text comprehension, Fowler and Barker (1974) found that subjects who were questioned a week after having read material were more likely to answer correctly the questions which related to the highlighted parts of the text than the non-highlighted material.

In summary, although the evidence suggests that highlighting may have beneficial effects on reading performance and comprehension, the over-use of such techniques should be cautioned against. Thus, it has previously been pointed out that visual search times can be increased if the operator is presented with too much information (or, more specifically, too much uncertainty). In this respect, too much information implies, perhaps, too many cueing categories. Whereas using one or two colours, for example, may increase searching performance, using too many may actually degrade it. (Jones, 1962, suggests that the normal observer can identify about nine or ten surface colours, primarily varying in hue.)

The second caution relates to the possible distracting influence of the cueing techniques and their deleterious effects on perceptual organization. For example, Engel (1980) argues that, although colour can be a powerful means of improving the legibility of text displays, over-use (or non-optimal applications) can break up the display's Gestalt. Perhaps more insidiously, colour can create artificial groupings of material and thus impair the Gestalt that are otherwise appropriate to specific sections of the display. This is particularly so for displays which consist of non-prose information such as tables or menus. As a check to ensure that this does not happen, Engel suggests converting the alphanumeric characters in the display into rectangles of the same size and colour. In this way the influence of the colours on the layout will become more apparent.

Speed of presentation

One of the major themes that has run through this book has been that performance will only be maximal when the information that is being transmitted between the operator and the machine is passed at an optimal rate—that is, the rate at which each component can process the information provided by the other. (This is not to imply, of course, that rate is the only important variable; the quality of the information is just as important.)

Since it is usually visual information that is transmitted from the computer to the operator, and since the normal modes of presenting such information include printers and visual display units, it is appropriate to consider whether there is an optimal speed of presenting such material. Common sense, of course, suggests that there should be: too slow a presentation rate is likely to slow down the whole communication process, leading to increased response time and also, possibly, to increased operator frustration with the system. Even more annoyingly, textual information presented at a slow rate might well interfere with the normal reading processes discussed earlier, placing more load on the operator's cognitive capacities—for example, having to remember groups of characters and words as they appear slowly in order to parse the sentence properly. At the other extreme, too fast a presentation rate may also interfere with reading performance—this time, either because the material cannot be read in time or because of the distracting effect of the characters flashing past on the screen. If the information is produced on a printer, a very fast printing speed will lead to the paper continually scrolling past the eyes, as each line is fed, so that pressures are put on operators' memory capacities as well as their speed of reading.

Very few studies have considered this question from an empirical viewpoint, although Bevan (1981) did investigate the presentation of totally textual information. He presented material at four rates: 10 characters per second (cps), 15 cps, 15cps in a word-by-word format, and 60 cps. The word-by-word format was included to overcome the objection levelled against slow printing speeds that they can interfere with the perception of whole words. In this case, then, whole words were presented with longer periods between words, so that an average speed of 15 cps was reached. As an additional variable, he divided his subjects into two groups: low and high ability, based on their performance on a comprehension, vocabulary and reading test.

In terms of errors, significantly more mistakes were made when subjects were presented with information at 60 cps than at either of the other three presentation formats. This occurred both for the low and the high ability groups. All subjects also took significantly *longer* to respond at 60 cps than at 15 cps. However, when the overall time spent at the terminal was analysed ('frame-rate'), subjects spent only about one-half of the time with the 60 cps display than at 10 cps. Considering that a 60 cps display presents text six times (and not twice) as fast as a 10 cps display, this result suggests that more 'cognitive' time is spent at the 60 cps display.

In a second experiment, Bevan added a very fast presentation rate of 480 cps (which, essentially, presents text in a page-wise fashion). Errors with this faster rate were approximately the same as at a 25 cps rate. Interestingly, the maximum number of errors were obtained at 18 cps, which suggests that whereas subjects could read and follow the text at 10 cps, and not at 25 cps so that they were left to their own devices, at 18 cps they were forced to read faster than they could take it in. At 480 cps the frame rate, again, was only about twice the speed as at 18 cps (and was the same speed as at 25 cps).

On the basis of these studies, and of subsequent interviews with the subjects, Bevan suggests an optimum rate of 10–15 cps for maximum understanding and retention of textual material.

Display and control compatibility

With this last section of this chapter, the information transmission wheel will have turned full circle. It is, again, time to consider the optimum 'man-machine' system that has been the theme of this book. Thus, information is not presented simply for the sake of it. On many occasions it is presented in order for the operator to respond in some way—to answer a question, to activate a cursor, etc. This section, therefore, will consider the ways in which information ought to be presented to the operator so that the 'return link' (the information pathways discussed in Part II) can be optimized. This will occur when the display and the corresponding control are compatible.

Compatibility effects can possibly best be exemplified by a simple experiment described by Welford (1976). Subjects were presented with up to eight stimulus lights, to any one of which they had to respond as quickly as possible by pressing the appropriate numbered key. In the first condition (highly compatible) each button was located below the light with which it was associated. In the second, the low compatible condition, the buttons were arranged in random order. The results demonstrated that a higher response time was produced when the lights (displays) were incompatible than when they were compatible. As Welford explains it:

Presumably in the first (condition), once the light was identified the key was also, whereas in the second arrangement the light had to be identified first and then its number used to locate the corresponding key. In other words, in the second condition the data had to be recoded from digital to spatial form before a response could be chosen, so that the translation mechanism had more 'work' to do than when each light was located above its corresponding key.

In other words, in the low compatible condition the display did not 'suggest' the appropriate key response.

The need to ensure compatibility arises for three reasons. First, as exemplified above, an incompatible display–control relationship is likely to lead to reduced response speeds. Secondly, the learning time for the operation of equipment on which the controls are compatible with the display will be much shorter than if they were incompatible. In the experiment described above, for example, the subjects had to learn the new (random) arrangement of buttons before they could respond quickly. Thirdly, and perhaps most insidious, when placed under stress an operator's performance on equipment with incompatible display–control relationships will deteriorate as he or she reverts to the relationship expected to occur. Such expectations (or 'stereotypes') will be discussed later.

Fitts and Seeger (1953) suggest that these three effects can occur because a response which a person makes can be considered to be a function of two sets of probabilities:

1 The probabilities (uncertainties) appropriate to the specific situation in which the operator is placed—training, instructions, past experience, successes, failures, etc.;
2 'The more general and more stable experiences or habits based on the operator's experiences in many other situations'.

They suggest that training will nearly always lead to changes in the former but will have relatively little effect on the latter. This argument is extended by Loveless (1962) who suggests that the new (trained) behaviours do not replace the old behaviours which were learned as a result of past experiences and expectations, they merely overlay them. Certain situations may arise in which the old behaviours may come to the fore:

> During training the old response is weakened sufficiently to allow the new response to appear, and the latter is then strengthened by further practice; but the old habit has been suppressed rather than eliminated. The suppression is likely to be in part temporary, so the old response may reappear after a period away from the task. ... It can be predicted on theoretical grounds that habit regression will occur when the operator's motivation is decreased, when he is fatigued and when he is subjected to any novel change in the working situation.

The suggestion is made, therefore, that compatibility arrangements are learned—that there are more examples of compatible than incompatible relationships in everyday living, and that the more that one is exposed to these relationships the more likely will be the tendency for the operator to expect these relationships to occur. If they do not occur then, depending on the degree of incompatibility, normal performance may be reduced by varying degrees. Under conditions of stress (for example time stress), however, performance is highly likely to be degraded significantly.

Two main ways of arranging compatibility between control and display exist. *Spatial compatibility* occurs when the position of items in the display suggest the appropriate control response. The lights and buttons in the experiment described by Welford had high spatial compatibility in the first condition, but very low compatibility in the second. Second is *movement compatibility*. In this case the movements of items in the display suggest the ways in which the associated control should be operated, and vice versa. For example, most operators would expect the right-hand cursor control key to move the cursor to the right of a screen, and the left-hand key to move it leftwards. Relationships which are expected by the majority of the population are described as population stereotypes. Oborne (1982) and Loveless (1962) provide details of these types of compatibility relationships and suggest means of predicting their direction.

In addition to the general display–control compatibility situations which apply to any machine with which a human operator needs to interact, computers present two further considerations. The first, a spatial compatibility problem, refers to the arrangement of information in displays when a response is required from the operator. The second is a movement compatibility problem and relates to the movement of the text, the cursor and the cursor control (which is usually a keyboard key but is sometimes a joystick).

When information is presented in such a way that the operator is required to respond to particular categories—for example, typing the name of the file or inputting particular numerical information—spatial compatibility problems can arise if the position of the cursor on the screen that indicates where the response is to be included does not imply the response key that needs to be pressed or, indeed, the type of response to be made. This can arise particularly if different parts of the display request different types of information in a less than ordered fashion—for example, alphabetic, followed by numeric, followed by numeric, followed by alphabetic, etc. In this respect Stewart (1980) argues strongly that the display should be organized in a logical sequence, both in relation to the system and to the users' or other information sources. For example, it is normally expected that the sequence 'name' followed by 'address' will occur on a written form or, dealing with a parts list, part A will be considered before part B. Displays which also conform to this sequence could be said to be spatially compatible with the user's expectations of the sequence of responses required. It is important to remember, then, that spatial compatibility can be infringed if the users' expectations are upset— irrespective of the control relationships.

With computer systems, the problems associated with ensuring movement compatibility are possibly more numerous than with spatial compatibility. Particularly when dealing with information presented via a VDU, the displayed information is generally moving in some way and the cursor certainly moves. Since in this case the two components, cursor and displayed text, are related in the operator's 'mind', it is important to ensure that their directions of movement are compatible.

Most software that allows the user to 'scroll' through the computer's memory (as, for example, in word processing) does so through the use of the cursor. In this case, pressing the 'CURSOR UP' key would generally have the action of moving the cursor up the screen; the 'CURSOR DOWN' key would have the opposite action. This, of course, is completely movement compatible—the action will occur within the expectations of the user. Unfortunately, however, since VDU screens have finite dimensions, when the cursor reaches the top (or bottom) line of the screen, the display–control relationship becomes incompatible. Because the action of the software is to scroll through the memory, and because the cursor cannot travel further upwards, the effect of moving *up* through memory is to move the text

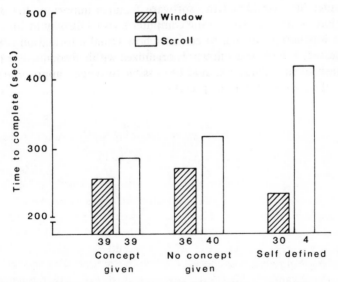

Figure 8.9. Average times taken to solve display problems using either a window or scroll cursor movement (adapted from Bury *et al.*, 1982). Reproduced by permission of the Human Factors Society.

downwards. Now, because the moving text becomes the 'figure' its movement appears incompatible with the operator's expectations. Bury *et al*. (1982) investigated this problem by comparing performance using a *scrolling* function of the cursor with that using *window* display. The two forms differ with respect to the operator's focus of attention. A window display suggests the VDU screen moving over the stationary text; a scrolling display suggests the reverse. Pressing the 'UP' key using a window display, therefore, would add one line of text at the top. The same key pressed using a scrolling display would add a line at the bottom of the text area.

In their study, subjects were allocated to one of five groups: the first (self-defined group) allowed subjects to define their own function. Thus they used the system according to their expectations. The remaining four groups used either the window or the scrolling function and were either told, or not told, of the concept behind the function's operation.

Two interesting results emerged from this study. First, out of the 34 'self define' subjects, 30 defined their direction keys to be the window function. It would appear, then, that some form of stereotype exists for this function. Secondly, for all groups of subjects, performance was faster for the subjects who used the window function than for those using a scroll function. These results are illustrated in Figure 8.9.

SUMMARY

This chapter has considered the software features important for presenting information to the operator via the computer's visual display facilities. In this respect it was important first to consider how visual information is perceived and processed, and secondly how it is organized within a cognitive framework. On the basis of such data, it should be possible to suggest appropriate ways of designing the information to be presented.

PART IV

Computer Applications at Work

In many respects this book could have been completed at the end of Part III. By now the interested reader will have considered in reasonable depth most of the important factors relating to the successful implementation of computers into a working situation—at least from the viewpoint of ensuring that those who are to work with the machines both accept the introduction of the new technology and are able to 'converse' with the system in a fruitful way. As has been stressed constantly through this book, only when the requirements and abilities of the operators match those of the computer system will performance and thus the organizational productivity be able to be maintained at the maximum that is possible.

To have completed the book at this point, however, would have prevented the reader from gaining some insight into how many of the principles discussed so far have been used in practice to implement computer systems in various situations. With the continual reduction in computing costs, and with a similar increase in computer power and flexibility, computing systems are being used in many different types of job and for varied reasons. As will be seen, they are being used for their large and (effectively) permanent memory capacities, for their ability to present a façade of almost infinite patience, for their fast (albeit very simple) decision making capabilities, for their computational abilities, etc. Different applications, then, require different features offered by the computer.

The use to which many of these faculties are put in practice will be discussed in the remaining three chapters. It must be stressed, however, that these applications will not be considered in great depth. The chapters will simply illustrate some of the principles discussed earlier and their application to particular situations. It is also important to realize that the applications discussed in Chapters 9–11 do not represent the full range of computer applications at work. Again, they are meant to provide a representative sample

311

of the situations in which computers are used and the problems which have arisen in their implementation and the solutions that have been suggested.

Chapter 9, therefore, will consider the use of computers in office environments; the introduction and the rise of technology and the problems involved in its use by people who have not been trained initially to use such technology. Finally, Chapter 10 will consider the introduction of computers to educational settings—teaching pupils of different ages and abilities. Their use in medicine will be considered in Chapter 11—both from the point of view of interacting with the patient and in helping medical practitioners make more accurate diagnoses. As was pointed out earlier, the main theme of each of the chapters in this section will be simply to discuss, in the light of the previous chapters, the application and success of introducing computer systems to the various situations. It is not intended to delve too deeply into the many issues that are raised by using computers in these situations—to cover the aspects fully would require at least a further book dealing with each of the topics.

CHAPTER 9

Computers in the Office

Offices are essentially information processing and transformation systems, and so almost all of the features that a computer offers—large memory capacities, fast processing, accurate computation, formalized decision processing—are employed nearly every day in controlling and running offices. Information about clients, stock, meetings, decisions, etc., constantly has to be recorded and retrieved; financial balances about the organization itself or small aspects of it need to be computed and presented quickly; modern decisions are often so complex, with the alternatives so finely balanced, that decision aids are often required. For all of these tasks, and many more, computers offer invaluable help—primarily because of their large and infallible memory. The purpose of this chapter will be to discuss the application of computers to some of these modern-day office practices, and to illustrate their problems and advantages. It will not discuss specific systems, programs or applications since their technology is advancing so quickly that any such discussion is likley to be out-dated even before this book reaches the bookshelves. The principles relating to the efficiency with which people interact with these machines within an office context, however, will remain. In this respect, it will be remembered that many of the social and attitudinal questions relating to the implementation of computers in offices were discussed in Chapters 2 and 3.

The history of technology in the office has had a long career, as Meyer (1982) has demonstrated. The innovative stages which he highlights began in the 1920s with telephones, that allowed personnel to communicate without leaving their workstation and enabled different communications infrastructures to develop. The 1940s introduced the era of industrial engineering and systems analysis, with the resultant studies of business transactions. This merged into the operations research era of the 1950s with its influence on business decision making and, in addition, the decade saw the introduction of computers for routine data processing. It should be noted that much of the literature dealing with the effects on employment and work practice of introducing computers into organizations was published during this decade.

The 1960s saw the emergence of more complex telecommunications systems, providing the facilities for tele-conferencing (using television networks to hold meetings with participants in different geographical locations) and data transmission using telephone lines. These two facilities enabled individual work groups and computers to be linked together so that they could communicate with each other, and the 1970s saw the beginning of such communication networks both within and between organizations. The introduction in the late 1970s of cheaper minicomputers and microcomputers enabled this distributive process to develop more rapidly than would have been the case had the cost of computing not fallen dramatically. The reduction in computing costs and the increased communication facilities have resulted in a decentralized shift in computing (and organizational) power, with the implications for the organization as discussed in Chapter 2. Furthermore, the existence of such networks, particularly between organizations, has led to an increase in 'cooperative computing' in which resources, data and software are shared—and this can lead to a number of technical and economic advantages for the participants. Unfortunately, as Bernard (1979) points out, the proposals for such sharing can fail if the managerial problems that can arise are not overcome. These can include some loss of autonomy for each participant, interorganizational conflicts, and a possible lack of finance and maintenance of the sharing system.

By taking a brief look at the history of technology in the office, then, it is possible to peceive the evolution that has occurred, and with it some of the changes in working practice. As a result of automation, the scene which now develops is towards the introduction of an integrated, automated office in which the functions of an ordinary office (performing information handling activities such as text and forms editing, filing documents, simple computations, verifying information, and communicating within and between offices and organizations) are performed using computer systems (Ellis and Nutt, 1980). Furthermore, as Olson (1982) points out, the introduction of computers for such tasks may result in the need to reconsider the concept of an office and how it functions with, perhaps, a dramatic change in the concept of office work. One of the biggest changes, she sees, will be in the definition of the physical location and organization of the office. With the ability to communicate electronically it will no longer be necessary for people to be physically located in a central place to perform their work nor, indeed, by making use of electronic mail and other such systems which do not require face-to-face communication, would it be neccessary for people to work during fixed hours.

A NEW CONCEPT OF PRODUCTIVITY?

When considering specific aspects of the computer and the interaction with humans, such as the software, hardware, environment, etc., a simple concept of probability has been implied. That is, the productivity of a static system (one in which there are no other influences on the system than simply 'input' and 'output') can be represented by the ratio of the input costs of the system (wages, hardware, maintenance, errors, etc.) to the output benefits (units sold, contracts won, etc.). For assessing the value of specific aspects of a system, this is a perfectly feasible equation (although it is often extremely difficult to quantify some of its variables). It is also possible (although again difficult) to produce a 'productivity figure' for individuals performing specific tasks. For example, a copy typist might be assessed in terms of the number of letters typed per unit time, the number of errors made, etc.

When dealing with a complex system such as an integrated office, however, this industrial-based definition of productivity is too simplistic. Workers in an information-integrated office are presented with a rich variety of information flowing from many different directions, both vertically and laterally within the organization and outside of it. Furthermore, this information flows both from and towards the worker, representing both information and feedback. Strassmann (1982), therefore, suggests that organizational productivity from the viewpoint of white-collar labour should be concerned more with the worker's ability to make appropriate choices from a set of possible options and to deal with ever-changing work conditions. The difference between the 'industrial-age' and the 'information-age' views of working practice, then, is that in the latter the workers make their own choices of how to use the machines and not *vice versa*.

Because of this increased flexibility that computers bring to the situation, new ways of thinking and collaborating can be introduced which should enable better (not just faster) work to be performed. Unfortunately for the definition of productivity, however, the system has not remained static—information is constantly being introduced into the input–output system from a number of different sources and so it is not possible to assign the benefit as having resulted from any particular source. For this reason, when considering information processing systems, the concept of productivity in terms of efficiency becomes one of productivity in terms of effectiveness. This is determined not only by the quantitative features of the output (number of letters typed, for example), but also by its quality, responsiveness and scope (Strassmann, 1982). Of course, the problem now becomes one of defining the variables that contribute to effectiveness, and Stabell (1982) discusses possible solutions.

WORKING PRACTICE

The changing concept of productivity in some ways arises as a direct result of a change in working practices that occurs as a result of introducing information systems into the office. Thus Olson's argument that increased communication facilities will enable more people to work away from the central office, perhaps at home, and at times more suited to themselves has already been discussed. She adds that one consequence of such decentralized working practices might be that office managers lose some control over their subordinates, with the result that more resistance to remote working might come from management than from employees.

Strassmann's suggestion that information technology in the office tends to increase a worker's flexibility in decision making has also been discussed. The effectiveness of the office worker in an information-structured office originates from an ability to recognize many variables simultaneously or to probe for answers that may not have been considered under former conditions. The effective information worker, then,

> 'makes more qualitative judgements, including whether the right task is being performed, whether the quality of the output is correct, whether the responsiveness is balanced with regard to the situation at hand, and whether the quantity of output is useful to whoever the service is delivered'.

From surveys of offices in which information systems were installed, Strassmann (1982) also points to other areas in which working practice changed as a result of the technology. Thus the positive features included:

1 *Shifting responsibility* for various tasks to those best suited to perform them, irrespective of status. For example, shifting responsibility for preparing, typing and distributing documents from secretaries, typists, etc. to the original author. Appropriate corrections can then be made at source.
2 As a consequence of this shifting of responsibility, and of the freer flow of information between individuals, *traditional roles* sometimes became blurred. Furthermore, the directions in which the information flowed tended to create new social and work groups, which often developed their own slant or special phraseology that emphasized their distinctiveness.
3 Again, as a result of shifting resources and changing roles, secretarial and support staff often had their *work enlarged* in a qualitative sense. Thus, the work became more varied, particularly in areas that required personal contacts. A similar observation was made by Hiltz (1982) when considering the effects of increased communication using video- and tele-conferencing. In this case he demonstrated significant changes in the use of reading and library facilities as a result of using these systems. Some groups of employees read significantly more books after participating in such conferences, although others read significantly fewer.

4 *Increased communication* also occurred with the rapid turn-round of messages that result from using electronic mail systems. The communication, however, transferred from verbal to written as a result of the data transmission being more reliable and quicker to use than telephones.

There were, however, some negative features of introducing information systems. These included:

1 An *increased exhibition of territoriality*. The concept of territoriality and its effects on behaviour was discussed in Chapter 6, and Strassmann noted examples of it in his pilot studies:

> One of the most interesting developments ... has been the discovery of an individual's identification and personal attachment to an electronic workstation. When a person had to give up his machine we noticed mild behavioral disturbances comparable to withdrawal symptoms such as anger, drop in effectiveness, and sometimes irrational efforts to restore the lost means for accomplishing work.

It is questionable, however, whether such behaviour occurred actually because of the perceived role changes which would result from suddenly not having access to a computer.

2 *Increased security*. With the free flow of information through the communication network traditional security measures such as locks become less useful. For this reason new security measures often have to be incorporated which sometimes disrupted working practice.

OFFICE AUTOMATION COMPONENTS

Any office manager considering implementing some form of computer system in the office will probably be bewildered with the number of different types and functions of systems available today. Both hardware and software systems are presently available to help make management decisions, to perform accounting tasks, to edit text and pictures, to coordinate work groups, to allow the user to record and process large amounts of information. These are often able to be purchased at comparatively little cost. Meyer (1982) suggests that this variety is a good thing, in that it offers flexibility and helps the implementor to adapt the technologies to the local business needs. Before being able to do so, however, some order must arise from the apparent chaos of available machinery, and this can be achieved by reference to the framework of the usual tools that are used in an office. Thus, the information systems available for offices generally fall into four types. Unfortunately, very little work appears to have been published relating to the behavioural issues involved in using these categories of information machines. The four types are:

1 *Text and graphics handling facilities*—the information technology equivalent of the typewriter. These are often called 'word-processors' and enable large quantities of text to be stored and edited at will, with the text having to be typed only once. Associated with these machines are others which deal with the text that has been produced—checking the spelling, formatting the printed output, etc. (see, for example, Peterson, 1980; Yannakoudakis and Fawthrop, 1983). Often, such functions are performed using the same piece of hardware (either a desk-top computer or a terminal attached to a large computer) but programmes with different software. The effects of word processing on office practice and on the material produced will be discussed below.

2 *Number handling facilities.* This is the information technology equivalent of mental arithmetic plus pencil-and-paper, or of the calculator plus pencil-and-paper. Again, these functions are normally produced using different software on the same hardware. Often, the software enables financial reports and charts to be generated by linking with the word processing software. They also generally allow mathematical and financial 'experimentation' to occur by employing user-generated models to analyse the numerical data to answer 'what-if' questions. Apart from considering the effects of such systems on employment, very little behavioural work has been performed to investigate the use of such facilities in offices.

3 *Information sources*—the information technology equivalent of files and filing cabinets. These are often called data bases, and can take two forms: either relating to the organization itself, for use in management decisions, or data relating to more public information such as library reference lists and bibliographies or public statistics. Such data bases also generally incorporate appropriate search facilities, for example allowing an author to search for all published articles dealing with 'human interaction with data bases'. Unfortunately, as Spence and Apperley (1982) point out, the human-computer interaction issues associated with how users choose items within large data bases have received very little attention. This is in sharp contrast to the large amount of research literature available concerning the design of data bases from the computing science viewpoint. Indeed, the design of office data bases should relate in some way to the normal organization of information within an office. For example, the ways that people organize their desks could imply a model for classifying and retrieving information and for producing reminders about matters to be seen to.

4 *Communications.* This is the information technology equivalent of the telephone and other human–human communication systems. Telecommunications and electronic mail systems are two examples of this form of office component, and are also examples of the two main divisions in office communication systems—synchronous and asynchronous.

Synchronous telecommunication tools allow people to communicate interactively when all parties are present at the same time. The systems range from complex telephone networks to full broadcasting facilities, the latter, of course, allowing much of the non-verbal communication that occurs during normal conversation to take place. Their drawbacks, however, relate to their very nature, that is everyone must be present at the same time. As Meyer (1982) points out, since hardware sometimes breaks down, conference calls often do not connect with all participants at the same time and so frustration with such systems can occur. Furthermore, the normal working practice needs to be adapted to the conferencing facilities. For example undertaking tele-conferences with participants located at different places on the globe means that some participants may be taking part during the early hours of the morning whereas, for others, it may be early evening or late at night.

Such problems do not occur with asynchronous communication systems such as electronic mail, for example Telex. In these cases the sender and receiver can communicate regardless of their schedule mismatches. By the nature of asynchronous systems, however, the communication is not interactive.

With both types of communication system, however, although a number of behavioural issues are raised (see, for example, Short, Williams and Christie, 1976) the computer has only a very small part to play, with its role being one essentially of controlling the communication equipment. The one independent role that the computer can play, however, concerns the use of message files—although, again, most research in this area has been directed towards the problems associated with the design of such systems, rather than the problems that may be faced by users (see, Tsichtritzis and Christodoulakis, 1983)

TEXT EDITING AND WORD PROCESSING

As was described above, word processors are simply minicomputers or microcomputers that are programmed to perform text editing functions. They are distinguished from electronic typewriters in that they have a permanent memory capable of storing almost limitless text (the limit is defined by the memory size of the storage medium—disks or tape) which can later be recalled for editing, reformating and printing. Word processors based on minicomputers may support a number of terminals with one computer. Microcomputers, on the other hand, are generally 'stand alone', 'desk top' machines, although modern data communication technology now allows them to be linked together with others of the same kind. Meyrowitz and Van Dam (1982a,b) describe many of the text editing systems that are currently available.

The basic word processing capabilities allow simply entry and correction of text. More advanced facilities which can be found on most modern machines, include moving blocks of text, editing between files, merging address lists with standard letters, accepting data from other programs such as financial calculations and spelling checking routines, and a variety of formatting facilities for use with printers. These include being able to define the margin positions, the start and finish positions on a page, page length, automatic page numbering, etc. Furuta, Scofield and Shaw (1982) describe various document formatting systems that are available.

On the surface, therefore, it would appear that word processing offers a number of advantages. From advertisements, for example, it would appear that the benefits that can accrue from word processing include: greater productivity; greater delegation of administrative tasks to the support personnel; more work satisfaction for administrative support personnel; and greater career opportunities. However, they also point to reports in the managerial literature which complain that word processing detrimentally affects working practice. Thus, they suggest, it can fundamentally alter the office social structure, affect roles, and encourage less accurate typing performance. Below the surface, therefore, the successful implementation carries a number of problems (many of which could have been predicted from the above discussion of changes in working practice that result from introducing information technology).

The main questions which relate to the successful implementation of office word processing, then, concern attitudes towards the system, the quality of the editor itself, and the quality of the composed text.

Attitudes towards word processing

Curiously, despite the explosion of computer sales to offices, many of which are for word processing applications, little empirical work has been undertaken to investigate secretarial attitudes to these systems. This is despite numerous studies that have demonstrated that an individual's resistance to a computer can limit the successful implementation of the computer application (for example, Byrnes and Johnson, 1981; Johnson *et al.*, 1978; Sherman, 1981).

Arndt, Feltes and Hanak (1983) distributed questionnaires to secretaries who used word processors. In addition to questions regarding their attitudes to word processors, their experience, etc., the authors also investigated the respondents' complexity (the extent to which the respondent was flexible and fond of novel situations) and locus of control (the degree to which the individual has a general tendency to view problems as arising from either externally or internally controlled factors).

Their major finding was that familiarity with the system led to more positive attitudes towards word processing and less anxiousness about using them. Simply using a word processor, therefore, creates a more positive attitude towards them. With regard to the 'personality' measures, the investigators found that secretaries who had demonstrated a high degree of complexity (of curiosity) were more eager to use the equipment; externally controlled individuals (that is, those who view events as being due to chance factors rather than to factors such as skill which are under their own control) were more reluctant to use the equipment.

Text composition and editing

It is the ability to store, retrieve and edit text that makes the word processing system a powerful office machine. The quality of the editing facilities, therefore, are of paramount importance to the efficiency of the machine. Indeed, Whiteside *et al.* (1982) have demonstrated that, irrespective of the nature of the word processor, performing editing functions take slightly more than 50% of the total time employed at a word processing keyboard. Their results illustrate the importance of the cursor control keys during word processing. Indeed, the full results suggest that free-text editing consists of about 50% typing, of about 25% cursor movement, of about 12% deletion, and of about 12% of other functions.

Research regarding the behavioural aspects of text editor use generally falls into one of three approaches. First are attempts to produce ideal models of text editing behaviour, against which the performance of subjects using various editors can be assessed. Secondly, consideration has been given to the creative process normally encountered when composing text, and the effects that direct entry to the word processing keyboard might have on this process and the literary quality of the material produced. Finally, some consideration has been given to the design of text editing features, both from the point of view of the software and of the hardware.

A model of text editing behaviour

Card, Moran and Newell (1980) describe an information processing model of editing behaviour which they suggest is an example of a 'routine cognitive skill'. Such behaviour occurs in situations that are familiar and repetitive, and which people master with practice and training, but where the variability in the task, plus the induced variability arising from errors, keeps the task from becoming completely routine and requires some cognitive involvement. The model that they developed to describe such a skill, the GOMS model, considers the user's cognitive structure to consist of four components: a set of Goals, a set of Operators, a set of Methods for achieving the goals, and a set of Selection rules for choosing between a goal's competing methods.

Goals, then, are the superior structures which define the task in hand: 'EDIT MANUSCRIPT', 'TYPE TEXT', etc. Each goal may be composed of a number of sub-goals. The *Operators* can be conceived of as the behaviours, both motor and cognitive, required to complete the goals; they are defined by specific effects and by a specific duration—for example, the keystroke required to input a character. The *Methods* describe procedures used for accomplishing the goals; they are the skills that are learned *before* the task is performed, they are not plans that are created during a task performance. For example, if the goal is 'TYPE TEXT', the methods include 'read characters', 'type characters', 'monitor visual and kinaesthetic feedback', 'correct errors', 'read characters', etc. Many of the processes discussed in Chapter 4, regarding the keyboard design and typing skills, are relevant to both operations and method rules. Finally, the *Selection* rules are determined by the specific goals at the time of performing the task; it is often the case that a single goal will have a number of methods available to accomplish it. In these cases, then, selection rules are used to determine which is the appropriate method to take. For example, 'If the number of lines to the next piece to be edited is less than 3, move the cursor line-by-line; otherwise scroll the page'.

Card, Moran and Newell tested their model and demonstrated that it was possible to use the model's rules to predict user behaviour about 80–90% of the time, both in terms of the proportions of time spent at various text modification tasks, and user accuracy.

Text composition using word processors

Before considering the effect of word processing on the composition process, it is necessary to investigate the *normal* composition process. Unfortunately, there are very few experimental data relating to the psychology of document composition other than some linguistic characteristics of various composition methods (Blass and Siegman, 1975) or investigations of the styles of famous authors. Nevertheless, some idea can be gained of the process involved in normal composition through a number of studies performed by Gould which have compared composition using different media (speaking, writing and dictation). The main finding arising from these studies was that the different modes for composition had no appreciable affect on the quality of the material produced (Gould, 1978a). With regard to dictation, for example, adult subjects who had never dictated before, with a few hours practice dictated one-page letters of various complexities as well as they wrote them. This was so even though the subjects themselves felt that their dictated letters were inferior to written ones (Gould and Boies, 1978). It would appear, therefore, that with regard to these three modes at least, any difference in performance will arise not through the mode of text composition, but through differences in individual's composition skills.

This aspect was investigated by Gould (1978b) who asked people having a variety of dictation experiences to perform the same type of letter-composition task as was used in his previous experiments. His results demonstrated, not unreasonably, that experienced executives were between 20% and 65% faster at dictating than at writing, and so at least the quantitative effects of the composition mode are related to experience with that mode. Nevertheless, comparing the temporal features of dictating and writing, Gould found that the preparation time used in both forms was roughly the same. The quantitative features aside, however, Gould's results demonstrated very few qualitative differences between the letter-styles produced by novices and those produced by the executives. The effect of experience and dictation skills appeared in terms of the composer's confidence:

'What is gained with experience at dictation seems to be a comfortable and confident feeling toward the method, including the secretary, who is a significant variable.'

Gould (1981) compared the composition performance of subjects using either a word processor to compose and print text, or using handwriting and giving the draft to a secretary to type. Again, the results demonstrated that the quality of the text-edited letters did not differ significantly from those composed using handwriting. Furthermore, as with the comparison of dictating and writing, roughly two-thirds of the total production time in both modes was spent planning the document. However, text-edited documents did take about 50% longer to produce than handwritten ones which were subsequently typed by a typist. This was due in part to more changes being made to the text, and to time taken in formatting and positioning the text for printing.

In summary, therefore, it would appear that word processing does not cause authors to change either their style or method of composition. However, they can be more time consuming for the perfectionist.

Word processing hardware and software

Many of the principles that guide the design of efficient word processors are the same as those discussed in Chapters 4, 5 and 6 and which relate to the design and use of keyboards, VDUs, and to the presentation of information to the operator, etc. Word processors, however, do have additional considerations because of the specialized nature of the input and display arrangements that can occur. Thus, the editing keys and functions and the ways in which the text is presented on the screen are important. With regard to the hardware aspects of editing functions, Thimbleby (1983) distinguishes between three types of functions: symbolic, manipulative, and gesture.

In *symbolic editing* the operator exits from the normal typing mode and uses command words or letters to perform a number of simultaneous operations. This can take two forms, 'instructional' and 'form'. In the instructional type, the user instructs the computer to perform the operations. For example, to replace all occurrences of the name 'Fred' in the text with the name 'Freda' the user might need to type:

Replace Fred Freda

With respect to syntax of this nature, many of the problems regarding cognitive compatibility raised in Chapter 7 need to be remembered.

In the form type of symbolic editing the user would type the relevant command (for example, replace) and two blank fields would be displayed, perhaps at the top of the screen, in which the user types 'Fred' and 'Freda'.

Thimbley suggests that this type of editing function has drawbacks insofar as there is no implicit synchrony between the commands and their effects. The commands typed at the keyboard, which appear at one part of the text display, can have an effect anywhere within the text, even text that is not on the screen. Nevertheless, he does point out that symbolic editing commands are useful when a number of similar operations need to be carried out within the text, without the need for continually moving the cursor.

Manipulative editing relates to the use of single keys, or groups of keys, to perform individual functions. These include the cursor control keys, screen scrolling keys, delete keys, etc. Thimbley suggests that this form of editing is possibly the superior of the three since it has a local and immediate effect on the text. There is a straightforward, direct, relationship between the user's editing goals, actions (or 'methods', in the terminology of the GOMS model) and the system feedback. As such users can be expected to develop some degree of non-cognitive ('routine cognitive') typing skill using the available manipulative editing features.

Brooks (1977) suggests, further, that such manipulative user interfaces improve the user's understanding of the system and, when text on the screen alters in direct response to the user's actions, the manipulation is perceived more as a real event and studied more intently. Such interfaces achieve a higher degree of 'transparency', and the user rapidly becomes unaware of the system as such and can concentrate on the underlying text. Furthermore, because the manipulative parts of an editing system are restricted to the manipulation of visible text, the consequences of errors are directly proportional to the amount of effort the user introduces to the task.

Thimbleby (1983) provides a number of suggestions for the design of various manipulative editing functions, including the use of deletion, insertion and highlighting functions.

Gesture editing uses input devices other than the keyboard (for example, a light pen) to instruct the machine to perform either symbolic or manipulative editing functions. As was discussed in Chapter 4, the problems that occur when using such devices relate to the interruption that they cause to the normal typing flow. Thus users need to perform motor acts, and adopt motor programs, that are different from those that they were using. For example, they might have to stop typing (essentially a ballistic process) and pick up a lightpen (essentially a manipulative process). Furthermore, given the cluttered nature of many office desks, they first have to find the lightpen!

With regard to the arrangement of manipulative editing keys on the keyboard, little work appears to have been performed in this area. However, the same principles should apply as those advocated for the design of alphanumeric keyboards—that is, keys are placed in relation to the frequency of their use (the more frequently used keys such as cursor control—Whiteside (1982)—should be placed near to the keyboard itself and not on a separate keypad) and their action ('dangerous' keys such as those which delete characters, sentences, etc., should be placed away from the more frequently used keys). Furthermore, the effect of ensuring compatibility between the display and control should not be forgotten. In this case, the display is generally represented by the cursor—it is the cursor that moves when the cursor key is pressed. Thus the key which moves the cursor to the beginning (left hand side) of a text line, for example, should be placed on the left side of the keyboard, etc.

Discussing the display control relationship leads to a consideration of the compatibility arrangement between the hardware (the control and display) and the user's cognitive processes (the user's model of how the text is stored and manipulated 'within' the machine). For example, scrolling text 'up' and 'down' the screen. This problem was discussed in Chapter 8, and relates to the fact that with a fixed screen, moving the cursor down a piece of text implies that the text itself moves upwards. This can create many problems for naive users using the cursor control keys. Other compatibility problems, which were again discussed in previous chapters, relate to the semantics of the keys themselves and the operations that they perform. 'Erasing', 'deleting', and 'rubout' keys often perform different variations of removing text.

SUMMARY

This chapter has considered how many of the principles discussed in Chapters 1–8 can be applied to the use of computers in the specific situation of the office environment. Interestingly, one of the primary messages to emerge from this review is that, to date, very few controlled behavioural studies have been reported in this area—despite the considerable increase in computer applications to office work that have occurred over the past few years following the introduction of smaller and cheaper computers. Only with respect to behavioural interactions with word processing and text editing facilities have any significant series of studies been reported.

CHAPTER 10

Computers in Education

On the face of it, computers should prove to be ideal aids in educational settings. Their very large and almost infallible memories, their infinite patience, their fast computing powers, and their novelty are only four of the factors which should contribute to produce the ideal system for use in situations in which individuals wish to find out about and to learn facts, concepts, ideas, etc. In short, computers ought to make ideal teachers.

Unfortunately, however, for a number of reasons (many of them having been discussed in the first three parts of this book) computers have not generally had a smooth introduction into educational environments. As this chapter will illustrate, deficiencies in the design of the dialogues which pupils have to use to interact with the computers, in the use of input devices for the specialized groups (children, handicapped, non-typists) who need them, and the formation of often negative attitudes towards the machines have contributed to a smaller penetration of computer systems into education than might otherwise have been expected. Indeed, Champness and Young (1980) reviewed a number of studies that investigated the use of technology in education and found

> 'repeated examples of writers expressing discrepancies between promise and performance right across the whole range of systems that come under the heading of educational technology, including the most recent of that genre, computer-aided instruction'.

Although the roots of educational technology can be traced back as far as the ancient Greeks (see, for example, Saettler, 1978), the role of computing machines for this form of teaching arose primarily in the 1950s and 1960s when the first minicomputers became more widely available. It was during this time that teaching machines were introduced to develop the idea of 'programmed instruction' whilst, almost at the same time, demands for increased

326

educational opportunities created the right environment for the development of more sophisticated and less labour-intensive teaching methods. Computers, with all of their abilities, clearly held out the promise of satisfying such demands (Annett, 1981).

The history of computer use in education, therefore, can be seen to have followed two distinct—albeit very similar—lines of development. On the one hand computers have been used to apply the learning theories of Boris Skinner to practical situations. 'Programmed learning' presents a method for pupils to learn information by their having to make some sort of active response to questions. Although, over the years, slight variations in technique can be seen (see, for example, Hartley and Davies, 1977), the essential features of this form of operant conditioning are that the pupil advances through the material in small steps only, and only as a result of making correct responses to each question. An incorrect response takes the pupil through another sequence of steps until the question is answered correctly.

The second line of development has been to use computers essentially as very knowledgeable and patient teachers. Thus the teaching process and material to be taught remain very much the same as in a classroom situation. Although special software needs to be written so that the information can be presented via a computer system, the material is still recognizable as that used in a 'normal' lesson; the complete course is not redesigned to 'program' the pupil to learn. Such techniques are encompassed in the synonymous terms 'computer aided instruction' (CAI) and 'computer aided learning' (CAL) which, as the names suggest, emphasize the fact that the computers act as an *aid* to teaching, rather than take over the process entirely.

PROGRAMMED LEARNING

The use of findings from behavioural laboratories in the 1940s and 1950s led to an academic revolution in the late 1950s which had important implications for the ways in which many pupils were taught subsequently. This revolution embodied the concept of programmed learning—teaching material in a controlled, programmed, way using principles of learning that were developed essentially from observations of pigeons and small mammals under laboratory conditions. The main proponent of the theory was B. F. Skinner who, in 1954, suggested that learning principles that had been deduced from laboratory situations could be incorporated into more mechanical 'teaching machines'. Indeed, he described his concept of a Utopian world in which such machines and principles are used to teach the young in his science fiction book *Walden Two*. Holland (1959) describes such machines:

> At Harvard there is a self-instruction room with ten booths, each containing a machine. The student gets one set of material from the attendant and places it in the machines. He closes the machine and begins his studies.

The machine presents one item of material at a time. The subject reads the statement which has one or more words missing and he completes the statement by writing in the answer space. He then raises the lever and a small shutter opens revealing the correct answer, and simultaneously his answer is moved under glass where it can be read and compared with the now-exposed correct answer. After comparing his answer with the correct answer the student indicates to the machine, with an appropriate movement of the lever, whether his answer was correct or incorrect and the next item appears in the window. All items answered wrongly are repeated after he completes the set of items. Correctly answered items are not repeated.

A critical feature of the machine is that it provides immediate reinforcement for correct answers.

It is not difficult to conceive of the role that a modern computer could play in such a situation.

The foundations for programmed learning lie in the results obtained from operant conditioning studies. In these experiments, animals are taught to learn quite complex sets of behavioural responses by building up the repertoires from simple conditioned responses. These responses, however, are different from those normally understood to be in the 'classical' mode and reported by experimenters such as Pavlov, who described only passive reactions to connections built up in relation to external stimuli. Pavlov's experiments, for example, involved combining the sound of a bell with food; whilst the normal response to food is salivation, there is no such natural response to the sound of a bell. When the two are repeatedly presented together, however, Pavlov demonstrated that the animals (dogs) soon salivated to the sound of the bell when it was presented alone. In short, the animal had 'learnt' (connected) that the bell implied food and responded accordingly.

The type of conditioning examined by Skinner is more enduring and is more likely to be successful with complex sets of behaviour. It is termed 'operant' conditioning. Again, two stimuli are presented together and the normal response to one becomes associated with the other stimulus. In an operant conditioning paradigm, however, the animal's response is some overt action such as pressing a button, rather than a passive (perhaps salivation) response obtained during a classical conditioning experiment. In a typical Skinnerian experiment then, an animal such as a pigeon might be presented with a lever (stimulus 1) and a light (stimulus 2). When the lever is pressed, in conjunction with the light, it produces a food pellet (reward). The animal associates the light with the lever as a reward producing stimulus and soon learns to press the lever when the light is illuminated. Much of Skinner's work was associated with varying the type, frequency and contingency of the reinforcement to determine the patterns which would produce the most enduring learning. It is also possible, using operant conditioning techniques, to make the animal perform quite complex combinations of behavioural responses—in other words, to learn complex material. This is done by 'teaching' one small step at a time so that eventually the total process will have been taught. In addition, of course, the presence of negative reward helps to extinguish the learned behaviour (it is such processes which form the bases of behaviour therapy in the field of clinical psychology).

The basis of operant learning, then, is the presence of reward and/or punishment and the patterns with which these are given to the learner. Coupled with the principle of presenting stimuli in small, linear steps so that students always make correct responses, such learning principles have formed the bases of programmed learning techniques.

Holland (1959) suggests seven principles which are important when designing a piece of programmed learning text:

(1) To provide *immediate* reinforcement for correct answers. Reinforcement is much like the concept of feedback discussed in previous chapters and both are important features of the learning of any skilled behaviour. The longer the delay in reinforcement, the less effective will it be as a learning aid. Computers, of course, can provide almost instantaneous reinforcement of, essentially, any type.

More recent research, however, suggests that the message which is fed back to the student following a response should not be regarded solely as a reinforcing stimulus but also as information which will help to locate errors and tell the student how to correct them (Anderson, Kulhavy and Andre, 1971, 1972). The importance of control over the learning process was also demonstrated by these workers when they included a condition in which subjects were forced to look ahead to the right answers before typing in their responses (i.e. to 'cheat'). The post-test results for these subjects were significantly worse than for all other groups, even one which was given no feedback at all. Clearly, this illustrates the advantage of using computers to present the program 'frames'—they do not allow students to look ahead as do, for example, books.

(2) Behaviour is only learned when it is 'emitted' and reinforced. In this respect, Holland is discussing the operant nature of learning, i.e. the student needs actively to make a response rather than the performance being of a passive, more cognitive, nature. Such a proposal, however, would conflict with later learning theorists who argue that cognitive learning can, and certainly does, take place. However, it is not the place of this book to discuss in detail the arguments for and against such assertions.

(3) The new pattern of behaviour to be learned should be presented in a gradual progression, through smaller steps, each of which are reinforced and relate to previously learned items. Holland suggests that this principle holds in normal teaching as well as in the operant conditioning laboratories:

> Obviously a child can't begin with advanced mathematics, but neither can he begin with $2 + 2 = 4$; even this is too complex and requires a gradual progression.

When developing a complex performance in a pigeon, we may first reinforce simply the behaviour of approaching the food tray when it is presented with a loud click. Later the pigeon learns to peck a key which reduces the click and the food tray. Still later, he may learn to peck this key only when it is lit, the peck being followed by the loud click and the approach to the food tray. In the next step he may learn to raise his head or hop from one foot to another, or walk a figure of eight, in order to produce the lighted key which he then pecks; the click follows; an he approaches the food tray.

(4) In parallel with the gradual progression of the response is the gradual withdrawal of support from the stimulus (fading). For example, whereas on one presentation the information might be fully detailed, on the next it might be referred to only by initials, etc.

(5) The learner must place full concentration on the material being presented; attention cannot be allowed to wander. It is at this point that the programmed learning concept invokes some idea of control: the student's observational and cognitive behaviour needs to be controlled to maintain active participation. Holland suggests that this can be achieved both via pace-making with the machine and through appropriate design of the presented software.

(6) At suitable points, the program needs to include some form of *discrimination training* to enable the student to distinguish between the more abstract concepts that arise: colour, shape, mathematical and scientific, meaning, etc.

(7) Finally, the program needs to be able to be continually adapted to the learners' requirements and abilities; it needs to have the facility of branching from one area to explore understanding in another on the basis, perhaps, of the student's responses. In a sense, this takes the role of a tutorial form of computer based educational technology; thus the ideal program would be one which undertook a Socratic form of branching.

In addition to these seven points, when designing a piece of programmed instruction text one also needs to consider the ways in which the learner makes a response. In this respect, two techniques appear to predominate: 'constructed' and 'multiple choice'. A constructed response is one in which the learner actually writes the response; in the multiple choice format he or she is presented with several possible answers from which one is chosen. This requires the memory processes involving recognition rather than recall. The evidence regarding the pros and cons of these two approaches generally has shown no systematic advantage of one over the other.

Another distinction to be made between the types of program is between 'linear' and 'branching' structures. With linear programs each subject responds to each frame of information in sequence, and must make a correct response before proceeding to the next. This is the form proposed by Skinner. A branching program is one that makes it more possible to adapt to the learner's abilities. This is done by providing specific branching points within the program—perhaps to skip some sequences of frames if the learner is demonstrating aptitude, or to take the learner through other frames if the material is not being mastered adequately. As an example, Shettel, Clapp and Claus (1963) used a by-pass type of branching technique to accommodate for the variability in prior knowledge when training supervisors. Compared with an identical linear program (which, of course, did not involve branching) learning efficiency was significantly increased.

Finally, there is some evidence to suggest that the type of learner has important implications for the way in which the material needs to be presented, and thus the efficiency of the system. A number of reviewers (for example, Newsham, 1969; Mackie, 1975) have concluded that older learners require different material with which to work. This is particularly so in two areas. Firstly, older learners probably like to work with programs, especially programs containing more activity, for longer sessions than do younger ones. Secondly, older learners prefer a more discovery-orientated approach than one which simply provides the information. Newsham (1969) provides suggestions for ways of overcoming such difficulties for older learners.

Programmed learning effectiveness

A number of studies have been performed to examine the effectiveness of programmed instruction. Hartley (1966) has pooled the results from over 100 such investigations and concluded (Hartley and Davies, 1977) that there is evidence that programmed instruction can be as effective as, or better than, conventional instruction in some cases. However, his figures shown in Table 10.1 do not suggest that programmed instruction is an unqualified success for all criteria of effectiveness—particularly when considering the amount of material that is retained. Thus, whereas it appears to be effective in reducing overall training time, in 73% of the studies in which subjects were retested after their original learning and testing period, no significant improvements were found using programmed instruction when compared with the

Table 10.1. The proportions of studies (per cent) showing improvements or deficits using programmed and conventional instruction (Hartley and Davies, 1977).

Measures taken	Number of studies	Significantly superior	Not significantly different	Significantly worse
Time taken	90	52	41	7
Test results	110	37	49	14
Retest results	33	18	73	9

conventional teaching method. Similar conclusions were reached in a similar type of study conducted by Nash, Muczyk and Vettori (1971).

Pooled results such as those shown in Table 10.1, however, do not reveal the full picture regarding programmed learning effectiveness: the different studies used different materials, types of subjects (generally primary and secondary school children), learning periods, etc., and the three categories of 'superior', 'no difference' and 'worse' cover a multitude of effects. Furthermore, what is not successful in scientific or statistical terms may be very successful in economic or organizational terms. This is particularly so when the reduced training time is taken into account as a significant economic consideration. As support for this argument, Table 10.2 is interesting. It provides a summary of the results of a series of industrial studies reviewed by Hartley (1972) which used cost-effectiveness as a measure of success. Clearly, in these cases, programmed instruction provided considerable savings.

In summary, therefore, it would appear that programmed instruction, using computers to aid the branching process, can be effective in educational settings—particularly in terms of training efficiency. Such effectiveness, however, needs to be weighed against the cost considerations of producing the programs. As was discussed in previous chapters, the cost of software development can be quite considerable—particularly if specific programs need to be developed for particular purposes.

COMPUTER AIDED INSTRUCTION

Although programmed learning can be a successful means of teaching, it has its drawbacks; cost and the complications of developing appropriate software being just two. In addition, over the years, with more liberal attitudes to education and learning there have developed more generalized feelings of dislike towards the concept of a controlled, token form of teaching—what Holland (1954) described as 'behavioral engineering'. Contemporary use of computers in education, therefore, involves the machines more as assistants to teachers; as aids in the normal teaching process. Computer aided instruction, then, uses the computer's faculties for storing large amounts of information (or answers), for performing complex branching processes, for displaying detailed and fast moving graphics, for being able to access and display information in a number of different forms, and for having infinite patience.

When presented in this form, the advantages of using computers to assist in the teaching process are numerous. Perhaps the most widely accepted is that CAI involves the individual student in active participation in the learning process. Rather than simply passively receiving information from a teacher in front of a large class, CAI generally requires the student to respond to particular questions or at particular stages in the information process. This very activity facilitates both interest and the learning process.

Table 10.2. Some cost/benefits of programmed instruction in industrial contexts. (After Hartley, 1972)

Investigators	Cost of program	Cost of conventional instruction	Estimated savings
American Bankers Association (Ofiesh, 1965)	—	—	20–50% of training time
American Telephone and Telegraph Co. (Ofiesh, 1965)	$218 per student hour	$309 per student hour	29% of instruction 27% of trainee time
Union Carbide Chemicals Co. (Ofiesh, 1965)	—	—	$90,000 in training to date ($30/man.)
Holme and Mabbs (1967)	£1500	£1500	£1500 per yr.
Hall and Fletcher (1967)	£20,000	—	1 week's trainee time Approx. £10,000 per yr.
Oates and Robinson (1968)	£12,500	—	8.2% of training time £24,700 after 2 yrs.
Watson (1968)	—	—	3 hr. per supervisor $90,000 per course
Mills (1968)	£550	—	£1275 annually
Howe (1969)	£13,500	—	£1000 for every 3 courses
Jones and Moxham (1969)	—	—	10 weeks' trainee time. Labour turnover reduced from 70% to 30%. Retention of skilled labour

Another obvious value of computerized instruction is that it allows the learner to proceed at his or her own pace, without there being any outward signs of impatience. The computer can evaluate the responses made and, by using the student's performance (both quantitative—how many—and qualitative—the *type*—of errors or correct responses made), it can make decisions suited to the individual learner. It is also able to provide fast and efficient feedback regarding the pupil's performance; feedback tailored to the needs of individuals students.

Computers can also allow students to experiment in safety—perhaps without the fear of teacher ridicule. At one end of the scale this can simply be to answer the 'what would happen if' type of questions that learners often ask: 'what would happen if the circle is made bigger?', 'What would happen if another argument is added to the equation?', 'What would happen if tax is raised to 50%?'. At the other end of the spectrum, perhaps using simulation programs and complex graphics, students might be able to learn and to experiment with theoretical interactions; to 'mix' chemicals in safety, to 'build' models of buildings and bridges and to test their strengths. Many of these investigations could use the computer to simulate instruments and methodologies which would otherwise be excessively costly or not possible at all.

In addition, the use of computers in this way can provide support for the teaching staff, freeing them for more individual tuition with those students who require it. Computer aided instruction, then, should allow the educational system to make more effective use of the teacher's time.

Unfortunately, however, there are also disadvantages in using the computer as a teaching machine. These lie, primarily, in two areas: their role in the teaching process and the current state of the art in program design. Both of these disadvantages, of course, may decrease in importance with time as the public computer consciousness increases and as more commercial programs appear.

To be used effectively, computer aided instruction requires teachers to move from accepted methods that work to a new and relatively untried method in which many individuals have little expertise and which (as was illustrated in Chapter 2) can arouse considerable fear and apathy owing to its heavy technological base. Some slight attitude and role changes, then, are required as well as alterations to working practice. In a study of over 100 teacher trainees, for example, Stimmell *et al.* (1981) found considerable negative affect towards computers; they were perceived as being 'oppressive' and 'remote' and similar feelings were expressed towards CAI. Barker (1982) suggests, too, that current educational practice has evolved to be the most efficient with the limited resources at hand and that computers may be perceived as machines which will upset this organized system. Furthermore:

> The very use of the term 'aid' is significant, implying a lack of conviction which educational technologists have been unable so far to counter. ... For the most part the media have been admitted as optional supplements, to be used voluntarily and peripherally by those teachers who are interested and to be discarded even by them when finance or technical support becomes scarce.

The success or otherwise of computer aided instruction clearly rests on the quality of the programs used. Unfortunately, however, here a 'mis-match' problem exists: those who know what is required (the teachers) do not normally have either the skills of efficient programming or, because of the pressures created by their own disciplines, the time to acquire them. Conversely, professional programmers do not generally have the curricular information in sufficient detail to produce meaningful programs. The result is that the majority of available CAI course materials are

'poorly constructed, largely undocumented, and able to be run on only selected computers for which they were written' (Chambers and Sprecher, 1980).

Hartley (1978) describes this state of affairs as being an example of the computer's 'limited modes of communication'. This relates not simply to communication limitations in the input/output directions discussed in Part III but, because of the communication barriers discussed above, to limited dialogues between the programmer and the student. Hartley and Bostrom (1982), for example, report a questionnaire study of 72 teachers' reactions to a number of available CAI programs for different types of school subjects. Few programs were considered to be relevant to the syllabus being taught in schools; over one-third of the teachers commented on the difficulties involved in unskilled personnel using the programs (more efficient screen and paper documentation being requested); whilst nearly one-third felt that the programs were not flexible enough to be used in teaching situations of different types— classrooms, small groups, individuals, etc. This flexibility was considered to be particularly important when the number of microcomputers available was limited owing to cost restrictions.

CAI effectiveness

Although descriptions of various CAI uses abound in the published literature, very few fully controlled evaluative studies are available. Where they exist, an assessment of the meaning of the evaluations is often difficult: the effectiveness of CAI is determined largely by the quality of the program used and the amount of additional tuition provided by the teacher (after all, the computer is used as an *aid* rather than a substitute for the teacher). Furthermore the effectiveness of CAI has been defined differently by different investigators. To some it means the amount of learning that takes place initially. To others it implies the amount of retention that occurs (measured by testing some time after the CAI course) or, indeed, whether the student remains on the course. Other studies are related to any change in the learner's attitude towards the computer as an instructional medium, whilst others are concerned simply with the acceptability or 'transportability' of the programs.

Despite these problems of assessment, some authors have attempted to arrive at some sort of summary of CAI effectiveness, with positive results.

Evaluating the use of CAI in secondary school courses for mathematics, reading and languages, for example, Suppes (1979) concludes that:

> The many studies reported in this survey show quite positive results for the use of computer-assisted instruction in basic skills, and these results seem to hold for a variety of measures of gain and for a wide variety of student populations. ... Perhaps the central role of computer-assisted instruction in basic skills is to provide an efficient and, from the teacher's standpoint, painless method of delivering a continual stream of individualized exercises to students and automatically evaluating their answers.

Chambers and Sprecher (1980) considered a number of CAI studies performed in different areas, using different techniques (tutorials, drill and practice, games, simulations) and varying educational levels of students. From this survey they concluded that the use of CAI:

1 either improved learning or showed no differences when compared with the traditional classroom approach;
2 reduced learning time when compared with the regular classroom situation;
3 improved student attitudes towards the use of computers for learning.

There were also some indications that low aptitude students gained more from the use of CAI than either average or high aptitude students. This advantage for lower aptitude students using CAI was also demonstrated by Spring and Perry (1981). They trained educationally handicapped children to read lists of three- and four-lettered words and demonstrated that, whereas 'normal' children performed no better after training (their performance mirrored, at a higher level, educationally handicapped children who had not been given the CAI course), the CAI-trained educational handicapped children performed significantly better.

Examples of CAI use

Computer aided instruction has been used in almost all areas of education from elementary schooling to universities, from teaching basic concepts (Hartley, 1978) to occupational training (Patrick and Stammers, 1977). A number of descriptive reviews of the packages presently available have been produced, for example Hartley and Bostrom (1982), Suppes (1979), Lewis and Tagg (1980), Hawkins (1977), Hunka (1978), and these have considered most areas of application.

Before discussing these applications, it is useful to consider the range of presentation modes that they can take. Psotka (1982) suggests that the various forms of computer-based instruction can be conceived as lying loosely along a dimension which ranges from passive to interactive. The most passive of these forms he describes as 'drill and practice' in which computers act essentially as testers. For mathematics, for example, pupils may have to supply answers to various problems; similarly languages can be taught with pupils having to type correctly, say, the French verbs. In these cases little interactive work takes place—information flows only in one direction each time according to a programmed pattern.

Secondly, and not very far removed from the drill and practice form, Psotka describes the 'information display' format, in which the computer acts simply as a vertical piece of paper. Information that would otherwise have been presented via a book page is presented via a VDU page. Depending on the software used, there may more cognitive interaction occurring with this format than with a drill and practice format, but this is not often the rule.

Thirdly, and at a more interactive level, Psotka suggests lie the games and simulation programs. These attempt to make education more interesting and exciting by involving the pupil in the process that is being taught. Many of the educational software that is presently being developed embodies this form of presentation as, too, are some new computer languages such as LOGO (an interactive language used to teach children mathematical concepts—see Howe, 1978).

Finally, the computer can be used as a fully interactive tutor, asking questions and, using multiple branching and feedback, varying the information presented and the questions asked in accordance with the student's knowledge and abilities. Such a Socratic method of teaching requires very comprehensive programming and a fast machine with large memory capacities. An example of the development of such a system is provided by Millward (Millward *et al.*, 1978; Millward, 1979). Unfortunately, the educational establishment appears to have made only a slow start in using computers in this context (see, for example, Hartley, 1978) although, as Chapter 11 will illustrate, such uses do occur within a medical context for the preliminary interviewing of patients. The problem inherent in this form of interaction, of course, is that (as discussed in Chapter 6) computers are not yet able to understand natural language. Whereas a teacher is able to use the student's own language to probe and to try to understand why a particular response was made or a particular word used in a particular context, this facility is denied the computer programmer at anything other than a very superficial—at least with present knowledge.

Two of these applications, drill and practice and games and simulation, will be discussed in more detail.

Drill and practice

This is possibly the most simple form of CAI, the teaching strategy involved being based on the notion that learning takes place by rewarding (i.e. reinforcing) correct associations between questions and answers. For example,

Terrell and Linyard (1982) describe an evaluative study of the 'Speak Spell' spelling aid. In this case the child simply types the spelling of a word that the machine 'speaks' and is rewarded either with 'That is correct' or with 'Wrong, try again'. Even using this very simple form of reinforcement, the authors demonstrated a significant increase in children's spelling ability. However, this performance fell to pre-machine levels once the opportunity to use the machine was removed.

This, then, provides another example of the need to apply many of the principles of reinforcement discussed with respect to programmed learning— for example, the work of Anderson and his colleagues which demonstrated the need for information being fed back to the student as well as simply performance data. Similar results were obtained in a CAI situation by Tait, Hartley and Anderson (1973). They used children of about ten years old undertaking multiplication practice, and compared the differential benefits of feedback given in the active and passive forms. With passive feedback the message was merely printed at the terminal, but in the active form the information was given as a question to which the student had to respond. If the answer was incorrect, the correct answer was given and the question repeated. The results of their study clearly demonstrated that, although the active form took longer, the performances of pupils given information feedback were significantly better than those of pupils who were simply given reinforcement feedback—particularly for pupils of poorer initial ability.

A further extension of using the feedback provided during CAI has been suggested by Park (1981). He argues for a 'response-sensitive strategy' to be incorporated in the CAI program in which the computer evaluates the *pattern* of mistakes made by the pupil in order to present the most effective aspect of the program. Thus, by the programmer having previously identified possible response patterns and relating them to implications for the learning stage reached (much like a doctor identifying patterns of symptoms and relating them to stages in a disease process), the CAI program would be able to adapt to individual student's learning needs. As Park argues:

> The response sensitive strategy can guide the student along the shortest track for achieving the expected learning outcome because it is a process which diagnoses the student's learning needs as early and as often as possible during instruction, and then adapts the instructional treatment immediately to his/her learning needs. Another important advantage ... is its capability to measure the student's competency or mastery level on the task during instruction.

Another important consideration when designing CAI material for drill-and-practice purposes is to take account of the student's own abilities. From the discussion of the memorization of computer programs, for example (see Chapter 6), it will be remembered that Ausubel (1968) has argued for the use of *advance organizers* to organize the student's learning strategies. Thus he suggests that the degree of meaningful learning of new material is related to its interaction with the student's cognitive structures:

'If his existing knowledge can be used to provide "ideational scaffolding" or anchorage for new material, then learning becomes facilitated.'

To help this process he suggests that, prior to instruction, relevant organizing material of greater generality or inclusiveness should be studied by the learner—the learner should be 'put in the picture'. In this respect, Hartley (1978) reports a study using chemistry undergraduates who were either given or not given prior organizers to their CAI course. Although both groups of students showed gains in the amount of material learnt, the 'organized' group demonstrated better performance in the practical application of the material presented. Further analysis of the results again demonstrated that the CAI differentially helped the students: the less able students were penalized more by not having the organizing material than were their more able counterparts.

In addition, the *type* of organization is important as Mayer and Greeno (1972) demonstrated. They devised two teaching treatments to investigate aspects of learning statistical probability theory. They first emphasized the *interrelations* between the tasks themselves, and then concentrated on formulae and quantitative relations. The second scheme tried to relate the *structure* of the subject matter to the existing knowledge structures of the student. The teaching emphasized meanings and relations and their attachment to common experience. This group of students scored lower on post-tests which contained numerical calculations and required algebraic techniques. However it was superior in recognizing plausible problems with no solutions and in other questions that emphasized the non-computational interpretations of probability measures. In essence, then, the students performed better in relation to the form of the advance organizer.

Finally, Pask (Pask and Scott, 1972; Pask, 1976) has provided further evidence that organization of material is an important variable in learning. He distinguishes between 'serialist' and 'holist students': serialists habitually learn, remember and recapitulate a body of information as a series of items related by simple links. Holists, however, work in more global terms, using higher-order relations and grouping material in more complex structures. Pask provides some evidence which shows that teaching is most effective when the sequencing of material is matched to an individual's particular type of cognitive competence.

Games and simulations

The main disadvantage of the drill-and-practice form of CAI discussed above lies in the fact that it can be perceived by the students as being very boring; it presents material, after all, in a fashion which is similar to traditional teaching techniques. With the increasingly sophisticated graphics facilities offered by many new computer systems, however, and with the increased power and reduced size of the machines themselves, the possibilities now exist for maintaining motivation by teaching through the medium of games and simulations. In these cases, the concepts being communicated are learned through active student participation with the machine. The computer program, then, is used to provide a model of the concept being taught which helps to build up the student's knowledge structures. In general, using such programs, the student is unable to edit or amend the programs themselves, but he or she can manipulate input values of different parameters within the model and observe their effects as displayed, usually, on the VDU. In this way the student can appreciate the properties of the underlying principles and can test out hypotheses and ideas about them.

Langton *et al.* (1980) suggest that games and simulations have four main advantages over traditional methods:

1 Complicated real-life situations can be reduced to manageable proportions and tailored to meet the specific needs of the target population.

   In this context Hartley (1978) adds that simulations can be used to teach techniques in situations in which it would be dangerous for an unskilled person to operate—for example, mixing chemicals or applying medical and surgical practices.

2 Well-designed games and simulations may achieve positive transfer of learning, implying the ability of participants to apply skills acquired during the exercise to other situations (Twelker, 1971).

3 Active student participation and motivation are extremely high.

4 Where a competitive element is included, this provides strong motivation for participants to commit themselves to the work of the exercise (Garvey, 1971). This competitive element may be overt (when individuals are in direct competition with one another) or it may be latent (when, for example, teams perform parallel activities and later report on their findings).

SUMMARY

This chapter has illustrated the way in which the use of computers in education has developed along two parallel paths. The first, an earlier path, employed the principles of operant conditioning to present information to students in a controlled, programmed fashion. The available evidence suggests that well-constructed programmed instruction can produce increases in learning, although the problems of producing suitable software are quite large.

The second approach has been to use computers essentially as extremely flexible and patient teaching assistants. Again the evidence suggests that, when used in this role, benefits can accrue. However the problems of obtaining suitable software are sometimes greater since those who produce the programs (the computer programmers) and those who use them (the teachers) often do not adequately communicate their requirements to each other.

CHAPTER 11

Computers in Medicine

In a sense, computer applications in medicine follow a very similar path to the ways in which they are presently being used in education; that is, as aids to the experts who practise in the system—in this case physicians and surgeons. Just as with using computer aided instruction it was the role of the teacher to teach and the computer to act as a willing assistant to enable some of the more mundane aspects of the job to be off-loaded, so the computer's role in medical practice can be seen essentially as one of a 'patient' medical assistant. Thus they can be used to aid practitioners in the interviewing process, remind them of possible medical decisions that they could make, monitor and maintain patients and their records. As will be seen later, however, this benign view of computer assisted medicine is not shared by all writers on the subject.

Unlike in education, the history of medical computing has not had such a long tradition. Fox (1977), for example, suggests that it was not until the early 1970s that the value of computers for performing various functions in medicine began to be demonstrated with any conviction. Since then the use of computers in health care has increased greatly to the extent that Glantz (1978) is able to point to predictions that this section of the market is likely to contribute to approximately 20% of the total U.S. data processing sales (this is to be compared with approximately 3.5% of sales in the education market).

The reason for this almost religious conversion of the medical establishment to computing, of course, is not difficult to perceive. Modern medicine strives constantly for quantification and more precise measurement, and the modern technology reinforces this trend. As Glantz (1978) argues, the desire for greater accuracy and for more comprehensive display of data encourages favourable reactions to anyone proposing the purchase of a new piece of equipment to fulfil these desires. Furthermore, the ownership of modern technology often provides an indicator of status and prestige:

342

'The preoccupation on the part of the professional as well as the popular press with technological "breakthroughs" reinforces the desire of individual practitioners and hospitals to acquire the most up-to-date equipment.'

Such proliferation in the use of computing equipment in medicine might be justified if it proved to be of value either to the medical profession or to the patient. It is the purpose of this chapter to investigate and to illustrate the areas where such success or failure has so far been shown to have occurred. The chapter will also consider the problems involved in using computers in a medical setting in which, as in education, they are employed by two distinct groups of people having different reasons for using them, abilities to operate them and understanding of their functions. These two functions and groups, of course, are as aids to the professionals (teachers and doctors) and as interactors with the clients (students and patients).

The role of computers in medicine falls primarily in five main areas. Firstly, they are used in all of the areas that constitute the initial diagnostic process. Their programmed ability to ask questions on the bases of patients' responses enable them to be used both in the initial interviewing stage and for psychometric assessment of patients. Again within the diagnostic process, computing devices are used to gather physiological data regarding the patient: blood pressure, electrocardiograms, etc. Finally, their computational powers and their ability to store large amounts of clinical data enable them to be used as aids to arriving at the final medical diagnosis.

The second area is very much related to the first. Having made a diagnosis the next stage in the health care field is, obviously, to treat the patient. Thus computers can be used in the planning, monitoring and execution of patient treatment—both for drug and for psychotherapeutic treatment.

Whereas the stages of diagnosis and treatment involve, primarily, software developments, the third use of computers utilizes their hardware and their ability to detect accurately small changes in patient condition. Thus they are used increasingly to monitor patients' vital processes in, for example, intensive care situations.

Although the main thrust with respect to the role of psychology in the application of computers to medicine must lie in the interaction between the computer and doctors and their patients, i.e. in the field of diagnosis and treatment, the fourth major role of computers in medicine has been the use of the very large storage capacities offered by computers to store patient information. The impact, in this respect, is to centralize records and make it easier for doctors to consult them, thus increasing communication and decision making. Furthermore, as Fox (1977) points out, with a centralized record keeping system, it could be ensured that all of the basic, but necessary, information about a patient is recorded, including allergic reactions to particular drugs, blood type, current medication, etc. With a conventional paper record it would be an extremely difficult task to ensure that all records were up-to-date, and equally comprehensive, comprehensible and accessible.

Fox points to two related movements that have grown up around this concept. The first, the THIS (Total Hospital Information Service), attempts to co-ordinate and integrate the information that each department needs on a hospital-wide basis. As the movement's name suggests, therefore, it is hospital-system orientated, recording and regulating such aspects as patient records, requests for prescriptions, bed allocations, laboratory instructions, and patient scheduling (see, for example, Collen, 1970). Lucas (1978) describes such a system in a hospital, whilst Clarkson *et al.* (1982) illustrate how a small, desk-top microcomputer can be used in specific units (in this case, an accident unit) to useful effect.

The second movement takes more of a patient-oriented approach. The Problem Oriented Medical Record (POMR) (reviewed by Feinstein, 1973) emphasizes the inclusion of all of the patient's problems over and above the immediate clinical illness. The argument, then, is that all of the patient's problems, whether at work, domestic or financial, may prove to be relevant to the immediate problem or to the patient's post-clinical support. As an extension of this type of approach, Kahn, Ramm and Gianturco (1981) describe the Therapy Oriented Computer Record System (TOCRS) for use in psychiatric settings. Again, the records contain information about the patient in addition to the illness and a concise summary of the patient, treatment and experience is provided for the therapist before each consultation.

The final use of computers returns, in many respects, to educational uses: the use of computers as aids to handicapped patients—both physically and mentally handicapped. Aids for blind, deaf, and immobile patients and for the mentally subnormal are appearing, many of which introduce specific problems of acceptance and use by those for whom they are produced. In this case, many of the problems and considerations discussed in Chapter 5 (dealing with hardware aspects) need to be taken into account. Useful reviews of some of the peripherals presently available for use with the handicapped are provided by Odor (1982), Thomas (1981), and Aylor, Johnson and Ramey (1981).

The remainder of this chapter will discuss in detail three of these five areas; gathering information about patients through interviewing and measurement, medical diagnosis and treatment planning. The principles and problems involved in using computers within the other areas have already been discussed in previous chapters in this book.

MEDICAL DECISION MAKING

Before discussing these areas in detail it is useful first to consider the stages through which the medical process passes, that is up to and after the diagnosis of the complaint.

The process by which a physician arrives at a patient's diagnosis and thus treatment regime is a very complex one and involves a number of definite stages, all of which allow the doctor to generate and to test various hypotheses regarding the nature of the illness presented. Thus, Elstein *et al.* (1972) demonstrated that clinical decisions are usually made first by the physician generating only a small set of hypotheses very early on during the first interview with the patient. Indeed, most of the important data required to make a reasoned judgement are obtained in the first few minutes of the interview, with the remaining time being taken to obtain further data to support or to refute the original hypothesis as to the nature of the illness. It is in terms of this initial hypothesis generation that Lusted (1976) attempts to categorize this form of medical skill. Thus he suggests that any differences between physicians in the efficiency of their reaching specific hypotheses might be attributed to experience, with the experienced clinician having a 'list of structures of attributes and diseases organized in more related and manageable "chunks" in his brain'. Indeed, Wortman and Greenberg (1971) have demonstrated that if information is presented in a form which is similar to disease definitions, it will also be organized in terms of hierarchical structures. This organization becomes more developed as individuals have to solve more problems using this information—that is, as they become more experienced.

Elstein and Bordage (1979) summarize the clinical reasoning processes, and suggest that there are four major components to it:

1 *Cue acquisition.* This forms the initial encounter with the patient and provides the major data from which hypotheses will be generated. Thus, information is obtained by a variety of methods including interviews, performing physical examinations and administering laboratory and psychological tests.
2 *Hypothesis generation.* On the basis of the information received, alternative formulations of the problem are considered and suggestions regarding possible diagnoses are entertained. Two related strategies are used to generate such hypotheses: firstly to use salient cues or clusters of cues to produce competing formulations; secondly to combine with other formulations to generate new ones. Elstein and Bordage suggest that strong links exist in memory between salient cues and certain hypotheses triggered by these cues. However, the maximum number of hypotheses entertained at any one time appears to be about four or five, although sometimes more than one hypothesis may be joined together or nested to produce a new formulation (Elstein, Shulman and Sprafka, 1978).
3 *Cue interpretation.* The data are interpreted in the light of alternative hypotheses under consideration. Gill *et al.* (1973) reported that diagnostic errors are due primarily to failure during this part of the process, that is to a failure to manipulate the large amounts of data correctly. Indeed,

De Dombal (1976) supports this contention with data relating to the diagnosis of peptic ulcers. Although over 90% agreement was reached between different physicians regarding the *symptoms* of 170 patients referred for abdominal pains, only 65% of the *diagnoses* agreed.

4 *Hypothesis evaluation.* The data are weighted and combined to determine if one of the diagnostic hypotheses already generated can be confirmed. If it cannot the process must be restarted, collecting new cues or clusters of cues and generating new hypotheses.

The medical decision process, therefore, is comprised essentially of two interrelated stages: obtaining information and entertaining hypotheses regarding the meaning of these data. The information is obtained from the patient through interviews and through physical and mental examination, and the diagnosis is arrived at through assigning probabilites to the appearance of the data within a given illness. In each of these stages, it could be argued, the computer could play a role: in the interviewing stage to collect data from the patient; in the physical examination stage as an accurate instrument; during the diagnosis formulation stage by comparing the data obtained with a very large store of medical information and arriving at a decision based on computed probabilities. In this latter respect a probability theorem known as Bayes' theorem is used which provides rules for revising probabilities in the light of new information that is itself probabilistic—see, for example, Elstein and Bordage (1978).

COMPUTER INTERVIEWING AND INTERROGATION

Since the process of hypothesis testing in diagnosis begins almost immediately during the physician–patient encounter, clearly the quality of the initial interview between the doctor and patient is extremely important. It is at this stage, the taking of the patient's 'history', that the patient is able to report the symptoms suffered and to begin the diagnostic process. On the face of it at least, computers should be able to be programmed to ask the relevant questions to relieve the physician of much of this relatively routine work.

Unfortunately, however, the process is not as simple as it may appear since any communication act between two or more people often includes at least two forms of communication: first the verbal, for example speech or written, communication which uses natural language; second a complex set of non-verbal communication acts such as gestures, grunts, sighs, body positions, etc., which enrich the language. In a clinical situation, for example, when describing a stomach pain the patient might simply be able to report that the pain is 'sharp', or 'stabbing' or 'moves across the stomach'. This, of course, is important information for the initial hypothesis forming stage. The movement of the patient's hands across the stomach, however, the speed of movement, its direction, whether the hand is clenched or open, the patient's facial expressions, etc., provide probably as much information regarding the possible illness as the initial verbal report. Unfortunately, a computer is unable to gather this type of information; the most non-verbal information that it might be able to gather is likely to relate to the patient's response times to particular questions or reliability in responding. (With regard to response times, the longer a patient takes to answer a question, the more uncertainty exists about the answer—Lucas *et al.*, 1976). For these reasons, the role for the computer for interviewing patients is limited, and Card and Lucas (1981) suggest that the process should be referred to as 'computer interrogation'.

A further difference between physician interviewing and computer interrogation lies in the adaptability of the operator. Thus, in addition to being able to use both forms of information to generate and to refine the initial hypotheses, the human physician is generally adaptable enough to be able to probe in areas other than those initially described. For example, patients reporting symptoms which would normally point to one diagnosis might, in fact, be suffering from another type of illness. Psychosomatic illnesses are an example of this form of behaviour—physical symptoms, such as stomach pains or lack of appetite, being produced as outward appearances of behavioural problems such as worry or, perhaps, sexual problems.

Despite these initially negative comments regarding the computer's role in patient interrogation, the available evidence suggests that computers are able to be used quite successfully in this area. As will be seen later, patients appear to be more 'honest' with computers and the data collected are often more thorough and consistent. One reason for this success probably lies in the social situation which is set up during an interview and which makes the normal human–human interview procedure something of an unreliable assessment tool. Thus, Hunt and MacLeod (1979) argue that although 'human' interviews are adequate for detecting gross defects associated with, say, moderate retardation or acute alcohol intoxication, their utility for making finer distinctions is suspect. Because of the roles that the participants are forced to play—that of 'doctor' (professional, knowledgeable, superior status, etc.) and 'patient' (ill, worried, inferior status, ignorant, etc.)—the scope for free communication can often be limited. Furthermore, if the expected norms of behaviour are violated, for example by the physician beginning to probe about psychological rather than physical problems, the person being interviewed may become either confused or hostile, with resultant strengthening of the communication barriers.

As an extension to their argument Hunt and MacLeod also point to the work of Weizenbaum (1976) and his computer-psychotherapeutic program ELIZA to suggest that the doctor is not the only member of the interviewing diad who generates and tests hypotheses regarding the patient's illness. The patient also does so—possibly well before the actual interview. It is, after all, often the patient who has diagnosed himself or herself to be ill enough to visit the doctor. Thus, they suggest that the patient is likely to provide the information which he or she considers to be relevant to the interview situation, with the result that the doctor's initial hypothesis forming behaviour is shaped as much by the patient's assessment of the illness as by the doctor's own assessment of the symptoms.

A further problem with the conventional interview situation relates to the lingusitic barrier that may be set up between the doctor and patient. The competence of each to 'talk in the language' of the other may not be good enough to allow the full flow of communication required to set up an efficient working hypothesis. This is particularly problematic when dealing with medical terms and, indeed, the problem is reminiscent of the naive users' problems of coming to terms with computer jargon! For example, discussing using the computer to aid an ophthalmologist in taking case histories, Marg *et al.* (1972) report that some of their patients failed (possibly not unreasonably) to understand the term 'Glaucoma', and that 'Ocular hypertension' did not help much! On a similar theme, Card and Lucas (1981) report that the term 'caries' is understood by only 19% of the population, and 'palliate' by 11% Even the term 'navel' is understood only by 75% of the population—as Card and Lucas question: what of the other 25%? Clearly, an efficient computer-patient communication system needs to take account of many of the dialogue and software display principles discussed in Chapters 5 and 6.

Techniques of computer interrogation

Fox (1977) describes two main types of system for interviewing patients: the completely automated interview and a hybrid system which acts simply as an aid to the clinician—as a 'notepad'.

In the completely automated system, the patient sits in front of the computer terminal and answers questions produced by either a linear or a branching program. The patient normally makes simple responses such as 'Yes', 'No', 'Don't know' or 'Don't understand' (see, for example, Bevan and Pobgee, 1981). Card and Lucas (1981) and Lucas (1979) also describe ways in which more confident or intelligent patients are able to provide further information, such as 'Certainly yes' or 'Probably no', the decision whether to ask patients to respond in this way being made by the computer on the basis of the patient's response times.

The computer 'notepad' system acts more in the way of a computer-assisted interviewer than a completely automated one. Using a system of this nature, the questions are asked formally by the physician, although prompted, unobtrusively, by the computer. In this way, the physician is reminded to ask the most important questions whilst, at the same time, being allowed to probe deeper in to specific areas and to take account of the non-verbal information that the patient supplies. Greist, Van Cura and Knepreth (1973) describe such a system designed for use in the emergency room, and Kendall and Bishop (1973) describe an evaluation of a notepad system.

Assessing computer interrogation

Lucas (1979) suggests that an assessment of the value of computers in the initial interrogation process must be made in terms of three criteria: accuracy in obtaining the information, acceptability both to the patient and to the doctor, and cost. Whereas it is feasible to consider the evidence relating to the first two of these criteria, because of the ever-reducing costs of computing and the ever-increasing power of computers, it is not sensible to spend time considering the economic benefits of computer interrogation. All that it is sensible to say is that the benefits or otherwise of installing such a system in terms of accuracy and acceptability need to be offset against the system costs at the time of installation. As was discussed in Chapter 1, however, the system costs are not simply the costs of equipment purchase: they include maintenance, software, peripherals, etc.

Accuracy

This has been studied in a number of cases in which patients are independently interviewed by several observers, including the computer, each recording whether predefined symptoms are present, absent, etc.

Perhaps one of the earliest studies of this nature was performed by Card *et al.* (1974). Seventy-two patients were each interviewed twice about 14 symptoms of dyspepsia, either by the computer and a consultant physician or by two consultants. The authors estimated error rates for the consultants varying between 9 and 12%, and for the computer interrogation varying between 10 and 18%. Clearly, in this case, the consultants were more accurate than the computer, possibly because of their experience at recognizing patterns of symptoms.

The computer fared rather more successfully in a study of patients with alcohol-related illnesses, however (Lucas *et al.*, 1977). In this study, the authors analysed the *types* of errors made, essentially errors of commission (false positives) and omission (false negatives). Comparing the computer with two psychiatrists, the results indicated no significant difference in error rate or type between the computer interrogator and its human counterpart.

The two previous examples dealt with specific illness types which, it could be argued, should prove easier to program a computer to ask the appropriate questions. Comparisons have also been made between the computer and human interrogator in more diverse settings. For example, in a mental health centre Angle *et al.* (1979) found that computer interviews yielded considerably more general and specific detail than did the clinicians. Moreover, the clinicians failed to identify, or at least to document, 76% of 20 critical items that a group of 55 patients revealed to the computer.

Angle *et al.*'s study, then, highlights a further aspect of the question of accuracy: that of the accuracy of the reported information. As was discussed earlier, patients may not report their symptoms accurately because of memory lapses, because of their own assessment of what the physician wishes to hear, or because of deliberate lying—perhaps through fear or embarrassment. This aspect of the data collection problem has been detailed by Lucas *et al.* (1977) during their study of the use of computers for interrogating patients with alcohol-related illnesses. Patients admitted to consuming significantly higher levels of alcohol (on average 30% higher) to the computer than they did to the psychiatrists. As Lucas *et al.* argue, if patients were more likely to understate than to exaggerate the amounts of alcohol that they drank, then it would appear that the computer interrogation was more accurate than the psychiatrist's interview. Similar findings are reported by Erdman, Klein and Greist (1983) regarding information concerning drug use.

Both quantitative and qualitative differences between the information gained using a computer and a human interrogator have also been documented by Slack and Slack (1977). They compared the information obtained from the two and demonstrated that the *content* of what the physician was told was affected by the time of day and by the interviewing sequences. This was not true, however, of the computer.

Acceptability

To be able to be implemented successfully, the computer must be accepted by both participants in the interrogation process. That is by both the doctor and the patient.

Clinician acceptance

Problems relating to the doctor's acceptance of the computer's role in medicine relate essentially to those situations in which the computer is used to perform the diagnoses (for example, De Dombal, 1979) and these will be discussed later. However, computer interrogations have been criticized on the basis of their providing *too much* information. Angle (1981), for example, has pointed out that computers can provide a more thorough assessment than can many clinicians. One program, for example, asks 3500 questions related to 29 problems. With such information, Angle suggests, there is a tendency for the computer to print out a detailed report that may be too 'overwhelming' and detailed for many clinicians. Presumably, therefore, clinicians would accept computers as interrogation aids provided the information that the computer produced was fully relevant.

Patient acceptance

The studies which have been performed to assess patient attitudes towards being confronted with a computer have generally produced positive results. For example, in 1968 Slack and Van Cura argued:

> 'Information which the patient has difficulty telling the doctor but wants the doctor to know about is, according to ... patients, more easily presented (and more likely to be given accurately) to the computer.'

This, of course, was illustrated during the Lucas *et al.* (1977) study of alcohol-related illnesses.

Lucas (1977) reports an attitude survey of 67 patients who had been interrogated by computer for dyspeptic complaints. Each patient answered the questionnaire anonymously and at home after interrogation. Altogether 82% (55) of the patients expressed favourable attitudes towards the use of computers for this purpose, although Lucas reports a significant difference in reactions between men and women (women had less favourable reactions than men), and a negative correlation between attitude and age (thus, younger patients were more favourably disposed towards the computer than were the older patients).

Similar positive reactions to the computer were also reported by Lucas *et al.* (1977) as a result of their alcohol-induced illness study. They used a semantic differential scale to investigate patients' reactions to the computer interrogation. (In this technique, subjects rate each concept on a number of bi-polar rating scales such as 'cold–hot', 'kind–cruel'—see Osgood, Suci and Tannenbaum (1957) and Heise (1969) for a more detailed description and rationale of the technique.) Seventy-five per cent of the patients who had returned the questionnaires had favourable attitudes. However, although the authors report that 50% of the patients' ratings of the concept 'medical interviews with a computer' were higher than those dealing with 'medical interviews with a doctor', these findings do suggest that an equal number of ratings were in the direction of preferring an interview with a doctor. Interestingly, the authors also asked their patients to rate 'the ideal medical interview'. As can be seen from Figure 11.1, both the 'doctor interview' and the 'computer interview' were often rated to be quite different from the 'ideal interview'. For many of the patients, therefore, neither was 'ideal'.

Finally, Dove *et al.* (1977) report a further positive aspect of patient's attitudes to computer interrogation—that of a perceived therapeutic effect as a result of having interacted with the computer. Patients attending a general practice were first interrogated by a computer before being seen by the general

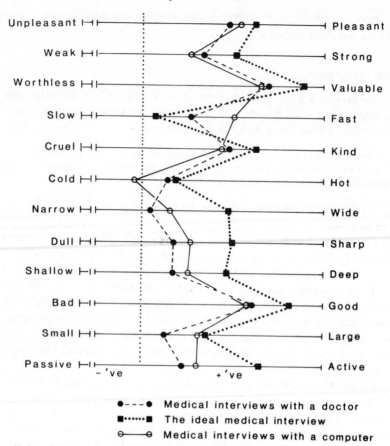

Figure 11.1. A semantic differential profile of patients' impressions of different forms of medical interview (Lucas *et al.*, 1977). Reproduced by permission of the Royal College of Psychiatrists.

practitioner. Dove *et al.* reported generally favourable responses to the computer and, because of the 'friendly nature of the computer's questions and the seclusion, comfort and leisure in which they were answered', a 'mood of introspection' appeared to be introduced into the subsequent interview with the doctor. Thus patients appeared to think more about the nature of their illness, were no longer 'apprehensive of the coming interview' and were 'relaxed and uninhibited' with the doctor.

Computerized medical and psychological testing

As was discussed earlier, in addition to gathering information and formulating and examining hypotheses during an interview with the patient, before the final medical decision is made further hypothesis testing also takes place as a result of information obtained during physical (and sometimes psychological) examinations. Again, computers have proved to be useful in such contexts: for examining the patient's physical state (using their ability to detect small variations in body conditions very accurately) and psychological condition (intelligence, personality, etc., using their ability to process large amounts of very structured information quickly).

Computers in physical examinations

The medical, computing and instrumentation literature abounds with examples of the use of computing machinery as medical instruments. Such instruments might range from simple peripherals to desk-top computers, to full systems in their own right, and range in complexity from thermometers costing only a few pounds, through chemical and blood analysis machines, to body scanning systems which cost upwards of £1 million. O'Kane and Haluska (1977) argue that acceptance of such automated systems in medicine will be most successful only when they are introduced in an evolutionary manner, after the employment of small-scale systems that have become commonplace in the daily activities of the medical profession.

There is such a proliferation of automated instruments that it would be both time- and space-consuming and, because of their fast growth, rather fruitless to consider them all here. However, one important medical computing system that should be mentioned, and that does appear to have had a major effect on diagnostic processes, is that of Computerized Axial Tomography (CT). These machines, which cost upwards of £1 million, allow a two-dimensional image of the body to be constructed from a series of one-dimensional X-ray projections of the segment's cross-section. These reconstructed cross-sections can then be memorized and made ready for any further automated processing. This machine appears to provided a powerful new aid to medical diagnosis with Backer (1975), for example, reporting that neurologists had used it to achieve a clinical accuracy of 95%. He also reports that after its introduction in the Mayo clinic in America, there was a decline in the use of every other technique for examining the brain except for electroencephalography (EEG).

One other important trend that appears to be occurring within the context of computerized instrumentation, is for hospitals and health centres to use analysis equipment linked to automated systems for the acquisition of samples, and collecting, collating, and reporting the results. Such systems are used in three areas: (i) automation of the logistics involved in obtaining the physical samples and results reporting, (ii) automation of acquiring the test results, and (iii) automation of the testing apparatus itself.

Spraberry *et al.* (1976) describe one such automated system in use at the University of Alabama Hospital. It makes test results available on terminals at the hospital's nursing stations as soon as they have been completed and entered into the system. With this system, routine test results were available two hours earlier and clerical error rates were reduced from 5% to 1%.

Laboratory automation, however, can have its drawbacks, as Grams (1976) suggests. The first relates to one of the problems suggested earlier with regard to computer interrogation—that of data proliferation. Thus Grams suggests that automated equipment is both so costly and so powerful that it may be feasible simply to run all of the tests of which a given instrument is capable— whether or not they were requested. The resultant mass of data might then obscure significant findings and create an additional burden on an automated record system. Furthermore, Glantz (1978) argues that an increase in the number of tests that can be performed might well lower the incentive for physicians to confine tests to those cases in which they have been demonstrated to be efficacious. Thus, even though the unit cost might be lowered, the use of unnecessary diagnostic procedures still increases the total cost of medical care.

The second problem regarding the efficiency of computer controlled physical testing is statistical and relates to the fact that decisions regarding 'normality' or 'non-normality' of a test result are generally made in terms of the extent to which the readings fall within defined limits—say the mean reading plus or minus 45% of the readings. In such cases, however, 10% of the population will have otherwise 'normal' values which fall outside of this range, causing a 'false-positive' decision to be made. As the number of tests performed increases there will be a correspondingly greater chance that one or more tests will be said to be outside the normal limits, whereas this is actually due only to the statistics of the situation.

Finally, although not necessarily used during the initial hypothesis formation stage, the application of computing equipment to *patient monitoring* should not be forgotten. For example, information provided whilst a patient is in an intensive care unit is important when deciding on possible courses of action that can be taken in an emergency. In these situations, a large number of physiological responses can be continuously recorded, and the computer is programmed to detect slight but important changes in the state of each.

The value of using computers in this context arises, essentially, in two areas. First, as O'Kane and Haluska (1977) point out, intensive care units operate on a very high nurse-to-patient ratio (typically about six times higher than in other parts of the hospital—Drazen, Wechsler and Wiig, 1975). Secondly, through boredom, fatigue, etc., human operators are often capable of missing important signals when having to perform continuous monitoring operations. Using computers to perform the monitoring function, then, might enable staff to be reduced in the intensive care unit to be employed elsewhere within the hospital and, for those who remain, to reduce the demands on their vigilance requirements and release them for other caring tasks within the unit.

As an example of the use of computers in this context Crawford (1975) describes a system for monitoring in the labour ward. Fetal heart rate and intra-uterine pressure help to give the clinical staff a picture of the stage of labour and its history. The information also helps in the prediction of fetal distress or delivery complications.

Computers in psychological examinations

In addition to information relating to the patient's physical state, complete medical diagnoses and treatment often require information that concerns the patient's psychological condition: intelligence, personality, personality defects, etc. Such information is generally obtained from the psychological equivalent of standard medical instruments such as stethoscopes or ophthalmoscopes— that is, from standardized psychometric tests, of which there are many hundreds available (Cronbach, 1970).

Psychometric tests are generally of a pencil-and-paper format, requiring subjects to answer questions using simple responses such as 'yes', 'no', etc., and are developed over long periods of time, using many hundreds of subjects to standardize them for particular populations or types of inquiry. For this reason, and because it is extremely difficult to measure accurately implied behaviours such as 'intelligence' or 'personality', such tests need to be presented in very standardized formats, and often by trained personnel. They often also require a fair amount of computation to be performed on each subject's 'raw score' responses so that sensible interpretations can later be made regarding the subject's personality, intelligence, etc., in relation to the rest of the population.

Psychometric testing, then, presents a situation in which standard presentations and questions are asked of the testee, in standardized settings, and often requiring complex, but nevertheless standardized, computations to be performed on the person's scores. Such conditions, it should be supposed, would be ideal for the computer which has already been shown to prove its value in less uniform settings during the initial medical interrogation. Nevertheless, despite the obvious benefits which could accrue from using computers in this context, the standardized nature required by a psychometric testing situation also brings its own drawbacks as far as a computer is concerned. This relates, of course, to the social rapport that a human tester normally has to establish with the testee. However, a number of authors have reported very high correlations when comparing the results from automated tests with those from more conventional means (for example, Ridgeway, MacCullough and Mills, 1982; Watts, Baddeley and Williams, 1982; Elwood, 1972) that it is unlikely that any lack of rapport has a major influence on the tests' validity.

As was the case when discussing the use of computers as medical instruments it would be both time-consuming and of little benefit to describe all of the tests that have been automated (see Thompson and Wilson, 1982, for a review). Rather this discussion will relate to some of the advantages of automated testing and to the success of this form of computer examination. These aspects will be considered from the points of view of the time and cost savings that an automated system brings, the acceptability of computerized testing, and the use of facilities which are associated with the computer such as branching and the possibility of recording additional data.

Time and cost

Psychometric tests of the 'question and answer' type generally take some considerable time to administer—often at least an hour and sometimes more. As was discussed above, they also take time to score: the testees' answers need to be translated from pencil marks to scores, which then have to be computed and related to standardized norms. Often the translation stage can, itself, take considerable time—sometimes longer than the test took to administer. The time taken to obtain information regarding each subject, therefore, can be quite considerable. Indeed, cost analyses (for example, Elwood, 1972) suggest that the administration and scoring of routine psychological tests by qualified psychologists incur a heavy drain on finances and man-hours. Denner (1977) suggests that it is these costs that have been the main cause of the fact that the 'psychometric tests of the traditional kind have been falling from favour among clinical psychologists' (Power, Muntz and Macrae, 1975).

Automated testing and analysis, therefore, provided it releases costly personnel to perform other functions, should reduce the cost of testing. Indeed, cost analyses have shown that cost savings of up to 50% can be made in personnel time. Thus Elwood (1972) analysed the salary levels and man-hours required for administering the WAIS (Weschler Adult Intelligence Scale) by both a technician operating a computer and by a professional psychologist. For each dollar spent testing by the psychologist, the same testing could have been performed by the technician and computer for $0.51. A technician and clerk typists working together could administer and score the WAIS for $0.42. Clearly, then, automated testing can reduce manpower costs, and can also free the psychologist for closer interaction with the patient or with other patients after having been tested. Indeed, Miller (1968) suggests that because automated testing releases the psychologist from the 'authoritarian role' required by the standardized procedure, this should enable the tester–testee relationship to develop more in a way that the psychologist wishes. Furthermore, because of the speed of automatic scoring from the computer it is quite feasible for the psychologist to have available the patient's test results soon after testing, so that some counselling can take place, or further questions asked, within the same session.

In addition to the direct manpower savings that can accrue from automated testing, the facilities available on some of the latest computers for allowing more than one user to operate the system at the same time (time-sharing) is also likely to reduce costs and increase system productivity.

The acceptability of computerized testing

The acceptability of computers for psychometric testing is an important consideration. Despite all of the cost benefits that arise from using computers in this situation, they would be valueless if either the doctors or the patients did not accept them.

The problem of patient acceptance of computerized testing relates, primarily, to the possibility that those who are not positively disposed towards the procedure produce responses which are either lies or are not complete. However, this problem may not be as important to the efficiency of the procedure as was the case when discussing acceptance of computerized patient interrogation. This is because most psychometric tests contain lie scales and/or social desirability scales: questions and analyses which are designed to screen false answers. Provided the automated test follows the pencil-and-paper form without modification, such scales should ensure that the interpretations of the testees' responses are at least 'honest'. However, as a further safeguard, Johnson *et al.* (1977) developed a screening instrument, the Q1, to detect interviewees who are overtly hostile to computer interviewing of any form or who are likely to be unreliable in their responses.

As with the case of computer interrogation, however, the fears of the computer being an impersonal tester do not appear to have any foundations. For example, Klinger, Johnson and Williams (1976) report that 68% of their patients liked being tested using a computer and 91% said that they were as truthful or more truthful than in the comparable non-automated situation. Space (1981) details a number of examples of situations in which both testees and clinicians have accepted the principles of automated testing.

Using the computers' additional facilities

Branching. This is sometimes termed 'adaptive testing' (Dewitt and Weiss, 1976) and relates to the ability of the testing program to branch to either specific questions or different sections on the basis of the testees' responses. As an example of such a program, Johnson, Gianetti and Williams (1979) report the use of such 'response contingent questions' in their Psychological Systems Questionnaire. For example, using branching procedures they were able to eliminate irrelevant questions, such as those relating to marriage when the respondent indicated that he or she was single. Sapinkops (1978) used adaptive strategies to reduce the number of items to be answered on the California Psychological Inventory by 67%. Although this approach did produce some problems relating to the reliability of the 'new' test, Sapinkops suggests that this approach merits further investigation.

Recording other data. In addition to obtaining data from the testee's active participation by answering questions, etc., the computer is also able to record more 'passive' data (Stout, 1981) such as response latency and psychophysiological information. Recording eye movements, heart rate and skin resistance, for example, might provide useful additional data relating to the testee's response to the questions.

With respect to response speed, Hunt (1980) has observed moderate correlations between verbal ability and speed of letter identification and speed for scanning for information in short term memory. It may be possible, therefore, to infer aspects of cognitive functioning from a testee's latency to particular test items. For example, Eysenck (1967) has argued that a meaningful measure of individual test performance could be based on the times taken to complete each item of a test. He suggested that performance measures (slopes) could be obtained by plotting response times against item complexity, with the slope intercept being related to subject ability. Some support for this contention was provided by Weinman, Elithorn and Farag (1981).

Unfortunately, although a number of authors argue that information regarding response latencies *ought* to be useful during psychological assessments, little empirical work is available to support or refute the contention. Stout (1981), however, did perform a small-scale study to test the possibility and concludes that although such ancillary data are useful, the response latencies themselves are very complexly determined and much more research is required to ascertain their meaning. For example, although increased latencies may be related to testee ability, they may also be related to other factors such as fatigue, to misunderstanding, to decisions to falsify responses, etc.

Using various input and output devices. The final use of computer facilities, of course, relates to the fact that information does not need to be presented either to the testees or to the computer in conventional verbal, written form. The variety of input and output devices discussed in Chapter 5 can be used by, for example, handicapped, geriatric or verbally deficient patients. For example, Wilson, Thompson and Wylie (1982) describe a testing system for severely physically handicapped using touch pads; Ridgeway, MacCullough and Mills (1982) describe a lightpen operated system. In such circumstances, however, and with such types of patients, the principles discussed in Chapter 6 become even more important for the efficiency of the system.

COMPUTER AIDED DIAGNOSIS

Having demonstrated how the computer can be used to aid physicians in gathering information about a patient, it is not unreasonable to suggest that they can also help to make decisions regarding the likely illness from which the patient is suffering. After all, it could be argued, the diagnosis process is essentially a sequence of decisions (Taylor, Aitchison and McGirr, 1971; Wortman, 1972) made on the basis of the information gathered. It might well be that a computer could make the same decisions with equal or better accuracy than the human clinician. This section will discuss some aspects of this question, although a comprehensive bibliography of the studies which have been performed to consider the truth of this assertion is provided by Wagner, Tautu and Wolber (1978).

In a detailed review of the techniques and problems of medical diagnosis, Wardle and Wardle (1978) point to the need for more rigorous diagnostic procedures and illustrate their argument by reference to studies which have compared the accuracy of diagnoses with results obtained from subsequent post-mortems. Their review suggests that diagnostic accuracy appears to be related to the type of illness being treated. For example, Rosenblatt, Teng and Kerpe (1973) examined the accuracy of cancer diagnoses and found accuracies ranging from 80 to 100%. When the cancer was in the lung, however, the accuracy rate appeared to fall to 44%, whilst 50% of carcinomas in the ovaries were missed. In a similar study, Gwynne (1965) detected four types of errors or omissions which led to one-third of the diagnoses in a sample of 1627 patients being false: (i) primary site wrongly recorded (5.9%); (ii) primary site not discovered (8.6%); (iii) diagnosis missed (10.3%); (iv) lesions not causing symptoms (8.6%).

Although such results imply that medical diagnoses are certainly fallible and can possibly be improved using some form of statistical decision making, they also emphasize the complex nature of illnesses and in many cases the difficulty of forming a decision. For example, Gwynne's analysis of the errors made illustrates the importance of adequate information gathering in the first place. Furthermore, in over 8% of the cases the symptoms which should have appeared were not present. Furthermore, as Card and Lucas (1981) point out, many conditions and symptoms are not mutually exclusive—particularly in adults—and so the clinical diagnosis has also to account for these possibilities.

The question that now needs to be asked is if computers are able to aid clinicians in their diagnosis, what decision rules need to be incorporated into the program to enable them to do so? At this point the topic becomes very complex, involving various probability theories, and outside of the requirements of this book. However the interested reader is referred to Wardle and Wardle's (1978) excellent review of the various models available and how they have developed over the years. Essentially, all of the techniques follow the same procedure: the patient's symptoms are compared with a database of symptom frequencies for populations of patients who were *finally* diagnosed as suffering from one of a set of related diseases (for example, gastric ulcer, duodenal ulcer, congenital heart disease). By means of a probability model (generally a form of Bayes' rules), each of the patient's symptoms is considered by the computer and evaluated to determine the amount of evidence it provides for each of the disease hypotheses. The final outcome is a set of *a posteriori* (after the event) probabilities of the diseases given the symptoms.

Once again, as when discussing the use of computers for interrogation and other information gathering, the important questions relate to their acceptability to the users and their accuracy in performing the task.

Acceptability

Unlike the case of computer interrogation, the only people who need to be considered in this respect are the clinicians themselves; computer aided diagnosis does not normally involve interactions with the patients. A number of reports have been produced, however, which suggest some unease amongst clinicians which arises, essentially, for three reasons: the lack of responsibility exercised by a computer, the implied certainty in a computer diagnosis, and the extent to which clinicians are involved in the production of computer diagnostic programs.

Responsibility

In his critique of the use of computers in medicine, Glantz (1978) points out that although computers are not human they are often given the appearance of human-like qualities; they make value-judgements and decisions *for* humans which the humans then often accept without question. In the majority of cases the clinician for whom the decision is made does not know what decision rules are being used, and so the question of who takes the responsibility for the decision needs to be asked.

In an equally spirited defence of computer aided diagnosis, however, Fox (1977) argues that clinicians *do* have the final responsibility for their decisions. He suggests that clinicians do not simply act as a 'delegate' to the computer and simply act on the computer's first choice of possible illnesses. Because clinical decisions are not simple and depend on a great deal of information not necessarily available to the computer program (like the patient's family circumstances, type of work, etc.), the final decision must remain in the clinician's hands.

A specification of ignorance

Computer aided diagnosis is often criticized, too, in that it presents too clear a picture to the clinician. The computer takes a process that involves gathering information about a wide range of topics and applies relatively simple probability rules to produce decisions about the state of a very complex human body. This must, at the best, be an imprecise process—the fact that, as will be shown later, it may be slightly more accurate than human decision making does not make the process any more precise.

Unfortunately, however, as Glantz feared computer decisions are often accepted uncritically, and are thus often assumed to be correct. Nevertheless, as has been discussed already, the whole process is based on a series of probability rules and, statistically at least, the more probabilities that are combined, the greater is the chance than an error will be made in the final decision. For this reason a statistician, when reporting a *statistical* decision, will also provide some indication regarding the confidence with which the decision should be accepted—this is known as the significance level of the decision. For the same reasons, Healy (1976) argues that computer-generated medical decisions should also be provided with a similar measure; in his terminology, a 'specification of ignorance'.

Physician involvement

When reporting the results of a survey of the use of computers to make clinical decisions, De Dombal and Hall (1979) point out that many attempts to implement computer systems or formal decision making in medicine have been made without adequate—or in some cases any—consultation with the clinicians involved. They suggest that this often constitutes a major reason for the 'failure' of clinical decision analysis with or without computers. De Dombal (1979) argues that a further reason for any failure in automated decision making systems is that their aims, and the criteria on which their results are judged, are not necessarily those of the clinician:

> 'All too often, computer systems and decision analysis systems are orientated towards the aims of the ... (health care planner).'

He also suggests, however, that many of these problems may be overcome by an appropriate presentation of the system.

Diagnostic accuracy

Despite the reservations expressed above regarding the appropriateness of computer aided diagnosis, many of its perceived evils are likely to be accepted and reduced in importance if it can be shown that more accurate diagnoses are made with, rather than without, computer assistance.

Any answer to a question concerning diagnostic accuracy must include the truism that the accuracy of any computer diagnosis will only be as high as the quality of the original program. Since the techniques and probability models that control the program have been improved and developed both with experience and with increasing mathematical knowledge, it is likely to be the case that the accuracy of computer assisted diagnosis will also improve over time. This, indeed, seems to be the case and a number of reports have appeared in more recent years that indicate that Bayesian methods of analysing a patient's symptoms can provide significant assistance in making differential diagnoses of specific classes of illnesses.

As examples of studies that have investigated the accuracy of computer diagnosis, De Dombal (1975) reports a 91% success rate for differential diagnosis of acute abdominal pain, and Horrocks and De Dombal (1975) suggest an 87% success rate for diagnosing patients complaining of dispepsia. Bouckaert (1972) reports 94% success rate for differential diagnoses of goitre (in thyroid disease), and Salamon *et al.* (1976) have obtained an 80% success rate in the difficult area of neurological disease. Wills, Teather and Innocent (1982) report a 68% success rate for deciding whether an image on a brain CT scan is or is not a tumour. Gustafson *et al.* (1977) successfully identified some 70 suicide attempts in a study based on medical records; roughly double the performance of the psychiatrists and clinicians who provided the data.

Such figures, of course, although impressive, are absolute and do not indicate the *relative* success of the computer compared with the human diagnostician. However, in their comprehensive review of studies in this area dating back to the mid 1960s, Wardle and Wardle (1978) provide data regarding a number of studies using different version of Bayes' rules. In those studies which actually compare physician and computer performance, the computer is on the average about 8–10% more accurate than the physician. In some cases the computer accuracy extends to over 95%.

In summary, therefore, it would appear that computers are able to aid clinicians in the formation and verification of their hypotheses. Their ability to 'ask' routine questions, sometimes embarassing ones, their ability to record fine and accurate measurements, and their ability to make complex probabilistic calculations all serve to produce a very useful medical tool.

TREATMENT PLANNING AND THERAPY

The computer's use in helping doctors to plan their patients' treatment falls, essentially, into two related categories. First are computer programs that act as extensions to the medical decision systems, taking patient data and, through the diagnostic stages, recommending forms of drug and other types of treatment. Young (1982) describes these as 'decision support systems'. Secondly some programs are available which aid the doctor in the application of the therapy, in particular its use during psychotherapeutic regimes. Finally, although no specific studies have been performed in this area, computers should be able to be used to good effect when communicating treatment information to patients. Thus, a number of surveys have demonstrated that patients frequently forget much of the important information given to them during a consultation: information such as the nature of their illness and the way that they should take the drugs prescribed (for example, Ley, 1979; Anderson, 1979). Providing patients with computer print-outs detailing their illness and treatment should help to reduce much of this forgetting.

Decision support systems

The essential feature of these programs is that they remind doctors in a given situation of a particular course of action. Unlike some of the diagnostic programs, they do not take from the doctor any powers of decision; they simply suggest the best choices for a particular set of circumstances. Young (1982) suggests that the basic features of a decision support system are (i) patient data are entered into the system; (ii) the system holds a data base of relevant information on patient care; (iii) on the basis of decision models the system suggests specific lines of action; (iv) the system shows the basis of its suggestions; (v) the user decides what action to take.

An example of one such system is MYCIN, which advises on the prescribing of antibiotics for various infections (Davis, Buchanan and Shortliffe, 1977). It asks for clinical and laboratory data about the patient and then attempts to determine whether an infection is present and to indicate the appropriate treatment. Yu *et al.* (1979) investigated the acceptability of MYCIN, and compared its performance with that of experts for the treatment of 15 patients. In 90% of the cases the MYCIN system and the experts agreed on the likely organism that was present, whilst in 8 of the 11 cases that required treatment the experts were willing to accept MYCIN's suggestions. Overall MYCIN's performance was judged to be acceptable in 14 of the 15 cases.

A more flexible system for evaluating the appropriate treatment for cardiac patients has been developed at Duke University and is called the 'Clinical Textbook of Cardiology' (Rosati, 1975). This system employs the knowledge that has been built up concerning different forms of cardiac diseases and treatment and, when a new patient arrives, a computerized profile of the patient is produced against which the data bank is searched for other patients who have had a similar clinical picture. This group of patients can then be analysed to determine what therapeutic regime has previously given the best outcome.

A final example of such programs, CARE, is a computer-based clinical assessment research and educational system designed to help surgeons make critical care decisions, particularly in the intensive care unit (Siegal *et al.*, 1976). It is able to advise on problems such as burns, gastric problems, major soft-tissue injury, dehydration, cardiac arrest, postoperative care, etc. During a review of the effects of CARE, Siegal *et al.* suggest that a reduction in non-cardiac surgical mortality occured from 18.8% in 1973 to 10.5% in 1978.

Trauma mortality was reduced from 25% to 7.5% and, in surgical patients with gastrointestinal complications, mortality dropped from 19.7% to 8.3%. The authors also point out that the use of the CARE system saved nearly 5% more lives overall.

Psychotheraputic uses

The application of computers in the field of psychotherapy has essentially occurred in two areas. Firstly attempts have been made to produce a computer program which would perform efficiently the psychotherapeutic interview. For example, Selmi *et al.* (1982) describe a computer program for interviewing and treating patients for depression. In many respects the successes and potential failures of this type of approach have been discussed already. The problems include generating a system which will understand and be able to respond to natural language, and ensuring that the failure to record the non-verbal communication that normally occurs during a psychiatric interview does not interrupt the rapport which needs to be built up between psychotherapist and client.

The primary application of computers to psychotherapy has been to use the computer hardware to present particular stimuli to patients at particular times under conditioning regimes. This is normally considered to be a form of treatment known as 'behaviour therapy' in which undesirable aspects of a patient's behaviour are conditioned out (removed) through non-reward or punishment, whilst more desirable behaviours are reinforced. The bases of behavioural therapy, therefore, are much the same as those of programmed instruction as discussed in Chapter 9.

An example of the use of computers to condition out unwanted behaviours is that of the treatment of autism. Autistic children generally withdraw from interacting with others at a verbal level, at the same time being disruptive in their behaviour. A number of studies have investigated the effects of conditioning on such behaviour and have found improvements to occur. For example, Ferster and DeMyer (1962) describe a situation in which a child was required to press a bar for tokens which could then be used in other games machines. The reward, in this case, was playing on the games machines; the child's behaviour was shaped by the secondary reinforcer which appeared as the tokens. The study demonstrated a reduction in tantrum activity.

Stodolsky (1970) also reports work by Colby (1967) which used computer controlled equipment to teach verbal behaviour to non-speaking children. He suggests that even the small amount of time spent in the computer-controlled environment (about 10 hours) led to a considerable improvement in 8 of the 10 cases.

A second example of the use of computer-controlled behaviour therapy concerns the desensitization of neurotic patients. In these cases the unwanted behaviour (usually fears of spiders, of heights, of open spaces, etc.) are conditioned out, usually by positively rewarding the patient at the same time as presenting a regime of stimuli that gradually build up to the feared object or thought. For example, a fear of spiders may be treated, through a conditioning paradigm, by gradually making the patient accept small objects with eight 'legs'; then plastic 'spiders'; then small living insects, etc. The value of using computers both to control the conditioning regime and to present the stimuli has been highlighted by studies that have indicated that the total cure rate for a human therapist is directly related to the amount of time that the therapist is willing to spend on the process of desensitization (for example, Eysenck and Rachman, 1965). With its infinite facilities for 'patience', the computer is likely to make an ideal tool in these situations.

Desensitization, then, provides an example in which unwanted behaviours are conditioned out and more acceptable behaviours conditioned into the patient's behavioural repertoire. Another example of this form of treatment, although one which stresses the *conditioning in* of acceptable behaviour rather than removing deviant behaviour, is that of biofeedback and relaxation training.

Numerous studies exist that have demonstrated the efficacy of training patients to 'attend' to particular body functions (for example heart rate, skin sweating) as a means of reducing stress (for example, Benson and Klipper, 1976). The rationale, in this case, is that such body functions are indicators of overall stress (arousal) level. By providing feedback relating to the arousal level (that is, by attempting to influence the particular body functions) it is possible to reduce arousal.

Because of their ability to measure and to record slight changes in physiological conditions computers make excellent biofeedback instruments for relaxation. Again, the computer's ability to control endless sessions with the patient without 'tiring', and the ability to display graphically the patient's physiological state and degree of success (Lang, 1980) can be used to good effect. Johnson *et al.* (1981) describe the use of a computer for relaxation training using a series of self-controlled and self-monitored discrete steps.

SUMMARY

This chapter has demonstrated that computers have a valuable role to play in the interrogation, diagnosis and treatment of patients. This role, however, necessarily remains one of an assistant; with present technology at least, the facilities available have not reached the level of sophistication needed to replace the physician.

REFERENCES

Aaronson, D. (1983). What's happening in CAI: A survey of ongoing projects. *Behaviour Research Methods and Instrumentation*, **15**, 262–269.

Adams, J. A. (1971). A closed-loop theory of motor learning. *Journal of Motor Behaviour*, **3**, 111–149.

Adams, M. J. (1979). Models of word recognition. *Cognitive Psychology*, **11**, 133–176

Addis, T. R. (1977). Machine understanding of natural language. *International Journal of Man–Machine Studies*, **9**, 207–222.

Ahl, D. H. (1975). Survey of public attitudes towards computers in society. *Creative Computing*, 77–79.

Ahrlin, U. and Rylander, R. (1979). Annoyance caused by different environmental noises. *Journal of Sound and Vibration*, **66**, 459–462.

Alden, D. G., Daniels, R. W. and Kanarick, A. F. (1972). Keyboard design and operation: A review of the major issues. *Human Factors*, **14**, 275–293.

Aldrich, H. E. (1972). Technology and organizational structure: A re-examination of the findings of the Aston group. *Administrative Science Quarterly*, **17**, 26–43.

Alpern, M. (1972). Effector Mechanisms in Vision. In J. W. Kling and L.A. Riggs (eds) *Experimental Psychology*. (New York: Methuen).

American Council of Life Insurance (1979). *Current Social Issues: The Public's View.*

American Standards Association (1960). *American Standards Acoustical Terminology S1*. (New York: ASA).

American Society of Heating, Refrigeration and Air conditioning Engineers (ASHRAE) (1972). Physiological principles, comfort and health. Chapter 7 in *Handbook of Fundamentals*. (New York: ASHRAE).

Anderson, J. L. (1980). Patients' recall of information and its relation to the nature of the consultation. In D. J. Oborne, M. M. Gruneberg, and J. R. Eiser (eds) *Research in Psychology and Medicine, Volume II*. (London: Academic Press).

Anderson, J. R. (1980). *Cognitive Psychology*. (San Francisco: W. H. Freeman).

Anderson, R. C., Kulhavy, R. W. and Andre, T. (1971). Feedback procedures in programmed instruction. *Journal of Educational Psychology*, **62**, 148–156.

Anderson, R. C., Kulhavy, R. W. and Andre, T. (1972). Conditions under which feedback facilitates learning from programmed lessons. *Journal of Educational Psychology*, **63**, 186–188.

Andersson, G. B. J. (1980). The load on the lumbar spine in sitting postures. In D.J. Oborne and J.A. Levis (eds) *Human Factors in Transport Research, Volume II*. (London: Academic Press).

Angle, H. V. (1981). The interviewing computer: A technology for gathering comprehensive treatment information. *Behaviour Research Methods and Instrumentation*, **13**, 607–612.

Angle, H. V., Johnsen, T., Grebenkemper, N. S. and Ellinwood, E. H. (1979). Computer interview support for clinicians. *Professional Psychology*, **13**, 49–52.

Anglin, J. M. and Miller, G. A. (1968). The role of phrase structure in the recall of meaningful verbal material. *Psychonomic Science*, **10**, 340–344.

Annett, J. (1981). Problems of man–computer interaction in education and training. In B. Shackel (ed) *Man Machine Interface: Human Factors Aspects of Computers and People*. (Netherlands: Sijthoff and Noordhoff).

Archer, B. U. and Margolin, R. R. (1970). Arousal effects in intentional recall and forgetting. *Journal of Experimental Psychology*, **86**, 8–12.

Argyle, M. and Cook, M. (1976) *Gaze and Mutual Gaze*. (Cambridge: Cambridge University Press).

Arndt, S., Feltes, J. and Hanak, J. (1983). Secretarial attitudes towards word processors as a function of familiarity and locus of control. *Behaviour and Information Technology*, **2**, 17–22.

Arroyo, F. V. (1982). Negatives in context. *Journal of Verbal Learning and Verbal Behaviour*, **21**, 118–126.

Atal, B. S. (1976). Automatic recognition of speakers from their voices. *Proceedings of IEEE*, **64**, 460–475.

Atwood, M. E. and Ramsey, H. R. (1978). Cognitive structures in the comprehension and memory of computer programs: An investigation of computer program debugging. *U.S. Army Institute for the Behavioral Sciences Report TR-78-A21*.

Ausubel, D. P. (1968). *Educational Psychology: A Cognitive View* (2nd Edition) (New York: Holt, Rinehart and Winston).

Awad, E. M. (1977a). Job satisfaction as a predictor of tenure. *Computer Personnel*, **7**, 7–10.

Awad, E. M. (1977b). Prediction of satisfaction of systems analysts, programmers. *Data Management*, **15**, 12–18.

Aylor, J. H., Johnson, B. W. and Ramey, R. L. (1981). The impact of microcomputers on devices to aid the handicapped. *Computer*, **14**, 35–40.

Backer, H. L. Jr., (1975). The impact of computer tomography on neuroradiologic practice. *Radiology*, **116**, 637–640.

Baddeley, A., Eldridge, M. and Lewis, V. (1981). The role of subvocalisation in reading. *Quarterly Journal of Experimental Psychology*, **33**, 439–454.

Bagley, W. C. (1900). The apperception of the spoken sentence: A study in the psychology of language. *American Journal of Psychology*, **12**, 80–130.

Bahrick, H. P. (1957). An analysis of stimulus variables influencing the proprioceptive control of movements. *Psychological Review*, **64**, 324–328.

Ball, R. G., Newton, R. S. and Whitfield, D. (1979). *The TOUCH PAD—A versatile interactive computer input device*. Applied Psychology Department Memo 211. Aston University.

Bansford, J. D. and Franks, J. J. (1971). The abstraction of linguistic ideas. *Cognitive Psychology*, **2**, 331–350.

Barber, R. E. (1979). *Response time, operator productivity and job satisafaction*. Ph.D. Thesis, New York University.

Barclay, J. R. (1973). The role of comprehension in remembering sentences. *Cognitive Psychology*, **4**, 229–254.

Barker, P. G. (1982). Some experiments in man-machine interaction relevant to computer assisted instruction. *British Journal of Educational Technology*, **13**, 65–75.

Barnard, P. J., Hammond, N. V., Morton, J., Long, J. B. and Clarke, I. A. (1981). Consistency and compatibility in human–computer dialogue. *International Journal of Man-Machine Systems*, **15**, 87–134.

Barnard, P. J., Hammond, N. V., MacLean, A., and Morton, J. (1982). *Learning and remembering interactive commands*. IBM Research report HF 055 (Hants: IBM).

Barnes, G. R., Benson, A. J. and Prior, A. R. J. (1978). Visual–vestibular interaction in the control of eye-movement. *Aviation, Space and Environmental Medicine*, **49**, 557–564.

Barron, J. (1973). Phonemic stage not necessary for reading. *Quarterly Journal of Experimental Psychology*, **25**, 241–246.

Barron, J. and McKillop, E. J. (1975). Individual differences in speed of phonetic analysis, visual analysis, and reading. *Acta Psychologica*, **2**, 386–393.

Bartol, K. M. (1977). Factors related to the EDP personnel commitment to the organization. *Computer Personnel*, **7** (3), 2–6.

Bauer, D. and Cavonius, C. R. (1980). Improving the legibility of visual display units through contrast reversal. In E. Grandjean and E. Vigliani (eds.) *Ergonomic Aspects of Visual Display Terminals*. (London: Taylor and Francis).

Begg, I. and Paivio, A. (1969). Concreteness and imagery in sentence meaning. *Journal of Verbal Learning and Verbal Behaviour*, **8**, 821–827.

Beldie, I. P. (1983). Fixed versus variable letter width for televised text. *Human Factors*, **25**, 273–277.

Bell, D. (1976). Programmer selection and programming errors. *The Computer Journal*, **19**, 202–206.

Benson, A. J. and Barnes, G. R. (1978). Vision during angular oscillation. The dynamic interaction of visual and vestibular mechanisms. *Aviation, Space and Environmental Medicine*, **49**, 340–345.

Benson, H. and Klipper, M. (1976). *The Relaxation response*. (New York: Avon Books).

Beranek, L. L. (1956). Criteria for office quieting based on questionnaire rating studies. *Journal of the Acoustical Society of America*, **28**, 833–851.

Beranek, L. L. (1971). *Noise and Vibration Control*. (New York: McGraw Hill).

Beranek, L. L., Kryter, K. D. and Miller, L. N. (1959). Reaction of people to exterior aircraft noise. *Noise Control*, **5**, 23–31.

Bergenthal, J. (1971). Preferred pushbutton switch operating forces. *IEEE Transactions—Man and Cybernetics*, **1**, 385–387.

Berliner, H. J. (1977). Some necessary conditions for a master chess program. In P. N. Johnson-Laird and P. C. Wason (eds) *Thinking*. (Cambridge: Cambridge University Press).

Berlyne, D. E., Borsa, D. M., Craw, M. A., Gelman, R. S. and Mandell, E. E. (1965). Effects of stimulus complexity and induced arousal on paired-associate learning. *Journal of Verbal Behaviour and Verbal Learning*, **4**, 291–299.

Bernard, D. (1979). Management issues in co-operative computing. *Computing Surveys*, **11**, 3–17.

Beshir, M. Y. and Ramsey, J. D. (1981). Comparison between male and female subjective estimates of thermal effects and sensations. *Applied Ergonomics*, **12**, 29–33.

Bevan, N. (1981). Is there an optimum speed for presenting text on a VDU? *International Journal of Man-Machine Studies*, **14**, 59–76.

Bevan, N. and Pobgee, P. (1981). MICKIE—A microcomputer for medical interviewing. *International Journal of Man–Machine Studies*, **14**, 39–47.

Bever, T. G., Garrett, M. F. and Hartig, R. (1973). The interaction of perceptual processes and ambiguous sentences. *Memory and Cognition*, **1**, 277–286.

Bezdel, W. (1970). Some problems in man–machine communication using speech. *International Journal of Man-Machine Studies*, **2**, 157–168.

Biegel, R. A. (1934). An improved typewriter keyboard. *The Human Factor*, **8**, 280–285.

Biermann, A. W., Ballard, B. W. and Sigmon, A. H. (1983). An experimental study of natural language programming. *International Journal of Man–Machine Studies*, **18**, 71–87.

Bird, P. F. (1977). 'Digilux' touch sensitive panel. In *Displays for Man–Machine Systems*. IEEE Conference Publication No. 150. (London: IEEE).

Bjorn-Andersen, N. (1979). Myths and realities of information systems contributing to organizational rationality. Proceedings of the IFIP 2nd HCC Conference (June). (Amsterdam: North Holland).

Bjorn-Andersen, N. and Pedersen, P. H. (1977). *Computer systems as a vehicle for changes in the management structure*. ISRG Working Paper No. 77-3. Copenhagen.

Bjorn-Andersen, N. and Rasmussen, L. B. (1980). Sociological implications of computer systems. In H.T. Smith and T.R.G. Green (eds) *Human Interaction with Computers*. (London: Academic Press).

Blackwell, O. M. and Blackwell, H. R. (1971). Visual performance data for 156 normal observers of various ages. *Illuminating Engineering Society Journal*, 1, 3–13.

Blake, M. J. F. (1971). Temperament and time of day. In W. P. Colquhoun (ed). *Biological Rhythms and Human Performance*. (London: Academic Press).

Blass, T. and Siegman, A. W. (1975). A psycholinguistic comparison of speech, dictation and writing. *Language and Speech*, 18, 20–34.

Blau, P. M., Falbe, C. M., McKinley, W. and Tracy, P. K. (1976). Technology and organization in manufacturing. *Administrative Science Quarterly*, 21, 20–40.

Blau, P. M. and Schoenherr, R. A. (1971). *The Structure of Organisations*. (New York: Basic Books).

Blauner, R. (1964). *Alienation and Freedom*. (Chicago: University of Chicago Press).

Bloom, A. M. (1980). Advances in the use of programmer aptitude tests. In T. A. Rullo (ed) *Advances in Computer Programming Management, Volume 1*. (Philadelphia: Heyden).

Bloomfield, J. R. (1979). Visual search with embedded targets: Colour and texture differences. *Human Factors*, 21, 317–330.

Blum, B. I. and Johns, R. J. (1980). Computer technology and medical costs. In S. H. Lavington (ed) *Information Processing '80*. (Amsterdam: North Holland).

Bodmann, H. W. (1962). Illumination levels and visual performance. *International Lighting Review*, 13, 41–47.

Boggs, D. H. and Simon, J. R. (1968). Differential effect of noise on tasks of varying complexity. *Journal of Applied Psychology*, 52, 148–153.

Bond, N. A. (1980). Human trouble shooting in very complex systems: An application of instructional technology. In K. D. Duncan, M. M. Gruneberg and D. Wallis (eds) *Changes in Working Life*. (Chichester: J. Wiley and Sons).

Bouckaert, A. (1972). Computer-aided diagnosis of goitres in a cancer department. *International Journal of Bio-medical Computing*, 3, 3–15

Bouma, H. (1973). Visual interference in the parafoveal recognition of initial and final letters of words. *Vision Research*, 13, 767–782.

Bouma, H. (1980). Visual reading processes and the quality of text displays. In E. Grandjean and E. Vigliani (eds) *Ergonomic Aspects of Visual Display Terminals*. (London: Taylor and Francis).

Bowen, H. M. and Guiness, G. V. (1965). Preliminary experiments on keyboard design for semi-automatic mail sorting. *Journal of Applied Psychology*, 49, 194–198.

Boyce, P. R. (1981). *Human Factors in Lighting*. (London: Applied Science Publishers).

Boynton, R. M. (1960). Summary and discussion. In A. Morris and E. P. Horne (eds) *Visual Search*. (Washington, D.C.: National Academy of Science).

Boynton, R. M. (1979). *Human Colour Vision*. (New York: Holt, Rinehart and Winston).

Boynton, R. M. and Gordon, J. (1965). Bezold–Brucke hue shift measured by color-naming technique. *Journal of the Optical Society of America*, 55, 78–86.

Bradley, J. V. (1969). Glove characteristics influencing control manipulability. *Human Factors*, 11, 21–36.

Bransford, J. D. and Franks, J. J. (1971). The abstraction of linguistic ideas. *Cognitive Psychology*, 2, 331–350.

Branton, P. (1966). *The Comfort of Easy Chairs*. Furniture Industry Research Report No. 22.

Branton, P. (1969). Behaviour, body mechanics and discomfort. *Ergonomics*, 12, 316–327.

Branton, P. (1972). Ergonomic research contributions to the design of the passenger environment. Paper presented to the Institute of Mechanical Engineers Symposium on Passenger Comfort, London.

Branton, P. and Grayson, G. (1967). An evaluation of train seats by an observation of sitting behaviour. *Ergonomics*, 10, 35–41.

Brayfield, A. H. and Crockett, W. H. (1955). Employee attitudes and employee performance. *Psychological Bulletin*, 52, 396–424.

Broad, D. J. (1972). Basic directions in automatic speech recognition. *International Journal of Man–Machine Systems*, 4, 105–118.

Broadbent, D. E. (1954). Some effects of noise on visual performance. *Quarterly Journal of Experimental Psychology*, 6, 1–5.

Broadbent, D. E. (1971). *Decision and Stress*. (London: Academic Press).

Broadbent, D. E. (1976). Noise and the details of ergonomics: A reply to Poulton. *Applied Ergonomics*, 7, 231–235.

Broadbent, D. E. (1978). The current state of noise research: Reply to Poulton. *Psychological Bulletin*, 52, 1052–1067.

Brooke, J. B. and Duncan, K. D. (1980). Experimental studies of flowchart use at different stages of debugging. *Ergonomics*, 23, 1057–1091.

Brookes, M. J. (1972). Office landscape: Does it work? *Applied Ergonomics*, 3, 224–236.

Brookes, M. J. and Kaplan, A. (1972). The office environment: Space planning and effective behaviour. *Human Factors*, 14, 373–391.

Brooks, F. P. Jr., (1977). The computer 'scientist' as a toolsmith—studies in interactive computer graphics. In B. Gilchrist (ed) *Information Processing '77*. (Toronto: IFIP Conference Proceedings).

Brooks, R. (1977). Towards a theory of the cognitive processes in computer programming. *International Journal of Man–Machine Studies*, 9, 737–751.

Brown, C. R. (1974). Human factors problems in the design and evaluation of key-entry devices for the Japanese language. In A. Chapanis (ed) *Ethnic Variables in Human Factors Engineering*. (Baltimore: The Johns Hopkins University Press).

Brown, I. D. (1965). A comparison of two subsidiary tasks used to measure fatigue in car drivers. *Ergonomics*, 8, 467–473.

Brown, I. D. and Poulton, E. C. (1961). Measuring the 'spare mental capacity' of car drivers by a subsidiary task. *Ergonomics*, 5, 35–40.

Brown, J. L. (1965). Flicker and intermittent stimulation. In C. H. Graham (ed) *Vision and Visual Perception*. (New York: John Wiley & Sons).

Brown, R. (1976). Reference in memorial tribute to Eric Lennenberg. *Cognition*, 4, 125–153.

Brown, R. and Lennenberg, E. H. (1954). A study in language and cognition. *Journal of Abnormal and Social Psychology*, 49, 454–462.

Brune, H. H. (1978). The social implications of information processing. *Information and Management*, 1, 143–156.

Burrows, A. A. (1965). Control feel and the dependent variable. *Human Factors*, 7, 413–421.

Burt, C. (1959). *A Psychological Study of Typography.* (Cambridge: Cambridge University Press).

Bury, K. F., Boyle, J. M., Evey, R. J. and Neal, A. S. (1982). Windowing versus scrolling on a visual display terminal. *Human Factors*, 24, 385–394.

Busch-Vishniac, I. J. and Lyon, R. H. (1981). Paper noise in an impact line printer. *Journal of the Acoustical Society of America*, 70, 1679–1689.

Buswell, G. T. (1935). *How People Look at Pictures.* (Chicago: University of Chicago Press).

Byrne, D., Baskett, G. D. and Hodges, L. (1971). Behavioural indicators of interpersonal attraction. *Journal of Applied Social Psychology*, 1, 137–149.

Byrnes, E. and Johnson, J. H. (1981). Change technology and the implementation of automation in mental health care settings. *Behaviour Research Methods and Instrumentation*, 13, 573–580.

Cahill, M. C. and Carter, R. C. Jr. (1976). Colour code size for searching displays of different density. *Human Factors*, 18, 273–280.

Cakir, A., Hart, D. J. and Stewart, T. F. M. (1980). *Visual Display Terminals.* (Chichester: John Wiley & Sons).

Campbell, D. P. (1971). *Handbook for the Strong Vocational Interest Blank.* (California: Stanford University Press).

Campbell, D. P. and Hansen, J-I. C. (1981). *Manual for the SVIB-SCII Strong Campbell Vocational Interest Inventory.* (Stanford: Stanford University Press).

Card, S. K., English, W. K. and Burr, B. J. (1978). Evaluation of mouse, rate-controlled isometric joystick, step keys, and text keys for text selection on a CRT. *Ergonomics*, 21, 601–613.

Card, S. K., Moran, T. P. and Newell, A. (1980). Computer text editing: An information processing analysis of a routine cognitive skill. *Cognitive Psychology*, 12, 32–74.

Card, W. I. and Lucas, R. W. (1981). Computer interrogation in medical practice. *International Journal of Man–Machine Studies*, 14, 49–57.

Card, W. I., Nicholson, M., Crean, G. P., Watkinson, G., Evans, C. R., Wilson, J. and Russell, D. (1974). A comparison of doctor and computer interrogation of patients. *International Journal of Man–Machine Studies*, 5, 175–187.

Carroll, J. B. (ed) *Language, Thought and Reality: Selected Readings of Benjamin Lee Whorf.* (New York: John Wiley & Sons).

Carroll, J. M. (1981). *Toward an integrated study of creative naming.* I.B.M. Research Report RC 9016 (No 39483) 8/31/81.

Carroll, J. M. (1982a). Creative names for personal files in an interactive computing environment. *International Journal of Man–Machine Studies*, 16, 405–438.

Carroll, J. M. (1982b). Learning, using and designing command paradigms. *Human Learning*, 1, 31–62.

Cashen, V. M. and Leicht, K. L. (1970). Role of the isolation effect in a formal educational setting. *Journal of Educational Psychology*, 61, 484–486.

Cavanaugh, W. J., Farrell, W. R., Hirtle, P. W. and Walters, B. G. (1962). Speech privacy in buildings. *Journal of the Acoustical Society of America*, 34, 475–492.

Cerullo, M. J. (1980). Computer usage in business and accounting. *Information and Management*, 3, 113–124.

Chambers, J. A. and Sprecher, J. W. (1980). Computer assisted instruction: Current trends and critical issues. *Communications of the ACM*, 332–342.

Chambers, J. B. and Stockbridge, H. C. W. (1970). Comparison of indicator components and push-button recommendations. *Ergonomics*, 13, 401–420.

Champness, J. and Young, I. (1980). Social limitations in educational technology. *European Journal of Education*, 15, 229–239.

Chapanis, A. (1960). Human engineering. In C. D. Flagle, W. H. Higgins and R. N. Roy (eds) *Operations Research and Systems Engineering.* (Baltimore: The Johns Hopkins University Press).

Chapanis, A. (1965a). On the allocation of functions between men and machines. *Occupational Psychology*, **39**, 1–11.

Chapanis, A. (1965b). Words, words, words. *Human Factors*, **7**, 1–17.

Chapanis, A. (1974). National and cultural variables in ergonomics. *Ergonomics*, **17**, 153–175.

Chapanis, A, Parrish, R. N., Ochsman, R. B. and Weeks, G. D. (1977). Studies in interactive communication: II The effects of four communication modes on the linguistic performance of teams during co-operative problem solving. *Human Factors*, **19**, 101–126.

Cheriton, D. R. (1976). Man–Machine interface design for time-sharing systems. *Proceedings of the Association for Computing Machinery National Conference*, 362–380.

Child, J. (1972). Organisation structure and strategies of control: A replication of the Aston studies. *Administrative Science Quarterly*, **17**, 163–177.

Child, J. and Mansfield, R. (1972). Technology, size and organization structure. *Sociology*, **6**, 369–393.

Chomsky, N. (1957). *Syntactic Structures.* (The Hague: Mouton).

Christ, R. E. (1975). Review and analysis of colour coding research for visual displays. *Human Factors*, **17**, 542–570.

Christie, A. W. and Fisher, A. J. (1966). The effect of glare from street lighting lanterns on the vision of drivers at different ages. *Transactions of the Illuminating Engineering Society*, **31**, 93–108.

Clark, R. E. (1961). The limiting hand skin temperature for unaffected manual performance in the cold. *Journal of Applied Psychology*, **45**, 193–194.

Clarke, R. E. and Cohen, A. (1960). Manual performance as a function of rate of change in hand skin temperature. *Journal of Applied Physiology*, **15**, 496–498.

Clarkson, D. McG., Gray, R. H., Jones, D. H. A., Smith, P. H. S. and Jones, I. W. (1982). Microcomputer system in an accident unit. *British Medical Journal*, **284**, 722–724.

Cleaver, T. G. and O'Connor, C. (1982). Prediction of success at typing. *Human Factors*, **24**, 373–376.

Cochran, D. J., Riley, M. W. and Stewart, L. A. (1980). An evaluation of the strengths, weaknesses and uses of voice input devices. *Proceedings of 24th Annual Meeting of the Human Factors Society*.

Coe, J. B., Cuttle, K., McClellon, W. C., Warden, N. J. and Turner, P. J. (1980). *Visual Display Units.* Report W/1/80. (Wellington: New Zealand Department of Health).

Cohen, G. and Freeman, R. (1976). Individual differences in reading strategies in relation to handedness and cerebral asymmetry. In J. Requin (ed) *Attention and Performance VIII.* (New Jersey: Lawrence & Erlbaum Associates).

Cohen, S., Glass, D. C. and Singer, J. E. (1973). Apartment noise, auditory discrimination and reading ability in children. *Journal of Experimental Social Psychology*, **9**, 40–47.

Colby, K. M. (1967). Computer-aided language development in non-speaking mentally disturbed children. Technical Report No. C585. Stanford University Department of Computer Science.

Cole, R. A. and Jakimik, J. (1978). Understanding speech: How words are heard. In G. Underwood (ed) *Strategies of Information Processing.* (London: Academic Press).

Cole, R. A., Jakimik, J. and Cooper, W. (1978). Perceptibility of phonetic features in fluent speech. *Journal of the Acoustical Society of America*, **64**, 44–56.

Cole, R. A. and Rudnicky, A. I. (1983). What's new in speech perception? The research and ideas of William Chandler Bagley, 1874–1946. *Psychological Review*, **90**, 94–101.

Collen, M. F. (1970). General requirements for a Medical Information System (MIS). *Computers and Biomedical Research*, **3**, 393–406.

Coltheart, M. (1978). Lexical access in simple reading tasks. In G. Underwood (ed) *Strategies of Information Processing*. (London: Academic Press).

Colton, K. W. (1979). The impact and use of computer technology by the police. *Communications of the ACM*, 10–20.

Connolly, D. W. (1977). *Voice data entry in air traffic control*. Paper presented to Conference on Voice Technology for interactive real time command/control systems applications. NASA Ames Research Center, California.

Conrad, R. (1960). Experimental psychology in the field of telecommunications. *Ergonomics*, **3**, 289–295.

Conrad, R. (1964). Acoustic confusion in immediate memory. *British Journal of Psychology*, **55**, 75–84.

Conrad, R. and Hull, A. J. (1968). The preferred layout for data-entry keysets. *Ergonomics*, **11**, 165–173.

Conrad, R. and Longman, D. J. A. (1965). Standard typewriter versus chord keyboard—An experimental comparison. *Ergonomics*, **8**, 77–88.

Coombs, M. J., Gibson, R. and Alty, J. L. (1982). Learning a first computer language: Strategies for making sense. *International Journal of Man–Machine Studies*, **16**, 449–486.

Cooper, M. B. (1976). The effect of keypad angle of a table telephone on keying performance. *Applied Ergonomics*, **7**, 205–11.

Cooper, R. and Foster, M. (1971). Sociotechnical systems. *American Psychologist*, **26**, 467–474.

Cooper, W. E., Egido, C. and Paccia, J. M. (1978). Grammatical conditioning of a phonological rule: Palatization. *Journal of Experimental Psychology: Human Perception and Performance*, **4**, 264–272.

Corlett, E. N., Eklund, J. A. E., Houghton, C. S. and Webb, R. (1983). A design for a sit–stand stool. In K. Coombes (ed) *Proceedings of the Ergonomics Society's Conference, 1983*. (London: Taylor and Francis).

Cornsweet, T. N. (1970). *Visual Perception*. (New York: Academic Press).

Couger, J. D. and Zawacki, R. A. (1978). What motivates D.P. professionals? *Datamation*, **24**, 116–123.

Cox, A. C. (1982). Human factors investigations into interactions with machines by voice. Paper presented to Man/Machines Systems Conference. IEE Document No. 212.

Cox, A. C. and Cooper, M. B. (1981). Selecting a voice for a specified task: The example of telephone announcements. *Language and Speech*, **24**, 233–243.

Crawford, B. H. and Stiles, W. S. (1937). The effect of a glaring light source on extra-foveal vision. *Proceedings of the Royal Society (Series B)*, **122**, 255–280.

Crawford, J. W. (1975). Computer monitoring of fetal heart rate and uterine pressure. *American Journal of Obstetrics and Gynaecology*, **121**, 342–350.

Crawley, R. and Spurgeon, P. (1979). Computer assistance and the air traffic controller's job satisfaction. In R. G. Sell and P. Shipley (eds) *Satisfaction in Work Design: Ergonomics and Other Approaches*. (London: Taylor and Francis).

Creamer, L. R. and Trumbo, D. A. (1960). Multifinger tapping performance as a function of the direction of tapping movements. *Journal of Applied Psychology*, **44**, 376–380.

Cromer, W. (1960). The difference model: A new explanation for some reading difficulties. *Journal of Educational Psychology*, **61**, 471–483.

Cronbach, L. J. (1970). *Essentials of Psychological Testing* (3rd Ed). (New York: Harper and Row).

Crook, M. A. and Langdon, F. J. (1974). The effects of aircraft noise in schools around London airport. *Journal of Sound and Vibration*, 12, 221–232.

Croome, D. J. (1977). *Noise, Buildings and People*. (Oxford: Pergamon).

Crouse, J. H. and Idstein, P. (1972). Effects of encoding cues on prose learning. *Journal of Educational Psychology*, 61, 484–486.

Cuff, R. N. (1979). *Database query systems for the casual user*. Report EE-MSS-CAS-79. (University of Essex: Department of Electrical Engineering Sciences).

Cunninghame-Green, R. A. (1973). Assessing the success of the computer. In I. StJ. Hugo (ed) *Computing Economics*. Infotech State of the Art Report No. 12 (London: Infotech Information).

Cushman, W. H. (1980). Selection of filters for dark adaptation goggles in the photographic industry. *Applied Ergonomics*, 11, 93–99.

D'Atri, D. A. (1975). Psychophysiological responses to crowding. *Environment and Behaviour*, 7, 237–252.

Dainoff, M. J. (1982). Occupational stress factors in visual display terminal (VDT) operation: A review of empirical research. *Behaviour and Information Technology*, 1, 141–176.

Dainoff, M. J., Happ, A and Crane, P. (1981). Visual fatigue and occupational stress in VDT operators. *Human Factors*, 23, 421–438.

Damon, A., Stoudt, H. W. and McFarland, R. A. (1971). *The Human Body in Equipment Design*. (Massachussetts; Harvard University Press).

Daniels, G. S. (1952). *The 'Average Man'?* Wright Patterson Airforce Base technical Note WCRD 53-7. Ohio.

Davis, R., Buchanan, B. and Shortliffe, E. (1977). Production rules as a representation for a knowledge-based consultation program. *Artificial Intelligence*, 8, 15–45.

De Boer, J. B. (1977). Performance and comfort in the presence of veiling reflections. *Lighting Research and Technology*, 9, 169.

De Dombal, F. T. (1975) Computer assisted diagnosis of abdominal pain. In J. Rose, and J. H. Mitchell, (eds) *Advances in Medical Computing*. (London: Churchill Livingstone).

De Dombal, F. T. (1976). How 'objective' is medical data? In F. T. De Dombal and F. Grey (eds) *Decision Making and Medical Care*. (Amsterdam: North Holland).

De Dombal, F. T. (1979). The psychology of diagnosis from a clinical point of view. In D. J. Oborne, M. M. Gruneberg and J. R. Eiser (eds) *Research in Psychology and Medicine, Volume II*. (London: Academic Press).

De Dombal, F. T. and Hall, R. (1979). Evaluation of medical care from the clinician's point of view: Can we trust our own assessments? In A. Alperovitch, F. T. De Dombal and F. Gremy (eds) *Evaluating the Efficiency of Medical Action*. (Amsterdam: North Holland).

Deatherage, B. H. and Evans, T. R. (1969). Binaural masking: Backward, forward and simultaneous effects. *Journal of the Acoustical Society of America*, 46, 362–371.

Deininger, R. L. (1960). Human factors engineering studies of the design and use of pushbutton telephone sets. *The Bell System Technical Journal*, 39, 995–1012.

Delaney, W. A. (1966). Predicting the costs of computer programs. *Data Processing Magazine*, 32.

Dempsey, C. A. (1963). The design of body support and restraint systems. In E. Bennett, J. Degan and J. Spiegel (eds) *Human Factors in Technology*. (New York: McGraw Hill).

Dempster, W. T. (1955). Space requirements of the seated operator: Geometrical, kinematic, and mechanical aspects of the body with special reference to the limbs. WADC Technical Report 55-159 (Ohio: WPAFB).

Denner, S. (1977). Automated psychological testing: A review. *British Journal of Social and Clinical Psychology*, **16**, 175–179.

De George, M. (1981). Experiments in automatic speech verification. *Electronic Engineering*, **June**, 73–83.

De Soto, C. B., London, M. and Handel, S. (1965). Social reasoning and spatial paralogic. *Journal of Personality and Social Psychology*, **2**, 513–521.

Dewitt, L. J. and Weiss, D. J. (1976). Hardware and software evolution of an adaptive ability measurement system. *Behaviour Research Methods and Instrumentation*, **8**, 104–107.

Dickmann, R. A. (1966). A survey of computer personnel selection methodology. Proceedings of the 4th Annual Computer Personnel Research Conference.

Dickmann, R. A. (1971). *Personnel implications for business data processing.* (New York: John Wiley and Sons).

Diebschlag, W. and Muller-Limroth, W. (1980). Physiological requirements on car seats: Some results of experimental studies. In D. J. Oborne and J. A. Levis (eds) *Human Factors in Transport Research, Volume II.* (London: Academic Press).

Diehl, M. J. and Seibel, R. (1962). The relative importance of visual and auditory feedback in speed typewriting. *Journal of Applied Psychology*, **46**, 365–369.

Ditchburn, R. (1955). Eye movements in relation to retinal action. *Optica Acta*, **1**, 171–176.

Doktor, R. (1976). Cognitive style and its use of computers and management information systems. *Management Datamatics*, **5**, 83–88.

Dooling, D. J. and Lachman, R. (1971). Effects of comprehension on the retention of prose. *Journal of Experimental Psychology*, **88**, 216–222.

Dove, G. A. W., Wigg, P., Clarke, J. H. C., Constandinidou, M., Royappa, B. A., Evans, C. R., Milne, J., Goss, C., Gordon, M. and de Wardner, H. E. (1977). The therapeutic effect of taking a patient's history by computer. *Journal of the Royal College of General Practitioners*, **27**, 477–481.

Downs, A. (1967). A realistic look at the final payoffs from urban data systems. *Public Administration Review*, **27**, 204–210.

Drazen, E., Wechsler, A. and Wiig, K. (1975). Requirements for computerized patient monitoring systems. *Computer*, **8**, 22–27.

Droege, R. C. and Hill, B. M. (1961). Comparison of performance on manual and electric typewriters. *Journal of Applied Psychology*, **45**, 268–270.

Duncan, J. and Ferguson, D. (1974). Keyboard posture and symptoms in operating. *Ergonomics*, **17**, 651–662.

Dunn, A. G. (1971). Engineering the keyboard from the human factors viewpoint. *Computers and Automation*, February, 32–33.

Earl, W. K. and Goff, J. D. (1965). Comparison of two data entry methods. *Perceptual and Motor Skills*, **20**, 369–384.

Eason, K. D. (1980). Computer information systems and managerial tasks. In *The Human Side of Information Processing.* N. Bjorn-Anderson (ed) (Amsterdam: North Holland).

Eason, K. D., Damodoran, L. and Stewart, T. F. M. (1975). Interface problems in man–computer interaction. In E. Mumford and H. Sackman (eds) *Human Choice and Computers.* (Amsterdam: North Holland).

Easterbrook, J. A. (1959). The effect of emotion on cue utilization and the organization of behaviour. *Psychological Review*, **66**, 183–201.

Easterby, R., Kroemer, K. H. E. and Chaffin, D. B. (1982). *Anthropometry and Biomechanics: Theory and Application.* (New York: Plenum Press).

Eddy, J. K. and Glass, A. L. (1981). Reading and listening to high and low imagery sentences. *Journal of Verbal Learning and Verbal Behaviour*, 20, 333–345.

Egly, D. G. (1982). Cognitive style, categorization, and vocational effects on performance of REL DATABASE users. *SIGSOC Bulletin*, 13, 91–97.

Ehrenreich, S. L. (1981). Query languages: Design recommendations derived from the human factors literature. *Human Factors*, 23, 709–725.

Eisenstadt, M. and Kareev, Y. (1977). Perception in game playing: internal representation and scanning of board positions. In P. N. Johnson-Laird and P. C. Wason (eds) *Thinking*. (Cambridge: Cambridge University Press).

Elias, M. F., Snadowski, A. M. and Rizy, E. F. (1965). Identification of televised symbols as a function of symbol resolution. *Perceptual and Motor Skills*, 21, 91–99.

Elizar, D. (1970). *Adapting to Innovation*. (Jerusalem: Jerusalem Academic Press).

Ellis, C. A. and Nutt, G. J. (1980). Office information systems and computer science. *Computing Surveys*, 12, 27–60.

Ellis, N. C. and Hill, S. E. (1978). A comparative study of seven segment numerics. *Human Factors*, 20, 655–660.

Elstein, A. S. and Bordage, G. (1979). Psychology and clinical reasoning. In G. C. Stone, F. Cohen and N. E. Adler (eds) *Health Psychology: A Handbook*. (San Francisco: Jossey Bass Publishers).

Elstein, A. S., Kagan, N., Shulman, L. Jason, H. and Loupe, M. J. (1972). Methods and theory in the study of medical inquiry. *Journal of Medical Education*, 47, 85–92.

Elstein, A. S., Shulman, C. S. and Sprafka, S. A. (1978). *Medical Problem Solving: An Analysis of Clinical Reasoning*. (Cambridge: Harvard University Press).

Elwood, D. L. (1972). Test-retest reliability and cost analyses of automated and face-to-face intelligence testing. *International Journal of Man-machine Studies*, 4, 1–22.

Engel, F. L. (1980). Information selection from visual display units. In E. Grandjean and E. Vigliani (eds) *Ergonomic Aspects of Visual Display Terminals*. (London: Taylor and Francis).

Erdman, H., Klein, M. H. and Greist, J. H. (1983). The reliability of a computer interview for drug use/abuse information. *Behaviour Research Methods and Instrumentation*, 15, 66–68.

Eriksen, G. W., Pollack, M. D. and Montague, W. E. (1970). Implicit speech. Mechanisms in perceptual encoding. *Journal of Experimental Psychology*, 84, 502–507.

Ernest, C. H. (1979). Visual imagery ability and the recognition of verbal and non verbal stimuli. *Acta Psychologica*, 43, 253–269.

Estes, W. K. and Wolford, G. L. (1971). Effects of spaces on report from tachistoscopically presented letter strings. *Psychonomic Science*, 25, 77–80.

Evans, C. R. (1979). *The Mighty Micro*. (London: Gollancz)

Evans, G. W. (1978). Human spatial behaviour: The arousal model. In A. Baum and Y. M. Epstein (eds) *Human Response to Crowding*. (Hillside, New Jersey: Lawrence Erlbaum Assoc.)

Evans, G. W. and Howard, R. B. (1973). Personal Space. *Psychological Bulletin*, 80, 334–344.

Eysenck, H. J. (1967). Intelligence assessment: A theoretical and experimental approach. *British Journal of Educational Psychology*, 37, 81–89.

Eysenck, H. J. and Rachman, S. (1965). *The Causes and Cures of Neurosis*. (London: Knapp).

Fanger, P. O. (1970). *Thermal Comfort*. (New York: McGraw Hill).

Feinstein, A. R. (1973). The problems of the 'Problem-Oriented Medical Record'. *Annals of Internal Medicine*, 78, 751–762.

Fellmann, Th., Brauninger, U., Giere, R. and Grandjean, E. (1982). An ergonomic evaluation of VDT's. *Behaviour and Information Technology*, 1, 69–80.

Ferguson, D. and Duncan, J. (1974). Keyboard design and operating posture. *Ergonomics*, **17**, 731–744.

Ferster, C. B. and DeMyer, M. K. (1962). A method for the experimental analysis of the behaviour of autistic children. *American Journal of Orthopsychiatry*, **32**, 89–98.

Fisher, B. A. (1978). *Perspectives on Human Communication*. (London: Collier MacMillan).

Fitter, M. J. (1979). Dialogues for users. In B. Shackel (ed) *Infotech State of the Art Report on Man–Computer Interaction*. (London: Infotech).

Fitter, M. J. and Green, T. R. G. (1981). When do diagrams make good computer dialogues? In M. J. Coombes and J. L. Alty (eds) *Computing Skills and the User Interface*. (London: Academic Press).

Fitts, P. M. (1954). The information capacity of the human motor system in controlling the amplitude of movement. *Journal of Experimental Psychology*, **47**, 381–391.

Fitts, P. M. and Seeger, C. M. (1953). S-R Compatibility: Spatial characteristics of stimulus and response codes. *Journal of Applied Psychology*, **46**, 199–210.

Flanagan, C., Fivars, G. and Tuska, S. A. (1959). Predicting success in typing and keyboard operation. *Personnel Guidance Journal*, **37**, 353–357.

Flanagan, J. L. (1976). Computers that talk and listen: Man–Machine communication by voice. *Proceedings of the IEEE*, **64**, 405–415.

Fleishman, E. A. and Rich, S. (1963). Role of kinaesthetic and spatial–visual abilities in perceptual-motor learning. *Journal of Experimental Psychology*, **66**, 6–11.

Flesch, R. (1948). A new readability yardstick. *Journal of Applied Psychology*, **32**, 221–233.

Folkard, S. and Monk, T. H. (1979). Shiftwork and performance. *Human Factors*, **21**, 483–492.

Fortuin, G. J. (1963). Age and lighting needs. *Ergonomics*, **6**, 239–245.

Foster, J. J. and Bruce, M. (1982). Reading upper and lower case on viewdata. *Applied Ergonomics*, **13**, 145–149.

Foster, J. J. and Coles, P. (1977). An experimental study of typographic cueing in printed text. *Ergonomics*, **20**, 57–66.

Fowler, R. L. and Barker, A. S. (1974). Effectiveness of highlighting for retention of text material. *Journal of Applied Psychology*, **63**, 309–313.

Fox, J. (1977). Medical computing and the user. *International Journal of Man–Machine Studies*, **9**, 669–686.

Fox, J. G. (1963). A comparison of gothic elite and standard elite typefaces. *Ergonomics*, **6**, 193–198.

Fox, J. G. (1971). Background music and industrial productivity—A review. *Applied Ergonomics*, **2**, 70–73.

Fox, J. G. (1983). Industrial Music. In D. J. Oborne and M. M. Gruneberg (eds) *The Physical Environment at Work*. (Chichester: John Wiley & Sons).

Fox, J. G. and Embrey, E. D. (1972). Music—an aid to productivity. *Applied Ergonomics*, **3**, 202–205.

Fox, J. G. and Haslegrave, C. M. (1969). Industrial inspection efficiency and the probability of a defect occurring. *Ergonomics*, **12**, 713–721.

Fox, J. G. and Stansfield, R. G. (1964). Diagram keying times for typists. *Ergonomics*, **7**, 317–320.

French, N. R. and Steinberg, J. C. (1947). Factors governing the intelligibility of speech sounds. *Journal of the Acoustical Society of America*, **19**, 90–119.

Fried, M. L. and DeFazio, V. J. (1974). Territoriality and boundary conflicts in the subway. *Psychiatry*, **37**, 47–59.

Furuta, R., Scofield, J. and Shaw, A. (1982). Document formatting systems: Survey, concepts and issues. *Computing Surveys*, **14**, 417–472.

Gagge, A. P., Stolwijk, J. A. J. and Nishi, Y. (1971). An effective temperature scale based on a simple model of human physiological regulatory response. *ASHRAE Transactions*, **77**, 247-262.

Gaines, B. R. (1981). The technology of interaction—dialogue programming rules. *International Journal of Man-Machine Studies*, **14**, 133-150.

Gaines, B. R. and Facey, P. V. (1975). Some experience in interactive system development and application. *Proceedings of the Institute of Electrical and Electronic Engineers*, **63**, 894-911.

Galitz, W. O. (1965). CRT keyboard human factors evaluation. UNIVAC, Systems Application Engineering, Roseville DPD, **March**.

Gane, C. P., Horabin, I. S. and Lewis, B. N. (1966). The simplification and avoidance of instruction. *Industrial Training*, **1**, 160-166.

Garner, W. R. and Whitman, J. R. (1965). Form and amount of internal structure as factors in free-recall learning of nonsense words. *Journal of Verbal Learning and Verbal Behaviour*, **4**, 257-266.

Garrett, J. W. (1971). The adult human hand: Some anthropometric and biomechanical considerations. *Human Factors*, **13**, 117-131.

Garvey, D. M. (1971). Simulation: A catalogue of judgements, findings and hunches. In P. J. Tansey (ed) *Educational Aspects of Simulation*. (London: McGraw Hill).

Gershefski, G. W. (1970). Corporate models—the state of the art. *Management Science*, **16**, 303-312.

Ghiringhelli, L. (1980). Collection of subjective opinions on use of VDUs. In E. Grandjean and E. Vigliani (eds) *Ergonomic Aspects of Visual Display Terminals*. (London: Taylor and Francis).

Gibson, E. (1969). *Principles of Perceptual Learning and Development*. (New York: Appleton-Century-Crofts).

Gibson, E. J., Pick, A., Osser, H. and Hammond, M. (1962). The role of grapheme-phoneme correspondence in the perception of words. *American Journal of Psychology*, **75**, 554-570.

Giddings, B. J. (1972). Alpha-numerics for raster displays. *Ergonomics*, **15**, 65-72.

Gilbert, M. and Hopkinson, R. G. (1949). The illumination of the Snellen chart. *British Journal of Ophthalmology*, **33**, 305-310.

Gilchrest, B. (1980). Computers and employment: The US experience. In S. H. Lavington (ed) *Information Processing '80*. (Amsterdam: North Holland).

Gilchrest, B. and Shenkin, A. (1979). The impact of scanners on employment in supermarkets. *Computers and Society*, **10**, 4-8.

Gilchrest, B. and Shenkin, A. (1981). The impact of scanners on employment in supermarkets—an update. *Computers and Society*, **11**, 31-33.

Gill, P. W., Leaper, D. J., Guillou, P. J., Staniland, J. R., Horrocks, J. C. and De Dombal, F. T. (1973). Observer variation in clinical diagnosis—a computer aided assessment of its magnitude and importance in 552 patients with abdominal pain. *Methods of Information in Medicine*, **12**, 108-113.

Glantz, S. A. (1978). Computers in clinical medicine: A critique. *Computer*, **11**, 68-77.

Glass, D. C. and Singer, J. E. (1972). *Urban Stress*. (London: Academic Press).

Gleason, H. A. (1961). *An Introduction to Descriptive Linguistics*. (New York: Holt, Rinehart and Winston).

Goodman, K. S. (1972). Psycholinguistic universals in reading. In F. Smith (ed) *Psycholinguistics and Reading*. (New York: Holt, Rinehart and Winston).

Goodman, T. and Spence, R. (1978). The effect of system response time on interactive computer aided problem solving. *SIGGRAPH '78 Proceedings*, 100-104.

Goodwin, N. C. (1975). Cursor positioning on an electronic display using lightpen, lightgun, or keyboard for three basic tasks. *Human Factors*, **17**, 289-295.

Gotlieb, C. C. (1980). Computers—A gift of fire. In S. H. Lavington (ed) *Information Processing '80*. (Amsterdam: North Holland).

Gotlieb, C. C. and Borodin, A. (1973). *Social Issues in Computing*. (New York: Academic Press).

Gough, P. B. (1965). Grammatical transformations and speed of understanding. *Journal of Verbal Learning and Verbal Behaviour*, **4**, 107–111.

Gough, P. B. (1972). One second of reading. In J. F. Kavanaugh and I. G. Mattingly (eds) *Language by Ear and by Eye*. (Massachussetts: MIT Press).

Gough, P. B. and Cosky, M. J. (1977). One second of reading again. In N. J. Castlellan, D. B. Pisoni and G. R. Potts (eds). *Cognitive Theory*, Vol 2. (Hillsdale: Erlbaum Press).

Gould, J. D. (1968). Visual factors in the design of computer-controlled CRT displays. *Human Factors*, **10**, 359–376.

Gould, J. D. (1975). Some psychological evidence on how people debug computer programs. *International Journal of Man–Machine Studies*, **7**, 151–182.

Gould, J. D. (1976). Looking at pictures. In R. A. Monty and J. W. Senders (eds) *Eye Movements and Psychological Processes*. (Hillsdale, New Jersey: Lawrence Erlbaum Associates).

Gould, J. D. (1978a). An experimental study of writing, dictating, and speaking. In J. Requin (ed) *Attention and Performance VII*. (Hillsdale, New Jersey: Lawrence Erlbaum Associates).

Gould, J. D. (1978b). How experts dictate. *Journal of Experimental Psychology; Human Perception and Performance*, **4**, 648–661.

Gould, J. D. (1982). Writing and speaking letters and messages. *International Journal of Man–Machine Studies*, **16**, 147–171.

Gould, J. D. and Boies, S. J. (1978). How authors think about their writing, dictating, and speaking. *Human Factors*, **20**, 495–505.

Gould, J. D. and Drongowski, P. (1974). An explanatory study of computer program debugging. *Human Factors*, **16**, 258–277.

Gould, J. D. and Shaffer, A. (1965). Eye movement patterns during visual information processing. *Psychonomic Science*, **3**, 317–318.

Graf, R. and Torrey, J. W. (1966). Perception of phrase structure in written language. *American Psychological Association Convention Proceedings*, 83–88.

Grams, R. R. (1976). Implications of mass automated instruments on medical practice. *Annual Review of Medicine*, **27**, 199–206.

Grandjean, E. (1973). *Ergonomics in the Home*. (London: Taylor and Francis).

Grandjean, E. (1980a). Ergonomics of VDUs: Review of present knowledge. In E. Grandjean and E. Vigliani (eds) *Ergonomic Aspects of Visual Display Terminals*. (London: Taylor and Francis).

Grandjean, E. (1980b). *Fitting the Task to the Man: An Ergonomic Approach*. (London: Taylor and Francis).

Grandjean, E., Hünting, W. and Piedermann, M. (1983). VDT workstation design: Preferred settings and their effects. *Human Factors*, **25**, 161–175.

Grandjean, E., Nishiyama, K., Hünting, W. and Piedermann, M. (1982). A laboratory study on preferred and imposed settings of a VDT workstation. *Behaviour and Information Technology*, **1**, 289–304.

Grant, E. E. and Sackman, H. (1967). An exploratory investigation of programmer performance under on-line and off-line conditions. *IEEE Transactions—Human Factors*, **HF8-8**, 33.

Green, B. F. and Anderson, L. K. (1956). Color coding in a visual search task. *Journal of Experimental Psychology*, **51**, 19–24.

Greene, J. M. (1970). The semantic function of negatives and passives. *British Journal of Psychology*, **61**, 17–22.

Green, K., Coombs, R. and Holroyd, K. (1980). *The Effects of Microelectronic Technologies on Employment Prospects; A Case Study of Thameside.* (Hampshire: Gower Publishing Co.)

Green, T. R. G. (1980). Programming as a cognitive activity. In H. T. Smith and T. R. G. Green (eds) *Human Interaction With Computers.* (London: Academic Press).

Green, T. R. G. and Manton, J. (1978). *What does problem representation affect; Chunk size, memory load, or mental process?* Memo No. 243. Medical Research Council Social and Applied Psychology Unit, Sheffield.

Greenberger, M., Crenson, M. A. and Crissey, B. L. (1976). *Models of the Policy Process: Public Decision-making in the Computer Era.* (New York: Russell Sage Foundation).

Gregory, M. and Poulton, E. C. (1970). Even versus uneven right-hand margins and the rate of comprehension in reading. *Ergonomics*, **13**, 427–434.

Greist, J. H., Van Cura, L. J. and Knepreth, N. P. (1973). A computer interview for emergency room patients. *Computers and Biomedical Research*, **6**, 257–265.

Grieve, D. W. and Pheasant, S. T. (1983). Biomechanics. In W. T. Singleton (ed) *The Body at Work—Biological Ergonomics.* (Cambridge: Cambridge University Press).

Gruneberg, M. M. (1970). A dichotomous theory of memory—Unproved or unprovable? *Acta Psychologica*, **34**, 489–496.

Gruneberg, M. M. (1978). The feeling of knowing, memory blocks and memory aids. In M. M. Gruneberg and P. E. Morris (eds) *Aspects of Memory.* (London, Methuen).

Gruneberg, M. M. and Oborne, D. J. (1982). *Industrial Productivity: A Psychological Perspective.* (London: MacMillan Press).

Guillien, J. and Rebiffé, R. (1980). Anthropometric models of a population of bus drivers. In D. J. Oborne and J. A. Levis (eds) *Human Factors in Transport Research Volume I.* (London: Academic Press).

Gunnarsson, E. and Osterberg, O. (1977). *Physical and mental working environment in a terminal-based data system.* Research Report No. 35 (Stockholm: Industrial Welfare Council).

Gunnarsson, E. and Soderberg, I. (1979). *Work with Visual Display Terminals in Newspaper Offices.* (Stockholm: National Board of Occupational Safety and Health).

Gustafson, D. H., Greist, J. H., Strauss, F. F., Erdman, H. and Laughren, T. (1977). A probabalistic system for identifying suicide attemptors. *Computers and Biomedical Research*, **10**, 83–89.

Gwynne, J. F. (1965). Fallacies in cancer mortality statistics. *New Zealand Medical Journal*, **64**, 146–151.

Haaland, J. (1973). Anatomic and physiological consideration of the use of the thumb for manual control in space flight. Honeywell Memo. July 1962. (Cited in Alden *et al.*, 1973).

Haaland, J., Wingert, J. and Olsen, B. A. (1963). Force required to actuate switches, maximum finger pushing force, and coefficient of friction of Mercury gloves. Honeywell Memo. February 1963. (Cited in Alden *et al.*, 1972).

Hackmeister, R. (1979). Focus on keyboards. *Electronic Design*, **11**, 169–175.

Hall, C. and Fletcher, R. N. (1967). Programmed techniques in the G.P.O. In *Programmed Instruction in Industry I.* (London: Pergamon).

Hall, E. T. (1976). The anthropology of space: An organising model. In H. M. Proshansky, W. H. Ittleson and L. G. Rivlin (eds) *Environmental Psychology (2nd Edition).* (New York: Holt, Rinehart and Winston).

Hammond, N. V., Long, J. B., Morton, J., Barnard, P. J. and Clark, A. (1981). Documenting human–computer mismatch at the individual and organizational levels. IBM Research Report HF 040. (Hampshire: IBM).

Hansen, D. and Rodgers, T. S. (1973). An exploration of psycholinguistic units in initial reading. In J. S. Goodman (ed) *The Psycholinguistic Nature of the Reading Process*. (Detroit: Wayne State University Press).

Hansen, W. J. (1971). User engineering principles for interactive systems. *American Federation of Information Processing Societies Conference Proceedings*, **39**, 523–532.

Hardin, E. (1967). Job satisfaction and the desire for change. *Journal of Applied Psychology*, **51**, 20–27.

Harding, G. F. A. (1979). Photosensitive epilepsy. In D. J. Oborne, M. M. Gruneberg and J. R. Eiser (eds) *Research in Psychology and Medicine, Volume I*. (London: Academic Press).

Harris, D. (1966). Effect of equipment complexity on inspection performance. *Journal of Applied Psychology*, **50**, 236–237.

Harris, L. R. (1977). User orientated database query with the ROBOT natural language query system. *International Journal of Man–Machine Studies*, **9**, 697–713.

Hartley, J. R. (1966). Research report. *New Education*, **2**, 29.

Hartley, J. R. (1972). *Strategies for Programmed Instruction*. (London: Butterworth).

Hartley, J. R. (1978). An appraisal of computer-assisted learning in the United Kingdom. *Programmed Learning and Educational Technology*, **15**, 136–151.

Hartley, J. R. and Bostrom, K. (1982). An evaluation of micro-CAL in schools. *International Journal of Man–Machine Studies*, **17**, 127–141.

Hartley, J. R. and Burnhill, P. (1976). *Textbook Design: A Practical Guide*. (Paris: UNESCO).

Hartley, J. R. and Davies, I. K. (1977). Programmed learning and educational technology. In M. J. A. Howe (ed) *Adult Learning: Psychological Research and Applications*. (London: John Wiley)

Hawkins, C. A (ed) (1977). *Computer-based Learning*. (The Netherlands: Department of Research and Development of Higher Education).

Healy, M. J. R. (1976). Computer-aided diagnosis—An overview of some theoretical problems. In F. T. De Dombal and F. Gremy (eds) *Decision Making and Medical Care*. (Amsterdam: North Holland).

Hebditch, D. (1979). Design of dialogues for interactive commercial applications. In B. Shackel (ed) *Man/Computer Communication*. (Maidenhead: Infotech).

Heise, D. R. (1969). Some methodological issues in semantic differential research. *Psychological Bulletin*, **72**, 406–422.

Hemingway, J. C. and Erickson, R. A. (1969). Relative effects of raster scan lines and image subtense on symbol legibility on television. *Human Factors*, **11**, 331–338.

Hershman, R. L. and Hillix, W. A. (1965). Data processing in typing: Typing rate as a function of kind of material and amount exposed. *Human Factors*, **7**, 483–492.

Hickson, D. J., Hinings, C., McMillan, J. and Schwitter, J. P. (1974). The culture-free context of organization structure: A trinational comparison. *Sociology*, **8**, 59–80.

Hickson, D. J., Pugh, D. S. and Pheysey, D. C. (1969). Operations technology and organization structure: An empirical reappraisal. *Administrative Sciences Quarterly*, **14**, 378–397.

Hill, D. R. (1971). Man–Machine interaction using speech. *Advances in Computing*, **11**, 165–230.

Hill, D. R. (1977). Using speech to communicate with machines. In B. Shackel (ed) *Man/computer Communication, Volume 2*. (Maidenhead: Infotech International Ltd.)

Hiltz, S. R. (1982). Impact of a computerized conferencing system upon use of other communication modes. In M. B. Williams (ed) *Pathways to the Information Society*. (Amsterdam: North Holland).

Hintzman, D. L.(1967). Articulatory coding in short-term memory. *Journal of Verbal Learning and Verbal Behaviour*, **6**, 312–316.

Hirsch, R. S. (1970). Effects of standard versus alphabetical keyboard formats on typing performance. *Journal of Applied Psychology*, **54**, 484–490.

Hitt, W. D. (1961). An evaluation of five different abstract coding methods. *Human Factors*, **3**, 120–130.

Hochberg, J. (1957). Effects of the Gestalt revolution: The Cornell symposium on perception. *Psychological Review*, **64**, 78–84.

Hochberg, J. and McAlister, E. (1953). A quantitative approach to figural 'goodness'. *Journal of Experimental Psychology*, **46**, 361–364.

Hochberg, J. and Silverstein, A. (1956). A quantitative index of stimulus-similarity: Proximity vs differences in brightness. *American Journal of Psychology*, **69**, 456–458.

Holladay, L. L. (1926). The fundamentals of glare and visibility. *Journal of the Optical Society of America*, **12**, 271–319.

Holland, J. G. (1959). Teaching machines: An application of principles from the laboratory. *Proceedings of the 1959 Conference on Testing Problems*. (Princeton: Educational Testing Service). Reprinted in W. I. Smith and J. W. Moore (eds) *Programmed Learning*. (Princeton: Van Nostrand).

Holland, J. L. (1973). *Making Vocational Choices: A Theory of Careers*. (Englewood Cliffs, New Jersey: Prentice Hall).

Holme, K. and Mabbs, D. (1967). Programmed learning—an expanding discipline. In M. Tobin (ed) *Problems and Methods in Programmed Learning Part 4*. (Birmingham: National Centre for Programmed Learning).

Holmes, V. M. and Langford, J. (1976). Comprehension and recall of abstract and concrete sentences. *Journal of Verbal Learning and Verbal Behaviour*, **15**, 559–566.

Horrocks, J. C. and De Dombal, F. T. (1975). Computer-aided diagnosis of 'dyspepsia'. *American Journal of Digestive Diseases*, **20**, 397–406.

Hopkin, V. D. (1971). The evaluation of touch displays for air traffic control tasks. *IEEE Conference on Displays: Publication No. 80*.

Hopkinson, R. G. (1972). Glare from daylight in buildings. *Applied Ergonomics*, **3**, 206–215.

Hopkinson, R. G. (1940). Discomfort glare in lighted streets. *Transactions of the Illuminating Engineering Society*, **5**, 1–30.

Hopkinson, R. G. and Collins, J. B. (1970). *The Ergonomics of Lighting*. (London: McDonald Technical and Scientific).

Hopkinson, R. G. and Longmore, J. (1959). Attention and distraction in the lighting of workplaces. *Ergonomics*, **2**, 321–333.

Hopkinson, R. G., Waldram, J. M. and Stevens, W. R. (1941). Brightness and contrast in illuminating engineering. *Transactions of the Illuminating Engineering Society*, **6**, 37–47.

Horrocks, J. C. and De Dombal, F. T. (1975) Diagnosis of dyspepsia from data collected by a physician's assistant. *British Medical Journal*, **II**, 421–423.

Houghton, F. C. and Yaglou, C. P. (1923). Determining lines of equal comfort. *ASHRAE Transactions*, **29**, 163–176.

Howarth, C. I. and Bloomfield, J. R. (1969). A rational equation for predicting search times in simple inspection tasks. *Psychonomic Science*, **17**, 225–226.

Howe, J. A. M. (1978). Artificial intelligence and computer assisted learning: Ten years on. *Programmed Learning and Educational Technology*, **15**, 114-125.

Howe, R. C. (1969). Programmed learning—a programmed initial installation training course. *Post Office Electrical Engineers Journal*, January.

Huddleston, J. H. F. (1974). A comparison of two 7×9 matrix alphanumeric designs for TV displays. *Applied Ergonomics*, **5**, 81-83.

Hultgren, G. V. and Knave, B. (1974). Discomfort glare and disturbances from light reflections in an office landscape with CRT display terminals. *Applied Ergonomics*, **5**, 2-8.

Hung, D. L. and Tzeng, O. J. L. (1981). Orthographic variations and visual information processing. *Psychological Bulletin*, **90**, 377-414.

Hunka, S. (1978). CAI: A primary source of instruction in Canada. *Technological Horizons in Education Journal*, **5**, 56-58.

Hunt, E. (1980). Intelligence as an information-processing concept. *British Journal of Psychology*, **71**, 449-474.

Hunt, E. B. and MacLeod, C. M. (1979). Cognition and information processing in patient and physician. In G. C. Stone, F.Cohen and N. E. Adler (eds) *Health Psychology: A Handbook*. (San Francisco: Jossey-Bass Publishers).

Hunter, I. M. L. (1977). Mental calculations. In P. N. Johnson-Laird and P. C. Wason (eds) *Thinking: Readings in Cognitive Science*. (Cambridge: Cambridge University Press).

Hünting, W., Läubli, Th. and Grandjean, E.(1981). Postural and visual loads at VDT workplaces. I Constrained postures. *Ergonomics*, **24**, 917-931.

Hurvich, L. M. and Jameson, D. (1957). An opponent–process theory of colour vision. *Psychological Review*, **64**, 384-404.

Illuminating Engineering Society (1977). *IES Code for Interior Lighting*. (London: IES).

Irwin, D. E., Bock, J. K. and Stanovich, K. E. (1982). Effects of information structure cues on visual word processing. *Journal of Verbal Learning and Verbal Behaviour*, **21**, 307-325.

Isensee, S. H. and Bennett, C. A. (1983). The perception of flicker and glare on computer CRT displays. *Human Factors*, **25**, 177-184.

Jackson, A. (1982). Some problems in the specification of rolling ball operating characteristics. Paper presented to IEE 'Man–machine systems' conference. (London: IEE).

Jansen, G. (1961). Adversive effects of noise in iron and steel workers. *Stahl und Eisen*, **81**, 217-220.

Jeavons, P. M. and Harding, G. F. A. (1975). *Photosensitive Epilepsy*. (London: Heinemann).

Jenkins, H. M. (1958). The effect of signal rate on performance in visual monitoring. *American Journal of Psychology*, **71**, 647-661.

Jenkins, W. L. and Connor, M. B. (1949). Some design factors in making settings on a linear scale. *Journal of Applied Psychology*, **33**, 395-409.

Jenkins, W. L. and Karr, A. C. (1954). The use of a joy-stick in making settings on a simulated scope face. *Journal of Applied Psychology*, **38**, 457-461.

Jerison, H. J. (1966). Remarks on Colquhoun's 'Effect of unwanted signals on performance in a vigilance task'. *Ergonomics*, **9**, 413-416.

Jerison, H. J. (1959). Effects of noise on human performance. *Journal of Applied Psychology*, **43**, 96-101.

Johnson, E. A. (1967). Touch displays: A programmed man–machine interface. *Ergonomics*, **10**, 271-277.

Johnson, J. H., Giannetti, R. A. and Williams, T. A. (1979). Psychological systems questionnaire: An objective personality test designed for on-line computer presentation, scoring, and interpretation. *Behaviour Research Methods and Instrumentation*, 11, 257-260.

Johnson, J. H., Williams, T. A., Giannetti, R. A., Klinger, D. E. and Nakahimas, R. (1978). Organizational preparedness for change: Staff acceptance of an on-line computer assisted assessment system. *Behaviour Research Methods and Instrumentation*, 10, 186-190.

Johnson, J. H., Williams, T. A., Klinger, D. E. and Giannetti, R. A. (1977). Interventional relevance and retrofit programming: Concepts for the improvement of clinician acceptance of computer-generated assessment reports. *Behaviour Research Methods and Instrumentation*, 9, 123-132.

Johnson-Laid, P. N. and Wason, P. C. (Eds) 1977. *Thinking* (Cambridge: Cambridge Univesity Press).

Jones, A. and Moxham, J. (1969). Costing the benefits of training. *Personal Management*, 1, 22.

Jones, D. M. (1979). Stress and memory. In M. M. Gruneberg and P. E. Morris (eds) *Applied Problems in Memory*. (London: Academic Press).

Jones, D. M., Chapman, A. J. and Auburn, T. I. (1981). Noise in the environment: A social perspective. *Journal of Environmental Psychology*, 1, 43-59.

Jones, I. (1976). The technology of visual display units. In D. Grover (ed) *Visual Display Units*. (Guildford: IPC Science and Technology Press).

Jones, M. R. (1962). Colour coding. *Human Factors*, 4, 355-365.

Jones, P. F. (1978). Four principles of man–computer dialogue. *Computer Aided Design*, 10, 197-202.

Jones, S. (1968). *Design of Instruction*. Training Information Paper 1. (London: HMSO).

Joseph, E. C. (1977). Future computer systems: beyond the next five years. In C. H. White (ed) *Future Systems*. (Maidenhead: Infotech International).

Judd, D. B. (1951). Basic correlates of the visual stimulus. In S. S. Stevens (ed) *Handbook of Experimental Psychology*. (New York: John Wiley).

Kahn, E. M., Ramm, D. and Gianturco, D. T. (1981). TOCRS- The Therapy-oriented computer record system. *Behavior Research Methods and Instrumentation*, 13, 479-484.

Kahneman, D. (1973). *Attention and Effort*. (London: Prentice Hall).

Kak, A. V. and Knight, J. L. (1980). Text formatting effects in speed reading. *Proceedings of the 24th Human Factors Society Meeting, Baltimore*. (Baltimore: HFS).

Kamman, R. (1975). The comprehensibility of printed instructions and the flowchart alternative. *Human Factors*, 17, 183-191.

Keegan, J. J. and Radke, A. O. (1964). Designing vehicle seats for greater comfort. *SAE Journal*, **September,** 72, 50-55.

Keele, S. W. (1968). Movement in skilled motor performance. *Psychological Bulletin*, 70, 387-403.

Keighley, E. C. (1970). Acceptability criteria for noise in large offices. *Journal of Sound and Vibration*, 11, 83-93.

Kelly, M. J. and Chapanis, A. (1977). Limited vocabulary natural language dialogue. *International Journal of Man–Machine Studies*, 9, 479-501.

Kelly, D. H. (1961). Visual responses to time-dependent stimuli. I Amplitude sensitivity measurements. *Journal of the Optical Society of America*, 51, 422-429.

Kendall, R. and Bishop, J. M. (1973). Evaluation of a new system for recording by computer the findings at physical examination. *Bio-Medical Computing*, 4, 161-172.

Kennedy, K. W. (1975). International anthropometric variability and its effects on aircraft cockpit design. In A. Chapanis (ed) *Ethnic Variables in Human Factors Engineering*. (Baltimore; Johns Hopkins University Press).

Kennedy, T. C. S. (1974). The design of interactive procedures for man–machine communication. *International Journal of Man–Machine Studies*, 6, 309–334.

Kernighan, B. W. and Plauger, P. J. (1974). Programming style: examples and counter examples. *Computing Surveys*, 6, 303–319.

Kimball, J. P. (1973). Seven principles of surface structure parsing in natural language. *Cognition*, 2, 15–47.

Kinkead, R. (1975). Typing speed, keying rates and optimal keyboard layouts. In *Proceedings of 1975 Human Factors Society Annual Meeting*. (Baltimore: HFS).

King, J. L. and Schrems, E. L. (1978). Cost-benefit analysis in information systems development and operation. *Computing Surveys*, 10, 19–34.

Klapp, S. T. (1971). Implicit speech inferred from response latencies in 'same different' decisions. *Journal of Experimental Psychology*, 91, 262–267.

Klare, G. R. (1963). *The Measurement of Readability*. (Des Moines, Iowa: Iowa State University Press).

Klemmer, E. T. (1969). Grouping of printed digits for manual entry. *Human Factors*, 11, 397–400.

Klemmer, E. T. (1971). Keyboard entry. *Applied Ergonomics*, 2, 2–6.

Klensin, J. C. (1982). Short-term friendly and long-term hostile? *SIGSOC Bulletin*, 13, 105–110.

Kling, R. (1974). Computers and social power. *Computing Society*, 5, 6–11.

Kling, R. and Scacchi, W. (1980). Computing as social action: The social dynamics of computing in complex organizations. *Advances in Computers*, 19, 249–327.

Klinger, D. E., Johnson, J. H. and Williams, T. A. (1976). Strategies in the evolution of an on-line computer-assisted unit for intake assessment of mental health patients. *Behaviour Research Methods and Instrumentation*, 8, 95–100.

Kobrick, J. L. and Fine, B. J. (1983). Climate and human performance. In D. J. Oborne and M. M. Gruneberg (eds) *The Physical Environment at Work*. (Chichester: John Wiley).

Kolers, P. A. (1976). Buswell's discoveries. In R. A. Monty and J. W. Senders (eds) *Eye Movements and Psychological Processes*. (Hillsdale, New Jersey: Lawrence Erlbaum Associates).

Korn, T. S. (1954). Effect of psychological feedback on conversational noise reduction in rooms. *Journal of the Acoustical Society of America*, 26, 793–794.

Kraemer, K. L. and Dutton, W. H. (1979). The interests served by technological reform: The case of computing. *Administration and Society*, 11, 80–106.

Kroemer, K. H. E. (1965). Comparison of a keyboard of a normal typewriter with a 'K'-keyboard. *Internat. zeitschchrift angewandt Physiologie*, 20, 453–464.

Kroemer, K. H. E. (1972). Human engineering the keyboard. *Human Factors*, 14, 51–63.

Kroemer, K. H. E. (1983). Work space and equipment to fit the user. In D. J. Oborne and M. M. Gruneberg (eds) *The Physical Environment at Work*. (Chichester: John Wiley).

Kroemer, K. H. E. and Robinette, J. C. (1968). *Ergonomics in the Design of Office Furniture: A Review of European Literature*. AMRL-TR-68-80.

Kryter, K. D. (1970). *The Effects of Noise on Man*. (New York: Academic Press).

Kryter, K. D. and Pearsons, K. S. (1963). Some effects of spectrum content and duration on perceived noise level. *Journal of the Acoustical Society of America*, 39, 451–464.

Lang, P. J. (1980). Behavioural treatment and bio-behavioural assessment: Computer applications. In J. B. Sidowski, J. H. Johnson and T. A. Williams (eds) *Technology in Mental Health Care Delivery Systems*. (Norwood, New Jersey: Ablex).

Langton, N. H., Addinall, E., Ellington, H. I. and Percival, F. (1980). The value of simulations and games in the teaching of science. *European Journal of Education*, **15**, 261–270.

Läubli, Th., Hünting, W. and Grandjean, E.(1981). Postural and visual loads of VDT workplaces. II Lighting conditions and visual impairment. *Ergonomics*, **24**, 933–944.

Leader, M. A. and Klein, D. F. (1977). Reflections on instituting a computerized psychosocial history in a clinical facility. *Comprehensive Psychiatry*, **5**, 489–496.

Lee, W. (1972). Keying while listening: The effect of input grouping. *Human Factors*, **14**, 89–94.

Leintz, B. P. and Swanson, E. B. (1981). Problems in application software maintenance. *Communications of ACM*, 763–769.

Leonard, J. A. and Carpenter, A. (1964). On the correlation between a serial-choice task and subsequent achievement at typing. *Ergonomics*, **7**, 197–204.

Lewis, R. and Tagg, E. D. (eds) (1980). *Computer Assisted Learning: Scope, Progress and Limits*. (Amsterdam: North Holland).

Ley, P. (1979). Improving clinical communication: Effects of altering doctor behaviour. In D. J. Oborne, M. M. Gruneberg and J. R. Eiser (eds) *Research in Psychology and Medicine, Volume II*. (London: Academic Press).

Licklider, J. C. R. (1960). Man–computer symbiosis. *Institute of Radio Engineers Transactions of Human Factors in Electronics*, HFE1.

Licklider, J. C. R. (1965). Man–computer partnership. *International Science and Technology*, May, 18–26.

Liebman, M. (1970). The effects of sex and race norms on personal space. *Environmental Behaviour*, **2**, 208–246.

Litterick, I. (1981). QWERTYUIOP—dinosaur in a computer age. *New Scientist*, **89**, 66–68.

Lockhart, J. M. (1968). Extreme body cooling and psychomotor performance. *Ergonomics*, **11**, 249–260.

Lockhart, J. M. and Keiss, H. O. (1971). Auxillary heating of the hands during cold exposure and manual performance. *Human Factors*, **13**, 457–465.

Loftus, E. F. (1975). Leading questions and the eyewitness report. *Cognitive Psychology*, **7**, 560–572.

Loftus, G. R. (1972). Eye fixations and recognition memory for pictures. *Cognitive Psychology*, **3**, 325–351.

Long, J. (1976). Effects of delayed irregular feedback on unskilled and skilled keying performance. *Ergonomics*, **19**, 183–202.

Loubser, J. J. and Fullan, M. (1970). *Industrial Conversion and Worker's Attitudes to Change in Different Industries*. Ottawa: Task Force on Labour Relations Study No 12.

Love, T. (1977). An experimental investigation of the effect of program structure on program understanding. *SIGPLAN Notices*, **12**, 105–113.

Loveless, N. E. (1962). Direction-of-motion stereotypes: A review. *Ergonomics*, **5**, 357–383.

Lovesey, E. J. (1971). *An investigation into the effects of dual axis vibration, restraining harness, visual feedback and control force on a manual positioning task*. RAE Technical Report 71213.

Lucas, H. C. Jr. (1978). The use of an interactive information storage and retrieval system in medical research. *Communications of the ACM*, **21**, 197–205.

Lucas, R. W. (1977). A study of patient's attitudes to computer interrogation. *International Journal of Man–Machine Systems*, **9**, 69–86.

Lucas, R. W. (1979). The role of one psychologist in a medical research project. In D. J. Oborne, M. M. Gruneberg and J. R. Eiser (eds) *Research in Psychology and Medicine, Volume I*. (London: Academic Press).

Lucas, R. W., Card, W. I., Knill-Jones, R. P., Watkinson, G. and Crean, G. P. (1976). Computer interrogation of patients. *British Medical Journal*, 2, 623-625.

Lucas, R. W., Mullin, P. J., Luna, C. B. X. and McInroy, D. C. (1977). Psychiatrists and a computer as interrogators of patients with alcohol-related illnesses: A comparison. *British Journal of Psychiatry*, 131, 160-167.

Luce, P. A., Feustel, T. C. and Pisoni, D. B. (1983). Capacity demands in short-term memory for synthetic and natural speech. *Human Factors*, 25, 17-32.

Lukiesh, M. and Holladay, L. L. (1925). Glare and visibility. *Transactions of the Illuminating Engineering Society*, 20, 221-252.

Lundervold, A. (1958). Electromyographic investigations during typewriting. *Ergonomics*, 1, 226-233.

Lunderg, U. (1976). Urban commuting: Crowdedness and catecholamine excretion. *Journal of Human Stress,* 2, 26-32.

Lusted, L. B. (1976). Clinical decision making. In F. T. De Dombal and F. Gremy (eds) *Decision Making and Medical Care*. (Amsterdam: North Holland).

Mackie, A. (1975). Consumer-orientated programmed learning in adult education. In L. F. Evans and J. Leedham (eds) *Aspects of Educational Technology*. (London: Kogan Page).

Mackworth, J. F. and Mackworth, N. H. (1958). Eye fixations on changing visual scenes by the television eye-marker. *Journal of the Optical Society of America*, 48, 439-445.

Mackworth, N. H. and Morandi, A. J. (1967). The gaze selects informative details within pictures. *Perception and Psychophysics*, 2, 547-552.

Maddox, M. E., Burnette, J. T. and Gutmann, J. C. (1977). Font comparisons for 5×7 dot matrix characters. *Human Factors*, 19, 89-93.

Maguire, M. (1982). An evaluation of published recommendations on the design of man–computer dialogues. *International Journal of Man-Machime Studies*, 16, 237-261.

Mahoney, E. R. (1974). Compensatory reactions to spatial immediacy. *Sociometry,* 37, 423-431.

Malone, T. W. (1983). How do people organize their desks? Implications for the design of office systems. *ACM Transactions on Office Information Systems*, 1, 99-112.

Mandal, A. C. (1981). The seated man (Homo Sedens). *Applied Ergonomics*, 12, 19-26.

Mann, F. C. and Williams, L. K. (1962). Some effects of the changing work environment in the office. *Journal of Social Issues*, 18, 90-101.

Marg, E., Crossman, E. R. F. W., Goodeve, P. J. and Wakamatsu, H. (1972). An automated case history taker for eye examination. *American Journal of Optometry*, 49, 105-112.

Marr, D. (1977). Artificial intelligence—A personal view. *Artificial Intelligence*, 9, 37-48.

Marschark, M. and Paivio, A. (1977). Integrative processing of concrete and abstract sentences. *Journal of Verbal Learning and Verbal Behaviour*, 16, 217-231.

Marslen-Wilson, W. and Welsh, A. (1978). Processing interactions and lexical access during word recognition in continuous speech. *Cognitive Psychology*, 10, 29-63.

Martin, A. (1972). A new keyboard layout. *Applied Ergonomics*, 3, 48-51.

Martin, J. (1973). *Design of Man-Computer Dialogues*. (New Jersey: Prentice-Hall).

Martin, T. B. (1976). Practical applications of voice input to machines. *Proceedings of IEEE*, 64, 487-501.

Martin, T. B. and Welch, J. R. (1980). Practical speech recognizers and some performance effective parameters. In W. A. Lea (ed) *Trends in Speech Recognition.* (New Jersey: Prentice-Hall).

Mason, M. (1978). From print to sound in mature readers as a function of reader ability and two forms of orthographic regularity. *Memory and Cognition*, 6, 568–581.

Mathews, K. and Canon, L. (1975). Environmental noise level as a determinant of helping behaviour. *Journal of Personality and Social Psychology*, 32, 571–577.

Matin, E. (1974). Saccadic suppression: A review and analysis. *Psychological Bulletin*, 81, 899–917.

Matsumoto, S. (1977). New multicolor liquid crystal display. *Toshiba Review*, 1–4.

Mayer, R. E. (1965). Different problem solving competencies established in learning computer programming with and without meaningful models. *Journal of Educational Psychology*, 67, 725–734.

Mayer, R. E. (1976). Some conditions of meaningful learning for computer programming: Advance organizers and subject control of frame order. *Journal of Educational Psychology*, 68, 143–150.

Mayer, R. E. (1979). Can advance organizers influence meaningful learning? *Review of Educational Research*, 371–383.

Mayer, R. E. (1979). A psychology of learning BASIC. *Communications of the ACM*, 11, 589–593.

Mayer, R. E. (1980). Elaboration techniques for technical text: An experimental test of learning strategy hypothesis. *Journal of Educational Psychology*, 72, 209–225.

Mayer, R. E. (1981). The psychology of how novices learn computer programming. *Computing Surveys*, 13, 121–141.

Mayer, R. E. and Bromage, B. (1980). Different recall protocols for technical text due to advance organizers. *Journal of Educational Psychology*, 72, 209–225.

Mayer, R. E. and Greeno, J. G. (1972). Structural differences between learning outcomes produced by different instructional methods. *Journal of Educational Psychology*, 63, 165–173.

Mazlack, L. J. (1978). Predicting student success in an introductory programming course. *The Computer Journal*, 21, 380–382.

Mazlack, L. J. (1980). Identifying potential to acquire programming skills. *Communications of the ACM*, 23, 14–17.

McBride, G., King, M. and James, J. (1965). Social proximity effects on galvanic skin responses of adult humans. *Journal of Psychology*, 61, 153–157.

McConkie, G. W. (1976). The use of eye-movement data in determining the perceptual span in reading. In R. A. Monty and J. W. Senders (eds) *Eye Movements and Psychological Processes.* (Hillsdale, New Jersey: Lawrence Erlbaum Associates).

McConkie, G. W. and Rayner, K. (1975). The span of the effective stimulus during a fixation in reading. *Perception and Psychophysics*, 17, 578–586.

McConkie, G. W. and Rayner, K. (1976). Asymmetry of the perceptual span in reading. *Bulletin of the Psychonomic Society*, 8, 365–368.

McCormick, E. J. (1976). *Human Factors in Engineering and Design.* (McGraw Hill: New Jersey).

McCusker, L. X., Hillinger, M. L. and Bias, R. G. (1981). Phonological recoding and reading. *Psychological Bulletin*, 89, 217–245.

McEwing, R. W. (1977). Touch displays in industrial computer systems. In *Displays for man–machine systems.* (London: IEEE).

McIntyre, D. (1973). A guide to thermal comfort. *Applied Ergonomics*, 4, 66–72.

McLaughlin, G. H. (1966). Comparing styles of presenting technical information. *Ergonomics*, 4, 257–259.

McLean, N. V. (1965). Brightness contrast, colour contrast and legibility. *Human Factors*, 7, 521-526.

McLean, P. D. (1969). Induced arousal and time of recall as determinants of paired-associate recall. *British Journal of Psychology*, 60, 57-62.

McNall, P. E., Ryan, P. W., Rholes, F. H., Nevins, R. G. and Springer, W. E. (1968). Metabolic rates at four activity levels and their relationship to thermal comfort. *ASHRAE Transactions*, Parts IV.3.1-IV.3.20.

McNamara, W. J. and Hughes, J. L. (1961). Review of research on the selection of computer programmers. *Personnel Psychology*, 14, 39-51.

Mead, P. G. and Sampson, P. B. (1972). Hand steadiness during unrestricted linear arm movements. *Human Factors*, 14, 45-50.

Megaw, E. D. and Bellamy, L. J. (1983). Illumination at work. In D. J. Oborne and M. M. Gruneberg (eds) *The Physical Environment at Work*. (Chichester: John Wiley).

Meyer, N. D. (1982). Office automation: A progress report. *Office, Technology and People*, 1, 107-121.

Meyrowitz, N. and Van Dam, A. (1982a). Interactive editing systems. Part I. *Computing Surveys*, 14, 321-352.

Meyrowitz, N. and Van Dam, A. (1982b). Interactive editing systems. Part II. *Computing Surveys*, 14, 353-416.

Michael, P. R. and Bienvenue, G. R. (1983). Industrial noise and man. In D. J. Oborne and M. M. Gruneberg (eds) *The Physical Environment at Work*. (Chichester: John Wiley).

Michaelis, P. R. (1980). An ergonomist's introduction to synthesized speech. In D. J. Oborne and J. A. Levis (eds) *Human Factors in Transport Research Volume I*. (London: Academic Press).

Michaelis, P. R., Chapanis, A., Weeks, G. D. and Kelly, M. J. (1977). Word usage in interactive dialog with restricted and unrestricted vocabularies. *IEEE Transactions on Professional Communication*, 20, 214-221.

Michaelis, P. R. and Wiggins, R. H. (1981). Speech synthesizers: the basics. *Bulletin of the Human Factors Society*, 24, 1-2.

Michaels, S. E. (1971). Qwerty versus alphabetic keyboards as a function of typing skill. *Human Factors*, 13, 419-426.

Miller, E. (1968). A case for automated clinical testing. *Bulletin of the British Psychological Society*, 21, 75-78.

Miller, G. A. (1956). The magical number seven plus or minus two: Some limits on our capacity to process information. *Psychological Review*, 63, 81-97.

Miller, G. A. (1962). Some psychological studies of grammar. *American Psychologist*, 17, 748-762.

Miller, G. A. and Licklider, J. C. R. (1950). The intelligibility of interrupted speech. *Journal of the Acoustical Society of America*, 22, 167-173.

Miller, G. R. (1972). *An Introduction to Speech Communication*, 2nd Edition. (Indianapolis: The Bobbs-Merrill Co Inc).

Miller, R. B. (1968). Response time in man-computer conversational transactions. *Proceedings of the Spring Joint Computing Conference*, 33, 267-277. (New Jersey: AFIPS Press).

Miller, R. B. (1977). A study in man-machine interaction. *Proceedings of the National Computer Conference*, 46, (New Jersey: AFIPS Press).

Mills, D. (1968). Clerical training in the quality department of Bryce Berger Ltd. *Progress in Instruction in Industry, Volume 2*. (London: Pergamon).

Millward, R. (1979). Teaching a computer to teach. *Behaviour Research Methods and Instrumentation*, 11, 101-110.

Millward, R., Mazzucchelli, L., Magoon, S. and Moore, R. (1978). Intelligent computer-assisted instruction. *Behaviour Research Methods and Instrumentation*, **10**, 213–217.

Minor, F. J. and Revesman, S. L. (1962). Evaluation of input devices for a data setting task. *Journal of Applied Psychology*, **46**, 332–336.

Mirvis, P. H. and Lawler, E. E. (1977). Measuring the financial impact of employee attitudes. *Journal of Applied Psychology*, **67**, 1–8.

Morfield, M. A., Wiesen, R. A., Grossberg, M. and Yntema, D. B. (1969). *Initial experiments on the effects of system delay on on-line problem solving*. Lincoln Laboratory Technical Report.

Morgan, C. T. (1965). *Physiological Psychology*, 3rd Edition. (New York: McGraw Hill).

Morgan, C. T., Cook, J. S., Chapanis, A. and Lund, M. (1963). *Human Engineering Guide to Equipment Design*. (New York: McGraw-Hill).

Morrill, C. S., Goodwin, N. C. and Smith, S. L. (1968). User input mode and computer aided instruction. *Human Factors,* **10**, 225–232.

Morton, R. and Provins, K. A. (1960). Finger numbness after acute local exposure to cold. *Journal of Applied Psychology*, **15**, 149–154.

Morton, J., Barnard, P., Hammond, N. and Long, J. B. (1979). Interacting with the computer: A framework. In E. Boutmy and A. Danthine (eds) *Teleinformatics '79*. (Amsterdam: North Holland).

Mountford, S. J. and North, R. A. (1980). Voice entry for reducing pilot workload. *Proceedings of the 1980 Human Factors Society*, 185–189.

Mourant, R., Lakshmanan, R. and Chantadisai, R. (1981). Visual fatigue and cathode ray tube terminals. *Human Factors*, **23**, 529–540.

Mumford, E. and Banks, O. (1967). *The computer and the Clerk*. (London: Routledge and Kegan Paul).

Munsell Colour Co. (1929). *The Munsell Book of Color*.

Murrell, K. F. H. (1969). Beyond the panel. *Ergonomics*, **12**, 691–700.

Murrell, K. F. H. (1971). *Ergonomics: Man in his working environment*. (London: Chapman and Hall).

Musatti, C. L. (1931). Forme e assimilazione. *Archivo Italiano di Psichologia*, **9**, 61–156.

Muter, P., Latrémouille, S. A., Treurniet, W. C. and Beam, P. (1982). Extended reading of continuous text on television screens. *Human Factors*, **24**, 501–508.

Nash, A. N., Muczyk, J. P. and Vettori, F. L. (1971). The relative practical effectiveness of programmed instruction. *Personnel Psychology*, **24**, 397–418.

Navon, D. and Shimron, J. (1981). Does word meaning involve grapheme–tophoneme translation? Evidence from Hebrew. *Journal of Verbal Learning and Verbal Behaviour*, **20**, 97–109.

Naylor, T. H. and Schauland, H. (1976). A survey of computer users of corporate planning models. *Management Science*, **22**, 927–937.

Nemecek, J. and Grandjean, E. (1973). Noise in landscaped offices. *Applied Ergonomics*, **4**, 19–22.

Newell, A. (1977). On the analysis of human problem solving protocols. In P. N. Johnson-Laird and P. C. Wason (eds) *Thinking*. (Cambridge: Cambridge University Press).

Newsham, D. B. (1969). *The Challenge of Change to the Adult Trainee*. Training Paper 3. (London: HMSO).

Nevins, R. G. and Gagge, A. P. (1972). The new ASHRAE comfort chart. *ASHRAE Journal*, **14**, 41–43.

Nickerson, R. S. (1969). Man-computer interaction: A challenge for human factors research. *Ergonomics*, **12**, 501-518.

Norman, D. A. and Fisher, D. (1982). Why alphabetic keyboards are not easy to use: Keyboard layout doesn't much matter. *Human Factors*, **24**, 509-519.

North, J. D. (1954). *The Rational Behaviour of Mechanically Extended Man*. (Wolverhampton, England: Boulton Paul Aircraft Co).

Noyes, J. (1983a). The QWERTY keyboard: A review. *International Journal of Man-Machine Studies*, **18**, 265-281.

Noyes, J. (1983b). Chord keyboards. *Applied Ergonomics*, **14**, 55-59.

Oates, A. A. and Robinson, C. F. (1968). Programmed learning for clerical work in the GPO. *Progress in Instruction in Industry*, Volume 2. (London: Pergamon).

Oatley, K. G. (1977). Inference, navigation, and cognitive maps. In P. N. Johnson-Laird and P. C. Wason (eds) *Thinking: Readings in Cognitive Science*. (Cambridge: Cambridge University Press).

Oborne, D. J. (1981). *Ergonomics at Work*. (Chichester: John Wiley).

Oborne, D. J. (1983). Vibration at work. In D. J. Oborne and M. M. Gruneberg (eds) *The Physical Environment at Work*. (Chichester: John Wiley).

Oborne, D. J. and Heath, T. O. (1979). The role of social space requirements in ergonomics. *Applied Ergonomics*, **10**, 99-103.

Ochsman, R. B. and Chapanis, A. (1974). The effects of 10 communication modes on the behavior of teams during co-operative problem-solving. *International Journal of Man-Machine Studies*, **6**, 579-619.

Odor, P. (1982). Microcomputers and disabled people. *International Journal of Man-Machine Studies*, **17**, 51-58.

Ofiesh, G. D. (1965). *Programmed Instruction*. (New York: American Management Association).

Ohlsson, K., Nilsson, L-G. and Rönnbert, J. (1981). Speed and accuracy in scanning as a function of combinations of text and background colours. *International Journal of Man-Machine Studies*, **14**, 215-222.

O'Kane, K. C. and Haluska, E. A. (1977). Perspectives in clinical computing. *Advances in Computers*, **16**, 127-182.

Olsen, D. R. and Filby, N. (1972). On the comprehension of active and passive sentences. *Cognitive Psychology*, **3**, 361-381.

Olson, M. H. (1982). Statement of concern. *Office: Technology and People*, **1**, 37-40.

Orth, B., Weckerle, H. and Wendt, D. (1976). Legibility of numerals displayed in a 4×7 dot matrix and seven-segment digits. *Visible Language*, **10**, 145-155.

Osanai, H. (1968). Ill health of key-punchers. *Journal of Science of Labour*, 367-371.

Osgood, C. E., Succhi, G. J. and Tannenbaum, P. H. (1957). *The Measurement of Meaning*. (Illinois: University of Illinois Press).

Oshika, B. T., Zue, V. W., Weeks, R. V., Nue, H. and Aurbach, J. (1975). The role of phonological rules in speech understanding research. *IEEE Transactions—Acoustics, Speech, Signal Processing*, **23**, 104-112.

Paivio, A. (1971). *Imagery and Verbal Processes*. (New York: Holt, Rinehart and Winston).

Paivio, A., Yuille, J. C. and Madigan, S. A. (1968). Concreteness, imagery and meaningfulness values for 925 nouns. *Journal of Experimental Psychology Monograph Supplement*, **76**, No. 1, Part 2.

Paivio, A. and Begg, I. (1981). *Psychology of Language*. (New Jersey, Prentice Hall).

Palmer, D. A. (1960). A system of mesopic photometry. *Nature*, **209**, 276-281.

Palormo, J. M. (1974). *Computer Programmer Attitude Battery*. (Chicago: Science Research Associates Inc).

Park, O. (1981). A response-sensitive strategy in computer-based instruction: A strategy for concept teaching. *Journal of Educational Technology Systems*, **10**, 187–197.

Parsons, H. M. (1976). Work environments. In I. Altman and J. F. Wohlwill (eds) *Human Behaviour and Environment*. Volume I. (New York: Plenum Publishing).

Pask, G. (1976). Styles and strategies of learning. *British Journal of Educational Psychology*, **46**, 128–148.

Pask, G. and Scott, B. C. E. (1972). Learning strategies and individual competence. *International Journal of Man–Machine Studies*, **4**, 217–253.

Pasmore, W. A. and Sherwood, J. J. (eds) (1978). *Sociotechnical Systems: A Sourcebook*. (California: University Associates Inc).

Pastoor, S, Schwarz, E. and Beldie, I. P. (1983). The relative suitability of four dot-matrix sizes for text presentation on colour television screens. *Human Factors*, **25**, 265–272.

Paterson, D. G. and Tinker, M. A. (1946). Readability of newspaper headlines printed in capitals and lower case. *Journal of Applied Psychology*, **30**, 161–168.

Patrick, J. and Stammers, R. (1977). Computer assisted learning and occupational training. *British Journal of Educational Technology*, **8**, 253–267.

Patterson, M. L. and Sechrest, L. B. (1970). Interpersonal distance and impression formation. *Journal of Personality*, **38**, 161–166.

Patterson, M. L., Mullens, S. and Romano, J. (1971). Compensatory reactions to spatial intrusion. *Sociometry*, **34**, 121–144.

Peacock, L. J. (1956). *A Field Study of Rifle Aiming Steadiness and Serial reaction Performance as Affected by Thermal Stress and Activity*. US AMRL Report 231.

Perry, D. K. (1952). Speed and accuracy of reading Arabic and Roman numerals. *Journal of Applied Psychology*, **36**, 346–347.

Perry, D. K. (1967). Vocational interests and success of computer programmers. *Personnel Psychology*, **20**, 517–524.

Perry, D. K. and Cannon, W. M. (1967). Vocational interests of computer programmers. *Journal of Applied Psychology*, **51**, 28–34.

Perry, D. K. and Cannon, W. M. (1968). Vocational interests of female computer programmers. *Journal of Applied Psychology*, **52**, 31–35.

Peterson, J. L. (1980). Computer programs for detecting and correcting spelling errors. *Communications of the ACM*, **23**, 676–687.

Petherbridge, P. and Hopkinson, R. G. (1950). Discomfort glare and the lighting of buildings. *Transactions of the Illuminating Engineering Society*, **15**, 39–79.

Pfauth, M. and Priest, J. (1981). Person–computer interface using touch screen devices. *Proceedings of the 25th Annual Meeting of the the Human Factors Society*.

Phillips, R. J. (1979). Why is lower case better? *Applied Ergonomics*, **10**, 211–214.

Pierce, B. F. (1963). Effects of wearing a full-pressure suit on manual dexterity and tool manipulation. *Human Factors*, **5**, 479–484.

Pike, K. L. (1972). General characteristics of intonation. In D. Bolinger (ed) *Intonation—Selected Readings*. (Harmondsworth: Penguin).

Pisoni, D. B. (1981). Speeded classification of natural and synthetic speech in a lexical decision task. *Journal of the Acoustical Society of America*, **70**, 598.

Pisoni, D. B. and Hunnicutt, S. (1980). Perceptual evaluation of MITalk: The MIT unrestricted text-to-speech system. *Proceedings of IEEE International Conference on Acoustics, Speech and Signal Processing*. (New York: IEEE).

Plath, D. W. (1970). The readability of segmented and conventional numerals. *Human Factors*, **12**, 493–497.

Pollard, D. and Cooper, M. B. (1979). The effect of feedback on keying performance. *Applied Ergonomics*, **10**, 194–200.

Porter, L. W. and Steers, R. M. (1973). Organizational work and personal factors in employee turnover and absenteeism. *Psychological Bulletin*, **80**, 151–176.

Porter, L. W., Steers, R. M., Mowday, R. T. and Boulian, P. V. (1974). Organizational commitment, job satisfaction, and turnover among psychiatric technicians. *Journal of Applied Psychology*, **59**, 603–609.

Postman, L. (1975). Verbal learning and memory. *Annual review of Psychology*, **26**, 291–350.

Pottier, M., Dubreuil, A. and Mond, H. (1969). The effects of sitting posture on the volume of the foot. *Ergonomics*, **12**, 753–758.

Poulton, E. C. (1967). Searching for newspaper headlines printed in capitals or lower-case letters. *Journal of Applied Psychology*, **51**, 417–425.

Poulton, E. C. (1969a). Searching lists of food ingredients printed in different sizes. *Journal of Applied Psychology*, **53**, 55–58.

Poulton, E. C. (1969b). How efficient is print? *New Society*, 5th June, 869–871.

Poulton, E. C. (1969c). Asymmetrical transfer in reading texts produced by teleprinter and typewriter. *Journal of Applied Psychology*, **53**, 244–249.

Poulton, E. C. (1974). *Tracking Skill and Manual Control*. (New York: Academic Press).

Poulton, E. C. (1976). Continuous noise interferes with work by masking auditory feedback and inner speech. *Applied Ergonomics*, **7**, 79–84.

Poulton, E. C. (1977). Continuous intense noise masks auditory feedback and inner speech. *Psychological Bulletin*, **84**, 97–101.

Poulton, E. C. (1978). A new look at the effects of noise: A rejoinder. *Psychological Bulletin*, **85**, 1068–1079.

Poulton, E. C. and Brown, C. H. (1968). Rate of comprehension of an existing teleprinter output and of possible alternatives. *Journal of Applied Psychology*, **52**, 16–21.

Poulton, E. C., Warren, T. R. and Bond, J. (1970). Ergonomics in journal design. *Applied Ergonomics*, **1**, 207–209.

Power, R. P, Muntz, H. J. and Macrae, K. D. (1975). Man and machine as a diagnostic tool: A comparison between clinical psychologists and discriminating function analysis. *British Journal of Social and Clinical Psychology*, **14**, 413–422.

Pritchard, D. (1964). Industrial lighting in windowless factories. *Lighting and Lighting Research*, **57**, 265.

Psotka, J. (1982). Computers and education. *Behaviour Research Methods and Instrumentation*, **14**, 221–223.

Pugh, D. S., Hickson, D. J., Hinings, C. R., MacDonald, K. M., Turner, C. and Lupton, T. (1963). A conceptual scheme for organizational analysis. *Administrative Science Quarterly*, **8**, 289–315.

Rabbit, P. (1978). Detection of errors by skilled typists. *Ergonomics*, **21**, 945–958.

Radl, G. W. (1980). Experimental investigations for optimal presentation-mode and colours of symbols on the CRT screen. In E. Grandjean and E. Vigliani (eds) *Ergonomic Aspects of Visual Display Terminals*. (London: Taylor and Francis).

Ramsey, H. R. and Atwood, M. E. (1979) *Human Factors in Computer Systems*. U.S. Office of Naval research Technical Report. SAI-79-111-DEN; AD-A075679.

Ratz, H. C. and Ritchie, D. K. (1961). Operator performance on a chord keyboard. *Journal of Applied Psychology*, **45**, 303–308.

Rayner, K. (1975). The perceptual span and peripheral cues in reading. *Cognitive Psychology*, **7**, 65–81.

Rayner, K. (1977). Visual attention in reading: Eye movements reflect cognitive processes. *Memory and Cognition*, **5**, 443–448.

Rayner, K. (1978). Eye movements in reading and information processing. *Psychological Bulletin*, **85**, 618–660.

Reddy, D. R. (1976). Speech recognition by machine: A review. *Proceedings of IEEE*, **64**, 501–531.

Reddy, S. P. and Ramsey, J. D. (1976). Thermostat variations and sedentary job performance. *ASHRAE Journal*, **18**, 32–36.

Reed, S. K. (1982). *Cognition: Theory and Applications*. (Monterey, C.A.: Brooks/Cole Publishing Co).

Reinstedt, R. N. (1967). Computer personnel research group programmer performance prediction study. *Proceedings of Fifth Annual Computer Personnel Research Conference*.

Reisner, P. (1981). Human factors studies of database query languages: A survey and assessment. *Computing Surveys*, **13**, 13–31.

Rey, R. P. and Meyer, J. J. (1980). Visual impairments and their objective correlates. In E. Grandjean and E. Vigliani (eds) *Ergonomic Aspects of Visual Display Terminals*. (London: Taylor and Francis).

Rholes, F. H. (1969). Preference for the thermal environment by the elderly. *Human Factors*, **11**, 37–41.

Rice, A. K. (1953). Productivity and social organization in an Indian weaving shed. *Administrative Science Quarterly*, **6**, 297–329.

Rice, A. K. (1958). *Productivity and Social Organization: the Ahmedabab Experiment*. (London: Tavistock Publications).

Ridgeway, J., MacCullough, M. J. and Mills, H. E. (1982). Some experiences in administering a psychometric test with a light pen and microcomputer. *International Journal of Man–Machine Studies*, **17**, 265–279.

Riggs, L. A. (1972). Vision. In J. W. Kling and L. A. Riggs (eds) *Experimental Psychology*. (New York: Methuen).

Ritchie, G. J. and Turner, J. A. (1975). Input devices for interactive graphics. *International Journal of Man–Machine Studies*, **7**, 639–660.

Roberts, D. F. (1975). Population dimensions, their genetic basis and their relevance to practical problems of design. In A. Chapanis (ed) *Ethnic Variables in Human Factors Engineering*. (Baltimore: The Johns Hopkins University Press).

Robey, D. (1981). Computer information systems and organization structure. *Communications of the ACM*, **24**, 679–686.

Robinette, K. M. and McConville, J. T. (1981). *An Alternative to Percentile Models*. SAE Technical Paper 810217. (Warrendale, PA: Society of Automotive Engineers).

Robinson, D. A. (1965). The mechanics of human smooth pursuit eye movements. *Journal of Physiology*, **180**, 569–591.

Rogers, J. G. (1963). The effects of target distance and direction on maximum velocity of the rolling ball control. *Human Factors*, **5**, 379–383.

Rosati, R. A. (1975). A new information system for medical practice. *Archives of Internal Medicine*, **135**, 1017–1024.

Rose, M. (1978). *Industrial Behaviour*. (Middlesex: Penguin Books Ltd).

Rosenberg, A. E. (1976). Automatic speaker verification: A review. *Proceedings of IEEE*, **64**, 475–487.

Rosenblatt, M. B., Teng, P. K. and Kerpe, S. (1973). Diagnostic accuracy in cancer as determined by post mortem examinations. *Progress in Clinical Cancer*, **5**, 71–80.

Rowlands, G. F. (1977). *The transmission of vertical vibration to the heads and shoulders of seated men*. RAE Technical Report TR77068.

Rubey, R. J. (1968) A comparative evaluation of PL/1. *Datamation*, 20.

Rumelhart, D. E. and Norman, D. A. (1982) Simulating a skilled typist: A study of skilled cognitive-motor performance. *Cognitive Science*, **6**, 1–36.

Rutenfranz, J. and Colquhoun, W. P. (1979). Circadian rhythms in human performance. *Scandinavian Journal of Work, Environment and Health*, **5**, 167–177.

Ruys, T. (1970). *Windowless Offices*. MA Thesis; University of Washington.

Saettler, P. (1978). The roots of educational technology. *Programmed Learning and Educational Technology*, **15**, 7-15.

Salamon, R., Bernadet, M., Samson, M., Derouesne, C. and Gremy, F. (1976). Bayesian method applied to decision-making in neurology—methodological considerations. *Methods of Information in Medicine*, **15**, 174-179.

Sapinkops, R. C. (1978). A computer adaptive testing approach to the measurement of personality variables. *Dissertation Abstracts International*, **38**, 10B, 4993.

Saunders, J. E. (1969). The role of the level and diversity of horizontal illumination in an appraisal of a simple office task. *Lighting Research and Technology*, **1**, 37.

Savinar, J. (1975). The effect of ceiling height on personal space. *Man-environment Systems*, **5**, 321-324.

Sayles, L. R. (1958). *The Behavior of Industrial Work Groups: Prediction and Control*. (New York: John Wiley).

Scales, E. M. and Chapanis, A. (1954). The effect on performance of tilting the toll-operator's keyset. *Journal of Applied Psychology*, **38**, 452-456.

Schiepers, C. W. J. (1980). Response latency and accuracy in visual word recognition. *Perception and Psychophysics*, **27**, 71-81.

Schmidt, F. L., Hunter, J. E., Mckenzie, R. C. and Muldrow, T. W. (1979). Impact of valid selection procedures of work-force productivity. *Journal of Applied Psychology*, **64**, 609-626.

Schmidtke, H. (1980). Ergonomic design principles of alphanumeric displays. In E. Grandjean and E. Vigliani (eds) *Ergonomic Aspects of Visual Display Terminals*. (London: Taylor and Francis).

Schoonard, J. W. and Boies, S. J. (1975). Short type: A behavioral analysis of typing and text entry. *Human Factors*, **17**, 204-214.

Scott-Morton, M. and Huff, S. (1980). The impact of computers on planning and decision-making. In H. T. Smith and T. R. G. Green (eds) *Human Interaction With Computers*. (London: Academic Press).

Segal, B. F. (1975). *Effects of Method of Interruption on Student Performance at Interactive Terminals*. Technical Report UIUCDCS-R-75-727. (University of Illinois Department of Computer Science).

Seguin, C. (1967). The individual space. *International Journal of Neuropsychiatry*, **3**, 108-117.

Seibel, R. (1962). Performance on a five-finger chord keyboard. *Journal of Applied Psychology*, **46**, 165-169.

Seibel, R. (1964). Data entry through chord, parallel entry devices. *Human Factors*, **6**, 189-192.

Selmi, P. M., Klein, M. H., Greist, J. H., Johnson, J. H. and Harris, J. H. (1982). An investigation of computer-assisted cognitive behaviour therapy in the treatment of depression. *Behaviour Research Methods and Instrumentation*, **14**, 181-185.

Severin, F. T. and Rigby, M. K. (1963). Influence of digit grouping on memory for telephone numbers. *Journal of Applied Psychology*, **47**, 117-119.

Shackel, B. (1979). The ergonomics of the man/computer interface. In B. Shackel (ed) *Man/Computer Communication, Volume 2*. (Maidenhead: Infotech International).

Shackel, B. (1980). Dialogues and language—can computer ergonomics help? *Ergonomics*, **23**, 857-880.

Shaffer, L. H. (1976). Intention and performance. *Psychological Review*, **83**, 375-393.

Shahnavaz, H. (1982). Lighting conditions and workplace dimensions of VDU-operators. *Ergonomics*, **25**, 1165-1173.

Sharp, J. C. and Waterworth, J. A. (1982). *Human Factors Aspects of Voice Recognition*. British Telecom Memo No. R19/019/82.

Shebilske, W. L. (1976). Extra retinal information in corrective saccades and inflow vs. outflow theories of visual detection constancy. *Vision Research*, **16**, 621–628.

Sheil, B. A. (1981). The psychological study of programming. *Computing Surveys*, **13**, 101–120.

Shepard, J. M. (1971). *Automation and Alienation: A Study of Office Factory Workers*. (Cambridge, Mass: MIT Press).

Sheppard, S., Curtis, B., Milliman, P., and Love, T. (1979). Modern coding practices and programmer performance. *Computer*, **12**, 41–49.

Sherman, P. S. (1981). A computerized CMHC clinical and management information system: Saga of a 'mini success'. *Behavior Research Methods and Instrumentation*, **13**, 445–453.

Shettel, H. H., Clapp, D. J. and Claus, D. J. (1963). *The Application of a By-pass Technique to Programmed Instruction for Managerial Training*. (Pittsburg: American Institute for Research).

Shipley, L. J., Gentry, J., Clarke, J. W. (1980). *VDT vs. Pencil: A Comparison of Speed and Accuracy*. (Columbia: University of Missouri Department of Journalism).

Shneiderman, B. (1976). Exploratory experiments in programmer behaviour. *International Journal of Computing and Information Sciences*, **5**, 124–143.

Shneiderman, B. (1977). Measuring computer program quality and comprehension. *International Journal of Man–Machine Studies*, **9**, 465–478.

Shneiderman, B. (1978a). Perceptual and cognitive issues in the syntactic/semantic model of programmer behaviour. *Proceedings of the Human Factors Society Symposium on Human Factors and Computer Science*. (California: HFS).

Shneiderman, B. (1978b). Improving the human factors aspect of database interactions. *ACM Transactions on Database Systems*, **3**, 417–439.

Shneiderman, B. (1979). Human factors experiments in designing interactive systems. *Computer-Institute of Electrical and Electronic Engineers Publication*, **12**, 9–19.

Shneiderman, B. (1980). *Software Psychology*. (Cambridge, Massachussetts: Winthrop Publishing Inc).

Shneiderman, B. and Mayer, R. (1979). Syntactic/semantic interactions in programmer behavior: A model and experimental results. *International Journal of Computer and Information Sciences*, **8**, 219–238.

Shneiderman, B. and McKay, D. (1976). Experimental investigations of computer program debugging and modification. *Proceedings of 6th Congress of the International Ergonomics Association*. (Baltimore: HFS).

Short, J., Williams, E., and Christie, B. (1976). *The Social Psychology of Telecommunications*. (Chichester: John Wiley).

Shrenk, L. P. (1969). Aiding the decision maker—A decision process model. *Ergonomics*, **12**, 543–558.

Siegel, J. H, Fitchthorn, J. and Monteferrante, J. (1976). Computer-based consultation in care of the critically ill patients. *Surgery*, **80**, 350–364.

Siegel, J. H., Fitchthorn, J. and Monteferrante, J. (1980). The effects on survival of critically ill and injured patients of an ITU teaching service about a computer-based physiologic care system. *Journal of Trauma*, **20**, 558–579.

Sime, M. E., Green, T. R. G. and Guest, D. J. (1973). Psychological evaluation of two conditional constructions used in computer languages. *International Journal of Man–Machine Studies*, **5**, 105–113.

Sime, M. E., Green, T. R. G. and Guest, D. J. (1977). Scope marking in computer conditionals—a psychological evaluation. *International Journal of Man–Machine Studies*, **9**, 107–118.

Sime, M. E., Arblaster, A. T. and Green, T. R. G. (1977). Structuring the programmer's task. *Journal of Occupational Psychology*, **50**, 205–216.

Simon, H. A. (1977). What computers mean for man and society. *Science*, **195**, 1186–1191.

Simpson, C. A. and Hart, S. G. (1977). Required attention for synthesized speech perception for two levels of linguistic redundancy. *Journal of the Acoustical Society of America*, Supplement 1, S7/D3.

Simpson, C. A. and Williams, D. H. (1980). Response time effects of alerting tone and semantic context for synthesized voice cockpit warnings. *Human Factors*, **22**, 319–330.

Skinner, B. F. (1954). The science of learning and the art of teaching. *Harvard Educational Review*, **24**, 86–97.

Slack, W. V. and Slack, C. W. (1977). Talking to a computer about emotional problems: A comparative study. *Psychotherapy: Theory, Research and Practice*, **141**, 156–164.

Slack, W.V. and VanCura, L.J. (1968). Patient reaction to computer based medical interviewing. *Computers and Biomedical Research*, 1, 527-531. Slobin, D. I. (1966). Grammatical transformations and sentence comprehension in childhood and adulthood. *Journal of Verbal Learning and Verbal Behaviour*, **5**, 219–227.

Sloboda, W. and Smith, E. E. (1968). Disruption effects in human short-term memory: Some negative findings. *Perceptual and Motor Skills*, **27**, 575–582.

Smith, A. G. (1981). Attitudes towards computers: A survey of diverse persons. *Australian Computer Journal*, **13**, 87–92.

Smith, C. H. and Dunsmore, H. E. (1982). On the relative comprehensibility of various control structures by novice FORTRAN programmers. *International Journal of Man–Machine Studies*, **17**, 165–171.

Smith, E. E. and Spoeher, K. T. (1974). The perception of printed English: A theoretical perspective. In B. H. Kantowitz (ed) *Human Information Processing: Tutorials in Performance and Cognition*. (Pontomac, M.D.: Erlbaum Press).

Smith, F. (1971). *Understanding Reading*. (New York: Holt, Rinehart and Winston).

Smith, F., Lott, D. and Cronnell, B. (1969). The effect of type size and case alternation on word identification. *American Journal of Psychology*, **82**, 248–253.

Smith, H. T. (1980). Human–computer communication. In H. T. Smith and T. R. G. Green (eds) *Human Interaction With Computers*. (London: Academic Press).

Smith, M. J., Stammerjohn, L. W., Cohen, B. G. F. and Lalich, N. R. (1980). Job stress in video display operations. In E. Grandjean and E. Vigliani (eds) *Ergonomic Aspects of Visual Display Terminals*. (London: Taylor and Francis).

Smith, M. J., Cohen, B. G. F, Stammerjohn, L. W. and Happ, A. (1981). An investigation of health complaints and job stress in video display operations. *Human Factors*, **23**, 387–400.

Smith, S. L. and Thomas, D. W. (1964). Colour versus shape coding in information displays. *Journal of Applied Psychology*, **48**, 137–146.

Smith, S. W. (1961). Visual search time and peripheral discriminability. *Journal of the Optical Society of America*, **51**, 1462(A).

Smith, S. W. and Rea, M. S. (1979). Relationships between office task performance and ratings of feelings and task evaluation under different light sources and levels. *Proceedings of the CIE 19th Session*, Kyoto.

Sommer, R. (1968). Intimacy ratings in five countries. *International Journal of Man–Machine Studies*, **3**, 109–114.

Sommer, R. (1969). *Personal Space: the Behavioral Basis of Design*. (New York: Prentice-Hall Inc).

Sommer, R. (1974). *Tight spaces: Hard Architecture and How to Humanize It*. (New Jersey: Prentice-Hall).

Space, L. G. (1981). The computer as a psychometrician. *Behaviour Research Methods and Instrumentation*, **13**, 595–606.

Spence, R. (1976). Human factors in interactive graphics. *Computer Aided Design*, **8**, 49–53.

Spence, R. and, Apperley, M. A. (1982). Data base navigation: An office environment for the professional. *Behaviour and Information Technology*, **1**, 43–54.

Sperling, G. (1967). Successive approximations to a model for short term memory. *Acta Psychologica*, **27**, 285–292.

Spraberry, M. N., Frety, P., Gascho, T. and Foft, J. (1976). A computerized data management system for the clinical laboratory. *American Journal of Medical Technology*, **22**, 201–208.

Spring, G. and Perry, L. (1981). Computer-assisted instruction in word-decoding for educationally handicapped children. *Journal of Educational Technology*, **10**, 149–163.

Stabell, C. B. (1982). Office productivity: A micro-economic framework for empirical research. *Office: Technology and People*, **1**, 91–106.

Stammerjohn, L., Smith, M. J. and Cohen, B. (1981). Evaluation of workstation design factors in VDT operations. *Human Factors*, **23**, 401–412.

Starr, S. J., Thompson, C. R. and Shute, S. J. (1982). Effects of video display terminals on telephone operators. *Human Factors*, **24**, 699–712.

Stephens, S. D. G. (1970). Studies on the uncomfortable loudness level. *Sound*, **4**, 20–23.

Stevens, G. C. (1983). User-friendly computer systems? A critical evaluation of the concept. *Behaviour and Information Technology*, **2**, 3–16.

Stevens, W. P., Myers, G. J. and Constantine, L. L. (1974). Structured design. *IBM Systems Journal*, **13**, 115–139.

Stewart, T. F. M. (1976). Displays and the software interface. *Applied Ergonomics*, **7**, 137–146.

Stewart, T. F. M. (1980). Communicating with dialogues. *Ergonomics*, **23**, 909–919.

Stiles, W. S. (1929). The scattering theory of glare. *Proceedings of the Royal Society (Series B)*, **105**, 131–146.

Stimmel, T., Connor, J. L., McCaskill, E. D. and Durrett, H. J. (1981). Teacher resistance to computer-assisted instruction. *Behaviour Research Methods and Instrumentation*, **13**, 128–130.

Stodolsky, D. (1970). The computer as a psychotherapist. *International Journal of Man–Machine Studies*, **2**, 327–350.

Stoudt, H. W. (1978). *Are people still getting bigger—who, where and how much?* SAE Technical Paper No. 780280. (Warrendale, P.A.: Society Of Automotive Engineers).

Stout, R. L. (1981). New approaches to the design of computerized interviewing and testing systems. *Behaviour Research Methods and Instrumentation*, **13**, 436–442.

Stranden, E., Aaras, A., Anderson, D. M., Myhre, H. O. and Martinsen, K. (1983). The effects of working posture on muscular-skeletal load and circulatory condition. In K. Coombes (ed) *Proceedings of the 1983 Ergonomics Society Conference*. (London: Taylor and Francis).

Strassmann, P. A. (1982). Overview of strategic aspects of information management. *Office: Technology and People*, **1**, 71–89.

Stymne, B. (1966). EDP and organizational structure: A case study of an insurance company. *Swedish Journal of Economics*, **68**, 4.

Suppes, P. (1979). Current trends in computer-assisted instruction. *Advances in Computers*, **10**, 173–229.

Tait, K., Hartley, J. R. and Anderson, R. C. (1973). Feedback procedures in computer-assisted instruction. *British Journal of Educational Technology*, **43**, 161–171.

Taylor, R. M. and Berman, J. V. F. (1982). Ergonomic aspects of aircraft keyboard design: The effects of gloves and sensory feedback on keying performance. *Ergonomics*, **25**, 1109–1123.

Taylor, T. R., Aitchison, J. and McGirr, E. M. (1971). Doctors as decision makers: A comparative study of diagnosis as a cognitive skill. *British Medical Journal*, **3**, 35–40.

Teichner, W. H. and Krebs, M. J. (1974). Visual search for simple targets. *Psychological Bulletin*, **81**, 15–28.

Teichner, W. H. and Mocharnuk, J. B. (1979). Visual search for complex targets. *Human Factors*, **21**, 259–275.

Terrana, T., Merluzzi, F. and Giudici, E. (1980). Electromagnetic radiation emitted by visual display units. In E. Grandjean and E. Vigliani (eds) *Ergonomic Aspects of Visual Display Terminals*. (London: Taylor and Francis).

Terrell, C. D. and Linyard, O. (1982). Evaluation of electronic learning aids: Texas Instruments' 'Speak and Spell'. *International Journal of Man–Machine Studies*, **17**, 59–67.

Thimbleby, H. (1980). Dialogue determination. *International Journal of Man–Machine Studies*, **13**, 295–304.

Thimbleby, H. (1983). Guidelines for 'manipulative' text editing. *Behaviour and Information Technology*, **2**, 127–161.

Thomas, A. (1981). Communication devices for the nonvocal disabled. *Computer*, **14**, 25–30.

Thomas, E. A. C. and Jones, R. C. (1970). A model for subjective grouping in typewriting. *Quarterly Journal of Experimental Psychology*, **22**, 353–367.

Thomas, J. R. (1978). Noise and memory. In M. M. Gruneberg, P. E. Morris and R. N. Sykes (eds) *Practical Aspects of Memory*. (London: Academic Press).

Thompson, J. A. and Wilson, S. L. (1982). Automated psychological testing. *International Journal of Man–Machine Studies*, **17**, 279–290.

Thompson, J. M. (1969). Why is everyone leaving? *Data Management*, **7**, 25–27.

Thorpe, C. E. and Rowland, G. E. (1965). The effect of 'natural' grouping of numerals on short-term memory. *Human Factors*, **7**, 38–44.

Tichauer, E. R. (1978). *The Biomechanical Basis of Ergonomics*. (New York: John Wiley).

Tiffin, J. and Phelen, R. F. (1953). Use of Kuder Preference Record to predict turnover in an industrial plant. *Personnel Psychology*, **6**, 195–204.

Timmers, H., Van Nes, F. L. and Blommaert, F. J. J. (1980). Visual word recognition as a function of contrast. In E. Grandjean and E. Vigliani (eds) *Ergonomic Aspects of Visual Display Terminals*. (London: Taylor and Francis).

Tinker, M. A. (1939). The effect of illumination intensities upon speed of perception and upon fatigue in reading. *Journal of Educational Psychology*, **30**, 561–571.

Tinker, M. A. (1963). *Legibility of Print*. (Iowa: Iowa State University Press).

Torle, G. (1965). Tracking performance under random acceleration: Effects of control dynamics. *Ergonomics*, **8**, 481–486.

Trist, E. L. and Bamforth, K. W. (1951). Some social and psychological consequences of the longwall method of coal getting. *Human Relations*, **4**, 3–38.

Tsichtritzis, D. and Christodoulakis, S. (1983). Message files. *ACM Transactions on Office Systems*, **1**, 88–98.

Turn, R. (1974). *The Use of Speech for Man–Computer Communication*. (Santa Monica: Rand Corporation Report R-1386-ARPA).

Twelker, P. A. (1971). Simulation and media. In Tansey, P. J. (ed) *Educational aspects of Simulation*. (London: McGraw Hill).

Tyler, L. E. (1974). *Individual Differences: Abilities and Motivational Directions*. (Appleton-Century-Crofts).

Umeda, N. (1977). Consonant duration in American English. *Journal of the Acoustical Society of America*, **61**, 846–858.

Usher, D. M. (1982). A touch sensitive VDU compared with a computer-aided keypad for controlling power generating plant. Paper presented to IEE Conference on Man/machine Systems.

Van Nes, F. L. and Bouma, H. (1979). Legibility of segmented numerals. Paper presented to 30th Annual Conference of the Ergonomics Society, Oxford.

Van Nes, F. L. and Bouma, H. (1980). On the legibility of segmented numerals. *Human Factors*, **22**, 463–474.

Vartabedian, R. H. (1971). Legibility of symbols on CRT displays. *Applied Ergonomics*, **2**, 130–132.

Vartabedian, A. G. (1973). Developing a graphic set for cathode ray tube display using a 7×9 dot pattern. *Applied Ergonomics*, **4**, 11–16.

Vaughn, W. S. Jnr. and Mavor, A. S. (1972). Behavioural characteristics of men in the performance of some decision-making task components. *Ergonomics*, **15**, 267–277.

Venezky, R. L. (1970). *The Structure of English Orthography*. (The Hague: Morton).

Vernon, H. M. and Warner, C. G. (1932). The influence of the humidity of the air on capacity for work at high temperatures. *Journal of Hygiene (Cambridge)*, **32**, 431.

Vickers, D. (1979). *Decision Processes in Visual Perception*. (New York: Academic Press).

Vroom, V. H. (1944). *Work and Motivation*. (New York: John Wiley).

Vygotsky, L. (1975). On the perception of words. In E. J. Gibson and H. Levin (eds). *The Psychology of Reading*. (Cambridge: MIT Press).

Wagner, G., Tautu, P. and Wolber, U. (1978). Problems of medical diagnosis—A bibliography. *Methods of Information in Medicine*, **17**, 55–74.

Walker, C. R. and Guest, R. H. (1952). *The Man on the Assembly Line*. (Cambridge: Harvard University Press).

Waller, R. A. (1969). Office acoustics—effect of background noise. *Applied Acoustics*, **2**, 121–130.

Waltzman, S. B. and Levitt, H. (1978). Speech Interference Level as a predictor of face-to-face communication in noise. *Journal of the Acoustical Society of America*, **63**, 581–590.

Wardle, A. and Wardle, L. (1978). Computer aided diagnosis—A review of research. *Methods of Information in Medicine*, **17**, 15–28.

Wason, P. C. (1965). The contexts of plausible denials. *Journal of Verbal Learning and Verbal Behaviour*, **4**, 7–11.

Wasserman, A. I. (1973). The design of idiot-proof interactive systems. *American Federation of Information Processing Societies Conference Proceedings*, **42**, M34–M38.

Watson, P. G. (1968). An industrial evaluation of four strategies of instruction. *Audio-Visual Instruction*, **13**, 156.

Watts, K., Baddeley, A., and Williams, M. (1982). Automated tailored testing using Raven's Matrices and the Mill Hill Vocabulary Tests: A comparison with manual administration. *International Journal of Man–Machine Studies*, **17**, 331–344.

Weale, R. A. (1963). *The Ageing Eye*. (London: H. K. Lewis).

Webster, J. C. (1973). S.I.L.—Past, present and future. *Journal of Sound and Vibration*, **3**, 22–26.

Weinberg, G. M., Gellar, D. P. and Plum, T. W-S. (1975). IF-THEN-ELSE considered harmful. *SIGPLAN Notices*, **10**, 34–44.

Weinman, J., Elithorn, A. and Farag, S.(1981). Test structure and cognitive style. In M.

Friedman, J. P. Das and N. O'Connor (eds) *Intelligence and Learning*. (New York: Plenum Press).

Weinstein, N. D. (1976). Human evaluations of environmental noise. In K. Craik and E. H. Zube (eds) *Perceiving Environmental Quality*. (New York: Plenum Press).

Weissman, L. (1974). *A Methodology for Studying the Psychological Complexity of Computer Programs*. Ph.D. Thesis; University of Toronto.

Welch, J. R. (1980). Automated speech recognition—putting it to work in industry. *Computer*, **May**, 65–73.

Welford, R. T. (1976). *Skilled Performance: Perceptual and Motor Skills*. (Illinois: Scott, Foresman & Co).

Wertheimer, M. (1958). Principles of perceptual organization. In D. C. Beardslee and M. Wertheimer (eds) *Readings in Perception*. (Princeton: Van Nostrand).

Wesner, C. E. (1972). Induced arousal and word-recognition learning by mongoloids and normals. *Perceptual and Motor Skills*, **35**, 586.

West, L. H. T. and Fensham, D. J. (1976). Prior knowledge or advance organizers as effective variables in chemistry learning. *Journal of Research in Science Teaching*, **13**, 297–306.

West, L. J. (1967). Vision and kinaesthesis in the acquisition of typewriting skill. *Journal of Applied Psychology*, **51**, 161–166.

Weizembaum, J. (1976). *Computer Power and Human Reasoning*. (San Francisco: W.H. Freeman).

Whisler, T. L. (1970). *The Impact of Computers on Organizations*. (New York: Praeger).

Whiteside, J., Archer, N., Wixon, D. and Good, M. (1982). How do people really use text editors? *SIGOA Newsletter,* **3**, 29–40.

Whitfield, D., Ball, R. G., Bird, J. and Garbett, T. (1979). On the use of touch input devices with computer generated displays. EDU Memo 7901, University of Aston, Birmingham.

Whyte, W. F. (1959). An interaction approach to the theory of organizations. In M. Haire (ed) *Modern Organizational Theory*. (New York: John Wiley).

Wijk, O. (1966). *Rules of Pronunciation for the English Language*. (London: Oxford University Press).

Wilkins, A. J. (1978). Epileptogenic attributes of TV and VDUs. Paper presented to Ergonomics Society Conference on Eyestrain and VDUs. Loughborough.

Wilkins, A. J., Darby, C. E. and Binnie, C. D. (1979). On the triggering of photosensitive epilepsy. In D. J. Oborne, M. M. Gruneberg and J. R. Eiser (eds) *Research in Psychology and Medicine, Volume I*. (London: Academic Press).

Williams, A. C. Jnr and Hopkins, C. O. (1958). *Aspects of pilot decision making*. WPAFB, Ohio: WADC Technical Report 58-522.

Willis, F. N. (1966). Initial speaking distance as a function of the speaker's relationship. *Psychonomic Science*, **5**, 221–222.

Willoughby, T. C. (1977). Computing personnel turnover: A review of the literature. *Computer Personnel*, **7**, 11–16.

Wills, K., Teather, D. and Innocent, P. (1982). An expert system for the medical diagnosis of brain tumours. *International Journal of Man–Machine Studies*, **16**, 341–349.

Wilson, A. *Noise—Final Report*. (London: HMSO).

Wilson, J. and Grey, S. (1983). The ergonomics of laser scanner checkout systems. In K. Coombes (ed) *Proceedings of the 1983 Ergonomics Society*. (London: Taylor and Francis).

Wilson, S. L., Thompson, J. A. and Wylie, G. (1982). Automated psychological testing for the severely physically handicapped. *International Journal of Man–Machine Studies*, **17**, 265–278.

Witeside, J., Archer, N., Wixon, D., and Good, M. (1982). How do people really use text editors? *SIGOA Newsletter*, **3**, 29–40.

Withington, F. G. (1969). *The Real Computer: Its Influences, Uses and Effects.* (Massachussetts: Addison-Wesley).

Witkin, H. A., Dyk, R. B., Faterson, H. F., Goodenough, D. R. and Karp, S. A. (1962). *Psychological Differentiation.* (New York: John Wiley).

Witkin, H. A., Lewis, H. B., Hertzman, M., Machover, K., Meissner, P. B. and Wagner, S. (1954). *Personality Through Perception.* (New York: Harper and Brothers).

Wohlwill, J. F., Nasar, J. L., DeJoy, D. M. and Foruzami, H. H. (1976). Behavioral effects of a noisy environment: Tast involvement versus passive exposure. *Journal of Applied Psychology,* **61**, 67–74.

Wolford, G. and Hollingsworth, S. (1974a). Retinal location and string position as important variables in visual information processing. *Perception and Psychophysics*, **16**, 437–442.

Wolford, G. and Hollingsworth, S. (1974b). Lateral masking in visual information processing. *Perception and Psychophysics*, **16**, 315–320.

Woodruff, C. K. (1980a). Data processing people—are they satisfied/dissatisfied with their jobs? *Information and Management*, **3**, 219–225.

Woodruff, C. K. (1980b). Data processing people—are they really different? *Information Management*, **3**, 133–139.

Woodward, J. (1958). *Management and Technology.* (London: HMSO).

Woodward, J. (1965). *Industrial Organization; Theory and Practice.* (Oxford; Oxford University Press).

Woodward, J. (1970). *Industrial Organization; Behaviour and Control.* (London: Oxford University Press).

Woodworth, R. S. (1938). *Experimental Psychology.* (New York: Henry Holt & Co.).

Wortman, P. M. Medical diagnosis: An information—processing approach. *Computers and Biomedical Research*, **5**, 315–358.

Wortman, P. M. and Greenberg, L. D. (1971). Coding, recoding, and decoding of hierarchical information in long term memory. *Journal of Verbal Learning and Verbal Behaviour*, **10**, 234–243.

Wright, P. (1977). Presenting technical information: A survey of research findings. *Instructional Science*, **6**, 93–134.

Wright, P. (1977). Decision making as a factor in the ease of using numerical tables. *Ergonomics*, **20**, 91–96.

Wright, P. (1978). Feeding the information eaters: Suggestions for integrating pure and applied research on language comprehension. *Instructional Science*, **7**, 249–312.

Wright, P. and Barnard, P. (1975). Effects of 'more than' and 'less than' decisions on the use of numerical tables. *Journal of Applied Psychology*, **60**, 606–611.

Wright, P. and Reid, F. (1973). Written information: Some alternatives to prose for expressing the outcomes of complex contingencies. *Journal of Applied Psychology,* **57**, 160–166.

Yaglou, C. P. (1947). A method for improving the effective temperature index. *ASHVE Transactions*, **53**, 307–326.

Yannakoudakis, E. J. and Fawthrop, D. (1983). An intelligent spelling error corrector. *Information Processing and Management*, **19**, 101–108.

Yarbus, A. L. (1967). *Eye Movements and Vision.* (New York: Plenum).

Young, D. W. (1982). A survey of decision aids for clinicians. *British Medical Journal*, **285**, 1332–1336.

Young, L. R. and Sheena, D. (1975). Survey of eye movement recording techniques. *Behavior Research Methods and Instrumentation*, 7, 397–429.

Youngs, E. A. (1974). Human errors in programming. *International Journal of Man–Machine Studies*, 6, 361–376.

Yu, V. L., Bucannon, B. G. and Shortliffe, E. H. (1979). Evaluating the performance of a computer-based consultant. *Computing Programs Biomedical, 9*, 95–102.

Zadeh, L. A. (1978). PRUF—A meaning representation language for natural languages. *International Journal of Man–Machine Studies*, 10, 395–460.

Zagoruiko, N. G. and Tambovtsev, Y. (1982). Aspects of human performance in an intensive speech task. *International Journal of Man–Machine Studies*, 16, 173–181.

Author Index

Subject Index